ETHICAL CHALLENGES TO LEGAL EDUCATION AND CONDUCT

Ethical Challenges to Legal Education and Conduct

Edited by
KIM ECONOMIDES,
Reader in Law
Exeter University

·HART·
PUBLISHING

OXFORD
1998

Hart Publishing
Oxford
UK

Distributed in the United States by
Northwestern University Press
625 Colfax
Evanston
Illinois 60208–4210 USA

Distributed in Australia and New Zealand
by Federation Press Pty
PO Box 45 Annandale, NSW
2038, Australia

Distributed in Netherlands, Belgium and Luxembourg by
Intersentia, Churchillaan 108
B2900 Schoten
Antwerpen
Belgium

Hart Publishing is a specialist legal publisher based in Oxford, England.
To order further copies of this book or to request a list of other
publications please write to:

Hart Publishing, 19 Whitehouse Road, Oxford, OX1 4PA
Telephone: +44 (0)1865 434459, Fax: +44 (0)1865 794482 or 434459
e-mail: hartpub@janep.demon.co.uk

British Library Cataloguing in Publication Data
Data Available
ISBN 1–901362–10–8 (cloth)
ISBN 1–901362–11–6 (paperback)

Typeset in 10pt Sabon
by Hope Services (Abingdon) Ltd
Printed in Great Britain on acid-free paper
by Bookcraft Ltd., Midsomer Norton, Somerset

Contents

Preface and Acknowledgements

This volume has its origins in the work of the International Sociological Association/Research Committee on Sociology of Law (ISA/RCSL) Working Group on Comparative Legal Professions, perhaps best known for the trilogy produced by Rick Abel and Philip Lewis in the late 1980s.[1] Following publication of these seminal volumes the Working Group, currently chaired by Bill Felstiner, has tended to concentrate on a wide range of more specialised projects.[2] Early in 1994, not long after joining the Secretariat of the Lord Chancellor's Advisory Committee on Legal Education and Conduct (ACLEC) on secondment from the University of Exeter, I proposed setting up a subgroup specifically on legal education with a view to feeding comparative research into ACLEC's Legal Education Review and ensuring that ACLEC's thinking was widely understood and disseminated throughout the community of international scholars engaged in the comparative sociology of legal professions. ACLEC's secretary at that time, Alistair Shaw, welcomed this idea, as did the Chair of the ISA/RCSL Working Group, Terence Halliday. The Legal Education sub-group was formally launched at a meeting of the Working Group held in Rouen, 13–16 July 1994, and immediately thereafter several members of the sub-group attended ACLEC's Second Consultative Conference informing the development and direction of its Education Review.[3] The present volume includes many of the founder members of the Legal Education sub-group but we have been joined by scholars from other disciplines also interested in exploring the implications of ethical challenges to legal education and conduct. All of these scholars are to be thanked not only for their contributions but also for agreeing to make an 'ethical investment' by donating royalties to the Working Group in order to facilitate further international and interdisciplinary exchanges.

ACLEC's vision in first investigating and then declaring an 'ethical challenge' provided much of the stimulus for this study and therefore I should like to place on record my gratitude to its former Chairmen, members and my

---

[1] R.L.Abel and P.S.C.Lewis (eds), *Lawyers in Society: Volume One, The Common Law World* (Berkeley, Los Angeles, London, Univ.of Calif.Press, 1988); *Lawyers in Society: Volume Two, The Civil World* (Berkeley, Los Angeles, London, Univ. of Calif. Press, 1988); *Lawyers in Society: Volume Three, Comparative Theories* (Berkeley, Los Angeles, London, Univ.of Calif. Press, 1989).

[2] Current projects of the ISA/RCSL Working Group include: cause lawyering; legal aid; cultural histories; professionals in family; judiciary; women in the profession; lawyers and politics; deregulation; lawyers and clients; legal education; and deontology. For further details contact Bill Felstiner: felstine@sscf.ucsb.edu

[3] Professor Harry Arthurs delivered an influential plenary address on "'Humane professionalism': lessons from the Canadian experience". See *Review of Legal Education: Report of the Second Consultative Conference—18 July 1994* (London, ACLEC, 1994).

colleagues in the Secretariat, all of whom between 1993 and 1995 taught me much about the ethical dimension to legal education, and professional practice more generally. Invidious as it may seem to single out individual members, nevertheless my special thanks go to ACLEC's first two Chairmen, Lord Griffiths[4]—and especially Lord Steyn who very kindly has agreed to find time to write a foreword—as well as to all the members of the Education Review Group[5] who shaped the Committee's overall philosophy on legal education which now firmly embraces legal ethics.

Working as a quasi-civil servant during this period was itself a training in the ethical values, disciplines and methods of the English Civil Service.[6] In this context I should like to mention Usha Prashar CBE, Graham Smith CBE and the late Mary Tuck CBE[7] all of whom drew upon their intimate knowledge of the internal workings of Government departments and who, along with the other Committee members, demonstrated a fearless independence and openness of mind throughout the protracted discussions over rights of audience which in turn raised many complex ethical issues.[8] I am particularly indebted to Alistair Shaw, Rael Zackon and Brenda Griffith-Williams for enabling me to gain first-hand knowledge of the very high standards of our civil servants and for communicating their professionalism by way of example, discussion and, somewhat less successfully, by instruction. I fear the only aspect of my civil service training to meet with any lasting success may have been my acquisition of certain office skills (e.g. where precisely to place a treasury tag)—and for this I have to acknowledge the patience, tact and good humour of Perry Bell, Linda Gray and, above all, the 'flexibility' of Jenny Patterson. Thanks for support are due also to Hilary de Lyon, Becky Lyon and Karen Low who, like me, were recruited from outside the Lord Chancellor's Department. Each member of the team made a huge contribution toward ACLEC functioning in a friendly and efficient manner, and making my time there thoroughly enjoyable. At the point where law schools are just beginning to reap real benefits from ACLEC's labours I should like to wish the present Committee a secure and successful future.

Several academic colleagues have assisted my re-entry into academic life and production of this volume—the move, as it were, from ACLEC to

---

[4] Lord Griffiths, "The Lord Chancellor's Advisory Committee on Legal Education and Conduct" (1994) 28 *The Law Teacher* 4.

[5] Professors Richard Card, Bob Hepple and Peter Scott, Dr Neville Hunnings, Mr Patrick Lefevre, Mr Ian McNeil, Dr Claire Palley and Mr David Wilkins.

[6] See R.Pyper, *The Evolving Civil Service* (Harlow, Longman, 1991), Chap.5; G.Drewery and T.Butcher, *The Civil Service Today* (Oxford, Blackwell, 1988), Chap.6 for discussion of ethics in the civil service and Robert Armstrong's *Note of Guidance on the Duties and Responsibilities of Civil Servants in Relation to Ministers* (Armstrong Memorandum).

[7] See obituary for Mrs Mary Tuck CBE, The Lord Chancellor's Advisory Committee on Legal Education and Conduct, *Annual Report 1996–1997* (London, The Stationery Office: 375, 1997) p.65.

[8] For an external view see, M.Zander,"Rights of audience in the higher courts in England and Wales since the 1990 Act: what happened?"(1997)4:3 *International J.of Legal Profession* 167.

ECLEC. Amongst the present contributors, Harry Arthurs encouraged me to persevere with this project and provided vital encouragement at a crucial time. Chris Gill and his colleagues in the Classics Department at Exeter have rekindled an interest in ancient philosophy. Richard O'Dair and Julian Webb both shared their innovative ideas about how to teach legal ethics and subsequently agreed, along with my Exeter colleagues Lesley Austen, Bryony Gilbert, Jackie Heath and Robert Mitchell in the Centre for Legal Practice, to help launch a new journal *Legal Ethics*. I should like to thank all of them most warmly, and especially Richard Hart for taking a risk in backing both ventures which I trust will uphold the commitment of Hart Publishing to publishing titles that are "interesting and intellectually important". I wish also to thank the University of Exeter for providing financial support enabling me to attend meetings of the ISA/RCSL Working Group in Glasgow and Peyresq, France in July 1996.

My greatest thanks, however, must go to my family who supported me throughout my absences both during and after my secondment to ACLEC. My wife Clare, a social worker who currently teaches on the 'Ethics and Values' course for trainee social workers at Exeter University, and my children Zoë and Alexander, have in their unique ways opened up new insights into moral education and ethical behaviour, as have my parents Bernice and Michael, whose exemplary lives and fighting spirit sum up for me the meaning and value of a "good life". My father Michael, a veteran of the Spanish Civil War who was made an honorary Spanish citizen shortly before his death in November 1996,[9] once made a powerful speech on the legacy of those who took a profoundly moral stand by fighting fascism in Spain in the 1930s. At several points during this speech he stressed that "Every generation has its challenges" and that "Every age has its volunteers for liberty." I should like to dedicate this volume to the memory of my father, and to the example of those like him, who volunteer to tackle the ethical challenges of their age.

Kim Economides,
Exeter, April 1998.

---

[9] L.Isla, "Michael Economides: Strong Voice Against Fascism" (1996) *The Guardian*, 28 December.

List of Contributors

Harry Arthurs is University Professor Emeritus, Osgoode Hall Law School and former President of York University, Canada.

Sophie Blencowe is a Research Assistant at the National Institute for Law, Ethics and Public Affairs, Griffith University, Brisbane, Australia. She is a co-editor (with Marge Hauritz and Charles Sampford) of *Justice for People with Disabilities: Assessing Legal and Institutional Responses* (1998).

Tim Dare is a Lecturer in Philosophy and Coordinator of the Diploma in Professional Ethics, Department of Philosophy, University of Auckland. He has practised law and worked as a clerk for the New Zealand High Court before completing his doctorate in Canada. He has also taught in both law schools and philosophy departments and publishes in the fields of political philosophy, ethics (including legal ethics) and the philosophy of law.

Costas Douzinas is Professor and Head of the Law Department at Birkbeck College, University of London, UK. He has recently co-edited a collection of essays on *Art and Law* and is currently finishing a book entitled *The End of Human Rights*.

Kim Economides is Reader in Law at the University of Exeter, UK and General Editor of the journal *Legal Ethics*. From 1993-1995 he was Education Secretary to the Lord Chancellor's Advisory Committee on Legal Education and Conduct (ACLEC).

Christopher Gill is Professor of Ancient Thought and Head of the Department of Classics and Ancient History at the University of Exeter, UK.

Andrew Goldsmith is Foundation Professor of Legal Studies at Flinders University, Adelaide, Australia. He taught for 7 years in the clinical programme at Monash University, as well as teaching legal professional responsibility at Monash. He has published articles on legal education, and is an editor of *Legal Education Review*.

Robert Granfield is Assistant Professor of Sociology, University of Denver, USA. He is the author of *Making Elite Lawyers: Visions of Law at Harvard and Beyond* (1992) and several articles on law school socialization, legal profession and drug policy.

Richard Grimes is currently Professor of Legal Education and Head of Law at the University of Derby, UK. Prior to taking up this appointment he was Associate Professor and Director of the Institute of Justice and Applied Legal Studies at the University of the South Pacific, based in Fiji (1995-97) whilst on secondment from Sheffield Hallam University, UK.

Leny E. de Groot-van Leeuwen is an Assistant Professor at Utrecht University and Nijmegen University, the Netherlands. She is author of several articles and books on the practice and ethics of the legal profession and has co-edited two books in this field. She is also editor of the Dutch and Belgian Law and Society journal `Recht der Werkelijkheid'.

Eliane Junqueira is Professor at the Catholic University of Rio de Janeiro where she teaches courses on sociology of law and criminology, and is the Director of the Instituto Direito e Sociedade (IDES), Brazil. In her latest book, *Direito e literatura: uma nova leitura do mundo das leis* (1998) she analyzed images of lawyers in Brazilian literature.

Thomas Morawetz is Tapping Reeve Professor of Law and Ethics at the University of Connecticut School of Law, USA. His books and articles include contributions to legal philosophy, criminal law, law and literature, professional responsibility, and philosophical ethics.

Richard O'Dair is a Lecturer in Law in the Faculty of Laws, University College London, London, UK and Book Reviews Editor of *Legal Ethics*.

Vittorio Olgiati is a lawyer in Milan; researcher at the Institute of the Philosophy and Sociology of Law, Faculty of Law, University of Milan; Lecturer in the Sociology of Organizations, Faculty of Sociology, University of Urbino, and in the Theory of Organizations, Faculty of Law, University of Macerata, Italy.

Guy Powles is Professor at Monash Law School, Melbourne, Australia. He has been associated for over 30 years with the development of legal systems in the South Pacific and, more recently, the new Law School of the University of the South Pacific. His work includes the study of legal professions and he teaches legal ethics at Monash.

Deborah Rhode is Professor of Law and Director of the Keck Centre on Legal Ethics and the Legal Profession, Stanford Law School, USA.

Robert Eli Rosen is Professor in the School of Law at the University of Miami, Coral Gables, USA.

Charles Sampford is Professor and Director of the National Institute for Law, Ethics and Public Affairs at Griffith University, Australia.

Avrom Sherr is Woolf Professor of Legal Education at the Institute of Advanced Legal Studies, University of London, UK.

Julian Webb is a Principal Lecturer in the Faculty of Law at the University of the West of England, Bristol, UK and Articles Editor of *Legal Ethics*.

Foreword by Lord Steyn

In the positivist tradition generations of law students have been taught that law and ethics or morals must be kept rigidly apart. In one sense this is inevitable since courts of law can ultimately only apply and enforce legal rules. But in another sense it is far too narrow an approach. Different forces play a role in the making and development of law. Justice Cardozo said that logic, history, custom, utility and morality were the shaping forces. Of these forces the role of morality is of crucial importance at all levels of lawmaking. When our legislators defend legislation at the bar of public opinion it is frequently morality, or a perceived conception of morality, that they invoke in support. When judges have to choose between different legal solutions in difficult cases—involving perhaps embryo experiments, surrogate motherhood, contraception by the young, withholding medical treatment to end a vegetative life, discrimination, and so forth—morality will often be the dominant influence. But that brings one to an intractable problem: often there will be great scope for debate as to what the moral answer is. The starting point of a modern English judge will probably be accepted standards of behaviour customary in a European liberal democracy. But he will also have to bear in mind the fact that we live in a multi-cultural society. Inevitably, there will be competing perspectives as to the dictates of morality.

Unfortunately our legal literature on this important and complex subject was sparse. Kim Economides and the essayists have admirably filled the gap. At the same time they have thoughtfully explored the introduction of legal ethics into law school *curricula*. While it is important that the role of morality should be taught as an integrated part of substantive teaching I have been fully persuaded that only by also teaching legal ethics as a separate subject can its potential be fully realized. Finally, I have found of great value the discussion of legal ethics and professional responsibility. In an age when crude commercialism is adversely affecting professional standards this discussion is most apposite.

I unreservedly recommend this book to all who are interested in the quality of our law and administration of justice.

4 May, 1998

The Right Honourable the
Lord Steyn
House of Lords
London

Introduction

Legal Ethics—
Three Challenges for the Next Millennium

KIM ECONOMIDES

For the past two hundred years law has been effectively separated from morality both jurisprudentially and pedagogically. The forces which sustain this separation—the positivist tradition, apathy, modernity's belief in the "technical fix" and the "ethics" of radical individualism prevalent in recent social and economic policy—while formidable are by no means inevitable.[1] This volume recognises the historical contingency of this separation and, through presenting the case for incorporating ethics into the curriculum of the modern law school, seeks to rise to the challenge of change at the cusp of a new millennium.

The present teaching of law, despite increasing contact between legal scholarship and ancillary disciplines, remains largely unaffected by other branches of normative science such as ethical and moral philosophy because of the enduring dominance of positivist legal science within the majority of law schools.[2] And law students nowadays seem more preoccupied than ever before with the acquisition of grades, knowledge, know-how and skills determining their entry into the legal services industry, while law schools themselves are subjected to perpetual audit and forced to pay increasing attention to grades which place them in national and international league tables. If values are detected in the informal curriculum they are likely to be commercial or competitive in character, and within the formal curriculum discussion of values tends to be confined to (increasingly optional) courses in jurisprudence or legal philosophy and packaged in terms of remote historic struggles between natural law theory and legal positivism.[3] Values, personal or political, are not supposed to enter the realm of legal analysis and if these cannot always be excluded from the business of interpreting law it is generally

---

[1] See, eg, R.Bellah et al, *Habits of the heart. Individualism and commitment in American life* (Berkeley, Univ. Calif. Press, 1985).

[2] P.A.Thomas (ed), *Legal Frontiers* (Aldershot, Dartmouth Publishing, 1997); R.P.George (ed), *The autonomy of law. Essays on legal positivism* (Oxford, OUP, 1996).

[3] H.Barnett, "The province of jurisprudence determined—again!" (1995) 15:1 *Legal Studies* 88.

accepted they must be contained as much as possible if law is to retain its status as an intellectual or professional discipline. Morals, like public policy, are seen as unruly hobby horses and dangerous to ride. Instead, problem questions based on fictitious or ridiculous characters enable law teachers to immunise their students from distracting real-life private and public moral dilemmas confronting lawyers, clients and communities in order that law teaching can imbibe appreciation and respect for the pure logic, beauty and symmetry of legal principle.[4] Law, as institutional, social or scientific fact, has—or should have—as little to do with values as possible and in a very real sense modern law is taught, and learnt, as if it is some kind of amoral natural science. Ethics have effectively been squeezed out of the modern law school at almost every level.

This traditional pedagogy, drained of all forms of ethical thinking, has come under increasing attack from scholars and teachers in recent years who reject the claims and methods of a crude positivist legal science. After all, it is accepted that natural scientists who reveal the secrets of splitting atoms, of human genes and life itself have moral responsibilities toward their research subjects, sponsors and findings and that it is not possible to exclude ethical consideration of the social consequences, intended or otherwise, of scientific discovery.[5] The detailed regulation of scientific discovery is frequently governed by complex secondary legislation influenced by the work of specialised ethics committees but for sure much of this work eventually falls into the hands of lawyers. In the realm of professional practice individual doctors, architects, engineers, accountants and social workers may submit themselves to disciplinary or investigative committees which arbitrate between what is right and wrong in the conduct of their members. Here too lawyers and judges are often found centre-stage of proceedings to ensure that process values are present when determining "the facts" and whether the evidence adduced supports a charge of professional misconduct, negligence or moral ineptitude. Positive law and evidential techniques, with some irony, frame the boundaries, discourse and outcomes of ethical debate across many areas of public and private life in contemporary society. The juridification of ethical debate arising out of scientific and technological discovery creates both new markets and moral responsibilities for legal professionals and regulators. Moreover, the application and manipulation of legal norms carries with it

---

[4] I do not wish to suggest that hypotheticals should have no place in law school and indeed they could have particular relevance for the future teaching of ethics, see, eg., L. de Groot-van Leeuwen, "Lawyers' moral reasoning and professional conduct, in practice and in education", Chap.12 *infra*; A.Hutchinson, *infra*, n.17. There is however a price to be paid for decontextualized knowledge, see further: Granfield, "The politics of decontextualized knowledge: Bringing context into ethics instruction in law school", Chap.15 *infra*. For an examination of the ethics of positivism and positivist ideals see: T.D.Campbell, *The Legal Theory of Ethical Positivism* (Aldershot, Dartmouth Publishing, 1996).

[5] V.Olgiati, "Risk, Professions, and the Claim for Human Rights" in: Oligiati et al (eds.) *Professions, Identity, and Order in Comparative Perspective* (Oñati: The International Institute for the Sociology of Law, 1998).

similar responsibilities which have an ethical dimension even if these are usually buried beneath a mass of technical legal rules.

One is entitled to ask what qualifies lawyers to assume these new roles and whether more should be done to make them aware of law's moral dimension in other areas of everyday legal activity. Is legal positivism a sufficient basis for the formation of the professional character of future lawyers—and what are its ethical foundations? Does the modern lawyer need instruction in the ethical consequences of professional action (or inaction)? What and for whom, we might ask, are modern lawyers, and law, really there for? This volume asks whether lawyers require a stronger ethical education and, if so, what could be taught them, when and how? What actually is involved in the ethicisation of law and lawyering?

1. THE MORAL WAVE IN CONTEMPORARY LEGAL EDUCATION

The range of issues and jurisdictions covered by the contributors to this volume suggests that there is in almost every corner of the globe a resurgence of interest in the teaching of ethics to future members of the legal profession. Nor is the Lord Chancellor's Advisory Committee on Legal Education and Conduct (ACLEC) alone amongst national reviews of legal education in laying down what it has called "the ethical challenge".[6] A recent report on the future of advanced legal research in the Netherlands (the Franken Report) had this to say on the role of ethics in legal education:

"We plead for strong intellectual ties with ethics. Law faculties must deliver conscientious lawyers, not simple implementation officers. A lawyer must be constantly aware of the ethical content of his decisions. Especially attorneys and corporate lawyers, sometimes out of necessity for partiality, move on the boundaries of what is ethically allowed. Lawyers are to an increasing extent confronted with politico-legal considerations. The developments of the private professional sense of values is necessary for a socially responsible professional practice. . . . Because numerous ethical, philosophical and political questions are submitted to the law nowadays, the search for normative starting points for the

---

[6] ACLEC, *First report on legal education and training*, para 1.19–20, 1996. Considered in B.Hepple, "The renewal of the liberal law degree" (1996) 55:3 *Cambridge L.J.* 470, 484; H.W.Arthurs, "Half a league onward: The report of the Lord Chancellor's Advisory Committee on Legal Education and Conduct" (1997) 31:1 *The Law Teacher* 1; J.Webb, "Ethics for lawyers or ethics for citizens? New directions for legal education" (1998) 25:1 *J. Law and Society* 134. In November 1997 the New Zealand Council for Legal Education, the professional body which sets the requirements for admission to the Bar, made it mandatory for all those admitted after July 2000 to have done a university course in legal ethics. See also, R.MacCrate, *Legal Education and Professional Development—An Educational Continuum. Report of the Task Force on Law Schools and the Profession: Narrowing the Gap.* (Chicago, American Bar Association, 1992); D.Pearce, *Australian Law Schools: A Discipline Assessment for the Commonwealth Tertiary Commission* (Australian Publishing Service, 1987); W.B.Cotter, *Professional Responsibility Instruction in Canada: A Coordinated Curriculum for Legal Education* (Montreal, Conceptcom, 1992)

law to deal with such complex and controversial social issues gets much greater urgency. What does a lawyer base his principles and fair judgements on when he is asked to weigh the visions of parties concerned that are diametrically opposed to one another?"[7]

There are several aspects to the new moral wave found in many law schools which forms part a common response to a perceived gap in the education of lawyers and a realisation that mastery in the technique of law is no longer sufficient for those entering the profession. While many might concede that such a gap exists there is no consensus on what should fill this moral vacuum or indeed whether it can or should be filled.[8] The most common response has been to ignore the issue, or if it is acknowledged, to deny that it is problematic. If the gap is now being acknowledged and seen as problematic then the real challenge emerges as to what can be done about it. The literature on legal ethics at the undergraduate level is, to say the least, scant and there are remarkably few courses outside North American law schools dedicated to this issue. And as some of the following chapters explain those courses on legal ethics which do exist produce few clear or consistent messages arising out of the experiences of those who teach or follow them. There is therefore no simple answer to the question, "can we teach legal ethics?" and no well-trodden path to follow through law's moral maze.

The call for ethical awareness amongst lawyers is of course not confined to educational debates within law schools and it is quite clear that the current demand for ethical instruction stems also from a desire to remedy perceived defects or deficiencies undermining professional practice. Professional standards and competence, it is hoped, might well benefit from the internalisation of ethical and legal values at a formative stage in the development of the lawyer's professional character. Ethics might also form a basis for shared identity in an increasingly diverse and confused profession coping with rapid change. We also know that professional regulation based on codes of conduct can only achieve so much, especially when the regulated group is by definition expert in manipulating and, where necessary, avoiding rules. What is it then that guides the handling of current professional codes of conduct: personal or client self-interest or is there some form of collective conscience which exerts influence over, if not determines, legal action? And we should not ignore the popularity of ethics in almost every other area of public life—ethics are without doubt fashionable in the political and business arenas of the 1990's which appear to be reacting against the base materialism of the 1980's. Is the ethicisation of law and lawyering at root part of this wider social trend or is it

---

[7] H. Franken, *Een eigen richting voor het recht . . . Eindrapport van de Verkenningscommissie Rechtsgeleerdheid.* (A sense of direction. . . The future of legal research in the Netherlands) Final Report of the Legal Education Review Commission, 1997, 55–56.

[8] A. Gutman, "Can virtue be taught?" (1993) 45 *Stanford Law Rev.* 1759. See further A. Paterson, "Legal ethics: Its nature and place in the curriculum" in R. Cranston (ed.), *Legal ethics and professional responsibility* (Oxford, OUP, 1995).

a logical next step to be taken within the evolution of legal science and professional practice?

The trend toward legal ethics would seem to fit comfortably within conflicting theories explaining the professional project of lawyers. Whether seen as a means to enhance "market control" or a consequence of the "renegotiation of professionalism" ethics arguably boosts both legal markets and professional status, without necessarily making lawyers any better as people or professionals.[9] How these divergent goals of pursuing profit whilst maintaining standards are balanced is crucial and possibly best understood inside what Arthurs describes as the "ethical economy" of the legal profession.[10] Yet we should not forget that the professional bodies, as much as their individual members, enjoy only so much autonomy and influence. The call for ethical instruction within law schools may at times form part of a more general reaction—if not moral panic—to some major constitutional crisis exposing the moral frailty of public figures (and their legal advisers) as, for example, in the infamous Watergate scandal or the corruption charges brought against President Collor in 1991 in Brazil. While cataclysmic events such as these offer some support for those who argue that a distinctive "ethical project"[11] can be seen at work within the wider professional project we should avoid adopting too narrow a view which might ignore the wider legal, social and political culture. In some countries where civil society itself is ethically grounded we may well find that instruction in legal ethics is considered otiose, and certainly no more necessary than either law or lawyers.[12] The present call for ethical instruction in law may be seen as naive, cathartic, cynical, altruistic, hypocritical, noble or futile—but whatever the motive behind this call its universal dimensions cannot be denied.

This moral wave in contemporary legal education and practice might be considered sufficient justification for the assertion that a "fourth wave" has now surfaced in the international Access to Justice Movement.[13] There are two distinct but related aspects to this fourth wave and both carry with them

---

[9] R. Abel, "Why does the ABA promulgate ethical rules?" (1981) 59 *Texas Law Rev.* 639; "The Decline of Professionalism?" (1986) 49 *Modern Law Rev.* 1; A. Paterson, "Professionalism and the legal services market" (1996) 3 *International J. of the Legal Profession* 137.

[10] H.W. Arthurs, "Why Canadian Law Schools do not Teach Legal Ethics", Chap.6 *infra*.

[11] P. Morgan & G. Reynolds, *The Appearance of Impropriety: How Ethics Wars Have Undermined the American Government* (New York, Free Press, 1997); L. Sheinman, "Looking for Legal Ethics" (1997) 4:1/2 *International J. of the Legal Profession* 139, 150.

[12] The Japanese legal system is sometimes held up to illustrate Donald Black's point that "law varies with other forms of social control": see D. Black, *The Behavior of Law* (New York, Academic Press, 1976). See also K. Economides, "Educating lawyers for the new millennium—the ethical dimension" (forthcoming, 1998) 31:3 *Chuo Comparative Law Rev.* [1997 Canon Foundation Visiting Professorship Lecture].

[13] See M. Cappelletti and B. Garth, *Access to Justice* (Milan and Alphen aan den Rijn, Giuffrè/Sijthoff & Noordhoff, 1978–79). See also K. Economides, 'Reading the waves of the "Access to Justice Movement": epistemology versus methodology' published as 'Lendo as ondas do "Movimento de Acesso à Justiça": epistemologia *versus* metodologia' in, *Justiça e Cidadania* (Rio de Janeiro, CPDOC-FGV/ISER, 1998, in press).

significant ethical responsibilities for the modern law school: first, citizens' access to legal education and entry to the legal profession; second, once qualified, lawyers' access and commitment to justice. Having surmounted the barriers to entry to the courts and the legal profession how can citizens ensure that either judges or lawyers will be equipped to understand and deliver "justice"? Although this volume concentrates primarily, but not exclusively, on the ethical challenges confronting law schools when "educating for justice"[14] we should not ignore the huge ethical responsibilities falling upon universities (and governments) everywhere which as gatekeepers regularly grapple with decisions over whom they fund or select and thereby determine who is able to enter law school and the legal profession.[15] In concentrating for now on this second aspect the hope is that eventually policy-makers inside and outside university law schools will actively promote access, equal opportunities and fairness regarding hitherto excluded groups, particularly if they themselves have been exposed to a rigorous legal education alive to issues such as how scarce resources should be allocated.[16] The goal to be striven for is to understand not only what makes a good lawyer, but also what makes a lawyer good.

In seeking answers to this question three related themes are tackled by the contributors to this volume: 1) the rediscovery of law's moral foundations; 2) introducing legal ethics into the law school curriculum and 3) what is involved in making lawyers good. While the disciplinary, jursisdictional and cultural backgrounds of the contributors differ all are united in presenting academic and critical perspectives on these interconnected challenges. It is perhaps also worth stating that the volume tries to unpack these challenges in order to comprehend and explain what lies behind them.

2. REDISCOVERING LAW'S MORAL FOUNDATIONS

Our first challenge is to understand better the relationship between law and ethics through examining more closely classical and literary texts and by explaining the forces which have kept these fields separate. From the various vantage points of classical, post (or late-) modern, normative and sociological thought we can observe the nature of professional obligation against the backcloth of moral as well as professional codes. These differing perspectives suggest new ways of conceiving and appreciating legal thought and action and above all challenge a mechanistic and subjective approach to studying or practising law. Legal rules and professional norms must be analysed taking

---

[14] See also J. Cooper and L. Trubek (eds.), *Educating for Justice: Social Values and Legal Education*, (Aldershot, Dartmouth Publishing, 1997).

[15] R. Dhavan et al.(eds.), *Access to Legal Education and the Legal Profession*, (London, Butterworths, 1989).

[16] See, eg., G.Calabresi & P.Bobbitt, *Tragic Choices* (New York, Norton, 1978).

into account higher principles and their effects on "the other". The perspectives offered here are of course only partial and to a large extent personal—Asian, African, Jewish, Islamic and Scandinavian philosophy could no doubt all add many other valuable and contrasting insights on law and ethics—but each of the present contributors in their own way encourages the reader to transcend traditional legal frameworks and engage directly with latent moral dilemmas. The challenge is not so much to see something new but rather to see afresh what is already there.

Christopher Gill (Chap. 1) reminds us that we have a vitally important resource in Greek and Roman philosophy to help us explore what lies at the root of contemporary Western legal ethics. His discussion of Plato's *Gorgias* and Cicero's *On Duties* Book 3 brings out many relevant points for lawyers but particularly valuable is his discussion of the ethical responsibilities of the advocate. What is the ethical status and function of those engaged in public persuasion and what does it mean to lead a "good" or "human" life within the practice of law? Law students may find it challenging, if not disturbing, to discover that there is no single agreed authoritative decision in answer to such a question. The ancient debates retraced by Christopher Gill demand from those who seek to follow them the application of moral reasoning and judgment rather than the blind application of precedent. More importantly, these debates overtly confront immoralism and offer the law student a set of moral precepts through which they could begin to work out their own independent ethical standpoint. And interestingly, these debates connect with universal as well as local considerations raising topical points concerning human rights and transnational legal orders. As such they provide a valuable antidote to parochial legalism. Costas Douzinas (Chap.2) also draws upon classical texts in order to explain the relationship between law, justice and ethics but from a distinct postmodern perspective which focusses our attention on "the other" (perhaps another useful antidote to lawyers' egotistical tendencies). He places legal justice in a wider philosophical and historical context opening up new possibilities for those lawyers wishing not to be totally dependent on the off-the-peg morality handed down by their professional codes. Both Gill and Douzinas set out a novel kind of ethical agenda which in time could conceivably shape a more enlightened and humane ethical framework for the practice of law.

Tim Dare's thorough discussion of the predicament of the lawyer-hero Atticus Finch, in Harper Lee's *To Kill A Mockingbird* (Chap.3), succeeds in teasing out some fundamental questions concerning the relationship between character, rules and principle and demonstrates exactly what rigorous ethical debate has to offer us. Every law student (and seasoned practitioner) might usefully read both Lee's novel and Dare's commentary in order to confront head on difficult ethical dilemmas likely to be ignored by written or unwritten social and professional codes of practice. This novel also raises something not normally classified as ethical, namely, the choice of where and for which social groups one practices law. Atticus opts for country practice and to defend a cause which seems lost from the outset and in so doing practices the "ethics of alterity". His example suggests that country practice and criminal defence work bring their own alternative rewards and opportunities even if very different to those of serving corporate clients in the City. As Allan Hutchinson has argued recently,[17] consciously choosing one's career path and place of practice, and therefore one's potential clients, can involve as much if not more of an ethical choice as the formal acceptance of a particular case in accordance with the cab-rank principle. Dare's discussion of Atticus also engages with classical thought and more recent debates on the changing basis of the legal professional ideal, notably Kronman's lament of the demise of the "lawyer-statesman",[18] in order to clarify what is at the heart of professional ethical obligation. His conclusion points not so much toward the need for a virtue-based ethics but rather for a deeper appreciation amongst lawyers of process and professional values governing relations with their clients and communities, as well as a much stronger grasp of the intrinsic value of both rules and principles.[19]

Staying with the theme of the lawyer as advocate, Robert Rosen (Chap. 4) examines critically some of the ethical contradictions which lie buried in this role: the idea of legal ethics as deontological ethics, the notion of "thinking like a lawyer"—as underpinned by the ideals of democracy and legalism—and the various "issue conflicts of interest" thrown up by the market place. In each instance Rosen exposes the ideological, economic and educational frameworks which circumscribe, if not determine, the narrow scope of current ethical debate amongst lawyers. This brake on the development of a truly progressive and humanistic legal education which Rosen describes poses the question, asked by Vittorio Olgiati (Chap.5), of whether "legal ethics" can become a matter of academic teaching. Olgiati fears that legal ethics, however conceived and taught, could simultaneously jeopardise both scientific and legal professionalism through its tendency to relativise and problematise, rather than reinforce, the validity of the professional model. Yet despite such problems Olgiati concludes that academics have no alternative but to rise to the challenge of linking professional responsibility to social claims for effective human rights enforcement mechanisms—to connect professional conduct with real social needs and in so doing entrench and re-establish law's moral foundations and authority. In order to achieve this he also suggests reviving the methods of ancient thought as revealed in classical texts.

---

[17] Lecture at Cardiff Law School, 4 March 1998, "Taking it personally: legal ethics in a diverse society". See also, A. Hutchinson, *Legal Ethics and Professional Responsibility: A Critical Introduction* (in press, 1998).

[18] A. Kronman, *The Lost Lawyer* (Cambridge, Mass., Belknap Press, 1993).

[19] See further M. McConville et al, *Standing Accused. The Organization and Practices of Criminal Defence Lawyers in Britain* (Oxford, Clarendon, 1994) and references at n.27 *infra*.

3. INTRODUCING LEGAL ETHICS INTO THE CURRICULUM

The second challenge concerns the problem of incorporating legal ethics into the curriculum. If students are to be made aware of law's moral foundations how should courses in legal ethics be organised to achieve this? The moral wave in contemporary legal education has highlighted a problem but without identifying any clear or obvious solutions. The contributors to this section all describe recent developments in undergraduate legal education which in several jurisdictions appear to have reached a crossroads. Underpinning all of these educational debates lies unresolved the problematic relationship linking the education and practice of law, perhaps best captured by the question "what are law schools for?"[20]

Harry Arthurs (Chap. 6) explains that in Canada law schools define their role in terms of providing a liberal education rather offering mere professional training. Their role is not subordinated to professional interests nor is it the business of a law school to inculcate on behalf of the profession the norms governing professional practice. Canadian law schools are, according to the Cotter Report[21], largely indifferent to legal ethics which as Arthurs explains is partly due to the absence of a significant body of scholarly domestic literature on the subject as well as the inaccessibility (and poor quality) of published primary source material. Apparently also inadequate is the enforcement of these ethical rules by the professional bodies. Without better indigenous source material, and contextual awareness of the application of ethical rules and the wider role of the legal profession in society, Arthurs argues that it is impossible to offer students a rigorous intellectual experience comparable to that offered in other parts of the curriculum. The Canadian experience illustrates well precisely the problem identified by Olgiati of how to balance scientific and legal professionalism.

Australian law schools, according to Andrew Goldsmith and Guy Powles (Chap. 7), have also been held back by the professional bodies from increasing ethical awareness amongst both students and practitioners but here part of the blame is levelled at law schools themselves. Goldsmith and Powles tell a very similar story to Arthurs and argue persuasively that there has been a serious dereliction of duty by most law schools and the Australian legal profession regarding the promotion of ethics. Ethical resources, whether primary or secondary, have been woefully deficient in both quantitative and qualitative terms and they argue forcefully that the time has now arrived for the construction of a new imaginative code to fill what they call "a strategic vacuum". Such a code might act as a kind of constitution for legal profes-

---

[20] See W. Twining, *Blackstone's Tower: The English Law School* (London, Sweet & Maxwell, 1994); "What are law schools for?" in W. Twining, *Law in Context: Enlarging a Discipline* (Oxford, OUP, 1997); "Rethinking law schools" (1996) 21 *Law and Social Inquiry* 1007; "Thinking about law schools: Rutland reviewed" (1998) 25:1 *J. Law and Society* 1.

[21] *Supra*, n.6.

sionalism and two contrasting models of professional preparation are advanced in order to fill this vacuum, a replicative and transformative model, which present a clear choice for policy-makers inside and outside law schools. The challenge in Australia, as elsewhere, is for academics and practitioners to forge an alliance in order that ethics can be researched, taught and practised in context, and thereby taken seriously.

The recent situation in English law schools regarding the teaching of legal ethics is summarised and discussed by Richard O'Dair (Chap. 8). The deficiencies of the professional codes and the need for their reform are also raised and the message that contextual awareness must be introduced into future legal ethics courses echoes that arising out of the Canadian and Australian experience. O'Dair examines the implications of the historic divide separating academic from practising lawyers in the UK and notes its retarding effect on the development of the teaching of legal ethics in undergraduate law degrees. The position of Brazilian law schools is analysed by Eliane Junqueira (Chap. 9) who also focusses on the role and relations with the professional bodies as well as the limitations of the professional codes. The teaching of ethics in the Catholic University of Rio de Janeiro is provided by the Department of Theology under the influence of the confessional character of Catholicism. Junqueira's description of the course on legal ethics shows just how eclectic, and exciting, teaching resources can be and ethical instruction may include discussion of historical events, film, progressive theological documents based on a Marxist theology of liberation, practical experience of working in a shanty town (*favela*) and an empirical research project on citizens' perceptions of the legal profession. Junqueira also considers the impact of this teaching on students both during their time at law school and thereafter. For most students, but not all, legal ethics become equated with those proclaimed in the professional codes with few willing to travel beyond them—but her explanation for this lies not so much in the prevailing attitudes of the legal profession, nor in those of the law school, but rather in those of Brazilian society itself. Richard Grimes (Chap. 10) examines the position of legal ethics in another tropical location, the South Pacific, which has recently been overhauling its system of legal education. Grimes also highlights the importance of contextual awareness and the need to develop ethical codes for the legal profession which are in tune with the norms and values of the local culture and its customs. Both of these studies point to a further challenge for anthropological and sociological research: the explanation of the relationship between social and cultural norms and the values espoused and practised by the legal profession.

Tom Morawetz (Chap. 11) finally brings together some of the more valuable lessons emerging from American law schools for those wishing to teach professionalism through ethics courses at the undergraduate level. His account of the available educational resources, defects and remedies for legal ethics teaching will provide invaluable guidance for those designing new courses from scratch. Morawetz proposes several reforms including moving the standard course on ethics to the first year. He also raises interesting points concerning lawyers' psychological health showing, for example, how the image and self-image of lawyers risks shattering due to the current sense of crisis, cynicism and ethical bankruptcy afflicting a profession working under increasing levels of mental and financial stress. He concludes with a reference to Plato's *Gorgias*, noting that the objectivity and accessibility of the concept of justice remains under seige, and asks whether lawyers today are capable of meeting the challenge of simultaneously serving the interests of their clients and justice. Can professionalism be represented as anything more than instrumental skill?

4. MAKING LAWYERS GOOD

The final challenge involves the construction of new frameworks for comprehending and transforming the structures which shape, and at times restrict, professional responsibility in order to promote the goal of the "good lawyer" and more refined understandings of professionalism. This will involve analysing the dominant forms of ethical reasoning present in current legal practice, incorporating new perspectives responsive to the values of groups, including clients, hitherto excluded from (or under-represented within) the legal profession; reforming vocational legal education to achieve a smoother transition from law school to law office or courtroom; strengthening contextual awareness in law school and legal practice so that lawyers are competent to give sound ethical advice and examining new regulatory frameworks which are beginning to evolve at the transnational level. Also important is the evolution of the adversarial framework for litigation currently being supplanted by alternative structures of a more informal nature and which in turn generate demand for new forms of lawyering and, consequently, new meanings for "legal" or "quasi-legal" ethics.[22]

Leny de Groot-van Leeuwen (Chap. 12) interviewed Dutch lawyers working in a range of legal practices about their handling of ethical dilemmas. Her findings offer a snapshot of current levels of ethical awareness amongst legal professionals and allow us to glimpse how ethical choices coexist alongside other decisions affecting the maintainance of economic and professional status in the market place. Moreover, distinct patterns of moral reasoning emerge, both amongst practitioners and students, who were required to reflect on the same hypothetical cases. The conclusion reached is that there is a need for ethical instruction to focus on the "ethics of care" and, supporting Morawetz, to time this instruction so that it takes place early on in the

---

[22] C. Menkel-Meadow, "Culture clash in the quality of life in the law: Changes in the economics, diversification and organization of lawyering" (1994) 44:2 *Case Western Reserve Law Rev.* 621; "The trouble with the adversary system in a post-modern, multi-cultural world" (1996) 1 *J.Institute for the Study of Legal Ethics* 801.

curriculum, but also important is the need to see this instruction as forming part of an educational continuum supporting lifelong learning. Because most of the lawyers interviewed in the sample would not have followed a course in legal ethics they placed heavy reliance on their professional oath and code of conduct and the jurisprudence of disciplinary committees. Deborah Rhode (Chap. 13) explains what is involved in adopting a feminist perspective on legal ethics and how feminist commitments radically challenge values embedded in law schools and professional legal practice. The challenges presented by feminist legal ethics are varied and operate at the methodological, substantive and structural levels. Sensitivity to context also implies taking responsibility for non-clients that are socially excluded and widening understanding of care and concern within the lawyer-client relationship. In this way feminist approaches both enrich and deepen professional commitment to access to justice.

Amongst the most difficult of the challenges facing law teachers is to know when and how to introduce their students to handling ethical conflicts. While a superficial grounding in the concepts and vocabularies of ethical discourse and reasoning can be transmitted at the undergraduate level it is far more difficult to find the right balance between principle and practice at the vocational stage, and thereafter. Julian Webb (Chap. 14) examines this issue in detail and points out defects in the teaching of legal ethics in vocational legal education. The problem here is not simply that of the limitations on (or of) the teacher since it appears common to several jurisdictions that students habitually resist, either through apathy or cynicism, ethical instruction. Can teaching legal ethics therefore make a real difference to professional conduct and, if so, under what conditions? In England the relaxation of the control exerted by the professional bodies over the content of the vocational courses creates novel opportunities for their development in partnership with legal academics. Webb argues that although some of these opportunities may have been missed the way forward lies through experimenting with developmental approaches based on realistic—if not real—problems arising out of the actual behaviour of practitioners. It follows that curriculum designers must be informed by the realities and experiences of the lawyers' working (and learning) environment—but this environment should not be considered either static or unmalleable. Part of this environment is constructed and maintained by the codes of conduct which provide an obvious starting point for reformers. Again, the way forward appears to lie in fusing and coordinating educational and substantive law reform. Robert Granfield (Chap. 15) explains how the context of professional practice might effectively be brought into the classroom without socialising students into too narrow a conception of professionalism. His longitudinal research which tracks the transition of a cohort of students from law school into practice, and assesses the impact of their courses in legal ethics, is instructive and should challenge the complacency of both law schools and professional bodies. Courses in legal ethics typically evade really tough personal and professional dilemmas, for example those arising out of whether and how to represent deviant, difficult or unpopular causes, including inchoate communitarian concerns, partly because traditional codes of professional ethics are either silent or simplistic regarding matters of power, inequality and community. The ethics of advocacy calls out for a far more theoretically and contextually informed treatment than it has received so far—it is one which presents academic lawyers with the double challenge of first discovering more about the nature of professional practice, and second, communicating the significance of this context to students in an interesting, lively and engaging manner.

It would be a mistake however to place all responsibility for educational reform onto law schools. Charles Sampford and Sophie Blencowe (Chap. 16) point to the need to expand our understanding of the professional context of lawyering beyond the narrowly legal and to see legal practice as inclusive of a range of advice-giving embracing, *inter alia,* advice on ethics. While they too argue that law schools should reverse their conventional practice of separating law from students' sense of morality by building ethics into the curriculum, and at all stages of the educational continuum, they also put forward the idea that lawyers should educate their clients regarding the value of ethical advice. This may be seen by some as little more than "demand creation" but perhaps comes closer to the notion of "consumer education". Their proposals in turn create novel organisational challenges for law firms which if implemented promise to enhance both individual and collective professional status through what they term "ethical risk management". Finally, we must not neglect the role and responsibilities of the professional bodies in educating and regulating the conduct of their members so as to promote practice standards at both the national and supranational levels. Avrom Sherr (Chap. 17) looks to the rules purporting to govern ethical conduct in just four jurisdictions inside the European Union (The Netherlands, Scotland, Germany, England & Wales). His survey comparing levels and systems of complaints across these jurisdictions, including also a comparison with the medical profession, reveals contrasting approaches toward the common problems of regulating professional conduct and policing misconduct. The problem which lies before us, however, is not simply one of preventing or correcting abuses and placing restraints on conduct for we must also begin the task of developing positive principles and attitudes—an ethical consciousness—which may inspire and actively promote the highest standards of professional behaviour, perhaps through informing the progressive evolution and creative interpretation of professional codes. The picture gradually emerging is one in which the inexorable demand for ethical education and regulation is pushing aside established jurisdictional and professional boundaries. Yet while the need for the "good lawyer" has never been so great, creating or finding this paragon remains as elusive as defining the model behaviour we might seek to promote.

5. ON MEETING THE ETHICAL CHALLENGE

The contributors to this volume present complementary academic perspectives on the nature of the ethical challenge which now lies before law schools and the professional bodies. These perspectives should serve to inform, inspire and caution reformers willing and able to take up (and unsettle those who decline) this challenge. Although the ideas and proposals which follow point in several directions it is possible to draw up three broad interconnected agendas concerning research, education and policy priorities, mirroring to some extent our three principal challenges, which might act as a catalyst for a comprehensive programme of reform.

(a) Research agendas

There is clearly further scope for original collaborative research on the relationship between law and ethics and Gill's appendix will hopefully guide and stimulate academic lawyers wishing to read, or re-read, classical texts. We should perhaps also acknowledge that the call for a link between law and ethics is not only intellectual but also, in part, embraces a range of emotional responses, including anger, at the effects of injustice.[23] Controlling and understanding the emotions is likely to prove amongst the most difficult of the challenges confronting those who wish to introduce a more systematic and rational approach to legal ethics education in the future.

Modern literature, as exemplified by Dare's chapter, similarly has much to offer lawyers wishing to understand the complexities and contradictions of moral reasoning inside legal contexts. And we should not forget that contemporary, even popular, culture can provide useful, if sometimes over-dramatised, materials from which to approach ethical dilemmas confronting legal practitioners.[24] As lawyers wishing to develop a deeper appreciation for

---

[23] See, eg., E. Cahn, *The Sense of Injustice—An Anthropocentric View of Law* (New York University Press, 1949); *Confronting Injustice* (London, Gollancz, 1967). M.C. Nussbaum, *Poetic Justice: The literary imagination and public life* (Boston, Beacon Press, 1996).

[24] See, eg., J.Flood, "Shark tanks, sweatshops, and the lawyer as hero? Fact as fiction" (1994) 21:3 *J.Law and Society* 396. The novels of John Grisham, television programmes such as *L.A. Law* or *Kavanagh Q.C.* frequently represent lawyers struggling with the decision over whether to take a moral stand and how to distinguish professional from private morality. In some jurisdictions it is judges who are forced to take a moral stand as in the Italian television series *Octopus*, produced by RAI, depicting attempts by the Mafia to subvert the judicial process through judicial assassination, as happened in the tragic case of the Sicilian Judge Falcone. Other films, such as *In the name of the father* (on the defence of the Guildford 4) and *Z*, based on the novel by V. Vassilikos, *Z* (Athens, Editions Themelio,1966) on the assassination of the left-wing politician Lambrakis in 1963 in Salonika, depict lawyers taking a heroic stand against authoritarian bureaucracies and regimes. See further, R.L. Abel, *Politics by other means. Law in the struggle against apartheid, 1980–1994* (New York and London, Routledge, 1995); A. Sarat and S.Scheingold (eds), *Cause lawyering. Political commitments and professional responsibilities* (Oxford, OUP, 1998).

the art of rhetoric and moral judgement we should recognise that sources such as film, literature, and even art may enlighten us as to the true nature of ethical obligation. Research on legal ethics should therefore be open to, and draw upon, literary, linguistic and artistic sources as well as diverse intellectual traditions within the social and normative sciences, and especially the field of applied ethics.[25]

These interdisciplinary approaches should not obscure the possibility of discovering and analysing legal values latent in the legal texts and processes which traditionally occupy the attentions of academic and practising lawyers.[26] There is no need to marginalise ethics by confining them to esoteric intellectual debates inaccessible to the majority of law teachers, students and practitioners and it is encouraging to note that in the English context there is currently a run of academic articles examining the ethical duties of practitioners.[27] Academic lawyers should seek to form collaborative alliances with both practitioners and those from other disciplines, but perhaps not simultaneously, in order to access and research the diverse contexts and meanings of ethical practice inside the law. It will also be necessary to connect legal ethics with broader normative and cultural frameworks outside the law and so put into practice the "ethics of alterity".

(b) Educational agendas

The educational agenda will need to be coordinated and informed by research uncovering the ethical context of legal practice. It will also be important to bear in mind the notion of the "educational continuum" and the timing issue in order to prevent overload at any given point within a legal career, while promoting a developmental—rather than instrumental—approach toward lifelong learning. Ethical reflection is arguably a competence which all legal professionals should continually refine throughout their careers. There is clearly much to be learnt from comparative experience, particularly that coming out of North America, but it would be a mistake to ignore ethical instruction and progressive practices currently being developed elsewhere and in other professions adopting proactive approaches motivated more by altruism

---

[25] See A. Young and A. Sarat (eds), "Beyond criticism: law, power and ethics" (1994) 3:3 *Social & Legal Studies* (Special issue); P.Singer (ed), *Applied ethics* (Oxford, OUP, 1986).

[26] D.R.F. O'Dair, "Ethics by the pervasive method—the case of contract" (1997)17:2 *Legal Studies* 305; D. Oliver, "Common values in public and private law and the public/private divide" (1997) *Public Law* 630; P. Cane, *The Anatomy of Tort Law* (Oxford, Hart, 1997); Stein and J.Shand, *Legal values in western society* (Edinburgh, Edinburgh Univ.Press, 1974).

[27] See, eg., M. Blake and A. Ashworth, "Some ethical issues in prosecuting and defending criminal cases" (1998) *Crim.L.R.*16; D.A.Ipp, "Lawyers' duties to the court" (1998) 114 *L.Q.R.*63; R. Henham, "Protective sentences: ethics, rights and sentencing policy" (1997) 25:1 *I.J.Sociology of Law* 45.

than profit.[28] While anti-discrimination law, and human rights law more generally, can be and are taught as any other branch of the law there are strong arguments in favour of elevating their status in the curriculum since commitment to these topics impacts directly on the collective integrity, responsibility and standing of lawyers as professionals.[29] It is to be hoped that the ethical challenge will unleash a new wave of experimentation resulting in improvements in teaching method and curriculum design.

In England and Wales, the forthcoming Joint Announcement on Qualifying Law Degrees soon to be issued by the Law Society and the Council of Legal Education offers precisely this opportunity and hopefully these bodies will respond to ACLEC's ethical challenge by incorporating "legal values including a commitment to the rule of law, to justice, fairness and high ethical standards"[30] amongst the educational outcomes all undergraduate law degrees should in future seek to meet. If this happens law schools in England and Wales will, at the very least, respond to—if not actually meet—the ethical challenge.

(c) Policy agendas

All of the above developments in the fields of research and education are likely to increase pressure on the professional bodies for reform of their codes of practice by highlighting omissions and pointing out alternatives. Applied comparative research on deontology—the formal rules governing conduct and professional responsibility—would be timely and has already commenced in a European context with Sherr's project.[31] Our understanding of compar-

---

[28] See, also, ethical awareness and competences currently being developed in social work training. The "Ethics and Values" course at the University of Exeter has the following aims: 1) to explore the value base of social work; 2) to develop understanding of ethical dilemmas in social work; 3) to examine the structure of power relationships and how they affect different groups in society; 4) to explore prejudice and discrimination, particularly in relation to class, gender, race, differing ability, sexuality, age, religion; 5) to enable students to develop awareness and understanding of anti-racist and anti-discriminatory practice; and 6) to enable students to apply learning from this sequence to all aspects of the programme. See further: R. Hugman and D. Smith (eds), *Ethical issues in social work* (London, Routledge,1995); S. Banks, *Ethics and values in social work* (Basingstoke, Macmillan, 1995); M. Horne, *Values in social work* (Aldershot, Wildwood House,1987); R. Adams, *Social work and empowerment* (London, Macmillan, 1996).

[29] See Olgiati, *supra* n.5. Emphasising the importance of these topics should not mean that we too readily abandon efforts to teach ethics throughout the law school curriculum: see D.L. Rhode, "Ethics by the pervasive method" (1992) 42 *J. of Legal Education* 31 and Chap.13 *infra.*; O'Dair *supra*, n.26. Arguments in favour of developing the ethical insights of the "legal humanities" (jurisprudence, legal history, law & literature) are also worth considering in this context, see Webb, *supra*, n. 6, 147.

[30] ACLEC *First Report supra* n.6, 72; note also the *Second Report* (London, ACLEC, 1997) para.2.33 calling upon the professions to make professional ethics mandatory during the first three years of practice.

[31] A. Sherr, "Legal Ethics in Europe", Chap.17 *infra*. See also J. Lonbay, *Training lawyers in the European Community* (London, The Law Society, 1990); G. Martin, *Déontologie de l'Avocat* (Paris, Editions Litec, 1995); R. Chadwick (ed.) *Ethics and the professions* (Aldershot, Avebury, 1994).

ative research should be broad enough to include international, inter- and intra-professional comparisons and consider, for example, the principles set out in ethical codes relating to other professions and their wider social significance.[32] The message from several jurisdictions seems to suggest that current codes are limited, limiting and unsatisfactory and, furthermore, that they are being badly supported by academic writing and analysis.[33] While it may be premature—even dangerous—to abandon or radically reform the professional codes a wide-ranging review of their current efficacy would be both valuable and informative. What do lawyers actually think of their codes of practice? Are they a help, hindrance or an irrelevance to the resolution of their ethical dilemmas? And finally, do the codes actually assist in the improvement and maintainance of professional standards—or do they instead retard the development of the "good" lawyer?

It is time that legal ethics became much more than a subject of passing debate within law schools and failure to respond creatively and imaginatively to these challenges will surely leave law schools and the wider legal community impoverished—not only intellectually, but also, and far more significantly, spiritually. Will law schools rise to this challenge and take responsibility for truly educating the next generation of lawyers by transmitting not only what Lon Fuller has called "the morality of duty" (law) but also "the morality of aspiration" (ethics)?[34]

---

[32] See, eg, British Association of Social Workers, *The Code of Ethics for Social Work* (Birmingham, BASW, 1996). C. Sampford with C. Parker, "Legal regulation, ethical standard-setting, and institutional design" in S. Parker and C. Sampford (eds), *Legal ethics and legal practice: Contemporary issues* (Oxford, OUP, 1995). It would be wrong to assume that codes of conduct are always essential: the English Bar, for example, had no code until 1980 relying instead for over six centuries on rules of conduct and etiquette being handed down by word of mouth. See A. Thornton, "Responsibility and ethics of the English Bar" in Cranston *supra* n.8. For a sceptical view of the value of ethical codes in an academic context see R. Dingwall, "Ethics and ethnography" (1980) 28:4 *Sociological Rev.* 871. See further R.M. MacIver, "The social significance of professional ethics" (1955) 297 *Ann.Am.Acad.Polit.Soc.Sci.* 118; E. Durkheim, *Professional ethics and civic morals* (London, RKP, 1957).

[33] See K. Economides and J. Webb, "Editorial : The ethical imagination" in the inaugural issue (Spring 1998) of *Legal Ethics* due to be published twice yearly by Hart Publishing, Oxford. See further: http://members.aol.com/legalethic/open.htm

[34] L. Fuller, *The morality of law* (New Haven and London, Yale Univ.Press, 1969),Chap.1.

Part 1

REDISCOVERING LAW'S MORAL FOUNDATIONS

1

Law and Ethics in Classical Thought

CHRISTOPHER GILL

INTRODUCTION

In this chapter, I examine two ancient discussions which both bear, in very different ways, on the relationship between law and ethics. The first, Plato's *Gorgias*, is a searching philosophical examination of the function and ethical status of rhetoric. With some historical imagination, we can read this work as raising issues which remain fundamental to the ethical status of legal practice and the legal profession. As the argument proceeds, it goes to the heart of such issues: what are the goals (the outcomes for living a human life) that legal practice and other forms of public persuasion aim at—and what should they aim at? The last part of Plato's dialogue is directed at an "immoralist", someone who argues that legal practice (and rhetoric generally) should be used to maximise your own interest and pleasure at the expense of other people. The *Gorgias* takes on the challenge of trying to show this immoralist that he fails to understand what he really wants in life, and therefore what he wants to achieve through public persuasion.

In Cicero's *On Duties* Book 3, the question explicitly raised is this: when right action and personal advantage conflict, what criteria do we use to resolve this conflict? Cicero, by contrast with Plato, assumes that his reader *wants* to lead a life centred on right action. So his question, more precisely, is this: what criteria can we use in such cases to ensure that our grasp of "right action" is objectively grounded? It is in Cicero's answer to this question that law enters the picture, in a way that both reflects Cicero's life-long experience in the Roman law-courts and bears on current debate about law and ethics. Although Cicero identifies certain universal principles as a basis for moral objectivity, he interprets these principles in the light of Roman legal precedents and concepts (such as "in good faith"). In effect, Cicero is arguing that moral objectivity is reached through correlating universal categories with the collective judgement and experience of one's community, as expressed in legal as well as ethical thinking and practice. I bring out the significance of this way of reading Cicero's discussion by partial contrast with Martha Nussbaum's reading, which stresses Cicero's use of universal categories, but which does not take account of the linkage between universal and localised or "embedded" legal and ethical thinking.

In this chapter, my aim is to bring out how the arguments put forward in these Greek and Roman philosophical discussions can contribute to contemporary debate about law and ethics. At the end of the chapter, I outline other Classical texts and topics that may be useful for this purpose and for teaching legal ethics.

PLATO'S *GORGIAS*

The argument of Plato's *Gorgias* centres on rhetoric, on its status as a form of expertise and on the goals with which it is, or should be, used. "Rhetoric", in Greek, signifies both the practice and the teaching of expertise in persuasive discourse. The scope of "rhetoric" is general, covering all fields of persuasion. But a field of special importance, both in Plato's dialogue and in late fifth-century Athens, where the dialogue is set, is that of public persuasion in the law-courts. The function of law-court rhetoric—and of punishment—is a key issue in the second stage of the dialogue. Also the questions raised about the status and proper use of rhetoric in general are similar to some of those raised in modern debate about the ethical status of legal practice and education. So, despite the institutional and social differences between Athenian and modern legal systems,[1] Plato's *Gorgias* can still serve as a powerful philosophical examination of issues in law and ethics.

The dialogue is conducted between the philosopher Socrates and three "interlocutors", Gorgias, Polus and Callicles, each of whom is engaged in dialogue in turn. The three parts are of increasing length and intensity, as the argument presses ever deeper into the issues. Broadly speaking, the first part centres on the status of rhetoric as an art or expertise, the second on the uses to which rhetoric should be put and the third on the proper goals of a human life, which determine how rhetoric and other forms of discourse should be employed. Another way of characterising the three parts of the dialogue is by the ethical stance of the interlocutor. Gorgias adopts a conventionally "respectable" ethical position; Polus equivocates between endorsing and subverting conventional ethics; Callicles adopts an explicitly "immoralist" stance. The dialogue implies that the third "immoralist" position is latent in the initial "respectable" one, and the argument sets out to expose radical ethical weaknesses in the conventional ethical understanding of rhetoric (including law-court rhetoric) and its uses.[2]

---

[1] Key differences are that Athenian juries are very large (e.g. 400), and that parties in disputes speak on their own behalf and refer freely to ethical considerations as well as the facts of the case. See further the references in n. 5 and Appendix below.

[2] See further C. Kahn, "Drama and Dialectic in Plato's *Gorgias*" (1983) 1 *Oxford Studies in Ancient Philosophy* 75–121.

The form of argument in the *Gorgias* is typical of Plato's early dialogues. Socrates puts a series of directed, general questions to his interlocutor (one person at a time) and exposes inconsistencies in the answers given by the interlocutor. More precisely, Socrates brings out inconsistencies between the answers originally offered by the interlocutor and those that the other person is prepared to accept when Socrates suggests them. This is a form of argument which places value on explicitness and logical consistency. The negative outcome of Socratic dialectic is clear: in this case, as suggested earlier, it exposes unrecognised inconsistencies in conventional beliefs about the ethical status and function of rhetoric. Less clear is the positive outcome. Some scholars think that Socrates believes that the conclusions of any given argument (which are stated with unusual explicitness and force at the close of this dialogue) have the status of known truths; more precisely, that only true statements can survive repeated examination in argument. Socrates, however, never makes such a strong claim. Here and elsewhere, the claim is, rather, that questioner and interlocutor are ethically and practically committed by the conclusion of the argument—until or unless they are able to provide each other with more logically consistent arguments for a different conclusion.[3] To this extent, ethics (the central topic of the Socratic dialogues) are presented as grounded in argument, an argument to which no external limit can be set.

GORGIAS: RHETORIC AND PROFESSIONAL EXPERTISE

The first stage of Socrates' argument is directed at Gorgias. Gorgias, in real life, was a famous "sophist", an itinerant expert and teacher; in particular, he was the most famous teacher of rhetoric in late fifth-century Greece. Socrates' questions focus on two, related issues. One is the status of rhetoric as a form of skill or expertise (*tekhnê*). On the one hand, Gorgias claims (what most people at the time would accept) that rhetoric *is* a form of expertise or knowledge (447c). On the other hand, he also makes admissions that enable Socrates subsequently to call into question whether rhetoric can count as a form of expertise (462b ff.). He admits that the function of rhetoric (as public persuasion) is to produce in its audience conviction or belief, which may be true or false, rather than knowledge, which can only be true (454c–455a). He also admits that the orator is more convincing than experts on a given subject, because he need not know the truth about it; he succeeds by *seeming* to non-experts to know more than the experts do (459b–c).

The second question on which Socrates focuses is whether someone who has expertise in rhetoric also has ethical expertise (knowledge of right and

---

[3] See e.g. *Gorgias* 505e–506a, 508e–509a (refs. to the standard Stephanus pages and page-divisions given at the side of the page in modern translations of Plato). See G. Vlastos, *Socratic Studies* (ed. M. F. Burnyeat, Cambridge, Cambridge University Press, 1994), chs. 1–2, for two seminal essays on Socratic method.

wrong) and the capacity to teach this to students. At one point Gorgias argues that the teacher of rhetoric should not be held responsible if students make ethically bad use of the rhetorical expertise they are taught (456e–457c). Subsequently, Socrates invites him to choose between two conceptions of the teacher of rhetoric: that of someone who merely seems to have, and to be able to teach, ethical knowledge, and someone who really has and can teach this knowledge. Gorgias chooses the latter option (459d–460a). Socrates then highlights the inconsistency between these two admissions of Gorgias (the orator claims to teach ethics, but is not to be held responsible if he fails to do so); and on this point their dialogue ends (460d–461c)).[4]

In this discussion, Plato goes straight to the heart of some of the issues we now associate with "professional ethics". The questions raised by Plato about rhetoric are all ones that apply with equal force to legal practice and education. As Socrates brings out, Gorgias equivocates between two conceptions of rhetoric. One is that it is an ethically neutral skill, the results of which (effective persuasion) can be defined without reference to the ethical content and effect of the persuasive rhetoric. (Associated with this conception is the idea that rhetoric can be taught—and, by implication, taught well—regardless of the ethical use made of rhetoric by the student.) The second conception of rhetoric is that it is an essentially ethical skill, and one whose function and effectiveness (like that of rhetorical education) cannot be defined without reference to ethical standards. The relevance of Plato's argument to questions of professional ethics is clearer in the case of law than in the case of some other professions, in that the force of law (to put it very broadly) is generally seen as bound up with its ethical function within society. Plato's argument thus serves to define two competing conceptions of the legal profession: as what Robert Rosen (in Chapter 4, Section 1, of this volume) calls "a lawful hired gun" and as a profession whose function is essentially ethical. The value of Plato's discussion lies in the starkness with which these options are defined, and in the rigour with which the argument brings out what each of these options imply and what they have to say to each other.

POLUS: ETHICAL AND NON-ETHICAL USES OF RHETORIC

In the second stage of the argument, Plato defines further the opposition between these two conceptions of rhetoric (and thus of professional expertise). He replaces Gorgias with an interlocutor (Polus) who, more or less explicitly, adopts the first of the two conceptions of rhetoric identified in the previous discussion, that of rhetoric as a value-neutral skill. Plato makes Socrates

---

[4] On the Socratic (and more generally Greek) idea of virtue as a *tekhnê* ("skill, expertise, craft"), see e.g. J. Annas, "Virtue as a Skill" (1995) 3 *International Journal of Philosophical Studies* 227–43; T. Irwin, *Plato's Ethics* (New York, Oxford University Press, 1995), 68–70.

argue, against Polus, for a conception of rhetoric as ethical through and through. Socrates' argument is also designed to bring into the open an equivocation in Polus' position. Despite his value-neutral view of rhetoric, Polus retains the conventional ethical belief that doing wrong is in some sense worse (as being more "shameful") than suffering it. Socrates argues that this admission is in conflict with his value-neutral view of rhetoric, and that it implies an ethically-laden view, which he draws out with paradoxical force. The contradiction exposed in this way is only resolved (at least temporarily) by the introduction of a third speaker, Callicles, who proclaims an "immoralist" position which matches Polus' non-ethical conception of rhetoric.

On entering the debate, Polus implicitly disowns Gorgias' agreement to the idea that rhetorical expertise includes knowing about right and wrong and teaching this to a student (461b). His subsequent comments about rhetoric develop this attitude: he sees it as an instrument of power, by which someone can pursue his own interests at the expense of others (whether rightly or wrongly). He views courtroom advocacy (whether in prosecution or defence) as a means of disadvantaging others and of advantaging oneself. This is achieved either by imposing disadvantages (such as fines and execution) on others or by securing acquittal from prosecution oneself regardless of the ethical rights and wrongs of the case (466b, 469a, 472e–473b). He thus defines the effectiveness of rhetoric as being distinct from its ethical quality and effect, and in this sense he holds a "value-neutral" conception of rhetoric, though his comments also imply a positive valuation of a certain kind of life. This comes out most clearly in his presentation as a paradigm of human happiness the tyrant Archelaus, who committed the most terrible crimes, but, instead of being punished for doing so, enjoys supreme power and its advantages (470d-471d). Rhetoric (including advocacy) is judged as effective insofar as it produces similar results; and to this extent Polus' conception of rhetoric is "immoralist", rather than "value-neutral", though this point is only made explicit by his successor in argument, Callicles.

Socrates, by contrast, argues (in an uncharacteristically positive way) for a thoroughly ethical conception of rhetoric, though one which, as Polus underlines, is paradoxically out of line with conventional ethical thinking. He argues for four interconnected claims. (1) Orators and tyrants only have power if they use it to bring about what is good, and not to bring about what they want, whether or not this is good (466b–468e). (2) Doing what is wrong, or unjust, to someone else is worse than suffering this at someone else's hands (469b–475e). (3) Doing what is unjust and escaping punishment is worse than doing it and being punished (476a–479e). (The argument assumes that punishment is a means of curing the "sickness" of character that makes someone do unjust acts.) On the basis of these points, Socrates reaches the following conclusion about the proper function of rhetoric. (4) Rhetoric should be used to ensure that you yourself, together with your family and friends, undergo punishment (and are thus cured) for any wrongdoing you commit, and to ensure that your enemies escape punishment for any wrongdoing they commit (480a–481b).[5]

Socrates draws out with particular relish the paradoxical quality of his conclusion. For modern readers too, although the ethic of friendship and enmity is no longer so powerful, the idea that the proper function of legal expertise is to secure conviction and punishment for oneself or one's client (if wrong has been done) retains its power to shock. What is the point of this confrontation of conceptions of rhetoric? Part at least of the aim is to bring into the open a conflict which Plato sees as latent in conventional Greek thinking (one which is also, arguably, part of conventional modern thinking). On the one hand, a lawyer is expected to exercise professional expertise in "getting the client off" or securing the opponent's conviction, whether or not this coincides precisely with the ethical rights and wrongs of the case, objectively considered. On the other, the acceptance of the authority of law-courts implies that the due process of trial and punishment (in which wrongdoers suffer for their wrongs) has an ethical validity whose force we recognise. Socrates' debate with Polus forces this contradiction into the open, demanding that it should be acknowledged and tackled.

As well as exposing this contradiction, the debate implies that Socrates' (ethical) conception of rhetoric has some leverage over Polus. This comes out most clearly in the way that Socrates secures Polus' assent to the claim that doing wrong is worse than suffering it (which Polus initially denies). The argument turns on the meaning of value-terms. Polus concedes that doing wrong is "more shameful", roughly, morally worse, than suffering it and accepts (what is uncontroversial) that the opposite of "shameful" is "fine", roughly, morally right. Socrates then secures his agreement to the idea that "fineness" should be defined by reference to usefulness (taken to be synonymous with goodness) or pleasure and that "shamefulness" should be defined by reference to badness (non-usefulness) or pain. He then applies the latter agreement, drawing out the implication of Polus' concession that doing wrong is "more shameful" than suffering it. If it is more shameful, it must exceed suffering wrong either in pain or in badness. Since it does not exceed it in pain, it must do so in badness. Therefore, as Socrates had originally claimed, and as Polus had denied, doing wrong is worse than suffering it (474c–475e).

Scholars disagree about the logical validity of this argument.[6] However, in the present context what matters most is what is implied about the scope of Socratic dialectic, and, more generally, of ethical debate. The function of the argument is not simply to highlight contrasting conceptions of rhetoric or to point out latent contradictions in conventional ethical thinking about this. It

[5] On the conception of punishment and moral psychology implied in these arguments, see M. M. Mackenzie, *Plato on Punishment* (Berkeley, Calif., University of California Press, 1981), chs. 9–11; T. J. Saunders, *Plato's Penal Code: Tradition, Controversy, and Reform in Greek Penology* (Oxford, Clarendon Press, 1991).

[6] See e.g. G. Vlastos, "Was Socrates Refuted?" (1967) 88 *American Journal of Philology* 454–60; Kahn, *supra* n. 2, at 86–97.

is also to show a way of moving forward from contradiction to (or at least towards) agreement through rational debate. What Socrates brings out is that Polus (here standing for conventional ethical thought) accepts that doing wrong is *in some sense* worse than suffering it. The argument offers—or rather, thrusts on—Polus one way of cashing in this idea. Although it is made clear that Polus is not convinced by the argument, he is at least awakened to the idea that he has ethical beliefs which are inconsistent with his view of rhetoric as an instrument of self-interested exploitation of others through the legal system. He is also introduced (though no more than this) to forms of argument by which he could develop this recognition into full-scale reflective understanding. To this extent, this part of the dialogue is an effective (though incomplete) demonstration of the power of philosophy in situations of ethical disagreement.

CALLICLES: RHETORIC AND THE GOALS OF A HUMAN LIFE

The question how far philosophy has the power to make progress in the face of ethical conflict [7] is also central to the third and final part of the dialogue. The argument with Callicles turns on a radical contrast between a morally committed and an immoralist conception of the function of rhetoric (including courtroom advocacy). Callicles suggests that the only reason Socrates was able to find inconsistency in the positions of Gorgias and Polus was because, out of "shame", they were not willing to avow in a full-blooded way the value-neutral, or immoralist, view of rhetoric that they really held (482c–e). (In this way, Plato suggests that conventional beliefs about rhetoric, such as that it is acceptable to try to "get" oneself or someone else "off" a charge, even if one is really guilty, contain a latent immoralism.) Callicles claims he can avoid any such self-contradiction by distinguishing between natural and conventional ethics. Conventionally, it is more shameful, as Polus admitted, to do wrong than to suffer it; but by the law of nature (the law that everyone would live by if they had the power) it is more shameful to suffer it. The naturally "fine" thing to do is to maximise your own self-interest and pleasure at the expense of others; Polus' admiration for the successful criminal who becomes a tyrant is generalised by Callicles into an ethical "law" of nature (483d–484b, cf. 470d–471d). The only reason that conventional ethical beliefs (such as that it is more shameful to do wrong than suffer it) have come into existence is because inferior people propagate them to try to prevent superior people from doing what everyone would really like to do (483b–c).[8]

---

[7] On this question (from an illuminating but sceptical standpoint), see B. Williams, *Ethics and the Limits of Philosophy* (London, Fontana, 1985), chs. 1–2.

[8] The immoralist position of Callicles is restated, in modified forms, in *Republic*, Books 1–2, 336–67. On the contemporary context of Callicles' position (the *nomos-phusis* debate), see Appendix below.

Callicles' position is, on the face of it, impregnable to the strategies Socrates has used so far: that of highlighting inconsistencies between his interlocutor's stance and conventional ethics, and of using conventional beliefs as the basis for reasoned ethical reflection. Socrates cannot build on the (alleged) moral content of legal institutions such as punishment, as he does with Polus. According to Callicles, legal institutions can derive no real moral validity from conventional ethics since conventional ethics have no real validity. The law-courts are seen, by implication at least, as simply one more social context in which people should use whatever means they can, including rhetoric, to fulfil nature's law of pursuing their own interest at others' expense (486a–c). Socrates needs to move to some more fundamental ground than conventional ethical beliefs to identify inconsistency in Callicles' position.

Socrates focuses on contradictions which emerge between Callicles' explicit objective of maximising and satisfying desires for pleasure and certain other value-beliefs he holds. Socrates appeals to a residual sense of shame that makes Callicles unwilling to endorse as good conventionally "shameful" plea-sures such as those of passive male homosexuality when indulged in from gross self-indulgence (494e).[9] Socrates also leads Callicles to acknowledge inconsistency between the idea that the maximising of pleasure is the highest good and Callicles' admiration of intelligence (specifically, the kind of intelli-gence expressed in exploiting others). Callicles is unable to resist Socrates' argument that there is no necessary connection between being intelligent and experiencing pleasures (497e–499b, cf. 489e–490a). The underlying thrust of Socrates' argument is this. Those, such as Callicles, who claim that immoral-ity (maximising one's interests and pleasures at others' expense) constitutes "the law of nature" imply that their conception of what is "natural" is both self-evident and self-evidently coherent. Socrates shows that Callicles' version of "the law of nature" contains an unacknowledged fusion of strands, includ-ing residual types of "shame" about sexual pleasures and competing ideals (intelligence and pleasure). Although Callicles' version of immoralism might be reformulated to take account of the specific objections made, the more gen-eral difficulty in defining a coherent, non-moral "law of nature" (which this debate highlights) remains real.[10]

Plato's dialogue as a whole suggests that arguments about law and ethics cannot cut very deep unless they move from conventional ethical beliefs to the kind of ground on which Socrates argues with Callicles, that of the funda-mental goals of a human life. Callicles implies that, underlying the view of the function of rhetoric (including advocacy) held by the previous two interlocu-tors is the kind of immoralism of which he tries to offer a coherent statement. Socrates makes the same assumption but on a radically opposed conception of the good or happy human life. Claiming, against Callicles, that the good

---

[9] This seems to be the connotation of the term *kinaidos*, usually translated as "catamite".

[10] On the difficulties that may arise in defining a coherent moral "law of nature", see *infra* n. 20.

life is one in which desires are internally "ordered" and the person is "self-controlled", he uses this to ground the account of the function of rhetoric and legal institutions he offered to Polus. "Law" in society designates the kinds of institutions that promote psychological "order" in those who obey laws; and the function of rhetoric, whether in the making or the enforcing of laws, is to act as a type of "medicine" which produces this type of psychological health (504b–505b, cf. 480a–481b).[11] The yawning gap, which the dialogue underlines, between this conception of law and rhetoric and the conventional beliefs expressed by Gorgias and Polus show that Plato is not trying simply to use philosophy to bolster up conventional institutions and the beliefs on which they rest. He is using the dialogue to ask fundamental questions about the ethical status and function of public persuasion, including the type of persuasion that goes on today in courtrooms or solicitors' offices and that is taught in law schools. The value of his dialogue to modern debate lies in the radical nature of his enquiry, and especially in the demonstration that reasoned argument, even with an immoralist, can yield the materials at least for defining an ethical basis for legal institutions and training.

CICERO, *ON DUTIES* 3: ETHICAL AND LEGAL REASONING

My second ancient text is very different in form and general character from Plato's *Gorgias*. Plato's dialogue is a rigorous dialectical argument, directed (increasingly) at arguing the immoralist out of immoralism. The other text is a more informal piece of philosophical exegesis, written by Cicero in his own voice and presupposing the validity of conventional law and ethics. But the two works converge in exploring the foundations of ethics (whether conventional or not) in a way that bears on law and legal practice. In Cicero's discussion, as in the last section of Plato's *Gorgias*, the idea of "the law of nature" figures, though used here to support, rather than to subvert, conventional ethics. But the more important point of connection between law and ethics in Cicero's text lies in the linkage between ethical and legal reasoning. In tackling an ethical issue, Cicero, a long-standing orator in the Roman courts, draws on the concepts and forms of arguments used by advocates and jurists. In so doing, he implies that ethical and legal reasoning are, essentially, either the same or interdependent. His argument also carries important implications about the relationship between universal moral norms and more localised or specific norms and forms of reasoning, and these implications are relevant to debate elsewhere in this volume.

The issue raised in Book 3 of *On Duties* is this. When right and advantage come into conflict, what criterion do we use to adjudicate between them? But this issue is raised from a certain standpoint, which requires us to state it more

---

[11] On the "therapeutic" conception of law, see Mackenzie, *supra* n. 5.

precisely. It is raised from the standpoint of Stoic ethical philosophy, which Cicero, broadly speaking, adopts in *On Duties*. For Stoic ethics, virtue, or the right, is the only thing that is good without qualification; and so there can be no *fundamental* conflict between right and advantage. Thus, for the "sage" or wise person, the normative figure in Stoicism, nothing can seem advantageous which is not also right. But, for ordinary but well-motivated people who are trying to make progress towards moral perfection or "wisdom", there can *seem* to be cases of conflict between right and advantage. Cicero's project is not that of trying to prove by argument that, where such conflicts occur, we should choose what is right. (In this respect, his aim differs sharply from Socrates' attempt to use argument to lead Polus and Callicles to recognise the force of ethical claims.) His aim is rather that of trying to help himself and others to recognise what criteria should be used to adjudicate such cases. Assuming that we want to do what is right, what standards do we draw on to ensure that our judgements of what is right are objectively grounded and correct?[12]

A key move made by Cicero in answering this question is to put forward a general "rule of procedure" for adjudicating cases of apparent conflict between right and advantage:

> "for one human being to take something from another and to increase his own advantage at the cost of another's advantage is more contrary to nature than death, than poverty, than pain and than anything else that may happen to his body or external possession" (*On Duties* 3.21).[13]

This formulation presupposes the central Stoic idea that the virtuous life is the natural one for human beings to lead (if they develop fully) and that the non-virtuous life is "contrary to nature". It is linked by Cicero with two other central Stoic ideas: that, in so far as human beings act virtuously, they contribute to a "brotherhood of humankind" or "world-city" (*kosmopolis*) and they obey the "natural" or rational "law" that underlies conventional laws and gives them their moral authority.[14] Cicero here draws on this set of ideas in order to give a general definition of what is advantageous without being right, and to distinguish this from the right that it is "natural" for us to choose.

[12] *On Duties* 3.7–18. On Stoic ethics, see e.g. A. A. Long and D. N. Sedley, *The Hellenistic Philosophers* (sources, commentary, and bibliography, 2 vols.) (Cambridge, Cambridge University Press, 1987), sects. 56–67. A helpful outline is given in R. W. Sharples, *Stoics, Epicureans and Sceptics: An Introduction to Hellenistic Philosophy* (London, Routledge, 1996), 100–13, 123–7.

[13] Trans. as in Cicero, *On Duties* (ed. and trans. M. T. Griffin and E. M. Atkins, Cambridge Texts in the History of Political Thought, Cambridge, Cambridge University Press, 1991), slightly modified. The idea of a "rule of procedure" (Latin, *formula*) is taken from Roman law, in which the magistrate set out in this form the point at issue in a case and the criteria that should determine the outcome (Griffin and Atkins, *supra* n. 13, 107, n. 3).

[14] On these Stoic ideas, see e.g. J. Annas, *The Morality of Happiness* (New York, Oxford University Press, 1993), 302–11; P. A. Vander Waerdt, "Zeno's *Republic* and the Origins of Natural Law" in Vander Waerdt (ed.), *The Socratic Movement* (Ithaca, NY, Cornell University Press, 1994), 272–308.

This move by Cicero is highlighted in a recent discussion by Martha Nussbaum, an expert in ancient philosophy whose recent work centres on law and ethics. Nussbaum takes Cicero's move as exemplifying a crucial contribution that ethical philosophy can make to legal debate, namely that of offering a definition of moral concepts that is based on sustained examination of the issues but is also formulated in a way that can inform legal practice. Nussbaum also stresses the importance of the fact that Cicero's criterion assumes the validity of *universal* human norms and categories such as "natural law" and "brotherhood of humankind", rather than norms which discriminate between genders, races or classes. She argues that the Stoic use of such ideas anticipates the modern move (which Nussbaum supports) of identifying certain universal "human rights" and of treating these as fundamental norms which should inform legal practice as well as ethical thinking.[15]

I think that Nussbaum is right to signal the relevance of Cicero's move to contemporary debate about law and ethics, but that we need to qualify her account of this move; this qualified account is of equal relevance to contemporary debate, though in a rather different way. I agree that it is important, for Cicero as for Stoic theory generally, that the "rule of procedure" is couched in terms of universal norms (what is "natural" for human beings), and that the moral authority of such norms derives partly from this fact. But Cicero's discussion is also important because it provides material for two further questions. One relates to the application of such universal norms in specific contexts: how far should this application be shaped by existing conventional standards and how far should it try to shape these standards? A similar question arises about the interpretation of such norms: how far is this necessarily shaped by more localised or "embedded" practices and forms of understanding? Although Cicero does not raise these questions explicitly as philosophical issues, they underlie his account; and their presence has a special relevance for the question of law and ethics.[16]

At one point Cicero reports a dispute between Stoic thinkers which bears on the first of these two questions. On the face of it, the dispute has to do simply with the ethics of buying and selling. One thinker (Diogenes) argues that the vendor need disclose only those defects of the item for sale (for instance, the property) which the civil law requires (3.51–5). The other (Antipater) argues that the vendor should disclose all those defects of which he is aware which might disadvantage the buyer, whether or not the civil law requires this. He should do so because that is what the "natural law" requires,

---

[15] See "Kant and Stoic Cosmopolitanism" (1997) 5.1, *Journal of Political Philosophy* 1–25 also, though without reference to Cicero, "Patriotism and Cosmopolitanism" in J. Cohen (ed.), *For Love of Country: Debating the Limits of Patriotism* (Boston, Mass., Beacon Press, 1996), 3–17.

[16] Underlying this discussion, as also Nussbaum's essay on "Kant and Stoic Cosmopolitanism" (*supra* n. 15) is the issue whether ethical principles should be conceived as universal principles or (even if they are universal) as necessarily understood from within the practices and tradition of a given community. See A. MacIntyre, *After Virtue* (London, Duckworth, 1981, 1985), *Whose Justice? Which Rationality?* (London, Duckworth, 1988), for the latter view.

according to which you should regard another's benefit as your own (3.52). Underlying this dispute, and also evident in Stoic thinking more generally, is a larger issue. This is the question how far the universal norms recognised by Stoicism are to be applied *within* the socio-economic and legal framework of our community, or whether their application requires us to live by standards which go beyond existing conventions.[17] Cicero stresses that this dispute is conducted *within* the framework of Stoic ethics, and that neither thinker advocates choosing what is advantageous at the expense of what is right. The question is how far the choice of what is right requires us to go beyond normal social and legal standards about obtaining what is advantageous (3.53).

Cicero supplements his account of Stoic casuistry (the analysis of issues raised by complex or borderline cases) by citing comparable Roman legal cases (3.58–88). In doing so, he refers especially to the idea of acting "in good (or bad) faith" (*bona* or *mala fides*), which was used by Roman jurists as a criterion of fraud (3.60–1, 64–7, 70). Although he cites attempts by Roman jurists to define in general terms what "bad faith" means (such as, "when one thing is pretended and another is done" (3.60), it is clear that any such definition needs to be specified further by reference to communally accepted judgements about the rights and wrongs of certain types of situation.[18] Cicero's procedure carries two further implications. One is that, to make full sense of the "rule of procedure" which was couched in universal terms, we need to refer to ideas such as "good faith", which derive their significance from a specific social and legal context. The other, which is implied in the whole form of Cicero's argument, is that the best practice of Roman law coincides with the realization of the universal moral categories referred to in Cicero's "rule of procedure".

Similar implications are carried by Cicero's climactic example in *On Duties*. This is that of Regulus, a Roman general captured in the First Carthaginian War, who was allowed to return to Rome on condition that he arranged the return of Carthaginian prisoners of war. In Rome he argued against returning these prisoners; instead of staying in Rome, he insisted on returning to certain torture and death in Carthage, having promised on oath to do so if he failed to arrange the return of prisoners. Cicero takes him as a supreme example of someone who chose to do what was right (and who correctly recognised what was right) rather than what was advantageous, although the two seemed to be in direct conflict (3.99–100). What is important for the present question is that, although Regulus' act exemplifies the other-benefiting behaviour elsewhere associated with "natural law" and "brotherhood of

---

[17] On this issue, see the references in n. 14 above, especially Annas, *Morality*, 309–10, on the Diogenes-Antipater debate; also C. Gill, "Musonius, Epictetus, Dio, Marcus Aurelius" in C. Rowe and M. Schofield (eds.), *Cambridge History of Greek and Roman Political Thought* (Cambridge, Cambridge University Press, forthcoming).

[18] Hence, the details given in 3.58–88 about the cases and the judgements made by jurists or Cicero himself form an integral part of the specification of what "good (or bad) faith" means.

humankind", Cicero explains Regulus' act by his commitment to the best standards of Roman practice (3.108–114). As in Cicero's discussion of "good faith", what is implied is that the realisation of these universal moral categories coincides with proper adherence to Roman law (here, the law of respecting oaths given "in good faith" to enemies, 3.104, 107–8). A further implication follows from the form in which Cicero considers this case: namely as a kind of "moot" (Latin *controuersia*), in which the arguments for and against Regulus' action are pitted against each other.[19] The arguments are strongly reminiscent of those used by Roman advocates (such as Cicero himself). The whole exchange suggests that legal reasoning is, at bottom, a species of ethical reasoning, thus confirming the link between good legal practice and general ethical concepts made elsewhere in the argument.

These points, taken together, lead to a rather different reading of the significance of Cicero's discussion for the relationship between law and ethics from that claimed by Martha Nussbaum. For Nussbaum, as noted earlier, its significance lies in the idea that ethical and legal reasoning should be shaped by universal moral categories, such as "human rights" or "natural law". I see Cicero's discussion as suggesting, rather, that the way in which such categories are understood and put into effect is crucially mediated by the best ethical and legal practice of the community. Apart from its general interest, this point has a special relevance to common law thinking at the present time. The English common law (like Roman law in Cicero's time) has traditionally developed piecemeal as case law, with authoritative status given to precedent and to the appeal to equity in order to resolve difficult cases. Recent developments, including our closer linkage with supranational European law, have introduced into domestic law consideration for universal principles such as "human rights". Cicero's combination of universal principles with more distinctively Roman forms of legal and ethical reasoning (expressed in his use of historical precedents and communally embedded norms such as "good faith") points to a way of accommodating these two approaches. Although there is, obviously, a danger that the universal force of the moral norms may be eroded in this way by local partialities, this accommodation also promises a way of making these norms a concrete and living force in the ethical and legal life of a given community.[20]

This feature has a special relevance to an issue which figures in different forms in other chapters in this part of the volume. Both Costas Douzinas and Robert Rosen argue, though on different grounds, that one route to restoring the ethical dimension to law is through respecting the moral force of specific

---

[19] 3.100–10.

[20] See further on this general issue Cohen (*supra* n. 15) in which Nussbaum's call for ethical and political "cosmopolitanism" generates responses from other thinkers, some of whom restate the case for patriotism or for an accommodation of the two norms. On problems in Cicero's accommodation of universal principles and Roman values elsewhere in *On Duties*, see C. Gill, "Personhood and Personality: The Four-*Personae* Theory in Cicero, *De Officiis* 1" (1988) 6 *Oxford Studies in Ancient Philosophy* 169–99.

interpersonal encounters within the legal context, rather than by appealing to universal norms of morality or rationality.[21] Tim Dare, by contrast, argues that moral particularism (which he associates especially with virtue-based ethics)[22] threatens the status of universal principles and uniformity of process that he sees as fundamental to legal institutions. (This point is made by reference to competing readings of Harper Lee's novel, *To Kill a Mockingbird*.) Cicero's discussion suggests that the contrast between moral universals and particulars assumed in these chapters is over-stated. *On Duties* 3, as interpreted here, implies that moral universals are incomplete until interpreted in the light of more "embedded" norms and practices, but also that universals constitute an important form of "control" over local partialities. A framework which offers a coherent accommodation between these two dimensions of ethics may offer a better basis for understanding the ethical content of law than one which focuses on only one of these dimensions.

It is also worth noting that Cicero, like Plato and the great majority of ancient philosophers, presupposes what we now call "virtue-ethics", that is, a framework centred on the conceptions of virtue and happiness. As Julia Annas stresses, although ancient forms of virtue-ethics differ in overall structure from the most dominant types of modern moral theory (consequentialism and deontology), they provide scope for features emphasised in those theories, including respect for rules and universal principles.[23] In both Plato's *Gorgias* and Cicero's *On Duties* 3, although the most fundamental question relates to the best form of human life (conceived as inhering in a life of virtue), the content of this life is drawn out by examination of the central principles and beliefs on which this life should be based. However, for ancient virtue-ethics, guiding principles and rules alone do not constitute a complete statement of the basis of morality.[24] They need to be located in an account of the best human life, including reference to human psychology and the socio-political structure in which the best life should be lived. In spite of Tim Dare's reservations, there is a strong case for thinking that virtue-ethics, of the type exemplified here, offer a coherent framework for accommodating respect both for universal principles and for the claims of specific interpersonal and com-

---

[21] See Ch. 2, Sect. 4 (an appeal to "the ethics of alterity"); Ch. 4, Sect. 4 (an appeal to the deontological claims of specific legal situations).

[22] See Ch. 3, Sect. 4. See *infra* n. 24 for an explanation of the stress on moral particularism which, as Dare notes, is sometimes (though by no means always) linked with virtue-ethics. It is notable that Nussbaum, whom Dare cites as a moral particularist, now places more emphasis on universal moral principles, though she does so, I think, from within a framework centred on virtue-ethics.

[23] Annas (*supra* n. 14), especially 84–115 and ch. 22.

[24] This partly explains the apparent moral particularism noted by Dare (*supra* n. 22). Aristotle and the Stoics, for instance, stress that the ethical knowledge of the normative wise person (the *phronimos* or *sophos*) cannot be articulated fully, either regarding the general principles the wise person follows or the specific decisions the wise person makes. However, formulating guiding principles and considering how they should be applied in specific cases forms an integral part of systematic progress towards moral perfection or "wisdom".

munal encounters. Above all, virtue-ethics focus attention on the question of the *motivation* for leading an ethically good life. Virtue-ethics offer a framework in which we can see why one should want to be an ethically good lawyer, namely as (part of) the realisation of human happiness. This is not, of course, to say that the particular ancient arguments for this claim here will necessarily win conviction. But the general (virtue-centred) character of these arguments deserves close attention as part of the project of re-examining the ethical basis of law.

In this chapter, I have examined two very different ancient texts bearing on the relationship between law and ethics. I have tried to bring out the fact that, in spite of the historical and cultural remoteness of these texts, they have substantive contributions to make to current debate in this area. Plato's *Gorgias* is especially valuable because of its philosophically searching examination of the ethical status of rhetoric and its confrontation of immoralism. Cicero's *On Duties* 3 has particular interest for the question of the relationship between universal moral principles and localised legal practice and norms. Both texts provide material for those wanting to see how virtue-ethics work in the area of law and morality. This chapter has focused exclusively on these two texts because I wished to bring out in some depth the quality of the thinking involved and the issues raised. But the following Appendix offers guidance for readers who wish to explore further the very wide range of Greek and Roman material relevant to the subject of law and ethics.

APPENDIX: CLASSICAL MATERIALS ON LAW AND ETHICS

The two texts discussed here were selected partly because they raise important questions without requiring specialist knowledge of their context. They are also available in good recent translations, with introductions, notes and bibliographies, and are thus potential teaching texts.[25] Indeed, Plato's *Gorgias* has been used for this purpose in the Miami Law School. The *Gorgias* has the additional interest that, especially in the Callicles section, it tackles head-on the kind of pervasive cynicism about the moral status of legal practice and education discussed by both Douzinas and Rosen in this volume and analysed recently by Kim Economides.[26]

Other Platonic texts that fulfil the same conditions (of raising issues without calling for detailed knowledge of the context) are Plato's version of Socrates' trial-speech (*Apology*) and a dialogue set when Socrates was in prison awaiting execution (*Crito*).[27] Both dialogues explore in quasi-dramatic

[25] E.g. Plato, *Gorgias* (trans. D. J. Zeyl, Indianapolis, Ind., Hackett, 1988); (trans. R. Waterfield, World's Classics, Oxford, Oxford University Press, 1994). For *On Duties*, see *supra* n. 13.

[26] "Cynical Legal Studies", in J. Cooper and L. Trubek (eds.), *Educating for Justice: Social Values and Legal Education* (Aldershot, Dartmouth Publishing, 1997).

[27] Helpful translations include Plato, *The Last Days of Socrates* (trans. H. Tredennick and H. Tarrant, Penguin Classics, London, Penguin, 1993).

form the issue treated at the end of the main text of this chapter: what ethical principles motivate a *life*, in this case, the life of Socrates terminated by a hugely controversial court case. One much-discussed topic arising from these texts is the apparent contradiction between Socrates' apparent defiance of the court's judgment in *Apology* 29c–30c and his principled submission in the *Crito* to the punishment imposed by the court and to the rule of law. Among the questions raised has been whether Socrates' defiance in the *Apology* can be appropriately characterised as "civil disobedience", and, if so, whether this can be squared with the ethical "contractualism" outlined in *Crito* 50–4.[28] Another Platonic text that has received less attention, partly because of its length, is Plato's *Laws*. An interesting section, which could be studied in isolation, is the proposal that laws should be framed with preludes or preambles, spelling out the ethical context and objectives of the law.[29]

A related subject, which is relatively accessible, despite involving more reference to the historical context, is the debate in the fifth century BC about the relationship between *nomos* ("law, convention, ethics") and *phusis* ("nature, reality"). Despite being the first debate on this subject in Western thought, it is surprising for the sophistication of the positions adopted and range of manifestations of the debate, including an argument between "just" and "unjust argument" in Aristophanes' comedy about Socrates, *The Clouds*.[30] A further question is whether Greek law-court speakers (or rhetoric teachers) in real life adopted a position on the ethical status of rhetoric which is closer to Socrates or to his interlocutors in the *Gorgias*.[31] A germane question, though one requiring more knowledge of the social context, is that of the broader ethical framework assumed by the Athenian law-courts (arguably, one centred on the ideas of reciprocity and honour rather than justice, as we normally understand this).[32]

[28] See e.g. A. D. Woozley, "Socrates on Disobeying the Law" in G. Vlastos (ed.), *The Philosophy of Socrates* (Garden City, NY, 1971), 299–318; *Law and Obedience: The Arguments of Plato's Crito* (Chapel Hill, NC, 1979). See also R. Kraut, *Socrates and the State* (Princeton, NJ, Princeton University Press, 1984), ch. 3; T. C. Brickhouse and N. D. Smith, *Socrates on Trial* (Princeton, NJ, Princeton University Press, 1989), 3.3.

[29] See *Laws*, Book 4, 718–Book 5, 734; a useful translation of *Laws* is T. J. Saunders, Penguin Classics (Harmondsworth, Penguin, 1970). On the preludes, see C. Bobonich, "Persuasion and Compulsion in Plato's Laws" (1991) 41 *Classical Quarterly* 365–88.

[30] *Clouds*, lines 889–1104; For translation, see e.g. Aristophanes, *Lysistrata, Acharnians, Clouds*, trans A. Sommerstein (London, Penguin, 1973), 149–58. On the *nomos–phusis* debate, see W. K. C. Guthrie, *A History of Greek Philosophy* (Cambridge, Cambridge University Press, 1969), iii, chs. 4–5; G. B. Kerferd, *The Sophistic Movement* (Cambridge, Cambridge University Press, 1981), ch. 10. For a translation of many of the relevant texts, see *Early Greek Political Thought from Homer to the Sophists* (ed. and trans. M. Gagarin and P. Woodruff, Cambridge Texts in the History of Political Thought, Cambridge, Cambridge University Press, 1995).

[31] Aristotle's (complex) position on this is explored in A. O. Rorty (ed.), *Essays on Aristotle's Rhetoric* (Berkeley, Calif., University of California Press, 1996), especially essays by Wardy, Engberg-Pedersen and Irwin. See also I. Worthington (ed.) *Persuasion: Greek Rhetoric in Action* (London, Routledge, 1994) esp. essays by Carey, Gagarin, Harris.

[32] For this view, see D. Allen, "A Situation of Punishment: the Politics and Ideology of Athenian Punishment", Cambridge University PhD thesis 1996; and P. Millett, "The Rhetoric of

Among topics treated in Cicero, *On Duties* 3, which bear on law and ethics, the obvious one to pursue is the Stoic idea of "natural law". There has been extensive discussion, for instance, about how far the Stoic idea influenced Roman legal thinking.[33] The question which Martha Nussbaum has raised (*supra* note 15), how Stoic thinking about natural law relates to modern thinking about human rights merits further discussion. For those wanting to explore the ancient form of virtue-ethics (discussed above in connection with *On Duties*), Julia Annas' *The Morality of Happiness* is, certainly, the best starting-point.[34] Nussbaum, in articles drawing out the relevance of ethical philosophy for legal education, highlights further aspects of ancient thought, including their theories of emotion, on which she has herself written an important and accessible study.[35]

Reciprocity" in C. Gill, N. Postlethwaite and R. Seaford (eds.), *Reciprocity in Ancient Greece* (Oxford, Oxford University Press, 1998). More generally, see S. C. Todd, *The Shape of Athenian Law* (Oxford, Oxford University Press, 1995).

[33] On natural law and its possible influence, see (in addition to the references *supra* in n. 14), G. Striker, "Origins of the Concept of Natural Law" in *Essays on Hellenistic Epistemology and Ethics* (Cambridge, Cambridge University Press, 1996), ch. 11; P. Mitsis, "Natural Law and Natural Rights in Post-Aristotelian Philosophy. The Stoics and their Critics" and P. A. Vander Waerdt, "Philosophical Influence on Roman Jurisprudence? The Case of Stoicism and Natural Law", both in W. Haase (ed.), *Aufsteig und Niedergang der römischen Welt*, vol. 2.36.7 (Berlin, De Gruyter, 1994), 4812–50, 4851–900.

[34] See *supra* nn. 14 and 23. On Stoicism and virtue-ethics, see also A. A. Long, *Stoic Studies* (Cambridge, Cambridge University Press, 1996), chs. 7–8. On Plato, see Annas' *An Introduction to Plato's Republic* (Oxford, Clarendon Press, 1981), especially chs. 6, 13; T. Irwin, *Plato's Ethics* (New York, Oxford University Press, 1995).

[35] See M. Nussbaum, "The Use and Abuse of Philosophy in Legal Education" (1993) 45 *Stanford Law Review* 1627–45; "Skepticism about Practical Reason in Literature and the Law" (1994) 107 *Harvard Law Review* 714–44. Also *The Therapy of Desire: Theory and Practice in Hellenistic Ethics* (Princeton, NJ, Princeton University Press, 1994).

2

Justice, Judgement and the Ethics of Alterity

COSTAS DOUZINAS

The most painful witness of the crisis of our time is the widely-felt sense that justice has miscarried. Justice has been aborted in miscarriages of justice and denials of access to justice, in racial and gender discrimination, in institutional violence and legal dogmatism. The British legal system, which only a few years ago was hailed as the best—the fairest and most efficient—in the world, has been enmeshed in a profound crisis. Miscarriages of justice are instances in which the whole legal system has failed, not in secondary and remediable ways, but in the most far-reaching and radical manner. There is much to be done to improve the civil and criminal justice systems and legal reforms are under way. But for the legal scholar the question is somewhat different. How is it that we came to the point where the legal system appears to be almost divorced from considerations of morality? What is the meaning of justice in our postmodern world of cognitive and moral uncertainties? Michel Foucault has called the great eighteenth-century civil lawyers who stood against the autocratic state "universal intellectuals": "[t]he man of justice, the man of law, he who opposes to power, despotism, the abuses and arrogance of wealth, the universality of justice and the equity of an ideal law."[1] Today we have lost our belief in the universality of law or in the ability of an ideal equity to ground its operations. Does that mean that we must abandon morality, unable to oppose "power, despotism, the abuses and arrogance of wealth"? Can we develop contemporary critical and reconstructive yardsticks for our legal system, after the end of the grand narratives of modernity and its attempts to ground the social bond on a principle of universal application? We need to re-examine modernity's (de)linking of legality and morality.

I. THE APORIA OF JUSTICE

The classical formulation of the problem of justice involves the denunciation of a double *injustice*: "the world is regarded as *unjust*, as the very negation of

[1] Michel Foucault, *Power, Truth, Strategy* (Sydney, Feral Publications, 1979), 43.

justice, and this negation of justice must itself be negated . . . men are unjust because they are corrupt and wicked, rather than righteous, and society (or the body politic) is unjust because it puts a premium on wickedness and allows the righteous to be trampled upon and perish".[2] This striking *ethico-political* idea of justice links justice with the moral idea of the good. But it also associates justice, the prime political virtue, with individual moral perfection. In the ancient definition of morality, citizens have a *telos*, which places them in the scheme of nature *physis* and justice *dike*. Virtuous action helps them move from what they are to what they ought to be according to their nature and occupy their proper place in the wider order of *cosmos*. But this can happen only within the political community and the law *nomos* should be a recognition of the normative aspects of this purposive order. A just city is the precondition of individual perfection, and happiness and virtuous citizens make the city just.

The classical writers present justice therefore as the prime virtue of the polity and the spirit and reason of law. A just constitution is a legitimate constitution and has a valid claim to the obedience of its citizens. From Aristotle to contemporary political philosophy, justice has been related to the law and legal decision-making. "Law exists among these between whom there is a possibility of injustice."[3] But he immediately adds that there is general and particular justice, and legal justice is only one aspect of particular justice. "Legal justice is different from justice in the primary sense . . . actions prescribed by law are only accidentally just actions. How an action must be performed, how a distribution must be made to be a just action or distribution [is a much harder task]."[4] The aim of general justice is the "good of the other".

Plato's metaphysical system exemplifies a second element in the classical conception of justice. In the *Republic*, Socrates offers no definition of justice. He replaces justice first with reason and later with the idea of the good, which is presented as its substance and ultimate value. Individual and common good provide the criteria for choosing between competing courses of action. But the good itself is not accessible to reason, it is declared to be *epekeina ousias*, beyond *Being* and essence. As Plato admits in his *Seventh Epistle*, we can never fully know the good "for it does not admit of verbal expression like other branches of knowledge".[5] Justice, too, the political expression of the good, cannot be discovered in laws and in written treatises, it has no essence or its essence lies in the "city in the sky". But the spirit of justice reveals itself to philosophers and lawgivers in mysterious ways and is expressed in the sense of injustice about the world and law. The quest for justice exemplifies the

---

[2] Agnes Heller, *Beyond Justice* (Oxford, Blackwell, 1987), 54.

[3] Aristotle, *Ethics* (London, Penguin Books, 1976), 291.

[4] *Ibid.*, 311.

[5] Plato, *The Republic* (London, Penguin Books, 1955). For a full discussion of the Platonic search for the meaning of justice and the good and his admission of defeat see Hans Kelsen, "The Metamorphoses of the Idea of Justice" in P. Sayre, *Interpretations of Modern Legal Philosophies* (New York, Oxford University Press, 1947).

paradox of reason formulated by Socrates "in the most extreme manner: reasoning leads to unreason".[6]

The Platonic dialogues started western philosophy. Yet the power of reason in morals and justice appears severely restricted. Behind the meandering dialogues on justice lies Socrates's ultimate argument: his sacrifice on the altar of a justice which cannot be defined or conclusively proven. Socrates represents not so much the triumph of reason but the first clear formulation of the *aporia of justice*: to be just is to *act justly*, to be committed to a frame of mind and follow a course of action that must be accepted before any final rational justification.[7] Political philosophy can be described as the history of the intellectual efforts to define justice. Philosophy's attempts have partially failed, but the sense of injustice has persisted and keeps building and reforming legal and moral systems. Justice is not fully of this world. It is caught in an unceasing movement between knowledge and passion, reason and action, this world and the next, rationalism and metaphysics.

For the Romans, law and justice come together in the order of right reason which is also the order of nature. "Law is the highest reason implanted in nature, which commands what ought to be done and forbids its opposite", writes Cicero.[8] We find many of these ideas in the writings of the classical common lawyers. As law's immemorial and unwritten foundation, justice links the common law with divine will and its expressions in nature and reason. After the Reformation, justice as equity is explicitly associated with the divine order and becomes law's spirit. "The chief end or lost mark of the law . . . is God's glory. But the next and immediate end which is allotted to it, is to administer justice to all, and in that sense it may be called the rule of justice: for religion, justice and law do stand together."[9] Justice is cumulatively the foundation, the spirit and the end of the law. It comes before and stands higher than the human artifice of the law and acts as a corrective to its harshness. When law and justice, in the form of equity, are in conflict, the law must give way to higher reason. In all these formulations, justice is seen as the "primitive reason"[10] of law, its virtue and ethical substance, an ideal or principle that gives rules their aim and limit and remedies their defects. But justice is also something outside or before the law, a higher tribunal to which

---

[6] Heller, *supra* n. 2, 73.

[7] The aporia of reason and justice is even stronger in the Jewish tradition. To be just, the Jew must obey the law, without any reason or justification. For Buber, Jews act in order to understand while Levinas denounces what he calls the western "temptation of temptation", the— "Greek"—demand to subordinate every act to knowledge and to overcome the "purity" and "innocence" of the act. See Emmanuel Levinas, *Nine Talmudic Readings* (Bloomington, Ind., Indiana University Press, 1990), 30–50.

[8] Cicero, *The Laws,* I, VI.

[9] William Fulbeck, *Direction or Preparative to the Study of the Law,* 1599 (1829 ed., London), 2–3.

[10] Sir Henry Finch, *Law, or, A Discourse Thereof in Four Books* (London, Society of Stationers, 1627), at fol. 57.

the law and its judgments are called to account. In this sense, a law without justice is a law without spirit, a dead letter, which can neither rule nor inspire.

II. THE SEPARATION OF LAW AND ETHICS

This internal relationship between the ethical and legal elements of justice has been severed. As Alasdair MacIntyre argues, modernity is the era of a profound "moral catastrophe", of a radical breakdown in ethical agreement and of the systematic annihilation of communities of value and virtue.[11] Modern theories of justice belong to the deontological school of ethics associated with Kant. Kant's project is to reconcile freedom, rationality and morality by concentrating on the form of law and duty. Ethics are identified with universal rules or principles, which are either grounded in reason or, in the writings of contemporary neo-Kantians, are reached through an understanding of the universal preconditions of argumentation and discourse. For Kant, the ancients made the mistake of positing a concept of the good first and deriving the law from it.[12] In so doing "their fundamental principle was always heteronomy, and they came inevitably to empirical conditions for a moral law".[13] Kant reverses the procedure; it is not the concept of the good that posits the law but the moral law that defines good and evil. Moral action meets certain universal or "transcendental" preconditions found in the free and rational action of the subject who follows the law of the categorical imperative out of a pure sense of duty and respect: "[a]ct in such a way that the maxim of your will can always be valid as the principle establishing universal law."[14]

This law is imperative, but it commands the will to follow the pure form of legality (the principle of the action should be always valid, in the form of a universal norm). While it forces the will, the law emanates from it. Kantian autonomy makes the modern self the law's *subject* in a double sense: he is the legislator, the subject who gives the law and the legal subject, subjected to the law. Kant's great discovery is that modern justice is the total and painful subjection to the law. But subjection to the law and conformity with duty do not give pleasure, they are the realm of pain, an insight which will be fully developed by psychoanalysis.[15] Justice does no longer commune with the aspirations of the soul; it works through the suffering reason imposes on desire.

[11] Alasdair MacIntyre, *After Virtue* (London, Duckworth, 1981), 1–5.

[12] "The ancients openly revealed this error by devoting their ethical investigation entirely to the definition of the concept of the highest good and thus posited an object which they intented subsequently to make the determining ground of the will in the moral law": Kant, *Critique of Practical Reason* (London, Macmillan, 1956), 66–7.

[13] *Ibid.*, 66.

[14] *Ibid.*, 30.

[15] Jacques Lacan, *The Ethics of Psychoanalysis* (London, Routledge, 1992); Costas Douzinas, "Law's Birth and Antigone's Death: On Ontological and Psychoanalytical Ethics" (1995) 16 *Cardozo Law Review* 3–4, 1325–62.

The second characteristically modern attempt to ground morality derives ethical commands and norms from grand theories about the just society, most notably in dogmatic Marxism. But theory of all types is a form of representation of reality, a description that claims to correspond to its referent. Knowledge and its object are declared to be equivalent. Theory can never occupy the space of ethics fully. Descriptive and theoretical statements place their utterer and their addressee in a position of equivalence because the referent of the sentence is "reality". Moral action, on the other hand, is a response to an ethical stimulus that originates in an other person and addresses the self; it is always still to come and it places the other who asks and the self who responds in a position of radical dissymmetry. No theory of the good society or account of justice can furnish the final word of ethical action. Theories are descriptions of determinate states of affairs while the ethical response is indeterminate, something to be done rather than something said.[16]

This moral catastrophe has been carried out in the most radical way in law, but law has also been presented as a substitute for the depleted value consensus. We are well aware of this de-ethicalisation of law, of the banning of morality from legal operations. For jurisprudence, the law is public and objective; its posited rules are structurally homologous to ascertainable "facts" which can be found and verified in an "objective" manner. Its procedures are technical and its personnel neutral. Any contamination of law by value will compromise its ability to turn social and political conflict into manageable technical disputes about the meaning and applicability of pre-existing public rules. Morality, on the other hand, is presented as private and subjective; it is about individual values, norms and preferences which are in principle incommensurable as no general value agreement exists. Indeed even this mutilated and publicly worthless morality is treated as a second-order legality. Morality is about moral codes and the following of rules and principles posited either by a divine authority, whose claims to universality in a multi-religious society are, however, suspect or, in the various neo-Kantianisms, by the autonomous and free subject who must discover in himself the laws of his universal subjection. Moral responsibility is measured according to the heartless subjection to the law and moral success according to criteria of instrumental rationality and conformity to the dictates of utilitarian calculations.

Morality as much as politics must be kept away from law; indeed the main requirement of the rule of law is that all subjective and relative value should be excluded from the operation of the legal system. In formal terms, justice is identified with the administration of justice and the requirements and guarantees of legal procedure. In substantive terms, justice loses its critical character and acts not as critique but as critical apology for the extant legal

---

[16] See J.-F. Lyotard, *The Differend. Phrases in Dispute* (Manchester, Manchester University Press, 1988); for an application of these ideas to law see Costas Douzinas and Ronnie Warrington, "A Well-Founded Fear of Justice", II *Law and Critique* 2, 1991, 1–36.

system. As a "disillusioned radical" barrister put it, "as a lawyer you don't have moral choice because the law makes the moral choices for you. I have no morality." And a former Chairman of the Bar went further: "[i]t's easy for the lawyer: there are rules. There are lighthouses all along the route for me and I haven't got to make moral judgements as I go. I am not a social worker. The rules fix my morality for me."[17] The radical gap in the normative universe created by the strict separation between legality and morality and the reduction of ethics to the private and subjective is filled by the law as the lighthouse on the way to universal and objective truth. This insulation of law from ethico-political considerations allegedly makes the exercise of power impersonal and guarantees the equal subjection of citizens and state officials to the dispassionate requirements of the rule of rules as opposed to the rule of men. And as adjudication is presented in common law jurisdictions as the paradigm instance of law, the demand for justice is equated with the moral neutralisation of the judicial process.

Justice loses therefore its ethical character and becomes a device for the legitimation and celebration of the law. Legal positivism argues that, as no generally acceptable criteria of justice exist, it should either be abandoned or its application should be restricted to the more manageable domain of legal procedures. Law is technical reason, a poor remnant of the right reason of the classics, while justice is associated with emotions and non-rational passions. To assert that a legal system is unjust, says Ross, is an "emotional expression. . . . To invoke justice is the same thing as banging on the table: an emotional expression that turns one's demand into an absolute postulate."[18] Non-formal conceptions of justice are "illusions which excite the emotions by stimulating the suprarenal glands". There is no hope of a rational foundation of justice, because the concept is ideological and "biological-emotional" and the science of law should abandon it.[19]

Chaim Perelman, one of the foremost theorists of justice, claims that "an attempt to judge the law in the name of justice is . . . confusion. . . . We must not say that the law is condemned in the name of justice, unless that is, we want to create confusion advantageous only to the sophists."[20] Justice is a confusion cultivated by sophists and dissidents. Plato has been totally reversed: his rational theory of justice was the tool to defeat the common sense of the Sophists. For the positivist, all claims to justice are dismissed as sophistry in the name of a common sense which mobilises in its arrogant defence the modern form of rationality, (pseudo) science. Justice becomes internal to the legal system, its principle identified as conformity with the law. The normative universe is now exclusively inhabited by the prescriptions of

---

[17] Interviews in the *Guardian* newspaper, 6 Feb. 1991, 21.

[18] Alf Ross, *On Law and Justice* (London, Stevens, 1958), 274.

[19] *Ibid.*, 275.

[20] C. Perelman, *The Idea of Justice and the Problem of Argument* (London, Routledge and Kegan Paul, 1963), 26.

the legislator and the decrees of the institution. Consequently, justice is not directly involved with ethics. As Lucas puts it, justice is "set in a somewhat low moral key . . . I can be just, and yet lack many moral virtues".[21] Hart too accepts that wicked and bad laws are not necessarily unjust nor are good laws necessarily just.[22]

Legality bestows authority on the law either through its origin in the organised power of the state or through its emanation from a long historical and "spiritual" process. In both cases however legality, as the nineteenth-century liberals explained, operates through external coercion. The morality of legality is totally heteronomous and acts through the fear of sanctions or the utilitarian calculation of rewards and punishments. But the paramount task of suppressing human wickedness endows the legality of coercion with the ethereal attributes of morality; moral values may not be the provenance or contribution of legal transactions or judgments but the operation of the law as a whole is the only expression and guarantee of public virtue that can tame private vices. The very absence of ethical value, the flight of justice, ensures the morality of the law. This is the basis of the jurisprudential claim that unjust laws should be obeyed as the morality of legality overrides any local injustices.[23] Moral content may have been abstracted from law, but the legal enterprise as a whole is blessed with the overall attribute of morality. On the surface, the transition from status to contract is supplemented by a parallel passage from value to norm and from the good to the right. The foundation of meaning and value has been firmly transferred from the transcendent to the social, and in this transition normativity has forfeited its claim to substance and value and has replaced them with blanket certifications of source and of conformity with form. In the world of law, justice and injustice refer to fairness, the restoration of balance and proportion and the redress of the *status quo* between individuals.

An idiosyncratic celebration of the morality of the law is found in the writings of Dworkin.[24] The law is no longer about rules *à la* Hart, and certainly it is not the outcome of the unlimited will and power of the omnipotent legislator *à la* Austin. Law's empire includes principles and policies and its operation involves judicial interpretations, which must construct creatively the "right answer" to legal problems; to do so judges must develop and apply political and moral theories about the legal system that should present the law in the best possible light and create an image of the community as integrity. Morality (and moral philosophy) now enters the law and is properly recognised as an inescapable component of judicial hermeneutics. But its task is to legitimise judicial practice by showing the law to be the perfect narrative of a

[21] J. R. Lucas, *On Justice* (Oxford, Clarendon, 1980), 262, 263.
[22] H. L. A. Hart, *The Concept of Law* (Oxford, Clarendon, 1961), 153–4.
[23] L. L. Fuller, *The Morality of Law* (New Haven, Conn., Yale University Press, 1964).
[24] Ronald Dworkin *Taking Rights Seriously* (London, Duckworth, 1977); *Law's Empire* (London, Fontana 1983).

happy community. Morality is no longer a set of subjective and relative values nor is it a critical standard against which acts of legal and judicial power can be judged. The law is assumed to possess an internal integrity and coherence which allows the construction of public and quasi-objective principles of morality which can then be used as its underlying grammar and help resolve "hard cases".

Law's morality becomes the guarantee that the law never runs out. If a right answer exists it can be discovered in every case through the mobilisation of the morality that law's internal criteria of coherence yield. Judges are never left to their own devices; the dreaded supplement of judicial discretion (in other words the individual morality of the judge) that Hart had reluctantly admitted at the cost of endangering the rational completeness, coherence and closure of law is firmly kept outside. Dworkin seems to reintroduce moral considerations into law. But his theory is the last step in the juridification of morality and in the assertion of the moral legitimacy of legalism, both common symptoms of the de-ethicalisation of the law. The radical gap in the normative universe, created by the strict separation between legality and morality and the reduction of ethics to the private and subjective, is filled by the discourse of law as the lighthouse on the way to universal and objective truth. But for those who are unrepresented, unrepresentable and excluded from the "integrated" community, for the victims of the exercise of power and legal force, law's empire has no place.

III. THE ETHICS OF OTHERNESS

We are "surrounded by injustice without knowing where justice lies".[25] Roberto Unger's statement links our contemporary bewilderment with the classical passion for the denunciation of injustice. Acts of power cannot be criticised solely according to other acts of power. Justice is either a critical concept or it is redundant, if not positively harmful, by encouraging an unquestioning attitude to law and power. Postmodernity recognises the exhaustion of the exalted attempts to ground moral action exclusively upon cognition, reason or the law and marks the beginnings of a new ethical awareness. But the re-linking of ethics and politics or of justice and the law must pass through another conception of the good, in a situation where classical teleology is historically exhausted and religious transcendence is unable to command widespread acceptance. We need a quasi-transcendental ethical principle and an associated theory of judgement which would allow us to criticise our moral and legal practices, while being firmly placed within our history and experience. Let us turn to an ethics that avoids the pitfalls of Kantian moralism.

Emmanuel Levinas bases ethics on the shifting relationships between self and other. Ethics are the unique encounter with the living other, in her pres-

[25] R. M. Unger, *Law in Modern Society* (London, 1976), 175.

ent and unrepresentable corporeality. The ethics of alterity call for the re-eth-icalisation of law but have nothing in common with the moralism of deon-tology. Levinas argues that western philosophy and ethics share a common attitude towards the world which reduces the distance between self and other and returns the different to the same. Since the time of classical Greece, philo-sophy has put speculation as to the meaning of *Being* at the centre of its con-cerns. Universal logos reflects and will reveal the structure of reality since the ontological realm follows the demands of theoretical necessity. The traces of this ontological totalitarianism litter the body of philosophy. In its modern version, individual consciousness has become the starting point of all know-ledge and as a result what differs from the selfsame has turned into a ques-tion of epistemology, an exploration of the conditions under which I can know the other's existence and understand her mental life.

For phenomenology, the ego acquires knowledge through the intentionality of consciousness and its adequation with the phenomenal world. Husserl asserts the primacy of the perceptions of self and claims that the world dis-closes itself fully to consciousness. Heidegger, on the other hand, emphasises the historical and social nature of self. There is no life which is not life with others. Self does not postulate the other in its own image but, in discovering itself, it simultaneously recognises the other. But Heideggerian ontology, by privileging the question of *Being*, makes the relationship between beings and *Being* the key concern of philosophy and explicitly abandons ethics in favour of a primordial *ethos*. For Heidegger, self and the other are equal participants in the "we" through which we share the world. But inevitably all speculation on the meaning of *Being* starts from the examination of my own being and returns to ontology's preoccupation with self.

Law and jurisprudence share fully these cognitive and moral attitudes. Cognitively, the law knows the world to the extent that it subjects it to its regulative operations. For the jurisprudence of modernity, the law and the world are potentially co-extensive. The legal system has all the necessary resources to translate non-legal phenomena into law's arcane discourse and thus exercise its regulative function. One key strategy is the legal person. In existential terms, the subject of legal and contractual rights and agreements stands at the centre of the universe and asks the law to enforce his entitlements without great concern for ethical considerations and without empathy for the other. If the legal person is an isolated and narcissistic subject who perceives the world as a hostile place to be either used or fended against through the medium of rights and contracts, (s)he is also disembodied, genderless, a strangely mutilated person. The other as legal subject is a rational being with rights, entitlements and duties like ourselves. We expect to be treated equally with the other and reciprocity of entitlement and obligation is placed at the basis of the legal mentality. But this conception of justice as fairness must nec-essarily reduce the concreteness of the other, it must minimise the differences of need and desire and emphasise the similarities and homologies between the subjects. The moral worthiness of the other's demand is to be sought more in what self and other share than in those differences and specificities that make the other a concrete historical being.

Legal rules ensure equality before the law and guarantee the freedom of the parties. But this equality is only formal: it necessarily ignores the specific history, motive and need that the litigant brings to the law in order to administer the calculation of the rule and the application of the measure. Similarly with legal freedom: it is the freedom to accede to the available repertoire of legal forms and rights, the freedom to be what the law has ordained accompanied by the threat that opting out is not permitted, that disobedience to a legal norm is disobedience to the rule of law *tout court* and that life outside the legal form ceases. Legal rules and their mentality are strangely amoral; they promise to replace ethical responsibility with the mechanical application of predetermined and morally neutral rules and justice with the administration of justice. But there is more; moral philosophy in its ontological imperialism needs and creates the generalised other.[26] The law on the other hand, sharing the preoccupation to abstract and universalise, turns concrete people into generalised legal subjects. But the legal subject too is a fiction and the natural (legal) subject is infinitely more fictitious than the corporate. The difference between the fictions of Rawls and those of the law is that the legal subject is a *persona,* a mask, veil or blindfold put on real people who, unlike the abstractions of moral philosophy, feel hurt, pain and suffering. It is doubly important therefore to remove the mask from the face of the person and the blindfold from the eyes of justice. But is there an ethical residue in the law behind the all concealing veil of formal legality?

The ethics of alterity question these ontological and epistemological assumptions. They always start with the other and challenge the various ways in which the other has been reduced to the same. The other is not the self's *alter ego,* self's extension. Nor is the other the negation of self in a dialectical relation that can be totalised in a future synthesis. Heidegger correctly emphasises the historical and social nature of self. But the other is not similar to self. Self and other are not equal partners in a Heideggerian "we" in which we share our world, nor is the other the threatening externality and radical absence of Sartrean existentialism that turns self into an object. The other comes first. (S)he is the condition of existence of language, of self and of the law. The other always surprises me, opens a breach in my wall, befalls the ego. The other precedes me and calls upon me: where do you stand? Where are you now and not who you are. All "who" questions have ended in the foundational moves of (de)ontology. *Being,* the I of the Cartesian *cogito* and

---

[26] A typical instance of this "generalised other" is found in John Rawls, *A Theory of Justice* (Oxford, Oxford University Press, 1972). For a philosophical critique see Sheila Benhabib, *Situating the Self. Gender, Community and Postmodernism in Contemporary Ethics* (London, Polity, 1992); for a jurisprudential one see Costas Douzinas and Ronnie Warrington, *Justice Miscarried* (Edinburgh, Edinburgh University Press, 1995), ch. 4.

the Kantian transcendental subject start with self and create the other as an *imitatio ego*. In the philosophy of alterity, the other can never be reduced to the self or the different to the same.

The sign of another is the face. The face is unique. It is neither an empirical entity, the sum total of facial characteristics, nor the representation of something hidden, the soul, self or subjectivity. The face does not represent an absent presence, and cannot therefore become a cognitive datum. Nor is the face the epiphany of a visage, or the image of a substance. The face eludes every category. It brings together speech and glance, saying and seeing, in a unity that escapes the conflict of senses and the arrangement of the organs. Thought lives in speech, speech is (in) the face, saying is always addressed to a face. The other is her face. "Absolutely present, in his face, the Other—without any metaphor—faces me".[27] In its uniqueness, the face gets hold of me with an ethical grip, myself beholden to, obligated to, in debt to, the other person, prior to any contracts or agreements about who owes what to whom. To comprehend is to make something my own. But the face of the Other cannot be domesticated or consumed; it demands that I accept my responsibility. In the face-to-face, I am fully, immediately and irrevocably responsible for the other who faces me. A face in suffering issues a command, a decree of specific performance: "Do not kill me", "Welcome me", "Give me Sanctuary", "Feed me". The only possible answer to the ethical imperative is "an immediate respect for the other himself . . . because it does not pass through the neutral element of the universal, and through respect, in the Kantian sense for the law".[28]

The demand of the other that obliges me is the "essence" of the ethics of alterity. But this "essence" is based on the non-essence of the other who cannot be turned into the instance of a concept, the application of a law or the particularisation of the universal ego. "The other arises in my field of perception with the trappings of absolute poverty, without attributes, the other has no place, no time, no essence, the other is nothing but his or her request and my obligation."[29] As the face of the other turns on me, (s)he becomes my neighbour, but not the neighbour of the neighbour principle in law. As absolute difference and otherness, my neighbour is at the same time most strange and foreign. The appeal of the other is direct, concrete and personal; it is addressed to me and I am the only one who can answer it. The demand does not depend on universal reason or law but on the concrete historical and empirical encounter with the other. It is this situated encounter and unrepeatable unique demand which assigns me to morality and make me a bound and ethical subject. Our relationship is necessarily non-symmetrical and non-reciprocal as her unique demand is addressed to me and me alone. Equity is not equality but absolute dissymmetry.

[27] Levinas, quoted in Jacques Derrida, *Writing and Difference* (London, Routledge, 1978), 100.
[28] *Ibid.*, 96.
[29] Lyotard, *supra* n. 16, 111.

The ontology of alterity is based on the absolute proximity of the most alien. When self comes to constitute itself, it faces before the I, I's relationship with the other. Subjectivity is constituted through this opening. All consciousness is intersubjective and all language is given, but as the other comes first the nature of (inter)subjectivity is not of two equal parties, nor is the other a projection of self. My *principium individuationis* is my inescapable call to responsibility, the result of the direct and personal appeal the other makes on me. The other addresses me and not a universal ego or a legal person. To be free is to do what no one else can do in my place. But how can we move from the ethics of responsibility to the law? What is the relevance of a discourse that claims a pre-ontological and pre-rational status and emphasises the uniqueness of the face for a legality that has universalistic pretensions and bases its empire upon the rationality of judgment and the thematisation of people and circumstances?

The law is about calculation and systematisation, it regulates and totalises the demands put before it. The law translates these requests in the universalisable language of rights, legal entitlements and procedural proprieties and synchronises them, makes them appear contemporaneous and comparable. Almost by definition and necessity, the law forgets the difference of the different and the otherness of the other. To say therefore that the law begins as ethics, as the infinite, non-totalisable and non-regulated moment of the encounter with another sounds counterfactual. But the ethics of alterity is unequivocal; the sense of responsibility, the "internal" point of view that speaks to me and commands me comes from the proximity of one to another, the fact that we are involved and implicated as we are faced and addressed by the other. In my proximity to the other, within the law or outside it, I am preoccupied by the absolute asymmetry of the one for the other and I find myself in an irreplaceable and irreversible relation of substitution. It is on this basis of the "legal as ethical" that we can visualise a politics of law that disturbs the totalising tendency of the legal system. Such politics would allow the other to reappear both as the point of exteriority and transcendence that precludes the closure of ontology and as the excluded and unrepresentable of political and legal theory.

But while ethical responsibility can be said to start with the all embracing demands of an unknown other, the law must also introduce the demands and expectations of the third party. "The other is from the first the brother of all the other men."[30] But the co-existence of "all the other men" places a limit on my infinite responsibility towards the other. When someone comes to the law, he is already involved in conflict with at least one more person and the judge has to balance the conflicting requests. The judge, seen from the perspective of the litigants, is the third person whose action removes the dispute from the domain of interpersonal hostility and places it within the confines of

---

[30] Levinas, *Otherwise Than Being or Beyond Essence* (London, Kluwer, 1991), 158.

the institution. Because the third is always present in my encounter with the other, the law is implicated in every attempt to act morally. Justice involves "comparison, coexistence, contemporaneousness, assembling, order, the *visibility* of faces, . . . a co-presence on an equal footing as before a court of justice".[31]

Justice is therefore grounded in the ethical turn to the other; it "is impossible without the one that renders it finding himself in proximity. . . . The judge is not outside the conflict, but the law is in the midst of proximity".[32] The judge and law teachers are always involved and implicated, called upon to respond to the ethical relationship by the other. We must compare and calculate, but we remain responsible and always return to the surplus of duties over rights. Injustice would be to forget that the law rises on the ground of responsibility for the other and that ethical proximity and asymmetry overflow the equality of rights. The law can never have the last word. Legal relations are just only if they recognise "the impossibility of passing by he who is proximate".[33] We cannot define justice in advance, because that would turn the injunction of ethics into an abstract theory. Justice is not about theories and truth; it does not derive from a true representation of just society. If the law calculates, if it thematises people by turning them into legal subjects, ethics is a matter of an indeterminate judgement without criteria, and justice is the bringing together of the limited calculability and determinacy of law with the infinite openness of ethical alterity.

IV. THE INDETERMINATE JUDGEMENT

The idea of indeterminate judgement refers us to two seemingly unrelated traditions, Aristotelian practical wisdom and casuistry. In Aristotle *phronesis*, or practical wisdom, becomes a coherent theory of judgment because it is inextricably linked with a clear teleology of persons and actions. The aim of ethics is the achievement of the good life, but similarly every practice, profession or engagement is unified through its "standards of excellence" which allow us to call an orator or a politician or a carpenter good. The good life is always situated, it is good for us, and involves an ongoing dialogue and adjustment between our actions, aiming at the standards of excellence of various practices we engage in, and our overall "life plan", the more or less clear set of ideas, hopes, dreams and expectations that make us believe that our life through its various good and bad episodes is a fulfilled life. Against this background, *phronesis* is the method of deliberation followed by the prudent in order to arrive at judgements that will help achieve the standards of excellence of the various practices as a part of the wider project of establishing the good life.

[31] *Ibid.*, 157.
[32] *Ibid.*, 59.
[33] *Ibid.*

Practical wisdom is therefore the virtue of praxis. Practical judgements, unlike theoretical statements, do not deal with essences or with necessary and immutable relations; they have a timely and circumstantial character, and they depend on a full and detailed understanding of the factual situation. The theoretical sciences examine general principles and the formal connections between phenomena, while practical knowledge deals with the changing and the variable, with "ultimate particulars" and tries to grasp the situation in its singularity.[34] Indeed Aristotle goes as far as to compare the singularity of practical judgement to that of perception *aisthesis*.[35] Thus, while the evolving knowledge of the aims of good life forms the horizon of Aristotelian ethics, *phronesis* recognises that moral norms and values are just that, a horizon. In his discussion of justice, Aristotle argues that equity, *epieikeia*, is the rectification of legal justice, in so far as the law is defective on account of its generalisations. While laws are universal, "the raw material of human behaviour" is such that it is often impossible to pronounce in general terms. Thus "justice and equity coincide, and both are good, [but] equity is superior".[36] Aristotle goes on to use the rule as a metaphor for law. But as the object to be regulated has an "irregular shape" the law too should be like the leaden Lesbian rule:[37] "just as this rule is not rigid but is adapted to the shape of the stone, so the ordinance is framed to fit the circumstances".[38] Justice and the variety of circumstances in which practical judgement is exercised require that the prudent go beyond the application of rules. Aristotle did not take the casuistic route and did not compile lists and classifications of good and bad acts like his medieval followers.[39] But the Aristotelian practical judgement is preoccupied with the specificity of the situation and with the perception, understanding and judging of the singular as singular, and is a major source of inspiration for medieval casuistry.

Casuistry is a method of resolving moral and religious conflicts, a church based form of moral reasoning.[40] Until at least the seventeenth century, matters such as the relations with one's family or neighbours, or with one's one body and soul as in the correct attitude to suicide,[41] how to behave in public, attitudes to sexuality, to the lending of money at interest and so on, all came within the casuist's scope. Indeed the Catholic church, assuming that the world was a *universitas christianorum*, decided that all aspects of conscience came under its jurisdiction. Christian casuistry, designed to help priests resolve borderline problems in a principled yet sensitive manner, reached its

[34] Aristotle, *supra* n. 3, 215.

[35] *Ibid.*, 219–20.

[36] *Ibid.*, 199.

[37] The "lesbian rule", used by the building trade in classical Mytilene, is made of soft lead and can bend around irregularly shaped objects to measure their circumference.

[38] *Ibid.*, 200.

[39] Douzinas and Warrington, *supra* n. 26, ch. 3.

[40] See generally A. R. Jonsen and S. Toulmin, *The Abuse of Casuistry* (Berkeley, Calif., University of California Press, 1988).

[41] Aristotle, *supra* n. 3, 200.

height of refinement and influence around the sixteenth and seventeenth centuries. For a time, it became a widely accepted and respected method for the resolution of disputes and problems faced by the all-encompassing church jurisdiction. Even when casuistry had become predominantly associated with a minority religion, as it did from Elizabethan times in England, it still affected the orthodoxy. Both as something "other", as a discourse of justice alien to the presumed majority opinion, and, even more insidiously, within the very orthodoxy that seemed to reject entirely the basis of casuistry's jurisdiction and method of operation, casuistry triumphed. For a time, even in Protestant England, it was ubiquitous. Casuistry fell out of intellectual favour from around 1650 after the violent attacks by religious enemies, who claimed that it was the sort of reasoning that could justify anything. Despite something of a recent revival, casuistry became, and is still now, frequently treated as synonymous with another debased tradition—"sophistry".

Casuistry as a form of moral judgement starts from the position of the unique individual in her natural and social environment and attempts to describe this singularity in morally relevant terms. In the words of casuistry's modern defenders, "the method of casuistry involved an ordering of cases by paradigm and analogy, appeals to maxims and analysis of circumstances, the qualification of opinions, the accumulation of multiple arguments, and the statement of practical resolutions of particular moral problems in the light of all these considerations". It is based on general maxims, but these are not "universal or invariable, since they hold good with certainty only in the typical conditions of the agent and the circumstances of action".[42]

These maxims were derived from three sources. First, principles came from God either through revelation or reason, which was God's way of allowing human beings to partake in divine wisdom. The obvious starting place, especially for Puritan casuistry, was the Bible.[43] Secondly, the casuists relied on the opinions of the learned who had, in the past, written about moral problems broadly conceived, and whose opinions, like those of common law judges, had come to be recognised as authoritative. Since at least the eleventh century, the Catholic Church had been wedded to the importance of "authority", and the casuists used it extensively.[44] Bishops, priests, doctors, saints, recluses, learned men of religion of all sorts had written, some of them in exhaustive quantities, on the detailed results that the confessors and advisers should reach in coming to conclusions in particular cases. Although mostly couched in terms of hypotheticals, the discussions were usually based on actual cases that had occurred. The endless works of casuistry were intended as a sort of handbook for those involved in day-to-day "adjudication" over

---

[42] Jonsen and Toulmin, *supra* n. 40, 256–7.

[43] D. R. Bellhouse, "Probability in the Sixteenth and Seventeenth Centuries: An Analysis of Puritan Casuistry", (1988) 56 *International Statistical Review* 63, 66.

[44] W. Ullman, *The Growth of Papal Government in the Middle Ages* (London, Methuen, 1962), 360–1.

matters religious and moral (if indeed such a distinction was a valid one in *societas christiana*).

But the most important source for the determination of moral disputes was "conscience". Conscience, like equity's conception of the term, was not merely individual thoughts or reactions to moral dilemmas and conflict. The irreducibly personal acts of conscience "weave norms and circumstances and opinions together into a strand of will and understanding called a judgement of right action".[45] Cases of conscience act "simultaneously as demonstrations of the principle that each human action is unique and as models of decision-making process to be imitated by all men with similar cases of conscience".[46] Conscience depended on individual circumstances, the who, what, when, where and how of the rhetoricians, and was always the final arbiter. But its judgement was intimately linked with the wisdom of past practices and the open-ended principles. The locus of this link is the "case", which brings together the various public and private aspects of the moral dilemma, the concrete persons with their unique histories, the time and place of the action and the wider considerations involved. Casuistry follows the rhetorical topics and organises its problems as narratives. This allows as many aspects of the situation as possible to come to bear on its narrative closure which is also the moral answer.

Aristotle had expounded carefully what the different virtues were, and that each had to be understood and applied around a notion of the mean. But, Aristotle had continued, such exposition of principles was insufficient: "[a] generalisation of this kind is not enough; we must apply it to particular cases".[47] The casuists took this injunction seriously, and set about detailing how principles should be applied in the vast area faced by Christian consciences. The doctors of the Jesuitical-casuistical tradition required the confessors and advisers, the dealers in heavenly approvals and damnable disapprovals, to determine the cases of conscience with a fine attention to the infinite detail of the myriad circumstances which flesh is heir to. And, notwithstanding their opponents and detractors, although they were concerned with principles (just as much as their common law counterparts) they had the wisdom to appreciate that all the principles in the world did not solve any specific problems. They would act as a guide to the conduct of the judge, they would always be relevant, but the final decision depended on the precise circumstances of the individual matter facing the arbitrator and trader in absolutions.

It is evident that one discipline that has taken the injunctions of casuistry seriously for centuries, with only very rare acknowledgements of its close

---

[45] J. Keenan and T. Shannon (eds.), *The Context of Casuistry*, Washington, DC, Georgetown University Press), xii.

[46] C. W. Slights, *The Casuistical Tradition in Shakespeare, Donne, Herbert and Milton* (Princeton, NJ, Princeton University Press, 1981), 297.

[47] Aristotle, *supra* n. 3, 103.

cousin, is the common law. Both casuistry and the common law treated the specific facts of any case with great respect; each claimed its decisions were based on principles; each was directly concerned with adjudications over "consciences", though by the end of the middle ages the scope of each jurisdiction's conscience applications had been separated. Especially in the jurisdiction of the court of equity conscience is paramount. For the equity courts, conscience is not just a knowledge of wrong doing. As the Court of Appeal once put it: for a claim of conscience to be pleaded successfully "it must be shown to have an ancestry founded in history and in the practice and precedent of the courts administering equity jurisdiction".[48] Conscience is both principle and individual mental comprehension of the possibility of right action. Finally, and above all, the common law, like casuistry, has the inherent potential to consider sensitively the specifics of the person before it. The common law's frequent failure to take seriously this possibility has been a main factor of its moral failings.

The growth of statutory interventions, the introduction of doctrinalism and of the "textbook tradition", the decline of casuistry as a church art undermined the casuistic method in law. In theory however the common law has never rejected the working procedures of the case method. Its particularity is to be found in the dialectical relationship between the general principles to be derived from common law, custom and statute, and the specific facts involved in any particular dispute. Past decisions are both sources of general but open-ended principle, precedents for future cases, and careful, often lengthy, examinations of all "relevant" surrounding circumstances which, in the best judgements, are woven into complete and æsthetically constructed narratives. In recognising the uniqueness of each case, the common law retains the potential for an ethical application of principles and the development of a notion of justice which is aware of the requirements of the individual before the court and of the contingency of decision-making.

If questions of justice and ethics are to be taken seriously, an understanding of the case law system, as a system of principles which are sensitive to the needs of the individual and the totalities of circumstances in the particular case, has to be brought to the forefront of legal reasoning. Of course, the common law's treatment of the "other" is generally harsh and sometimes brutal.[49] We need to develop a secular form of casuistic reasoning for use in the law. The common law has the resources for turning into a form of decision-making which is fully cognizant of the needs of the other, as well as the requirements of principle. There is all the more reason, therefore, to draw out the possibilities implicit in the common law for arguing and acting otherwise. A contradictory notion it may be, but a secular form of casuistry, fully aware of the call of the other, is a potent source of principled action. If the other is a transcendent principle for the law, casuistry tells us how to acknowledge her

---

[48] *Re Diplock* [1948] Ch. 465.

[49] For examples of such treatment see Douzinas and Warrington, *supra* n. 26, ch. 6.

call. This combination of an ethics of alterity that posits an external entity whose needs must be respected with the prudential and concrete casuistic decision-making is the starting and finishing point for the re-ethicalisation of law. The law is committed to the form of universalism and abstract equality; but a just decision must also respect the requests of the contingent, incarnate and concrete other; it must pass through the ethics of alterity in order to respond to its own embeddedness in justice. In this unceasing conjunction between the most general and calculating and the most concrete and incalculable, or between the legality of form and the materiality of the person lies the postmodern aporia of justice.

3

"The Secret Courts of Men's Hearts", Legal Ethics and Harper Lee's To Kill a Mockingbird

TIM DARE

"Atticus had used every tool available to free men to save Tom Robinson, but in the secret courts of men's hearts Atticus had no case. Tom was a dead man the minute Mayella Ewell opened her mouth and screamed."[1]

I. INTRODUCTION

Lawyers are widely thought to be callous, self-serving, devious, indifferent to justice, truth and the public good. The profession could do with a hero. It has seemed to some that Atticus Finch of Harper Lee's *To Kill a Mockingbird* fits the bill. Claudia Carter, for instance, has urged lawyers to use Atticus as a model: "I had many heroes when growing up", she writes. "Only one remains very much "alive" for me. . . . Atticus made me believe in lawyer-heroes".[2] Not all lawyers and commentators have been so ready to laud Atticus as an appropriate ethical model for his real-life colleagues. Most influentially, Monroe Freedman has argued that Atticus was hardly a man to be admired since, as a state legislator and community leader in a segregated society, he lived "his own life as the passive participant in that pervasive injustice".[3]

Though there is plainly disagreement between Freedman and the "Atticans", as Freedman dubs his opponents, there is also an important point of agreement. Both take it that Atticus's suitability as a role model for lawyers

---

[1] Harper Lee, *To Kill a Mockingbird* (London, Heinemann, 1960), 266. Subsequent references appear in parentheses in the text of the article.

[2] Claudia Carter, "Lawyers as Heroes: The Compassionate Activism of a Fictional Attorney as a Model We Can Emulate", *Los Angeles Lawyer* (July–Aug. 1988).

[3] Monroe Freedman, "Atticus Finch, Esq., R.I.P." *Legal Times* (24 Feb. 1992), 20.

is to be settled by his character. Freedman argues against giving Atticus the job on the ground that he is not the mythical figure portrayed by the Atticans: Atticus does not take on Robinson's defence willingly, but only when appointed by the court. Atticus admits that he had hoped "to get through life without a case of this kind" (98). Atticus excuses the leader of a lynch mob as "basically a good man" who "just has his blind spots along with the rest of us" (173). Atticus sees that "one of these days we're going to pay the bill" (243–4) for racism, but hopes that payment, and so justice for blacks, will not come during his children's life times.[4] Freedman argues, then, that Atticus's character makes him unsuitable as a role model. On the other hand, a leading Atticus supporter, Thomas Shaffer, argues that Atticus shows us precisely that what matters in professional ethics is character rather than moral principle:

> "One thing you could say about Atticus is that he had character. . . . We say that a good person has character, but we do not mean to say only that he believes in discernible moral principles and, under those principles, makes good decisions. We mean also to say something about who he is and to relate who he is to his good decisions. When discussion proceeds in this way, principles need not even be explicit. We can say, 'How would Atticus see this situation?' or 'What would Atticus do' rather than, 'What principles apply?' ".[5]

Cast in this light the debate about Atticus connects with the recent resurrection of virtue ethics, and with concomitant suggestions that a virtue or character-based ethics might provide a particularly promising approach to professional ethics in general and to legal ethics in particular.[6] I argue that this appeal to Atticus is misplaced. Though Atticus can teach us important lessons for legal ethics, they are not about the priority of virtue or character. Neither side to the debate, then, has Atticus quite right. Sorting out what it is about him which makes him an appropriate or inappropriate role model for lawyers will both enrich our appreciation of a fine novel and further our understanding of what it is to be an ethical lawyer. More widely, it suggests that virtue ethics have little to offer toward an understanding of the moral responsibility of lawyers.

---

[4] Monroe Freedman, "Atticus Finch—Right and Wrong" (1994) 45 *Alabama Law Review* 473–82.

[5] Thomas L Shaffer, *Faith and the Professions* (Provo, Utah, Brigham Young University Press, 1987), 5.

[6] I say a little more about the general resurrection of virtue ethics in Sect. IV below. For applications to the legal profession see Anthony Kronman, *The Lost Lawyer* (Cambridge, Mass., Belknap Press, 1993) and Gerald Postema, "Moral Responsibility in Professional Ethics" (1980) 55 *New York University Law Review* 63–89.

II. AN OVERVIEW OF *TO KILL A MOCKINGBIRD*

In the simplest terms, *To Kill a Mockingbird* is the story of the trial of a black man, Tom Robinson, for the rape of a white woman, Mayella Ewell, in racist Alabama in the 1930s. Appointed to defend Robinson, Atticus Finch takes the task seriously, so drawing upon himself and his children the slurs and taunts of neighbours. At trial he proves that Robinson could not have raped Mayella, showing her attacker to have been left handed with two good arms while Robinson had lost the use of his left arm in a cotton gin accident. The plain implication of the evidence is that Mayella's father, Bob Ewell, beat her after seeing her with her arm around Robinson's waist. Robinson is convicted nonetheless. Lee presents the jury as facing a choice: believe a black man or a white woman. Even though Mayella is "white trash", her word—and thus rejection of the implication that a white woman had sought a liaison with a black man—was to be preferred to the evidence and to accepting the word of a respectable black man. The verdict does not surprise Atticus. Racism, "Maycomb's usual disease"(98), has made it a foregone conclusion. But Atticus is not led to compromise the zealous pursuit of Tom's interests by his appreciation of the hopelessness of the case. Indeed, he tells his children that you display real courage "when you know you're licked before you begin anyway and you see it through no matter what. You rarely win, but sometimes you do"(122). Atticus's principal act of courage is standing up for Tom against the prejudices of his community, though he knows it will in the end come to nothing.

After the trial verdict Atticus tells Tom that they will have a good chance on appeal, but Tom refuses to be comforted: "Good-bye, Mr Finch", he responds, "there ain't nothing you can do now, so there ain't no use tryin' "(258). Sure enough, shortly afterward Tom is killed, shot seventeen times while trying to climb a prison fence in full view of guards. Atticus describes the event as showing that Tom was "tired of white men's chance and preferred to take one of his own"(260), though it reads as easily as suicide, and some commentators assume it was murder.[7] Tom's death completes one story in *Mockingbird*: an innocent black man has been falsely accused, wrongfully convicted and killed.

"Tom's story" occurs in the middle parts of the novel, flanked by another. A central figure in this other story is the Finches' mysterious neighbour, Arthur "Boo" Radley. Neither the Finch children nor their friend Dill have ever seen Boo. He has been kept a recluse inside his family's house for close to twenty-five years, and has not been seen since stabbing his father with a

[7] Monroe Freedman treats the episode as showing Atticus's naïvety: "You can believe this improbable story [that Tom broke into a blind, raving charge in a hopeless attempt to climb over the fence and escape], as Finch purports to. But I believe (and Harper Lee appears to believe) that Tom was goaded into a desperate, futile run for the fence on threat of being shot where he stood": "Atticus Finch—Right and Wrong", *supra* n. 4, 478.

pair of scissors about fifteen years into this period of isolation. The children regard him as a bogey man, and play what seem to them dangerous games of brinkmanship with him. The reader sees that Boo is not as the children perceive him: rather he is a gentle person—he leaves gifts for the children, he wraps a blanket around Scout as she watches a fire in the cold, he attempts to mend the trousers Jem has torn and abandoned in flight from a raid into the Radley property.

The two stories—Tom's and Boo's—come together at the end of the novel. Walking home from a school pageant the Finch children are attacked by Bob Ewell. Scout is saved by her pageant costume. Jem is knocked unconscious and has his arm badly broken. They are saved by a mysterious rescuer who turns out to be Boo Radley. Boo kills Bob Ewell. In what will be an important moment for my account of the novel, Atticus ultimately decides to go along with the Sheriff's recommendation that they do not charge Boo over Ewell's death. Instead Atticus and the Sheriff adopt the fiction that Ewell fell on his knife.

Each story is a vehicle for the moral fable which runs through *Mockingbird*. In the simplest terms still, this is a fable of innocence confronting evil and learning from the experience. Scout the narrator personifies the theme. Her childish innocence is a crucial aspect of her narration. The senselessness of the racism and class divisions which rend Maycomb is highlighted by her genuine lack of comprehension, just as her inability to comprehend Tom's conviction makes explicit the senselessness of justice being destroyed by prejudice. The innocent narrator finds all of these things mysterious, and through her eyes readers too are invited to cast aside any jaundice or resignation which may dull the impact of what is, after all, a tragically familiar story. During the course of the novel Scout's innocence wanes. It gives way, however, not to prejudice but to informed goodness. The transformation is most evident in Scout's attitude to Boo. At the beginning of the story she regards Boo as an outsider and misfit—fit to be tormented and feared. The novel closes with her taking his hand to lead him home and seeing that things look the same from the Radley porch as they do from her own.

Much of the credit for Scout's moral development is owed to Atticus, the spokesman for the moral philosophy of the novel. He is a loving, patient and understanding father who consciously and conscientiously guides his children to virtue while respecting them as individuals capable of judgement and decision. He teaches them compassion and tolerance, frequently advising Scout to "step into the shoes" of others such as the Ewells and Boo Radley. Scout's final response to Boo is an indication that she has learnt this central moral lesson. Atticus treats everybody, regardless of class or colour with respect. Atticus is courageous, both in the sense which leads him zealously to pursue Tom's defence despite knowing that it will not succeed, and in the more straightforward sense evident when he arms himself only with a newspaper though anticipating a confrontation with a lynch mob. In sum, Atticus's is a

voice of decency, wisdom and reason, courageously speaking out against bigotry, ignorance and prejudice.

III. *MOCKINGBIRD'S* THREE GREAT MOMENTS FOR LEGAL ETHICS

There are three moments in *Mockingbird* of particular significance for lawyers
and for legal ethics. The first is the final part of Atticus's summation to the
jury. One often hears, he remarks, that all men are created equal. On some
constructions the assertion is simply ridiculous: as a matter of fact, people are
not born equally smart or equally wealthy. But, says Atticus:

> "there is one way in this country in which all men are created equal—there is one
> human institution that makes a pauper the equal of a Rockerfeller, the stupid
> man the equal of an Einstein and the ignorant man the equal of any college pres-
> ident. That institution, gentlemen, is a court. It can be the Supreme Court of the
> United States or the humblest J.P. court in the land, or this honourable court
> which you serve. Our courts have their faults, as does any human institution, but
> in this country our courts are the great levellers, and in our courts all men are
> created equal" (227).

The passage requires no further elucidation. It is as plain a statement of the
role of courts as one could hope for. Whatever inequalities people suffer outside the court, within it they are to be treated as equals.

The second great moment occurs after Tom's death. Mr Underwood, the
editor of the local newspaper, has published a courageous editorial condemn-
ing the death as sinful and senseless, likening it to the "slaughter of songbirds"
(265). Initially, Scout is puzzled by the editorial: how could Tom's death be
sinful when he had been granted due process of law and vigorously defended
in an open court, but, she continues:

> "Then Mr Underwood's meaning became clear: Atticus had used every tool avail-
> able to free men to save Tom Robinson, but in the secret courts of men's hearts
> Atticus had no case. Tom was a dead man the minute Mayella Ewell opened her
> mouth and screamed" (266).[8]

Again, the meaning of the passage seems clear: Tom was convicted, despite
the evidence, because he had not been tried in a court of law at all. His trial
had been conducted "in the secret courts of men's hearts". These courts were
governed not by presumptions of equality and innocence, but by the prejudices and bigotry which comprised Maycomb's usual disease. Atticus's plea to
the jury, to ensure that Tom was tried in the public courts of law, had been
ignored and Tom had been convicted and killed as a result.

In his final speech Atticus makes clear his commitment to the ideal of a rule
of law—where a rule of law is to be understood precisely as rule by public

---

[8] Extraordinarily, I think, this key passage was omitted from Horton Footes' screenplay of
Mockingbird and hence from the classic movie of the novel.

standards rather than by the private wishes and inclinations of individuals. In Scout's explication of Mr Underwood's editorial we have a further elucidation of that commitment. An innocent man has died because a jury chose to try him secretly by its own standards rather than by those of the public system of law. Thus far, then, the message of *Mockingbird* to lawyers seems to be that they should fight for and maintain commitment to the rule of law rather than to the rule of individuals. They should honour and protect the public judgments of courts, not only in preference to but from the private judgements of individuals.

The third great moment in the novel occurs in its last few pages, when Tom's and Boo's stories come together. Bob Ewell has attacked Atticus's children as they walk home through the woods after dark. Boo Radley comes to their rescue and Bob Ewell is killed. Initially all that is clear is that the children have been attacked and that their attacker lies dead, "a kitchen knife stuck up under his ribs" (294). Atticus thinks that Jem has killed Ewell, wresting the knife away during the attack, and he simply takes it for granted that Jem will go before a court, though he will be acquitted since "it was clear cut self defence" (300). Mr Tate, the Sheriff, interrupts, telling Atticus that Jem did not stab Ewell, that he fell on his own knife. Atticus assumes Tate is trying to hush up what has happened to protect Jem, and refuses to go along with the subterfuge. But soon Atticus realises that it is not Jem that the Sheriff is trying to protect. Boo Radley stabbed Bob Ewell, and it is Boo who will be spared a trial by the fiction that Ewell fell on his own knife. It would, Tate maintains, be a sin to bring Boo before a court:

> "To my way of thinking taking the one man who's done you and this town a great service an' draggin' him and his shy ways into the limelight—to me, that's a sin. It's a sin and I'm not about to have it on my head. If it was any other man it'd be different. But not this man. . . . I may not be much, Mr Finch, but I'm still sheriff of Maycomb county, and Bob Ewell fell on his knife" (304).

Atticus sits, looking at the floor for a long time before finally raising his head and saying to Scout "Mr Ewell fell on his knife. Can you possibly understand?" (304). Scout's response demonstrates that she understands perfectly well that there has been a decision to accept a fiction. "Yes sir", she says "I understand. . . . Mr Tate was right. . . . Well, it'd be sort of like shootin' a mockingbird, wouldn't it?" (304).

These three episodes pose an obvious challenge. In the first two we have a clear message in favour of the rule of law, put quite specifically as a warning about the danger of deciding upon guilt or innocence within the "secret court's of men's hearts" rather than by the public processes of the courts of law. But this seems to be exactly what Atticus countenances in the final episode. Atticus and the Sheriff have decided that Boo should be spared a trial. They have tried him in the secret courts of their own hearts and declared him innocent, and their decision is endorsed by Scout: to try Boo would be like shooting a mockingbird. What was a wicked thing in Tom's case is a good thing in Boo's case.

IV. *MOCKINGBIRD* AND THE RETURN TO VIRTUE

The challenge has not gone unnoticed. Some commentators have been mildly critical. Even Attican Thomas Shaffer describes Atticus's decision to go along with the Sheriff's account of Ewell's death as a mistake.[9] For the most part however, commentators, including Shaffer, applaud both Atticus's position in his final speech and his decision to spare Boo. Indeed, the apparent inconsistency in Atticus's responses in the two episodes is taken to show his praiseworthy character and his laudable attitude toward the law. Claudia Johnson writes at length of Atticus's respect for law, before commenting on the Ewell/Radley decision:

> "Despite Atticus's respect for the law, he believes that reason must prevail when law violates reason. . . . Even a human and civilised system of law sometimes becomes, under certain circumstances, severely limited when primitive, hidden codes of lawlessness emerge so powerfully. In the case of Boo Radley's killing of Bob Ewell, law is proven inadequate, because on occasion reason dictates that laws and boundaries must be overridden for justice to be done. Circumstances must override honour; a human being's needs must supersede principle. . . ."[10]

Here the apparent inconsistency between Atticus's views in Tom's and Boo's cases is taken to illustrate Atticus's "wisdom" or practical judgement. He is not a mere automaton, mindlessly following the law wherever it may lead. Where following law would defeat justice, Atticus is prepared to abandon law in order to preserve or further more fundamental values. And even Thomas Shaffer, who describes Atticus's decision to adopt a fiction over Ewell's death as a mistake, does not think the mistake diminishes Atticus as a hero. Rather it shows us precisely "how a good man makes a doubtful choice" and once again reminds us of the importance of character, since the episode demonstrates "that more is involved than whether the choice is sound in principle".[11] These authors take the importance of *Mockingbird* to lie in its demonstration of the importance of the character of practitioners in professional ethics. In effect, they render Atticus's character coherent by subsuming his conduct under the notion of "judgement". His conduct may well

---

[9] Thomas L. Shaffer, "The Moral Theology of Atticus Finch" (1981) 41 *University of Pittsburg Law Review* 181–224, 196. We will see in a moment that Shaffer does not think this a criticism of Atticus.

[10] Claudia Johnson, "Without Tradition and Within Reason: Judge Horton and Atticus Finch in Court" (1994) 45 *Alabama Law Review* 483–510, 499. See too, Timothy Hall who, arguing for the ethical centrality of character, defines character by reference to Atticus, and concludes that Atticus allows us to see and teach how virtue and character guide the practice of law: "Moral Character, the Practice of Law and Legal Education" (1990) *Mississippi Law Review* 511, 525.

[11] Thomas L. Shaffer, "The Moral Theology of Atticus Finch", *supra* n. 9, 196.

be inconsistent when viewed from the perspective of this or that general principle or rule of right conduct, but this just shows the inadequacy of principle- or rule-governed approaches to ethical conduct.

I suggested earlier that the debate about Atticus connected with wider developments in contemporary ethics. It will be useful to add a little detail to these remarks. One of the most striking features of contemporary moral philosophy has been the rediscovery of Aristotle. At the heart of this renaissance is the idea that moral deliberation and justification cannot proceed deductively through the application of general principles to particular cases. Aristotle supposes that the phenomenon with which ethical inquiry is concerned is marked by mutability, indeterminacy and particularity, such that they can never be unproblematically subsumed under general principles of right action. His view of the limitations of general principles of right action led him to stress the importance of "practical judgement" (*phronesis*), a practical reasoning skill which is a matter neither of simply applying general principles to particular cases nor of mere intuition. *Phronesis* is a complex faculty in which general principles and the particularities of the case both play a role.[12] The *phronimos* relies upon his judgement to identify the right thing to do in light both of principles and the exigencies of the particular case. This emphasis upon judgement brings the character of the practical reasoner to centre-stage. We cannot look to general principles to settle what is the right thing to do, hence we must look to the character—or virtues—of those doing the judging.

Although the Aristotelian model once dominated normative theory, including legal theory, it fell into disfavour around the time of the scientific revolution.[13] Recently there has been a dramatic return to Aristotle. Though it is difficult to characterise virtue theory so as to capture all that has been gathered under that rubric, it will do for our purposes to understand a virtue theory as one which holds that judgements about the character of persons, independently of assessments of the rightness or the value of the consequences of their actions, is what is most fundamental in moral evaluation. Bluntly, virtue theories are character-based in so far as they eschew principle- or rule-based moral reasoning and place emphasis instead upon the judgement of moral agents. A flavour of the new wave of virtue theory, understood in this rather broad fashion, may be gained from John McDowell, who maintains that morality is "uncodifiable", and writes that "one knows what to do (if one

---

[12] "Practical wisdom is not concerned with universals only; it must also recognise particulars, for it is practical and practice concerns particulars"; Aristotle, *Nicomachean Ethics*, 1141b14–16.

[13] Newton had shown that the whole of nature could be explained by a small set of fundamental principles, and moral philosophers sought to follow his example. Thus philosophers such as Spinoza and Hobbes explicitly described their work as following the scientific or geometric method, and Bentham's entire philosophical project may be characterised as an attempt to provide a single and fundamental principle—the principle of utility—from which all practical discourse might proceed by "moral arithmetic". "[A]ny . . . work of mine . . . on the subject of legislation or any other branch of moral science", he wrote, "is an attempt to extend the experimental method of reasoning from the physical branch to the moral": quoted in W. S. Holdsworth, *History of English Law* XIII (Methuen, London, 1952), 53.

does) not by applying universal principles but by being a certain sort of person: one who sees situations in a certain way",[14] and Martha Nussbaum who states that "[t]he conception of ethical theory on which I rely is, roughly, an Aristotelian one",[15] while arguing for the priority of perception over rules and claiming that "to confine ourselves to the universal is a recipe for obtuseness".[16]

We should regard the Attican's response to *Mockingbird* as a part of this wider rediscovery of Aristotle and virtue ethics. The Atticans present Atticus as the *phronimos*, an expert practical reasoner sensitive both to general principles and the particularities of cases. Atticus is one who knows what to do not by applying general principles, but by being the sort of person he is, by having the sort of character he has. Atticus recognises that confining himself to general principles such as those he defended at Tom's trial would be a recipe for obtuseness. Again, his lesson for us is the priority of character over rules and principles.

V. AN ALTERNATIVE APPROACH TO THE THREE MOMENTS: ATTICUS AS A TRAGIC FIGURE

I am not convinced that Atticus is an appropriate ethical role-model for lawyers. He fails in this regard not—as Monroe Freedman would have it—because his character makes him unsuited to the role, but because the character approach itself is unable to provide an appropriate grounding for the ethical obligations of lawyers and similar professionals and *that*, I believe, is Atticus's lesson for us. My starting point is essentially a reiteration of the challenge posed by the three episodes set out in Section III above. Accepting the Atticans" account of the significance of the Boo decision leaves us with task of explaining just what is to be made of the "other" two passages; of Atticus's final speech to the jury and of Scout's "secret courts" explanation of the injustice suffered by Tom. Why did Atticus say the things he did at Tom's trial? Why tell the jury that the courts were the great levellers when really he thought they were not? Perhaps the Atticans will respond to these queries by pointing to a dramatic dissimilarity between Tom's and Boo's cases. Although the cases are hauntingly similar—and a good deal of the force of the novel turns on this similarity—in one respect at least Tom's and Boo's cases are dramatically and importantly different. By the time Atticus is called in, the wheels of Maycomb justice already have Tom firmly in their grip. In Boo's case, by

[14] John McDowell, "Virtue and Reason" in Stanley G Clarke and Evan Simpson (ed.), *Anti-Theory in Ethics and Moral Conservatism* (Albany, NY, State University of New York Press, 1989) 87–109, 105.

[15] Martha Nussbaum, *The Fragility of Goodness: Luck and Ethics in Greek Tragedy and Philosophy* (New York, Cambridge University Press, 1986), 10.

[16] Martha Nussbaum ," 'Richly Aware and Finely Responsible': Literature and the Moral Imagination" in *Anti-Theory in Ethics and Moral Conservatism, supra* n. 14, 122–34, 126.

contrast, Atticus and the Sheriff have the opportunity to avoid exposing Boo to public trial altogether. Why tell the jury that the courts were the great levellers then? Because in the circumstances that was the best Atticus could do. Tom's best, albeit forlorn, hope was that Atticus could convince the jury to try Tom according to those public standards intended to render the courts the great levellers rather than in the secret courts of their own hearts. Claudia Johnson appears to have this response in mind when she writes that even as he delivered the soliloquy "Atticus is grieved by what he cannot at this moment say: that the law of the land is one thing and 'the secret court of men's heart' quite another".[17] The Atticans might go on to argue that Atticus was speaking to the jury prescriptively rather than descriptively when he said the courts were the great levellers. He did not mean to describe the actual practice of the courts, the Atticans might claim, but instead to identify their intended social role; a role possessed by all courts even if honoured by only a few. Atticus believed everything he said to the jury as a prescriptive matter, but given the descriptive truths that most courts failed to perform their intended role and that Tom's court was predictably going to do so, he was prepared to avoid the courts when he judged, *qua phronimos*, that that was the way to attain justice.

But there are considerable costs to adopting either of these responses. Both require deeply problematic interpretations of central passages in the novel and, consequently and more importantly, quite dramatic reassessments of Atticus's character as well. If we adopt the responses, we must think that Atticus's stirring final speech did not say what it rather plainly seemed to say. The most dramatic version of this conclusion portrays Atticus as a dissembler. Though he told the jury that the courts were the great levellers he did not really believe that, since—to put it bluntly—he thought that he and his kind were the great levellers, not the courts. Even as he spoke, he was "grieved" by what he thought but could not say. Atticus's much remarked commitment to truth-telling was not all it seemed.[18] Now of course, Atticans are likely to resist this strong conclusion. Even if Atticus did tell the jury something he did not believe, one can imagine them responding, his doing so amounted to an appropriate departure from rigid principles of truth-telling. But even if we stop short of the strong conclusion, we must at least give the final speech a much narrower compass than we may have thought appropriate: it was not a general account of the nature of courts at all, but a plea to *this* court on *this* occasion. According to the first response he did not really mean what he said; he made the plea only because Tom was already enmeshed in the court system and he had no chance to intervene more directly and effectively. According to the second response we must ignore the rather plain

---

[17] Claudia Johnson, *To Kill a Mockingbird: Threatening Boundaries* (New York, Twayne Publishers, 1994), 95.

[18] "[Atticus] was uncommonly devoted to the truth. He would not even lie a little to comfort his client": Shaffer, "The Moral Theology of Atticus Finch", *supra* n. 9, 185.

language of Atticus's principal soliloquy, so rewriting one of the most powerful and evocative passages of the novel and one of the most eloquent insights into Atticus's character. For Atticus certainly does not seem to be speaking prescriptively when he speaks to the jury: "there is one institution that makes men equal" and "our courts are the great levellers", he says, not "there is one institution which *should* make men equal" or "*it is the job* of the courts to be the great levellers". Perhaps we should forgive these rhetorical flourishes, but we should not ignore the fact that recognising them as such changes their meaning.

The "secret courts" passage raises these difficulties even more bluntly. In the passage Scout tells us why it was legitimate and insightful to liken Tom's death to the senseless slaughter of songbirds; why, that is, we should regard Tom as a mockingbird. The problem, remarked Scout, was that Tom had been tried "in the secret courts of men's hearts". Here Atticus had no case and Tom had no chance. But notice how we must revise our reading of this passage if we accept the Atticans' responses. If we accept that Atticus would have intervened if only he could have, then we see that Tom's misfortune was not to be tried in the secret courts of men's hearts *tout court*, at all. The problem was just that he was tried in the secret courts of the *wrong* men's hearts. Again, it becomes a remark not about courts in general but about *this* court on *this* occasion. This seems to be a dramatic rewriting of a passage with no lesser role than explaining the link between one of the novel's principal themes and the title-motif of the work. Furthermore, while we can come up with a "particularist" explanation of Atticus's final speech to the jury— perhaps giving *that* speech to *that* jury in *those* circumstances is exactly what the *phronimos* would have done—it is harder to explain the secret courts passage along these lines. Here Scout has the opportunity to tell us what went wrong in Tom's case. If the problem lay with this jury in this case, then surely Scout had the opportunity to say as much. Perhaps there are grounds to think Atticus did not mean what he said to the jury, and that in the circumstances what he said was appropriate, but it is harder to see what reason Scout, *qua* narrator, had for not simply saying that the difficulty was with *those* men's hearts, if that is what she meant.

The discussion in this Section may not seem to have taken us very far. We began with the idea that Atticus seems to have acted inconsistently in the three episodes I have highlighted. I have resisted the idea that he would have acted consistently if only he had had the opportunity in Tom's case. Atticus was not merely making the best of a bad job. We are back, then, at the conclusion that Atticus seems to have acted inconsistently, and that, we have seen, is a conclusion which the Atticans are happy to embrace, subject to the ambition of rendering Atticus's apparently inconsistent behaviour consistent under the idea of practical wisdom. But I think there is a more natural reading of all of this.

We seek an interpretation of Atticus's conduct which allows that, though he acted inconsistently, he acted honestly, and under which the central passages I have focused upon mean more or less what they seem to mean on their face. We have such an interpretation if we appreciate that Atticus is a tragic figure. *Mockingbird* has at least some elements of tragedy: an innocent man falls victim to evil despite the best efforts of the novel's hero. Atticus's story, too, is tragic. He is a man who regards the rule of law as of tremendous importance. He presents his arguments in its favour with passion and all of his professional ability, recognising that the life of an innocent man rests upon his success. But he fails and Tom dies. When a decision over Boo is required, Atticus is struck not by the differences between the cases, but by the similarities. From Atticus's perspective, Boo's case is hauntingly familiar. Both Tom and Boo are mockingbirds: innocents whom it would be sinful to harm. Both Tom and Boo are "outsiders": Tom because he is black and Boo because he is simple and has lived as a recluse, isolated from the dominant community. In each case, an outsider must rely upon the dominant community to ignore the fact that he or she is an outsider. In Tom's case the community did not do so. When confronted with the fact that Boo stabbed Bob Ewell, Atticus must decide whether he will allow another outsider to face that threat. And, of course, Atticus is cast as protector of both men. In Boo's case he has the power to do what he tried and failed to do in Tom's case. When faced with the possibility of another tragedy in Boo's case, Atticus's faith in the rule of law and perhaps his courage as well fail him. He cannot bear the possibility that he will be party to the "death" of another mockingbird. In the end Atticus abandons a principle that he has passionately defended, in terms of which he has understood himself, which has to a large extent secured his unique and valuable role in Maycomb. That is the stuff of tragedy: a principled man has been confronted by the inability of principles by which he understands himself to resist evil, and realises that he cannot risk another loss. He abandons the principles and adopts a fiction. Whether or not it is wicked to try people in the secret courts of men's hearts now depends upon which men's hearts.

Understanding Atticus as a tragic figure allows us to see that he was speaking honestly to the jury, that he was neither dissembler nor mere strategist. It also allows us to understand what happened in Boo's case. We need not strain for an interpretation which makes Atticus's conduct consistent: it was not consistent. It is not that Atticus was throughout acting as the *phronimos*, an eye firmly on substantive principles of justice and fairness. He was a more accessible figure, who tragically, though understandably, was not prepared to risk a vulnerable person who was effectively in his care, having so recently seen how his legal system mistreated another similarly placed outsider.

It is important not to misunderstand the significance of interpreting Atticus as a tragic figure. The point is not to brand Atticus as less than admirable and *therefore* as unsuited to the job the Atticans would give him. I propose the reading of Atticus as a tragic figure as an alternative to the conclusion that Atticus deliberated as an Aristotelian *phronimos* and as an alternative to the assumption shared by both sides of the debate that his significance for legal ethics is to be settled by reference to his character. Cast as a tragic figure Atticus has a very different message for us from that he conveys as a wise figure. We are not meant to *admire* what he does *qua* tragic figure. Rather, we are meant to be struck by the gravity of his loss. If he is seen as a tragic figure his message is one about the value of the principles he has abandoned, not one about the desirability of regarding them as disposable or trivial or burdensome.

VI. PRACTICAL WISDOM AND BOO'S CASE

A tenacious Attican might claim that even if Atticus did abandon the principles he defended in Tom's case, the decision to do so was "a wise one", and does not show Atticus to have acted other than as a *phronimos*. But there are reasons to reject this assessment. Some of these reasons are specific to Boo's case: they undercut the claim that Atticus's decision in Boo's case was a wise one. I examine these "Boo-specific" issues in this Section. Other reasons to reject the assessment are more general, having to do with the social roles of law and lawyers. I turn to these more general issues in the following Section.

Perhaps the most striking Boo-specific feature in this context is the fate from which Atticus and Sheriff Tate are attempting to save Boo. In portraying Atticus as a tragic figure I suggested that he could not bear the thought of being party to the death of another mockingbird. The talk of "death" is rhetorical. The rhetoric is warranted if we seek to characterise the phenomenological structure of Boo's case for Atticus. It is the appropriateness of "death" in this context which explains why Scout speaks so effectively when she likens putting Boo on trial to "shootin' a mockingbird". But the reference to death *is* rhetorical. None of the parties to the decision to spare Boo seems to think that there is any very real chance Boo will suffer Tom's fate. They take it for granted that he has committed no crime and that he will be acquitted. It is not even the trauma of the trial which is foremost in Atticus' or the Sheriff's minds. Sheriff Tate makes this clear when he says to Atticus that:

> "I never heard tell that it's against the law for a citizen to do his utmost to prevent a crime being committed, which is exactly what he did, but maybe you'll say it's my duty to tell the town all about it and not hush it up, Know what'd happen then? All the ladies of Maycomb includin' my wife'd be knocking on his door bringing him angel food cakes. To my way of thinkin', Mr Finch, taking the one man whose done you and this town a great service an' draggin' him and his shy ways into the limelight—to me, that's a sin" (304).

The worst Sheriff Tate can imagine for Boo is that he would be besieged by grateful Maycomb ladies! Now plainly none of Scout, Atticus or the Sheriff think this a trivial matter for Boo. Given Boo's shy ways this public attention would be an ordeal. But surely this cannot be an appropriate ground upon which to reject what, on anybody's reading of the novel, is a fundamental principle of justice.

This is to suggest that Atticus made a mistake in Boo's case. He too easily put aside fundamental principles in the face of insufficiently countervailing considerations. It is not hard to see why he might have done so. At least two features of the case offer themselves naturally to an explanation. First, I have suggested that the most significant fact about Boo's case from Atticus's perspective was its similarity with Tom's case. I propose that Atticus's deliberations about Boo were dominated by these similarities, and in particular by the perception that Boo was, like Tom, an outsider. The significance of Boo's status as an outsider is highlighted by Atticus's insistence that Jem would not be spared a court appearance. There is no need to save Jem from the system. Jem is not an outsider and Atticus assumes that his guilt or innocence will be decided upon institutional criteria rather than within the secret courts of men's hearts: "Of course it was clear cut self defence" (300). But while Boo was indeed an outsider, he was an outsider of a very different sort from Tom, and the difference was both plain and important. We see it illustrated starkly in the Sheriff's very different responses to Boo and Tom. After a somewhat perfunctory investigation of each episode, he immediately arrests Tom, with no apparent qualms about the reliability of the Ewells' accusation. He does not, for instance, think it necessary to obtain medical evidence of the assault, an omission to which Atticus draws critical attention at the trial. Yet he decides on the spot to adopt a fiction to spare Boo a trial, evidencing a sensitivity to Boo quite absent from his dealings with Tom. It apparently does not occur to Sheriff Tate that Tom is as much a mockingbird as Boo. Atticus says not a word about the Sheriff's apparent change of heart. But it shows clearly that Boo was not the same sort of outsider as Tom. Ironically the very fact the Sheriff recommends treating Boo unequally shows that Boo had nothing to fear except the trauma of the appearance itself and public gratitude. At least as compared with Bob Ewell, Boo was a privileged outsider and Atticus seems not to have noticed or to have given too little weight to this fact. The second obvious explanation for Atticus's lapse is the involvement of his own children in Boo's case. His gratitude to the man who saved his children is surely understandable and one can see that a parent in his position would be loathe to be the very one to insist that his children's rescuer be put through a public trial and—in Boo's case—the ensuing ordeal of displays of public gratitude. By the same token, however, surely the involvement of Atticus's children should have led him to be especially careful about trying Boo in the secret court of his own heart.

One might worry here both about the reliability of Atticus's own assessment of the appropriate thing to do in Boo's case and about the way in which his decision might be interpreted by others who come to hear about it. Note that no "middle grounds" are canvassed—there is no discussion of the possibility of putting Boo on trial and forbidding the Maycomb ladies from bombarding him with angel cakes for instance. Nor is there any discussion of whether the public had a legitimate interest in knowing what had happened. It is surely only a little churlish to point out that Boo had already had special consideration from the legal authorities, and that it was far from obvious that it had been to his benefit. "According to neighbourhood legend", at least, he had been released into his father's custody rather than being sent away to a state industrial school after some youthful high jinks. While his fellow hooligans "received the best secondary education to be had in the state; one of them eventually working his way through to engineering school in Albany", Boo was not seen or heard of for fifteen years (11). He did not come to public attention again until he gratuitously stabbed his father with a pair of scissors. Again, he received special consideration: after a period in the local cells he was once more released into his family's custody rather than being sent for psychiatric help, his father insisting "no Radley was going to any asylum" (12). By the time of the episodes recounted in *Mockingbird*, Boo has been held a recluse in his family home for some twenty-five years. Now surely one need not be terribly hard hearted to think that the local community has an interest in knowing that a person with Boo's history had been about with a honed kitchen knife with which he had dispatched Bob Ewell, no matter how much Ewell deserved his fate or how clearly Boo had merely been trying to prevent a crime. And, of course, one might wonder whether Boo would have been better served precisely by bringing him out of the shadowy world he had occupied for so long.

In light of all of this there seem grounds to wonder whether Atticus got it right in Boo's case and just how we should interpret his decision. We have seen that Thomas Shaffer also describes Atticus's decision to spare Boo as a mistake, though he thinks it is one which shows us "how a good man makes a doubtful choice", and once again reminds us of the importance of character, demonstrating "that more is involved than whether the choice is sound in principle".[19] But I think that Sheriff Tate had it right when he said:

> "Mr Finch I hate to fight you when you're like this. You've been under a strain tonight no man should ever have to go through. Why you ain't in bed from it I don't know. But I do know that for once you haven't been able to put two and two together" (303).

There is of course a link between this reading of Atticus's decision in Boo's case and the interpretation of him as a tragic figure. He makes a poor decision in Boo's case because his focus on the common themes between the cases prevents him from paying sufficient detail to the particularities of Boo's situation. Indeed, the considerations, and Atticus Finch's response to them, may be regarded as a further defence of the reading of Atticus as a tragic figure: it is difficult to believe they would not have moved "Atticus the wise", but we

---

[19] Shaffer, "The Moral Theology of Atticus Finch", 196. See text accompanying nn. 9 and 11 *supra*.

would might expect "Atticus the tragic" to respond just as Atticus Finch responds. This however is not their only significance. They also speak to the difficulty even a character like Atticus will face from time to time in making decisions in particular cases, and in this role they are reasons to be wary of the character approach in general. If even Atticus cannot avoid the sort of understandable cognitive dissonance which seems on reflection to mark his deliberations in Boo's case, then we should favour an alternative approach which places less emphasis upon the particular judgements of individuals. A rule- or principle-based approach, though not of course eliminating the need for judgement, is such an alternative.

There is another point to be drawn from this discussion. Behind much of it has been the idea that the decision to spare Boo would have been more reasonable had there been a genuine risk that Boo would have suffered Tom's fate. I have suggested that the facts of Boo's case simply do not support that conclusion. But suppose for a moment that we accept it; we suppose, that is, that Boo's status as an outsider would have led a Maycomb jury unjustly to convict him of wrongdoing in the death of Bob Ewell. The supposition renders *Mockingbird* the story of legal system in crisis. We may think, indeed, that Tom's fate alone is enough to show that this is just what *Mockingbird* is. But what would its lesson be for lawyers if this were correct? It would not, I think, be the lesson identified by the Atticans. Rather, assuming that it is the story of a system in crisis, *Mockingbird*'s lesson is that lawyers should not admire and emulate Atticus's alleged attitude to rules and principles. For, on the reading of the novel which portrays it as the story of a legal system in crisis, it is precisely the jury's *disregard* for these constraints which generates the crisis. Here, once again, Atticus's lesson for us would be one about the importance of rules and principles, not one about their triviality.

VII. VIRTUE AND THE ROLE OF LAW

I remarked that there were two sorts of reasons to doubt that Atticus's decision in Boo's case was a wise one, some specific to Boo's case and others which were of more general import. In this section I turn to the reasons of the second sort. As well as bearing again upon the question of Atticus's wisdom, these are reasons to think that we should reject the "character" approach to legal ethics themselves, quite apart from the grounds for thinking Atticus was led astray in Boo's case.

I begin with an account of the nature and function of law. One of Atticus's most important moral lessons to his children is that of tolerance and the appreciation of difference: "you never really understand a person", he tells Scout, "until you consider things from his point of view—until you climb into his skin and walk around in it"(33). Here Atticus gestures at what has recently been described as the most significant fact about modern western societies, namely the existence of a plurality of reasonable views of how one should live: the problem of political liberalism, writes John Rawls, is "[h]ow is it possible that there may exist over time a stable and just community of free and equal citizens profoundly divided by reasonable religious, philosophical and moral doctrine?".[20] A central part of the liberal response to this question has been the establishment of procedures and institutions which aspire to an ideal of neutrality between the reasonable views represented in the communities to which they apply. The members of a pluralist community, the idea goes, will often be able to agree on the structure of neutral institutions and practices even where they cannot agree on the right outcome of a policy question as a substantive matter. Of course these institutions and practices cannot guarantee outcomes which will suit all the reasonable views: often there will be no such universally acceptable outcomes. The hope of liberalism, however, is that even those whose substantive preferences do not win the day on this or that occasion will have cause to accept the decisions of these institutions as fair and just. At the very least, they must have reason to believe that their views have been taken seriously and that the decision procedures have not simply turned the individual preferences of some members of the community into public policy to be imposed on all.

Precisely these sorts of general political concerns lie behind the requirement that individuals are to be tried by public standards in public courts rather than by private or secret tribunals. Why object to trials in the secret courts of men's hearts? Not because we are worried about whether or not we have the right men's hearts. It is because a crucial part of the role of law in pluralist communities is to allow individuals to see the mechanisms by which public decisions are made and to see that those mechanisms have indeed been used in particular cases. Liberal community so understood is undercut by those who insist upon appeal to their own substantive views of the good rather than to the procedures. Appeals to individual judgement are likely to be conceptually confused as well: to suppose it legitimate to override public process when it conflicts with private judgement is to ignore the fact that it is the inappropriateness of appeal to private judgement which leads us to adopt public decision processes in the first place.

Atticus had it right in his final speech to the jury. A commitment to tolerance and equality leads to decision procedures which render trial within the secret courts of men's hearts illegitimate. Atticus's decision to spare Boo a public trial is a mistake, not just because it fails to take account of the particular facts of Boo's case, but because it undercuts the role of law in securing community between people who hold a range of diverse and reasonable views. This view about the role of law in pluralist societies has consequences for the ethical obligations of lawyers. They act improperly when they substitute their own judgements for the proper procedures, acceptance of which makes pluralist community possible. An appreciation of the role of law should lead us away from, rather than toward, a character-based approach to legal ethics. The issue is not whether we have the right men's hearts, but whether any individual's heart will do.

This discussion provides a response to a recent and important contribution to the legal ethics debate. Anthony Kronman has argued that the legal profession is in the grips of "a spiritual crisis which strikes at the heart of [the lawyer's] professional pride" and threatens the very soul of the profession itself.[21] The crisis has resulted from the demise of a professional ideal—the ideal of the "lawyer-statesman"—which portrayed the outstanding or model lawyer as, in essence, Aristotle's *phronimos*: not a mere technician but a person of practical wisdom possessed of a range of honourable and more or less peculiarly legal character traits. This Aristotelian professional ideal served as a model for lawyers for the better part of two centuries, providing compelling reason to believe the various "law jobs" worthwhile. With its demise lawyers have come to regard law as an essentially technical discipline requiring no particular character or virtue on the part of its leading practitioners, judges and teachers. Kronman aims to revise and revive the Aristotelian ideal in the hope that "we may hope to find a foundation for the belief that to be a lawyer is to be a person of a particular kind, a person one may reasonably take pride in being".[22]

As the "lawyer-statesman" epithet suggests, Kronman takes lawyers to have a significant leadership role. In the political sphere, the lawyer-statesman seeks a certain kind of political integrity, namely one which obtains despite the existence of significant and ineliminable conflict. The lawyer-statesman directs us to a condition of political wholeness in which "the members of a community are joined by bonds of sympathy, despite the differences of opinion that set them apart on questions concerning the ends, and hence the identity, of their community".[23] By establishing bonds of fellow feeling among the members of a community, bonds based upon a willingness to sympathise with others' interests and concerns, political fraternity helps to counteract the destructive forces posed by groundless yet identifying choices which confront both individuals and communities.

The discussion of the role of law and lawyers given above allows us a better account of these matters. First, note that the "procedural" story is directed precisely at securing political community in the face of ongoing substantive

---

[21] Anthony Kronman, *The Lost Lawyer*, *supra* n. 6, 2.

[22] The remark appears in "Practical Wisdom and Professional Character" (1986) 4 *Social Philosophy and Policy* 203–34, 208, in which Kronman anticipates many of the central themes of *The Lost Lawyer*.

[23] *The Lost Lawyer*, *supra* n. 6, 93. It is no coincidence that Kronman appeals to historical examples of the lawyer-statesman, just as the Atticans appeal to the fictional figure of Atticus. Both are led to characterise the *phronimos* ostensively, since they are suspicious of the possibility of doing so by appeal to anything like "principles" of deliberation or good character. The use of such principles would undercut the suppositions of the character approach.

dispute. The neutral institutions of political liberalism aim to give us ways of going on as a community which take the reasonable views represented within our midst seriously, and which assure even those whose personal preferences have failed to carry the day that neither they nor their views have been ignored. Law is an essential part of the effort to secure stable and just political community between the advocates of diverse views of the good. Given this role, the procedural approach provides a response to Kronman's spiritual crisis as well: on the procedural account the various law jobs are extraordinarily important in pluralist communities and hence are ones in which lawyers can and should take pride. One might think, indeed, that some such story would be a source of considerably more comfort to lawyers than Kronman's—it tells them, after all, that what most of them are doing has moral and political value. It seems not unlikely that any current crisis of morale would be made worse by Kronman's conclusion that contemporary lawyers belong to the generation which killed the lawyer-statesman. The lesson for legal ethics, I believe, is not that lawyers need to throw over the rule- and principle-based model of professional ethical obligation, but that they should be bought to appreciate the significance of the social roles they serve, and to understand and take pride in fulfilling the duties which flow from those roles.

VIII. VIRTUE AND THE CLIENT/PROFESSIONAL RELATIONSHIP

The discussion in this section has so far focused upon what we might call "macro-normative" concerns. I have suggested that the role of law in pluralist communities has significance for the ethical obligations of lawyers working within those communities. There are also "micro-normative" reasons to be wary of character-based approaches to legal ethics, reasons which focus not upon the political or social significance of law in general, but upon the nature of lawyer–client relationships. We can relate these concerns to *Mockingbird* by noting a difference between Atticus's position and that of most contemporary lawyers. *Mockingbird* is importantly the story of an intimate community. A good deal of the book is concerned to place Atticus and his family within Maycomb, to show how he and his forebears came to the town, to show that the neighbours and the community knew him well. As a result, we might suppose, Atticus's professional relationships have much in common with relationships such as those between family-members or friends. But this is not typical. We do not tend to know our lawyers as the Maycomb folk knew Atticus. Nonetheless, we often, of necessity, place ourselves in positions of vulnerability to our professionals in a way and to an extent which we would typically reserve for much more intimate relationships. In these latter relationships we have grounds—our intimate or personal knowledge of the individual—to make assessments of the character of the people to whom we are vulnerable, of their motivations, their priorities and so forth, which explain our willingness to place ourselves in their hands. But because most of us do not have this kind of detailed knowledge of our professionals—because most of us do not live in Maycomb or anywhere much like it—we cannot rely upon the characters of our professionals as we rely upon the characters of friends. The clients of professionals, this is to say, typically rely upon relative strangers, to whom they stand in relationships of considerable inequality of expertise, for things of importance, when they cannot reliably assess or constrain the diligence or expertise which the professional applies to their task. The result is that the "character aspect" of the virtues approach makes it inappropriate for professional and legal ethics. Clients do not have access to information about the characters of their professionals in a way which would make it reasonable to ask them to place themselves in positions of vulnerability in reliance upon character-based considerations.[24]

Given this analysis of professional–client relations, it is important not only that professionals are ethical, but that clients and potential clients have some way of knowing the ethical stance of practitioners, even though they do not know them or their moral views personally. The adoption and promulgation of a distinct professional morality is a way of making the ethics of the profession public in a way that the personal ethics of its members cannot be. Clients get the benefit of these "public ethics" however, only if they are indeed given priority over personal ethics in members" dealings with the public. The client need know only what values the professional role requires the professional to adopt and that the professional is a role-occupant to know what values at least should govern the professional's conduct in the relationship. In a different world, perhaps one characterised by the positive communal aspects of life in Maycomb, we may not need these guides to the ethical views of our professionals. But Maycomb, both thankfully and sadly, is not our world.

IX. CONCLUSION

The appeal to Harper Lee's *To Kill a Mockingbird* in the legal ethics literature is part of a broader development in recent normative theory, namely the rediscovery of virtue- or character-based ethics. Atticans take the lawyer-hero of the novel to show the importance of character over rule- or principle-based approaches to professional ethics. His willingness to set aside the rules of law in Boo's case is taken to show the value of judgement and flexibility; of *phronesis*, the Aristotelian master virtue. I have argued, however, that this is not the right way to look at Atticus. He is, I have suggested, a tragic rather

---

[24] This analysis may capture the compelling aspects of the idea that the professional is the client's "special purpose friend". See Charles Fried, "The Lawyer as Friend: The Moral Foundations of the Lawyer–Client Relation" (1976) 85 *Yale Law Journal* 1060–89.

than a wise figure. As a tragic figure, his message for us is one about the importance of the principles he defended in Tom's case, not one about the desirability of abandoning them in favour of an appeal to character. Atticus is tragic because he took the principles he defended in Tom's case seriously. He abandons them not because he judges it right to do so, but because he cannot face the risk of being implicated in the death of another mockingbird.

The plausibility of this reading is heightened by the fact that the decision in Boo's case is not a particularly good one on the facts of the case. It is not the decision we would have expected from Atticus, cast as a wise figure. At the same time, appreciating the difficulty of the decision in Boo's case from Atticus's point of view gives us general grounds to favour rule- or principle-based approaches to legal ethics over character-based alternatives. And, at this point, we can see a dilemma for those who defend Atticus's decision. The most plausible defence of his conduct seems to be one which portrays him as working in a legal system in crisis. But if that is right, *Mockingbird* is an illustration, not of the desirability of abandoning principle and rule in favour of the judgements of individuals, but of the dangers of doing so. The appropriate conclusion here, I believe, is that both sides of the debate about Atticus have him wrong. His significance for legal ethics does not turn upon his character at all. His lesson is one about the value of rules and principles.

There are also general reasons to think this the right conclusion about legal ethics. Atticus teaches his children the importance of tolerance and equality. These values are best protected by procedural systems which do not reserve to some the right to appeal to their own judgements in preference to public decision procedures. A crucial part of ensuring tolerance and equality is to ensure that individuals are dealt with by public procedures and not in the secret courts of *anybody*'s heart. Furthermore, if lawyers appreciate how important their role is in securing community through these institutions, we should expect them both to take pride in their profession and to take seriously the ethical obligations of their professional roles. An important task of legal ethics is to teach these institutional lessons, and Atticus is a useful tool for doing so. Finally, Atticus allows us to note the importance of the nature of lawyer–client relationships. Clients do not have access to information about the character of their professionals, such that it would make sense for them to place themselves in positions of vulnerability in reliance upon character-based considerations. Clients require and professionals have an obligation to provide and abide by more publicly accessible indications of the obligations under which professionals act than character-based approaches allow.

The result is that Atticus does indeed have important lessons for legal ethics. The lessons, however, are not about the importance of character over rules and principles. On the contrary, Atticus allows us to see the importance of the principles of law he defends so eloquently in Tom's case and abandons so tragically in Boo's case. In doing so he shows why we cannot found an adequate professional ethic on the character of practitioners. Such approaches make it less rather than more likely that professionals will fulfil the ethical obligations appropriate to their roles.

4

Devils, Lawyers and Salvation Lie in the Details: Deontological Legal Ethics, Issue Conflicts of Interest and Civic Education in Law Schools

ROBERT ELI ROSEN

"The advocate may urge any permissible construction of the law favorable to his client, without regard to his professional opinion as to the likelihood that the construction will ultimately prevail."[1]

"When a lawyer . . . advocate[s] a position with respect to a substantive legal issue that is directly contrary to the position being urged by the lawyer (or the lawyer's firm) on behalf of another client in a different and unrelated matter . . . the persuasiveness and credibility of the lawyer's arguments in at least one of the two pending matters would quite possibly be lessened, consciously or subconsciously, in the mind of the judge."[2]

In modern legal ethics, the advocate engages in strategic action, instrumental and responsive to client ends, circumscribed solely by the bounds of law. This account is challenged by the possibility of pure "issue conflicts of interest"— where it is to the instrumental advantage of different clients that lawyers argue opposing positions on an issue of law. Issue conflicts reveal that advocates engage their credibility when they speak. Their persuasiveness depends on their being able to claim that they are truthfully advocating a true and correct position. They are involved in communicative, that is moral, not merely, strategic action.[3]

---

[1] American Bar Association, *Model Code of Professional Responsibility* (Chicago, Ill., ABA, 1970), EC 7–4.

[2] American Bar Association, *Formal Ethics Opinion 93–377* (Chicago, Ill., ABA, 1993).

[3] The distinction between communicative and strategic action is drawn from Habermas. See, e.g., J. Habermas, *The Theory of Communicative Action*, (T. McCarthy, trans., Boston, Mass., Beacon, 1981), ch. III.

Courses in legal ethics are a supplement to traditional legal education in "thinking like a lawyer". This vague phrase denotes an activity that becomes sacred to law students. Not the moral value of the rules of legal ethics, I will argue, but the sanctity of "thinking like a lawyer" is what makes legal ethics appear to be morally obligatory for lawyers.

This dependency of legal ethics is ironic for "thinking like a lawyer", as traditionally taught in common law law schools, would be better described as "thinking like a judge". From the analysis of judicial opinions, activities of argument and analysis are taught in substantive law courses. These activities create possibilities for legislatures, judges and other public officials both to be restrained and to further the public interest.

This dependency is self-defeating for legal ethics because in practice lawyers do not have to be restrained or further the public interest. They can "urge any permissible construction of the law". In fact, unlike judges and other public officials, lawyers claim no moral responsibility for the legal decisions reached.

The profession has failed to articulate content to make professional judgements able to sustain morally meaningful action. What meaning there is to be found in the practice of law comes from the market. By choosing sides—and a limited client base—lawyers can "think like a lawyer", avoid issue conflicts and gain the freedom to engage in both communicative and strategic action. This freedom has its cost: the lawyer forsakes independence from clients and that which was sacred in "thinking like a lawyer" is open to spoliation.

I. LEGAL ETHICS AS A DEONTOLOGICAL ETHIC

Legal ethics demand strange things from lawyers. Certainly, the practice of law is not a knitting society, and a lawyer ought to do that which in other situations morality might not command. A lawyer in court, like Hamlet in his mother's chamber, sometimes "must be cruel, only to be kind. Thus bad begins and worse remains behind."[4]

One approach to justifying an ethic is to consider it as a deontological one. Legal ethics can be viewed as elaborating the requirements of the lawyer role, the duties of lawyer stations, rather than "the place of the idea of an End or form of goodness to be realized in life".[5] The alternative to deontology, a consequentialist interpretation of legal ethics, in fact, does not take the ethics' internal point of view: the consequences of lawyers' and clients' actions do not count for much in legal ethics. Denial of lawyer responsibility for morally significant consequences, captured in the imagery of a "lawful hired gun", is a hallmark of legal ethics.

---

[4] W. Shakespeare, *Hamlet*, Act 3, sc. 4.

[5] J. H. Muirhead, *Rule and End in Morals* (Oxford, Oxford U P, 1932), 6 (summarizing non-deontological ethics), quoted in B. Herman, *The Practice of Moral Judgment* (Cambridge, Mass., Harvard U P, 1993) 208 n. 1.

Considering legal ethics as a deontological one immediately raises the problem that lawyers contradict themselves. Proverbially, a lawyer is "capable of talking out of the two sides of his mouth". "He is no lawyer who cannot argue both sides of a case."[6] Thus the lawyer stands accused of "turning black to white",[7] using "the law as shoemakers use leather, rubbing it, pressing it, and stretching it with their teeth",[8] "perverting, confounding and eluding" the laws.[9]

Lawyers thus seem to offend not only against the Kantian requirement of universalizability, but also against the more general deontological requirement of consistency. Not only do they so offend, but lawyers are obligated to take inconsistent positions when doing so advances the interests of their clients.[10] When lawyers act within the bounds of law, inconsistencies are normalized by legal ethics:

> "So long as there are non-frivolous legal arguments to be made, lawyers should be proud to acknowledge that as detached professionals they are capable of asserting either side."[11]

To understand how it is possible for a deontological ethic to allow inconsistency, one might resort to thinking of legal practice as a language game. The game restricts lawyers from engaging in communicative speech, limiting them to strategic speech. Moral justification entails communicative action. The validation of lawyer action, then, must be the product of a domain of speech in which what lawyers do as lawyers, purely strategic speech, is not heard. That is, whatever it is that lawyers do (within the bounds of law, of course) does not figure in its moral warrant.

Legal ethics appear to take such a turn. As legal ethics put it, "[L]awyers do not personally vouch for the soundness of their legal arguments".[12] Lawyers act strategically to pursue the objectives of their clients. Their purposive behavior makes claims about facts and law, but, within normatively established limits, lawyers do not claim they are stating the truth, are being truthful about their intentions or that their actions are normatively valid. Effectiveness, not truth, sincerity or correctness, tests their lawful actions. Litigators, at least in adversary systems, imagine that their work in law is a

---

[6] Charles Lamb, "Letter to Samuel Rogers", Dec. 1833, cited in B. Stevenson (ed.), *The Macmillan Book of Proverbs, Maxims and Famous Phrases* (NY, Macmillan, 1948, 1976), 1372.

[7] Rabelais, *Pantagruel*, Bk iii, ch. 44 (1545) cited in Stevenson above.

[8] Ascribed to Louis XII of France (1462–1515), cited in H. L. Mencken (ed.), *A New Dictionary of Quotations* (NY, Knopf, 1960), 666.

[9] J. Swift, *Gulliver's Travels* II (1726), in Mencken, above at 667.

[10] I am aware that the rule, quoted *supra* at n. 1, reads in the permissive form. But only at the risk of being charged with inadequate zeal will a lawyer reject a course advantageous to a client. In the absence of strong professional or legal defenses, a rational, but not necessarily morally justified response, what is formally granted as permission becomes an obligation.

[11] G. C. Hazard, Jr., and W. W. Hodes, *The Law of Lawyering: A Handbook on the Model Rules of Professional Conduct* (NY, Prentice Hall, 1996), sec. 1.7:106.

[12] American Law Institute, *Restatement of the Law: The Law Governing Lawyers* (Tent. Draft No. 4) (Phila., ALI, 1991), sec. 209, cmt. f.

battle or a sport and winning is the only mark of success.[13] The principle of lawyer non-accountability is conjoined to the notion that legislatures, judges and other public officials are responsible for allowing the immorality clients do: it is the system's fault. Ascriptions of accountability belong to those actors engaged in communicative action.

The lawyer approaches the system instrumentally, as an obstacle to and mechanism for client objectives. Like computer hackers, not Luddites, lawyers threaten to sabotage the system, seeking out gaps in legal norms or enforcement. Like computer hackers, lawyers send unvalidated messages and create unplanned events, breaking the security seemingly afforded by the system.

In legal education, all too often, questions about lawyer responsibilities are answered by the rules of the lawyer's job, "the law of lawyering". When students ask fundamental moral questions about who they are as lawyers, they receive legalistic responses. "The law of lawyering" is not concerned with the lawyer's good will, but with compliance. A lawyer subordinates herself to the law of lawyering for prudential, not moral, reasons. It demands only avoiding the forbidden, not the doing of what is ethical. It sets objective, coercive public norms to answer morality's concern with the subjective and voluntary. While it may be prudential to comply with it, the law of lawyering does not make it morally obligatory to comply.

The law of lawyering fails to explain why the moral particularism which is the law of lawyering overrides other obligatory regimes a lawyer may inhabit. Where once lawyering was constrained by plural norms of family, religion and community,[14] the law of lawyering assumes, but does not morally obligate, the absolute priority of its restraints. Lawyers may be authorized to be "lawful hired guns", but why ought someone so to act? How is it that acting like a lawyer is morally obligatory for lawyers? What conditions support a deontological legal ethics?

Analyses of legal ethics as ethics displace communicative speech, the deontological justification of legal ethics, to the lawyer role "as detached professionals", to the rights of clients and to the legal system as a whole.

Role-morality, the duties of one's station, insists on the absolute priority of the lawyer obeying the obligations of her role. It is because of his or her role that a lawyer operates within a purely strategic domain, not responsible for inconsistencies, let alone the ends of the client or the consequences of the lawyer's representation. The problem with a role theory *simpliciter* is that it assumes the lawyer role as currently constituted. It does not justify it. And what must be justified is that lawyer inconsistency is necessary for the role,[15] for lawyers cannot escape the question we all face, "is this what we *ought* to do?"

---

[13] E. G. Thornburg, "Metaphors Matter: How Images of Battle, Sports, and Sex Shape the Adversary System" (1995) 10 *Wis. Women's LJ* 225.

[14] B. Frohnen, "The Bases of Professional Responsibility: Pluralism and Community in Early America" (1995) 63 *Geo. Wash L Rev.* 931.

[15] D. Luban, *Lawyers and Justice: An Ethical Study* (Princeton, NJ, Princeton UP, 1988).

Justification for legal ethics may then be displaced to the rights of clients as citizens. In a legally complex world, lawyers must be client "hired guns" if clients are to be autonomous actors, "first-class citizens".[16] Building on the civic responsibility of lawyers to protect individuals from state power, this theory is seemingly very powerful.

The difficulty with this account is that it relies on an underdeveloped political theory: it starts and ends with accounts of the client as abstract citizen. It ignores differences between citizens as well as the moral interests of affected third parties. It ignores duties to the system of justice. It ignores duties clients owe to their lawyers and those which lawyers owe to themselves. Autonomous citizens need a polity to constrain their immorality, and more needs to be demonstrated to immunize the lawyers who aid and abet them.

Analysis of legal ethics may then displace the discussion to lawyer and client roles within the legal system. Such an explanation is an important one because it ties lawyer ethics to the justice of the legal system.[17] Criticism is made possible of lawyers who claim they are only doing their jobs in regimes that are unjust. Furthermore, to the extent that there is injustice perpetrated by the legal system, excuses by lawyers that turn on the legal system are less warranted. When combined with the requirement that seemingly immoral behavior obligated by legal ethics must be necessary for the lawyer role, a deontological account must show that lawyer inconsistency, for example, is necessary for the legal system to produce justice.

From a deontological perspective, justifying lawyer actions by the legal system is problematic because it is difficult to understand how the entire legal system becomes "the ultimate internal condition of rational agency".[18] A deontological account of legal ethics must describe a regulator of lawyer reason, a categorical imperative, generated by the legal system.

One requirement of any such regulator of lawyer reason is that it must provide what Lionel Trilling called, "moral realism": the ability to respond to the contingency of moral reason in particulars. It must be able to direct moral reasoning, in Barbara Herman's phrase, "all the way down".[19] As she explains in her account of deontological ethics:

> "In order for agents to read the moral facts of the world, they require recognitional resources that render these facts perspicuous. Both rules and standard cases introduce possibilities of pattern recognition, but neither offers the agent the kind of rationale that could support full deliberative judgment. The questions we ask are too hard, the moral data too complex. If our reading of the moral data is crude, the moral problems we encounter will to that degree be less tractable, the resolutions less convincing. Lack of suppleness in basic moral categories leads to

---

[16] S. L. Pepper, "The Lawyer's Amoral Role: A Defense, A Problem, and Some Possibilities" [1986] *Am. Bar. Fndn. Res. J.* 613.

[17] See Luban, *supra* n. 15.

[18] B. Herman, *supra* n. 5, at 210.

[19] B. Herman, *supra* n. 5, at 228 (quoting I. Kant, *Grundwerk*, Third Ch.).

epicycles of ad hoc exceptions and conditions or to a desire either to limit or to explain away deontological constraints."[20]

Two prominent explanations of legal ethics that might meet such a requirement are that lawyers are obligated as officers of the court and by duties of lawfulness. As officers of the court, lawyers' reason is always regulated by their role, the rights of clients and the needs of the legal system:

> "[I]nvocation of counsel as officer of the court is designed to constrain the excessive amalgamation of the lawyer's interest with that of his client and to forestall the transformation of privately managed litigation into a melée of self-seeking."[21]

Whatever purpose this imagery is supposed to serve, however, it does not function as a regulator of lawyer reason:

> "Vague notions that attorneys owe a duty to the judicial system by virtue of their status as court officers are feeble counterweights in making day-to-day tactical decisions."[22]

"Lawfulness" too does not function as a regulator of lawyer reason. Without further explanation, it remains open to the charge that what is lawful may not be moral. Such an account would do violence to Kant's project of providing an account of ethics "between the poles of naturalism and metaphysical realism about value".[23] Moreover, lawfulness in practice is the product of lawyer moral reasoning, not its regulator. Law's transcendence is not believable to lawyers: "[L]awyers learn not to take law seriously".[24]

I would like to suggest "thinking like a lawyer" as the regulator of lawyer reason. In one sense, it is obvious that "thinking like a lawyer" regulates what lawyers do. Notice, it also can satisfy the two conditions set out above. In practicing law, "thinking like a lawyer" is seemingly necessary for the role. "Thinking like a lawyer" also seems capable of moral realism: It requires recognitional resources making the particularities of the case perspicuous and demands suppleness in analysis. By examining the concept of "thinking like a lawyer", we can "reveal the sense in which rationality as a regulative norm [of lawyers' actions] represents a distinctive conception of value".[25]

---

[20] B. Herman, *supra* n. 5, at 211.

[21] M. R. Damaska, *The Faces of Justice and State Authority* (1986) 142–3, quoted in Thornburg, *supra* n. 13, at 263, n. 278.

[22] A. R. Miller, "The Adversary System: Dinosaur or Phoenix" (1984), 69 *Minn. L Rev.* 1, 18, quoted in Thornburg, *supra* n. 13, at 227, n.11.

[23] B. Herman, *supra* n. 5, at 210.

[24] D. Riesman, "Toward an Anthropological Science of Law and the Legal Profession" in D Riesman, *Individualism Reconsidered* (emphasis omitted) (NY, Free Press, 1964, 450). See also D. B. Wilkins, "Legal Realism for Lawyers" (1990) 104 *Harv. L Rev.* 468.

[25] B. Herman, *supra* n. 5, at 213.

II. "THINKING LIKE A LAWYER" AS THE REGULATOR OF LAWYER REASON

When the philosopher Judith Jarvis Thompson was teaching her "Trolley Problem" article to a class at Yale Law School, it is said that a student demanded she stop "hiding the ball" and articulate a way to resolve the problem. In telling this story, one might stress the need for certainty of law students, even at the Yale Law School. To approach civic education in law schools, I wish to stress not the demand for an answer, but the assumption that there is a way to resolve the problem.

The classic style of law teaching, sometimes (mis)called the Socratic method, is the spinning of hypotheticals. Students are asked to resolve a case, similar but (significantly) different from a prior case. Then they are asked to resolve another case, with only time and energy preventing endless permutations from being presented.

With a response always demanded, students learn that the law can resolve any case properly presented: whatever stories Clotho spins out, like Atropos, the law can cut. In the student's question to Professor Thompson, there was the demand that she apply a power they had been taught about law: law has what might be called "resolution power". Moral problems may be puzzling and intractable, but there is a legal resolution to such problems.

This feature of legal education has been recognized by other observers: "[L]aw, considered as an intellectual discipline, consists of certain methods of argument . . . able to apply . . . to the 'ever-tangled skein of human affairs' ".[26] "At their best, lawyers serve as society's general problem solvers, skilled in avoiding as well as resolving disputes and in facilitating public and private ordering."[27] Legal education has "encompassing tendencies," lawyers have "a zest for problem solving", and "for each dispute there is either a rule or else a rule can be derived".[28]

Future lawyers are trained that there is a legal resolution to their clients' problems. This is clearly a market asset. It supports their entrepreneurialism—the extension of law's jurisdiction—which is one of the distinctive features of US legal professionalism.[29] The resolution power of law gives lawyers "the particular courage to work ahead of the cases and statutes in order to give powers to corporations [and other clients] which had never been tested (and often have never yet been tested) in court".[30]

---

[26] S. Brewer, "Exemplary Reasoning: Semantics, Pragmatics, and the Rational Force of Legal Argument By Analogy" (1996) 109 *Harv. L Rev.* 925 (quoting C. C. Langdell, "Preface to the First Edition", *A Selection of Cases on the Law of Contracts* (2nd edn., Boston, Mass., Little, Brown & Co., 1879), viii.

[27] P. Brest and L. Krieger, "On Teaching Professional Judgment" (1994) 69 *Wash. L Rev.* 527, 529.

[28] M. C. Miller, *The High Priests of American Politics: The Role of Lawyers in American Political Institutions* (Knoxville, Tenn., U Tennessee P, 1995), 22–4 (citations omitted).

[29] R. L. Nelson and D. M. Trubek, "New Problems and New Paradigms in Studies of the Legal Profession" in R. L. Nelson, *et al.* (eds.), *Lawyers' Ideals/Lawyers' Practices* (Ithaca, NY, Cornell UP, 1992), 8.

[30] D. Riesman, *supra* n. 24, at 448.

The legal system's jurisdiction grants much of the law's resolution power. In one sense, courts do resolve problems.[31] The cases which reach the highest court are finally resolved, because the court is the final legal arbiter. "Thinking like a lawyer", however, also may be valued outside law's jurisdiction. The law may be valued because it appears to make lucid aspects of problems generally. Even where legal finality is not at issue, a lawyer may have advice to give.

Lawyers' zeal to legalize may be realized, regrettably. Hubris, economic self-interest and other instrumental reasons may explain why lawyers extend law's reach. Yet this zeal also is part of lawyers' moral education.

It is not just that lawyers are trained in casuistry, the process of deciding cases. It is not just that an expansive conception of law's resolution power gives lawyers practical advantages. It is that for lawyers extending law's resolution power is obligatory. It is because the lawyer is enacting law's resolution power that there exists the absolute priority to the hired gun of the defense that the lawyer was acting within the law. Not because the actions are lawful, but because the lawyer is bringing the law to bear, by "thinking like a lawyer", that the lawyer feels justified.[32]

In his account of legal education, William Twining emphasizes the central symbolic place of the Law Library. Legal education engenders "The Fascination of the Law Reports". To understand this fascination, Twining suggests a thought experiment:

> "[I]magine a vast anthology of stories, each one of which raised a moral or social dilemma or problem. In order to be included in the anthology the problem was such that people genuinely disagreed about the best solution. In addition to each story closing with an ending, denouement or other resolution, it also contained a sub-plot in which arguments for and against competing endings were advanced and then one or more wise persons announced their solution and their reasons for adopting it."[33]

Twining emphasizes three characteristics of the law reports, the heart of the law library, that explain their moral force: "they are authentic; they are detailed; they are interconnected".[34] Taken together, "the law reports are more like a seamless web than a wilderness of single instances".[35]

Legal education produces "enormous and sometimes wrenching changes in how an individual sees and understands the world around them".[36] It is moral

---

[31] And only in one sense. Life goes on.

[32] Pierre Schlag defines the logic as follows: "The perception of successful legal acts (winning a case) is attributed to the performance (the 'doing of law') that is attributed back to a 'knowing' of the ropes that is then reified and attributed back to a 'discipline' of law, namely the 'knowledge' of an imaginary object-form known as the 'law.' ": P. Schlag, "Law and Phrenology" (1997) 110 *Harv. L Rev.* 877, 911.

[33] W. Twining, *Blackstone's Tower* (London, Sweet & Maxwell, 1994), 102.

[34] *Ibid.*, 103.

[35] *Ibid.*, 105.

[36] M. C. Miller, *supra* n. 28, at 21.

education. At the root of this education is that "thinking like a lawyer" is morally obligatory. There is no need for the transcendence of law, for lawyers to believe that "thinking like a lawyer" is transcendent. In the 1950s, David Riesman observed that legal education takes place by the "impious treatment of cases".[37] The law is a false god. It is "thinking like a lawyer", the process modelled by law professors, which merits piety. As Riesman observed, lawyers have "exploited a long tradition of legal learning in order to lend meaning to their daily lives".[38]

"Thinking like a lawyer" shares much with the philosophical position that has been called "legalism", which evinces a

> "dislike of vague generalities, the preference for case-by-case treatment of all social issues, the structuring of all possible human relations into the form of claims and counterclaims."[39]

Pettifoggery is a charge that often has been laid against lawyers. It is in the small, in the details, where a lawyer often is to be found, wrangling and quibbling about small petty points. Law's resolution power structures human relations by claims and counterclaims, and vague generalities are not part of lawyer's reason.

As Roger Cotterrell has emphasized, what we know about lawyers is that they dwell in the details, making little use of abstract interpretive skills of doctrine manipulation.[40] Geoffrey Hazard opines:

> "In days past, at least some practitioners regularly addressed their thoughts beyond the imperatives of pending matters. . . . [M]odern law practice has narrowed the practitioner's intellectual frame of reference . . . Detail is significant partly as a matter of viewpoint, partly as a matter of the mental constructs in terms of which experience is interpreted, and partly as a matter of responsibility."[41]

As Erwin Griswold noted, legal education tends "to focus the mind on narrow issues" and tends "to obscure the fact that no reasoning, however logical, can rise above the premises on which it is based".[42]

III. "THINKING LIKE A LAWYER" AND DEMOCRACY

Perhaps "thinking like a lawyer" can function as a regulator of lawyer reason and it is treated as sacred in legal education and practice. But this does not explain why a deontological account should be based on it. What makes it

---

[37] Riesman, *supra* n. 24, at 442.
[38] Riesman, *supra* n. 24, at 462.
[39] J. N. Shklar, *Legalism* (Cambridge, Mass., Harvard UP, 1964), 10
[40] R. Cotterrell, *The Sociology of Law* (2nd edn., London, Butterworths, 1992), 194–200.
[41] G. C. Hazard, Jr., (untitled testimonial for Robert Stein) (1995) 80 *Minn. L Rev.* 14, 16.
[42] E. Griswold, "Intellect and Spirit" (1967) 81 *Harv. L Rev.* 292, 299, quoted in R. C. Cramton, "The Ordinary Religion of the Law School Classroom" (1978) 29 *J. Legal Educ.* 247, 260.

valuable? How is it specified so that it can be understood to represent a distinctive conception of value?

> "The lawyers who do the Lord's work, as well as that of the Devil, have the same cognitive apparatus and use it much of the time in the same way: making decisions, evaluating possibilities, advising courses of action in the light of the possible consequences."[43]

If the same cognitive apparatus produces morality and immorality, how can it be obligatory, constitute a normatively desirable regulator of reason for lawyers?

"Thinking like a lawyer" may be understood as the civic responsibility of a lawyer in a particular conception of democracy, developed by a student of Kant's philosophy, Emile Durkheim. To Durkheim, in a democracy law has maximal resolution power. Democracy is "the political form of society governing itself, in which the government is spread throughout the milieu of the nation".[44] As Durkheim noted, democratic societies are characterized by "a greater range of government consciousness":[45]

> "Compare the small number of things that government deliberations covered in the seventeenth century and the thousand-and-one objects they apply to nowadays."[46]

The rise of democracy from various forms of absolutism demonstrated that

> "it is an error to believe that governments we term absolute are all powerful. It is one of those illusions that comes from a superficial view. They are indeed powerful against the individual and that is what the term "absolute" means, as applied to them; in that sense it is justified. But against the social condition (*état*) itself, against the structure of society, they are relatively powerless. Louis XIV, clearly, was able to issue his *lettres de cachet* against anyone he wished, but he had no power to modify the existing laws and usages, the established customs or accepted beliefs".[47]

In this account, nothing is potentially outside the "range of the government consciousness". Totalitarian power, of course, is not the sole defining characteristic of democracy to Durkheim. As Durkheim noted, democratic regimes are characterized by "closer communications between this [government] consciousness and the mass of individual consciousness". In a democracy:

> "all these obscure things come more and more to the surface in that region of social consciousness that is lucid, which is the government consciousness. As a result, it becomes all the more malleable."[48]

---

[43] G. L. Blasi, "What Lawyers Know: Lawyering Expertise, Cognitive Science, and the Functions of Theory" (1995) 45 *J. Legal Educ.* 313, 320.

[44] E. Durkheim, *Professional Ethics and Civic Morals* (C. Brookfield, trans., London, Routledge, 1992), 82.

[45] *Ibid.*, 88.

[46] *Ibid.*, 86.

[47] *Ibid.*, 87.

[48] *Ibid.*, 87. In pre-democratic societies, "[t]he whole of the law worked automatically in an unconscious way; it was a matter of custom": *ibid.*, 86.

This makes it "the political system that best conforms to our present-day notion of the individual" who is "loathe to" be used "as a mechanism to be wielded from without by a social authority".[49] Demonstrating his Kantianism, Durkheim continues: "[t]he clearer ideas and sentiment become, the more completely they are dominated by reflection and the greater its hold on individuals."[50]

Durkheim did not think that lucidity and morality were the ordinary outcomes of governments claiming to be democracies. Because law has great resolution power does not mean that it goes "all the way down", enacts moral realism, morally responding to particularity. In democracies,

> "all, in practice as in theory, becomes a matter of controversy and division, and all is in a state of vacillation. There is no firm ground under the feet of society. Nothing any longer is steadfast. And since the critical spirit is well developed and everyone has his own way of thinking, the state of disorder is made even greater by all the individual diversities. Hence the chaos seen in certain democracies".[51]

To maintain respect for law in a democracy, according to Durkheim, there must be the "confidence" that a certain law is not just the result of democratic voting but also, and more crucially, that the law

> "is a good one—that is, appropriate to the nature of the facts. . . . [T]his confidence depends equally on that inspired by the organs that have the task of preparing it. What matters then is the way in which the law is made, the competence of those whose function it is to make it and the nature of the particular agency that has to make this particular function work."[52]

Durkheim explicitly addressed the question of what social practices were capable of responding to this problematic. As is well known, Durkheim focussed on the particular importance of secondary organizations, including the professions. Two related functions are performed by the "moral particularism"[53] which constitutes the obligation of professional ethics according to Durkheim. These obligations have the functional competence to create the confidence he described, "going all the way down" by being morally "appropriate to the nature of the facts". Professional ethics also, as one would expect in a deontological account, provide the regulator of reason and the source of professional virtue.[54]

If Durkheim's description of the democracy we can fashion is correct, it certainly is very hospitable to lawyers since "all . . . becomes a matter of controversy and division" and law's resolution power is at a maximum where

[49] *Ibid.*, 90.
[50] *Ibid.*, 87–8.
[51] *Ibid.*, 94.
[52] *Ibid.*, 108.
[53] *Ibid.*, 5.
[54] "If we follow no rule except that of a clear self-interest, in the occupations that take up nearly the whole of our time, how should we acquire a taste for any disinterestedness, or selflessness or sacrifice?": *ibid.*, 12.

nothing is potentially outside the "range of government consciousness". "Thinking like a lawyer" will be valuable, for it is a concomitant of democracy that "all is in a state of vacillation". Individualism, at the least, will demand the particular treatment of claims and counterclaims, in norms of more or less general applicability, that fosters legalism.

If we take Durkheim's account of democracy as correct, if we take it as a hypothetical imperative, what obligations does it impose on lawyers? What ought to be lawyers' civic responsibility in realizing such a democracy? What should regulate their reason so that lawyers help realize democracy? What would make "thinking like a lawyer" not only valuable but also valued?

What has been described as Durkheim's functionalism helps answer these questions. Durkheim's description purports to present an emergent social fact of our form of social organization: "democracy" (as we can (perhaps) realize it). Commitment to such a social fact is a moral one, i.e. it is a commitment to realize more morally worthy democratic forms. To be functional, the moral particularism generated by the commitment to democracy, in part, must protect against the realization of less worthy forms.

The civic responsibility of lawyers, in part, then must be to respond to the well-known pathologies of legalism. Lawyer reason must be regulated to prevent the realization of legalism's morally less worthy forms. And the allowance of purely strategic behavior by lawyers appears well-suited for that function.

At least at the most abstract level, legal ethics can point to the avoidance of the pathologies of legalism to justify itself. Of course, detailed examination would be required to know if the sanctioned behaviors bore any relation to creating a more worthy democratic society. But "thinking like a lawyer" when combined with strategic action appears to respond to the pathologies of legalism: its aloofness from politics, rigid categorizations and analysis, overweening commitments to order and formality and tendency to conservatively accept established rules and conventions.

Legalism presents a "policy of justice, which despises arbitration, negotiations, bargaining, as mere 'politics' arbitrary and expedient".[55] For the lawyer, engaging in strategic action, not needing to be truthful or correct allows expediency and bargaining to be jurisgenerative in law practice.

Legalism through its rigid categorizations and analysis excludes values necessary for moral realism. The strategic action of one who "thinks like a lawyer" knows that law is anything but set in black letters. "[T]he foremost task of legal education is to inculcate a skeptical attitude towards generalizations, principles, concepts and rules."[56]

Legalism threatens to elide morality as it takes the question of legal validity as the sole moral question. Lawyers, as we have seen, are permitted to adopt an instrumental attitude toward law and argue "any permissible con-

---

[55] J. N. Shklar, *supra* n. 39, at 19.
[56] R. C. Cramton, *supra* n. 42, at 249.

struction of the law", taking legal validity as but a boundary issue. Legal education that delegitimates legalism, that questions whether legal validity is the
sole test of lawyer actions, as in critical legal education of various sorts, helps
prepare lawyers for a practice responsive to this pathology of legalism.

"Thinking like a lawyer", unlike legalism, does not create a politics ordered
by the "fear of the arbitrary".[57] Tocqueville said about lawyers: "[i]f they
prize freedom much, they generally value legality still more; they are less
afraid of tyranny, than of arbitrary power".[58] Like computer hackers, today's
lawyers are "tough-minded".[59] Practicing for individuals in a democracy who
"loathe" being "wielded from without by a social authority", lawyers, bringing the government in "closer communication" with the "mass of individual
consciousness", are permitted by their strategic action to further arbitrariness.
They know that:

> "There is no right answer . . . discovered by the reasoned elaboration of pre-
> existing principles, but a conscious act of choice on the part of the decider."[60]

If lawyers need to engage in strategic speech to respond to the pathologies of
legalism, then their speech as lawyers may be contradictory. Those who say
"lawyers lie" either are pointing to unethical lawyers or they do not understand
the language game lawyers play. While "the devil can cite Scripture for his purpose",[61] lawyers are obligated by our commitments to democracy to do so.

Thinking like a lawyer, however, reproduces the pathology of legalism's
case-by-case analysis. Operating in the details, lawyers are not regulated to
respond to a legal system that has instituted principles of injustice: operating
at low levels of generality, the lawyer never confronts the principle naked. The
wrong is always mediated in a series of claims and counterclaims. "Thinking
like a lawyer" does not give the lawyers the tools to ask vital questions about
the justice of the system lawyers inhabit.

"The devil is in the details" is an old aphorism. Lawyers are there, too,
authorized to be strategic actors, doing work that may be of the devil. And,
being in the details, "thinking like lawyers", lawyers do not pursue the salvation of justice, or recognize the devil they may be serving. But lawyers do
carry the civic responsibility of preventing one of democracy's less worthy
forms, one beset by legalism.

IV. "THE DEVIL IS IN THE DETAILS" AND ISSUE CONFLICTS OF INTEREST

That lawyers may be obligated sometimes to being purely strategic actors does
not require they always be so. Democracy is not the only emergent social fact.

---

[57] J. N. Shklar, *supra* n. 39, at 15.
[58] A. de Tocqueville, quoted in J. N. Shklar, *supra* n. 39, at 15.
[59] R. C. Cramton, *supra* n. 42, at 250.
[60] *Ibid.*, 251.
[61] W. Shakespeare, *The Merchant of Venice*, Act 1, sc. 3.

Some forms of legalism may be a price well paid in the service of other values. And in a morally worthy democracy, law will not only have great resolution power, it will morally respond to particularity. It was not a lawyer who reminded us that "God is in the details".[62] In response to the charge of pettifoggery, could not lawyers respond that they are engaging in communicative action? Or, in the guise of Pietism, that "[t]he devil is in the details, but so too is salvation"?

Those who ascribe to lawyers the capacity of practical judgement (_phronesis_) suggest that the moral worth of lawyering is in its capacity to lie in the details, going "all the way down".[63] It is in the details that the rule of law is worked out so that we avoid what Blake knew, that "One law for the Lion and Ox is Oppression".[64]

Only by being communicative actors can lawyers engage practical judgement in their work. As communicative actors, lawyers are making moral choices. Lawyers must be able to justify their judgements, although protecting client confidences will mean that publicity often is not available for these justifications. Ascribing practical judgement to lawyers imposes heavy responsibility on lawyers, although this often is not fully acknowledged. In the details, as communicative actors, lawyers are responsible for producing and reproducing patterns and perceptions of social action, ideology, identity, consent and legitimacy.

Accepting that lawyers engage in communicative action is compatible with much of lawyer behavior being strategic speech. Depending on the moral values and communicative issues at stake, lawyers would be justified in assisting clients in ends lawyers would not morally chose. Even if the best lawyers engaged in communicative speech, delivering morally praiseworthy judgements, telling clients they "were damned fools", clients also can engage in communicative action, or just not listen. Criminal defense attorneys defend the guilty, if the police have done their jobs properly. Realizing a morally worthy democracy may require granting a large strategic domain to lawyers.

But allowing salvation to join the devil and lawyers in the details, accepting that sometimes lawyers engage in communicative speech, raises again the problem of lawyer inconsistency. If lawyer action is not purely strategic, it sometimes is bound by communicative norms. Sometimes lawyer reason must be regulated so that a lawyer is prevented from contradicting himself or herself.

---

[62] Although this idea could be derived from various philosophers, perhaps best from the G. W. F. Hegel of _The Philosophy of Right_, this aphorism has been attributed to the architect Mies van de Rohe (e.g. M. Lewis, 208(16) _New Republic_ 20 (19 Apr. 1993) but see M. Dowd, 204(19) _New Republic_ 28 (13 May 1991 ("It was not Mies van der Rohe who said that god is in the details.")), Aby Warburg ("Aby Warburg is supposed to have said _Der liebe Gott steckt im Detail_ ("God dwells in the detail"). That's been said of the Devil too.)": C. Hitchens, 261(19) _The Nation_ 696 (4 Dec. 1995)) and André Gide (J. Cottingham, 58 _Am. Artist_ 42 (Jan. 1994)).

[63] See e.g. A. Kronman, _The Lost Lawyer_ (Cambridge, Mass., Bleknap Press, 1993).

[64] W. Blake, "The Marriage of Heaven and Hell" in D. V. Erdman (ed.), _The Complete Poetry and Prose of William Blake_ (Berkeley, Calif., U California P, 1982), 33, 44.

The rules governing "issue conflicts of interest" limit lawyers from engaging in some forms of contradiction. They do not impose a very strong regulator on lawyer reason. Even though they recognize that lawyers engage in communicative speech, without any violations of lawyer obligations, it was said that "for half a million dollars you could buy any legal opinion you wanted from any law firm in New York."[65]

Issue conflicts of interest can arise in either litigation or business-planning contexts:

> "The classic positional [or issue] conflict of interest arises in litigation when a lawyer or law firm argues for one interpretation of the law on behalf of one client and for a contrary interpretation on behalf of another client. . . . These conflicts may further arise in the transaction context when the lawyer or law firm drafts a particular arrangement for one client and for another client attacks the propriety of a similar arrangement."[66]

"Issue conflicts of interest" are distinct from conflicts of interest created by the interests of a lawyer's other clients or the lawyer's own interest. They arise because: "[w]hen a trial judge views a lawyer making opposite conclusions for different clients, the judge may discount the attorney's arguments".[67] The recognition of issue conflicts admits that lawyers are not engaged only in strategic action. As the prefatory quotation indicates,[68] lawyers stake their credibility in their arguments. Consequently,

> "if a lawyer were contemporaneously to assert both sides of an unsettled point of law before the same tribunal on behalf of different clients . . . [a]bsent informed consent . . . the lawyer would be required to withdraw from one of the matters because of the conflict of interest."[69]

Issue conflicts can require lawyers to withdraw even when they are not speaking out of both sides of their mouths before a single judge. When the cases are before different appellate judges in the same jurisdiction, American ethics rules require the lawyer to withdraw because he would be creating a precedent against the second client.[70] An Arizona Ethics Committee explained:

> "It requires little imagination to foresee a circumstance where an appellate judge would question either lawyer as to whether her partner was mistaken in making legal arguments directly contrary to those being presented."[71]

---

[65] Edward J. Kane, a banker, former lawyer, quoted in D. Luban, "The Social Responsibilities of Lawyers: A Green Perspective" (1995), 63 *Geo. Wash. L Rev.* 955, 958.

[66] J. S. Dzienkowski, "Positional Conflicts of Interest" (1993) 71 *Texas L Rev.* 457, 460.

[67] *Ibid.*, 489.

[68] See *supra* n. 2.

[69] American Law Institute, *supra* n. 2.

[70] American Bar Association, *Model Rules of Professional Conduct*, Rule 1.7, cmt. para. 9 (Chicago, Ill., ABA, 1983).

[71] Ariz. State Bar Comm. on the Rules of Professional Conduct, Op. 87–15 (27 July 1987), at 3, quoted in J. S. Dzienkowski, *supra* n. 66, at 477.

The appellate judge who would imagine that the lawyer was mistaken, or one who discounts the contrary arguments, must understand that the lawyer is making a claim about the truth or correctness of the legal position asserted. The judge must be assuming that the lawyer is engaging in communicative action. And it is not only the judge. As Dzienkowski suggests, issue conflicts may have an "effect on the public's confidence in lawyers and the legal system".[72]

In one case, a federal judge argued that when faced with an issue conflict a lawyer "[u]nconsciously . . . will be tempted to 'soft pedal' his zeal" on behalf of one of the conflicting positions.[73] This cognitive dissonance theory assumes, does it not, that the lawyer is being truthful and believes in the truth or correctness of one of the positions? Are lawyers consciously strategic, but unconsciously communicative, actors?

Furthermore, the rule that requires a lawyer to withdraw when he may make precedent contrary to his other clients' interest assumes the lawyer is responsible for the decision reached.[74] Legal ethics, however, assume a division of responsibility: the judge makes the decision and the lawyer is not responsible if it is ill-advised. The logic of the rule also would demand, *ceteris paribus*, that a lawyer not attack a precedent the lawyer helped establish.

The logic has not been extended. Issue conflicts are not even interpreted in terms that respond to their source in lawyer communicative action. Issue conflicts are interpreted in terms of loyalty to client: One of the things current clients can buy is that lawyers will not compromise their strategic behavior by their duties to other current clients. Former clients, to whom lawyers have minimal loyalty obligations, have no such right. So interpreted, issue conflicts do not challenge the belief that lawyers are only strategic actors.

It is the accepted wisdom that recognizing issue conflicts would pose massive problems for two reasons. First, lawyers' low level of generalization would make it difficult for issue conflicts to be detected.[75] The claims of integrity, let alone consistency, are not perspicuous to lawyers. Secondly, under current practice conditions, issue conflicts occur "[a]lmost daily":[76]

> "One reason the practicing bar has largely refused to acknowledge that positional conflicts of interest pose a problem of professional responsibility is the vast implications that such legal conflicts would have for their business. After all, lawyers within firms are constantly arguing for slightly different interpretations of the applicable legal rules for their clients."[77]

---

[72] J. S. Dzienkowski, *supra* n. 66, at 496 n. 166.

[73] *Estates Theatres, Inc. v. Columbia Pictures Indus.*, 345 F Supp. 93, 99 (SDNY, 1972).

[74] *Contra*, American Law Institute, *supra* n. 12.

[75] Maine State Board of Bar Overseers, Professional Ethics Commission, Opinion 155, 15 Jan. 1997.

[76] State Bar of Cal. Standing Comm. on Professional Responsibility and Conduct, Formal Op. 1989–108 at 3 (1989), quoted in J. S. Dzienkowski, *supra* n. 66, at 476 n. 85.

[77] J. S. Dzienkowski, *supra* n. 66, at 509.

Dzienkowski assumes, correctly, that standards for lawyer argument do not constrain these interpretations. Although lawyers are forbidden from making "frivolous arguments", this has boiled down to the laugh test: can lawyers make the argument without breaking out in laughter? The weakest of communicative action norms (can I be truthful in appearance?) regulates their reason. "Thinking like a lawyer" poses little restraint on the strategic actions of lawyers.

Lawyers use law's resolution power, but under current rules of legal ethics have no obligation to see that it is in service of moral realism. Communicative action, and consequently practical judgement, have no place in legal ethics. Lawyers then may help us avoid the pathologies of legalism, but give us no confidence in the functioning of law. Lawyers and devils lie in the details, not salvation.

V. MARKET NORMS AND CIVIC RESPONSIBILITY IN LEGAL EDUCATION

Not only does accepting that lawyers are purely strategic actors fail to place them in a position to judge the justice of the legal system, fail to create capacities for moral realism, fail to advance democratic commitments except by the avoidance of pathologies of legalism, fail to account for the possibility that judges believe that lawyers are engaging in communicative action, it also fails to accord with the reality of practice.

Part of the emotional labor of lawyering is that lawyers come to believe in their case. People generally seem to need to believe that what they are doing is right. But, on the basis of my observations, lawyers generally believe not only that serving clients is a good thing, but also that their theories of the case or transaction form are true and correct. After the engagement, they may acquire a different view. But, when lawyers are acting, they believe they are engaged in both strategic and communicative action. For lawyers, especially, where you stand depends on where you sit.

Lawyers' beliefs in their cases, of course, may be an elaborate form of deception. To appear believable, they have to believe, but their belief is known to them as a deception. Lawyers may be untroubled about taking inconsistent positions. They may understand the communicative action of their speech as outside their domain. And Elihu Root, who sought to keep Louis Brandeis off the US Supreme Court for this reason, may have been right: a lawyer who "thinks like a judge" does a disservice to his client.[78]

There is strong evidence to suggest that lawyers do not engage in this deception.[79] Issue conflicts, contrary to what has been assumed, do not occur on a

---

[78] See D. Levy, "The Lawyer as Judge: Brandeis' View of the Legal Profession" (1969) 22 *Okla. L Rev.* 374.

[79] On different evidence, William Simon reaches the same conclusion: "In the dominant understanding, judgments about legality and justice are grounded in the norms and practices of the

daily basis. Normally, lawyers do not contradict themselves. They truthfully believe that they are presenting a true and correct version of the issue. What makes this possible? The accepted wisdom forgets that lawyers may choose their clients so that they can endorse them and their activities. In the marketplace, lawyers choose sides. Loyalty to clients allows lawyers to engage in communicative action and avoid issue conflicts.

That lawyers may view themselves as engaging in communicative action, in spite of a legal ethic that restricts them to strategic action, is not too surprising. Lawyers, we know, take responsibility for situations and results when it suits their purposes. Ideologies of lawyer ethics can coexist with sharply different realities.[80] For example, there is ample evidence that routine processing of cases is more the norm of practicing lawyers than is zealotry, let along diligence.

"The age of the general practitioner is over. This is the age of the lawyer as specialist", we have been told. Through specialization, coupled with the rules on avoiding material or confidentiality conflicts of interest, lawyers are likely to take legal positions favorable not only to the instant client, but also to the type of clients the lawyer normally represents. In Chicago, Heinz and Laumann found that the legal profession was divided into two-hemispheres: lawyers who represent organizations and those who represent individuals.[81] As a consequence, for the body of law relating to industrial relations, lawyers will have clients who are only management, or only labor unions or only employees. This type of specialization aligns lawyers with one side. Even within the hemispheres, there is further alignment by side: some firms who only represent organizations will do plaintiff but not defense antitrust or white-collar crime work.

Doctors specialize by disease, lawyers by side. There are plaintiff or defense lawyers of all types. Lawyers normally choose sides early in their careers. The only apparently large shifts of side are for those lawyers who go in and out of government, for example prosecutors who become defense counsel.

By choosing sides, lawyers usually are able to meet the claims of consistency and integrity.[82] They come to adopt the "industry outlook" or "pro-

surrounding legal culture. These norms and practices are objective and systematic in the sense that they have observable regularity, and are mutually meaningful to those who refer and engage in them. Even when lawyers disagree about such judgments, they usually do not regard them as subjective and arbitrary. One indication of this fact is that they do not articulate or experience their disagreement as 'an opposing assertion of subjective preference or arbitrary will.' Rather, they oppose decisions on the ground that they are wrong—wrong in terms of norms and practices that they plausibly believe binding on the decisionmaker": W. Simon, "Ethical Discretion in Lawyering" (1988) 101 *Harv. L Rev.* 1083, 1120.

[80] See R. L. Nelson and D. M. Trubek, *supra* n. 29.

[81] J. P. Heinz and E. O. Laumann, *Chicago Lawyers: The Social Structure of the Bar* (NY, Russell Sage, 1982).

[82] Explaining why it is important to restrict the rules regulating issue conflicts, a tentative draft from the American Law Institute (not intentionally ironic) claims that "if the rule were otherwise law firms would have to specialize in a single side of legal issues": American Law Institute, *Restatement of the Law: The Law Governing Lawyers*, sec. 209, cmt f (Prelim. Draft No. 11) (Philadelphia, Penn., ALI, 1995).

plaintiff" bias. At times of paradigm shifts in the law, inconsistencies may result. This occurred when the management theory of corporations was replaced by a shareholder theory.[83] But lawyers have more than self-interest in adapting their actions to be consistent with the new paradigm.

When it is the market that controls how lawyers avoid issue conflicts of interest, then "thinking like a lawyer" becomes "thinking like a lawyer for these sorts of clients". The lawyer gains freedom to engage in communicative action at the expense of independence from clients. Furthermore, the entire enterprise of "thinking like a lawyer" is open to spoliation. Market control of the profession is ill-equipped to provide lawyers with professional judgement, which requires cultural reproduction and social integration. Market control, furthermore, introduces non-professional forms of reasoning, making it harder for lawyers to derive meaning from having a distinctive way of regulating their reason, by "thinking like a lawyer".

Letting the market regulate lawyer communicative action brings back to the foreground a crucial issue of legal ethics: while a lawyer may not be responsible for the results of his or her work as a lawyer, he or she is responsible for the choice of clients. A lawyer who chooses to be *consigliore* to a criminal enterprise is castigated. The deontological perspective extends this condemnation. The outlooks and biases lawyers form by choosing sides and which regulate their reason are morally relevant to judging lawyer actions. This extension of the principle of judging lawyers by their clients is especially important because more and more lawyers are practicing in large organizations. As a consequence, lawyers are less tied to the moral decision about whether or not to represent a client.

Instead of client norms regulating lawyers as communicative actors, professional norms could regulate lawyers. Lawyers may argue any permissible construction of the law, but this liberty need not become a license. To free lawyers from domination by clients, the profession could "create norms powerful enough to constrain the lawyer's conscience and calculations".[84] In the USA, legal ethics require that with respect to tax reporting. lawyers may advocate not any non-frivolous position, but only those that have "a likelihood of success closely approaching one-third".[85] Outside tax reporting, the laugh test still prevails.

Traditionally, legal education appeared to set professional limits on lawyer communicative action, developing independent professional judgement. Students learned how "to think like a lawyer" by "thinking like a judge". For all the rule-skepticism in legal education, "it is astonishing how strongly the

---

[83] See M. J. Powell, "Professional Innovation: Corporate Lawyers and Private Law Making" (1993) 18 *L & Soc. Inq.* 423.

[84] R. W. Gordon, "The Independence of Lawyers" (1988) 68 *BUL Rev.* 1, 34.

[85] American Bar Association, "Report of the Special Task Force on Formal Opinion 85–832" (1985), quoted in D. L. Rhode and D. Luban, *Legal Ethics* (2nd edn., Westbury, NY, Foundation, 1995), 464.

image of the judge stands as the image of the lawyer-hero".[86] The case system idealized the ability to speak to the law. Whatever techniques lawyering skills teach, they can do no better a job than the case-method in training lawyers for communicative action.

While the judge-as-hero appears to give meaning to a life lived "thinking like a lawyer", its support is of little value to one engaged in only strategic speech. Legal ethics can be a dangerous supplement to the rest of legal education. Scott Turow saw law students being educated "to cultivate opinions which were 'rational' but which had no roots in the experience, the life, they'd had before".[87] And, we can add, "or since".

Legal ethics' narrow construction of communicative action promotes analytic rigor, but also corrosive skepticism. Legal ethics teaches that the bases for reaching moral agreement are limited. Lawyers who seek to justify their actions "withdraw into technique, into the professional cult of craftsmanship and competence for its own sake, or just into the cynicism that seems to be our profession's main defense mechanism".[88]

Instead of creating commitments to democracy, legal education becomes simply education for power. In teaching how authority is exercised, law school only minimally regulates lawyers not to abuse power. It develops "a technocratic perspective which elevates power and control at the expense of other values".[89] Legal education teaches cynicism about the possibility of communicative speech. As a result law students' "aptitude for verbal articulation increases, but they rarely stop to listen to others".[90] When "thinking like a lawyer" is combined with a legal ethics of purely strategic speech, legal education instructs its graduates to reproduce the existing social hierarchy:

> "Instead of transforming society, . . . [legal education's] approach tends to become dominated by society, to become an apologist and technician for established institutions and things as they are, to view change as a form of tinkering rather than a reexamination of basic premises. Surface goals such as 'efficiency,' "progress,' and "the democratic way' are taken at face value and more ultimate questions of value submerged . . . One of the factors which makes it easy to avoid explicit discussion of values and goals in law school is "the often less than consciously held idea that the proper role of the lawyer is always merely to take someone else's goals and values—those of the private or public client and 'go from there.' "[91]

Legal education, in other words, promotes as a social outlook the philosophical position of legalism. Lawyers come to believe that legal validity is the sole moral question and become apologists for the *status quo*. They answer

[86] Riesman, *supra* n. 24, at 441.
[87] S. Turow, One L 86–87 (NY, Penguin, 1977), quoted in M. C. Miller, *supra* n. 28, at 22.
[88] R. W. Gordon, *supra* n. 84, at 57.
[89] R. C. Cramton, *supra* n. 42, at 258.
[90] *Ibid.*, 262.
[91] *Ibid.*, 254, 255 (citation omitted).

moral questions about their work as lawyers by referring to the law of lawyering as currently constituted.

Ironically, their work as lawyers is justified by appeals to values that are inconsistent with the social outlook they are trained to adopt. It is no accident that cynicism and retreats into craftsmanship for its own sake pervade the profession. Civic education in law schools roots this schizophrenia. Failing to develop norms of communicative action for lawyers, failing to provide meaningful content for "thinking like a lawyer", the profession requires lawyers in their practices to contradict the social outlook that lawyers are trained to adopt.

5

Can Legal Ethics Become a Matter of Academic Teaching? Critical Observations from a Late-Modern Perspective

VITTORIO OLGIATI

I. INTRODUCTION

Can "Legal Ethics" become a matter of academic teaching? If so, what options have to be considered and what sort of socio-institutional consequences can be expected? In contemporary—late-modern—western societies, these (and other similar) questions have recently been placed at the top of the agenda of professional bodies. Law schools too—increasingly concerned with changes in the educational system—are now debating the opportunity to include legal ethics in law students' curricula.

Even at first blush, to answer such questions is no mere scholarly exercise. The problems which arise are both socially and professionally significant: the teaching of "legal ethics" at an academic level not only suggests a strategy for re-shaping the image of lawyers in society, it might also be one way to reconsider lawyers' power/knowledge as an action system, a device that has to be both institutionally "plausible" and socially "adequate".

As a consequence of these political implications, competing theoretical and methodological options are at stake. Various experiments carried out to date have raised doubts about the features of legal ethics courses (should they take place at the pre- or post-qualifying stages?) as well as about how and what should be taught. In particular, it is *not* commonly accepted yet how field-work should be approached and whether this is relevant to legal ethics *per se*, or whether it is necessary also to take into account the broader dynamics of the socio-normative realm. In short, the search for an optimum format for teaching and learning legal ethics is progressing cautiously, with any consensus on the wider issues apparently still some way off (Paterson, 1995). This chapter seeks to move beyond this controversial starting point and, more particularly, aims to reformulate the above questions by problematising the very notion and content of what is commonly understood by "legal ethics."

II. LEGAL ETHICS: A CONTROVERSIAL ISSUE

As is well-known "legal ethics," either as a concept or as a topic, have been and still are a highly controversial issue amongst lawyers. Ever since the claim made by the Italian jurist Alberico Gentili, an Oxford law professor at the time of the schism between temporal and spiritual power—*silete theologi in munere alieno*! ("Shut up theologians outside your jurisdiction!")—the term "legal ethics" has achieved the status of a true oxymoron, and remains useful in creating the impression that within the western legal tradition law and morality go hand-in-hand, provided certain short cuts in social interaction are present.

Moreover, ever since the proposal made by Jeremy Bentham to conceive the "ought-to-be" of social interactions not as an unavoidable compulsory duty, but simply as a useful performative guideline, it evokes—under the label of "deontology"—the embodiment of individual utilitarian standards to reward certain valuable relationships, rather than top-down official enforcement of disciplinary measures set up to ensure the social control of certain intellectual and/or behavioural potentials.

For these reasons "legal ethics" have also been, and remain, a highly contested legal field. The impact of Westphalian principles on legal theorising at the time of early Absolutism—which stated that the only valid law is that of the State—seriously undermined the core *rationale* and coherence of its long-standing symbolic and pedagogic regulatory functions. Furthermore, the ideology of the Napoleonic Code and positivistic legal modelling also succeeded in downgrading its structural traits—so much so that, *de jure* and *de facto*, the vast majority of western lawyers apparently consider legal ethics a mere social device justifying "personal" choices rather than contributing to the enhancement of "transpersonal" socio-professional ideals.

On the other hand, those who attempt to reduce the complexity of the problem through the drafting of written codes inevitably succumb to a harsh reality, i.e. to the fact that professional performances ultimately rely on multi-dimensional contexts and relationships, the microphysical variability of which has little to do with formal-official decisionism expressed in the form of professional codes.

It is therefore clear that if a law school wishes to introduce a new course in legal ethics, the dubious academic status of "legal ethics" becomes, in addition, a problem of determining what "legal ethics" really means at any given spatial or temporal juncture, and whether in scientific terms jurists, moral philosophers, sociologists or social psychologists might be considered better equipped to teach this subject under present conditions.

III. LEGAL ETHICS: A PROBLEMATIC TOPIC FOR SCIENTIFIC INQUIRY

A cautionary paradox arising out of traditional experience informs us that to be fully aware of a problem is only to be close to, and not at, its solution. In what follows I will take this paradox seriously and argue that the extent of theoretical and practical difficulties which must be taken into account if the academic teaching of "legal ethics" is to evolve is also a constitutive part of the problem which can be neither hidden nor ignored.

Before entering into a detailed discussion, and in order to avoid conceptual misunderstanding, let me "suspend"—as Foucault might say—use of the term "legal ethics" for the time being. As I have argued elsewhere (Olgiati, 1991), according to a socio-legal perspective the entire province of professionally oriented values, rules, uses, standards, precepts, restatements, advices, etc. concerning the actual exercise of powers of autonomy (self-goverment), autarchy (self-management) and autocriny (self-jurisdiction) of a profession constitute its domestic (interior) system of self-regulation.

Significantly, the peculiarity of such a system is that it is structurally and functionally Janus-headed: (1) it is a truly constitutional framework, for it defines the overall professional regulatory standards in relation to the exercise of professional power/knowledge nexus from the strict point of view of the professional group (professional self-regulation as professional *jus proprium*, i.e. as a proper, unique normative order); and consequently (2) it is also the constitutional model of the given process of professionalisation, for it contains the ideal-typical standards of experience necessary to assess the social identity and technical specificity of the professional group *vis-à-vis* the broader social system (professional self-regulation as a meaningful sign of an actual/ideal professional project, in accordance with the principle *necessitas jus constituit*).

As one can readily appreciate, it is not arbitrary to stress the double-faced character of this issue in socio-legal terms: it corresponds to empirical fact, is theoretically "reasonable" and useful in practice. By definition, the sociology of law focuses on the two principal dimensions of any form of social regulation: the legal and the social. In so doing, it is also typically oriented toward the methodological coupling of empirical and factual, as well as symbolic and material, factors. In short, as a scientific domain the sociology of law is particularly appropriate for dealing with any professional socio-legal order as a veritable *unitas multiplex* of physical and ideal variables, i.e. as a dual/unitary *corpus mysticum*.

Looking at this from a socio-legal standpoint, both the "is" and "ought" dimensions which constitute current/prospective status-roles and expectations of the professional group can be directly connected. These elements can therefore also be referred to as the combination of rule-oriented behaviour and principle-oriented ideals which define the degree of suitability and plausibility of the same group at a broader social (epistemological) level. In turn, the relationship between the group's members and those having direct competence/authority in the creation and enforcement of the system—i.e. the *honoratiores* (élite members)—can be clarified. Consequently the process (performances) and policy (ideals) of the profession can be related also to other living legal spheres (including positive official law), as well as the hierarchy of social stratification, i.e. to the intertwinement—typical in modern western societies—of legal pluralism and socio-institutional corporatism. Finally, the coupling of cultural and normative standards in the internal reproduction of the professional group can be assessed in general, as well as particular, terms. Hence the contrast between, for example, professional responsibility and professional misconduct in relation to the efficacy of the system as a whole can be seen not only as an offence or disfunction, but also as a vital condition for individual and collective "secondary adjustments" (consistent with the fact that any illict conduct is a co-essential part of the value assessment of the same conduct).

Having explained this, let me now move on to consider what is commonly understood by the term "legal ethics". This is not far from what has just been described, i.e. a multi-layered constitution-in-action that not only links standards of professional practice (facts) with the meaning of professional discourses (values), but "translates" the "is" and "ought" patterns in problem solving-oriented guidelines. That is a double mix which is nothing more, but also nothing less, than the sedimentation by embodiment of the binding force of all cautionary experiences derived from the power/knowledge nexus implicit in overall courses of professional action. Put another way, "legal ethics" are merely a label which facilitates conceptualising the exchange between an "organism" (professional body) and its "organisation-set" (professional arena), i.e. the (often) implicit *organisational texture* (Cooper and Fox, 1990) of the professional action system which moulds the part within the whole, and *vice versa* (not unlike a hologram), according to a permanent creative process of order and change.

If the above hypothesis is correct, it follows that the intertwinement of qualitative and quantitative, material and symbolic, variables is so tight and mobile at any one given time that it cannot be broken or dropped at whim. Even less can it be fixed for pedagogic purposes into predefined didactic schemes. Being a unity of continuity (of tradition and exemplary memory) and movement (of context and performance) it cannot be framed within the domain of any single analytical scientific inquiry for—as the ancient Greek philosoper Heraclitus would say—it is impossible "to enter to the same river twice". Thus, it is extremely important to be aware from the outset that, whether or not a socio-legal modelling is adopted, it is almost inevitable for intrinsic reasons that, either in the short or long term, the academic teaching of "legal ethics" will pose serious theoretical, methodological and practical problems.

To the extent that "legal ethics" are, as we have seen, in practice a cluster of professional values (cultural patterns) which transustantiate into professional behaviours (pragmatic actions) and *vice versa*, it is impossible to locate the boundary between the two dimensions. By contrast, academic teaching in the West continues to be constructed according to the principle of functional differentiation between work (practical know-how) and thought (formal knowledge). Consequently, it is separated from actual professional practice by its scientific foundations. Moreover, as regards content and method, it can only be executed by means of out-of-context examples of professional discourses or case simulations. Such a functional detachment and selective reductionism can never be totally overcome. Sooner or later, therefore, the matter might be transformed (via scientific systematisation) into a veritable discipline, thereby endangering the whole dynamic of the process of legal professionalization.

Furthermore, to the extent that "legal ethics" are conceived as the means through which professional authority/competence is linked to broader cultural/practical mainstreams of law in society, and *vice versa*, academic teaching—coherently devoted to its scientific (critical) mission—cannot but take into account data at its disposal, i.e. the extraordinary gap between the "is" and "ought" of professional fact-values. The result is to relativise and problematise, instead of re-inforcing, the validity, efficacy and legitimacy of the professional model. As shown by the history of both the professions and academic institutions, these two prospective scenarios are far from remote. One might therefore reasonably speculate: how can both trends be neutralised without simultaneously jeopardising scientific method and professional experience?

IV. LEGAL ETHICS: AN EMBODIED SOCIO-LEGAL SYSTEM

In order to grasp the theoretical and practical significance of institutional constraints imposed on academic courses in "legal ethics", one can draw attention to a simple but too often neglected fact, namely, that professionalism abhors discourses which are either *more geometrico demonstrata* or require compulsory obedience towards *ex-cathedra* codified "truths". More precisely, professionalism tends to reject any sort of systematic scientific disciplinary regulation related to ideological and political authoritarianism. In fact, systems of professional action always imply, by definition, experimentation and innovation—the break up of officially negotiated settlements based on mere institutionalised power relations—in order to deal with the endless problematic changes caused by social dynamics. In other words, professionalism necessarily requires what has been defined in theoretical terms as "the level of creative indeterminacy of knowledge" (Jamous and Peloille, 1970). So much so that, as historical experience shows and the theory of organisations confirms, the more professional power/knowledge is denied such "creative indeterminacy" the more professionalism becomes mere bureaucratic managerialism (Etzioni, 1961). Or, put another way, the more professional authority-competence is "cultivated" solely by means of formal controls and codified discourses, the more professionals lose their peculiar social function as "organic intellectuals" and become mere technical intermediaries. In both instances, in the short or longer term, they will act as real *gardiens de l'ipocrisie collective* (Bourdieu, 1991) up to the point of endangering the evolutionary patterns of the broader social system.

It goes without saying that such perverse outcomes typically recur alongside the historic development of legal professions. Legal professions are always involved in the ascendancy and assessment of particular ideological and material powers which are most in need of "unproblematic", "systematisable" and "loyal" competences. It is not by chance, therefore, that lawyers universally try to flee from such recurrent "iron cages" which inevitably lead to processes of "degradation of the self", i.e. to actual de-professionalisation. As we shall see, it is not unusual that they also assert professional "independence" and "autonomy" in order to detach, so far as is possible, their status-roles and functions from any sort of doctrinal or factual *Grundnorm* (Olgiati, 1990).

Given this, it is by no means fortuitous that professional self-regulation cannot easily be systematically ordered according to monothematic scientific discourses, one-dimensional causal chains, and even less by means of *ad hoc* formal codes or codified "truths". Indeed, professional self-regulation neither follows nor respects disciplinary boundaries set up in accordance with the principle of the "social division of cultural labour" characterised by academic institutions. The reason for this is clear: the *rationale* of the professions' autonomy rests on their ability to grasp the *totality*—and not merely an arbitrarily "divided" and perhaps "pre-defined" part—of socio-professional issues which determine institutional hegemony.

Moreover, professional self-regulation particularly abhors the crystallisation of contents and apriorism of means and ends which typically characterise "official" theories, especially when they are taught as legitimation-oriented theorems. Finally, is it or is it not self-evident that such officialising mechanisms contradict the complex *continuum* of social dynamics? Doubtless one cannot ignore that many of its cultural patterns reflect the state of current scientific debates. This, however, is done in a very instrumental, unpredictable and opportunistic way and, it is worth noting, without rejection of insights drawn from historical experience rooted in, or related to, mere "common sense".

By way of conclusion on this point, we can say that professional self-regulation does not deal with social problems according to the Cartesian method—i.e. by continuously raising doubts and using clear and distinct concepts. Its primary concern is not with the "reduction" of social complexity, but rather with the framing of socio-professional issues as a whole by means of a veritable "bounded rationality", i.e. a type of rationality which does not claim to explain social facts, but rather tries to handle them notwithstanding their intrinsic and irrepressible complexity. In this sense professional self-regulation is a highly eclectic and unstable socio-normative domain because: (1) professionalism is a means to transform, for whatever reason, all kinds of formal academic knowledge into a useful and socially plausible practical know-how; and (2) professionals, while "carrying on" such transformation—*bon gré mal gré*—put into it all the limitations and promise of their "flesh" and "blood", i.e. the idiosyncratic ups-and-downs of their bodies and wills (Freidson, 1986).

For this very reason, one should well aware that what is called "legal ethics" is not merely a discursive formation easily adaptable for incorporation in text-books. It is, moreover, what lawyers actually are, do, predict and what they believe in. In short, it is the relative and situational embodiment of *a priori* values-in-action, i.e. the psycho-physical "corruption" of any given "pure" (institutionally rationalised) social ideal. This being so, to what extent can the academic teaching of "legal ethics" properly take into account the constitutive peculiarities of this model?

V. LEGAL ETHICS: AN "UNLOADING" AND "RE-EMBEDDING" FUNCTIONAL DEVICE

The above question is not purely rhetorical, since radical changes within the province of law have over recent decades undermined and/or eroded not only traditional technical expertise but also the socio-institutional settings to which legal professions were linked. New, disorganic and unrefined socio-normative arrangements now have come to the fore. So much so that professional patterns can no longer be conceived as given data; instead they have become problematic puzzles. In such circumstances, it seems there is only one reasonable way to proceed, that is to focus on the basic epistemological preconditions of the professional action system in order to re-appraise its most meaningful features. For the sake of brevity and clarity, let us now concentrate on the functional traits before focussing on the other dimension of its highly complex socio-technical structuration.

If one considers the cultural tradition of professions and professionalism it is possible to distinguish at least two general dimensions which sum up the entire functional realm of professional self-regulation. The first dimension could be labelled the "exemption" or "unloading" function, while the second might be defined as the"re-embedding" function. As we shall see, in both instances we are concerned with a common organisational problem: how the process of "transposition of ends" (a process which arises in every institutionalised setting) transubstantiates a limit into a potential resource, and *vice versa*.

Professionalism—not to be confused with expert occupationalism—is in fact a means of treating social problems and existential needs which otherwise are irresolvable and/or irrepressible. Outstanding examples of this inherent characteristic are offered by the most ancient of professions, i.e. doctors, lawyers and priests (nowadays psychotherapists). Each of these professions is concerned with issues relating to life/death facts/values in the first instance. Thus, doctors deal with *physical* life/death fact/value dimensions of the human condition, such as illness, birth, etc.; lawyers deal with the *civil* life/death dimensions such as economic misfortune, social conflicts and power struggles, etc.; while priests (psychotherapists) deal with the *spiritual* life/death dimensions such as the quest for faith, meaning and hope surrounding these same life/death dimensions. Since these issues derive from basic bio-items (and cultural taboo/interdicts) of both individual and collective bodies they can be neither repressed nor resolved, only dealt with through ritual and/or procedural therapeutic treatment. Moreover, since in the final analysis all major life/death events associated with the human condition far transcend any technical skill or knowledge, it follows that no one—not even doctors, lawyers or priests—is able to guarantee a final outcome through professional therapy. Therefore any such professional treatment, although of interest as a comment on the conventional/instrumental social acceptance of the artificial trust/security offered by professionals, is in reality little more than a device for the "transposition of ends".

(a) The "Unloading" Function

Following on from what has just been said, it is well known that professionalism treats social problems and existential needs by means of *ad hoc* sociotechnics. On the one hand, the treatment is mainly performed by virtue of relational-type contracts. This implies the achievement of given quality standards (the so-called "economy of quality") based on given credentials (i.e. reputation). These two achievements are absolutely necessary because they are the only social devices that allow a prospective replay of socio-professional relationships without endangering the whole framework of a given professional setting. In fact, quality standards and credentials are based ultimately on opinions and judgements made throughout social communication rather than on actual professional achievements. As social communication never ends, it provides an interpersonal shelter confronting the fact that: (a) professional interaction is always undetermined (due to the everchanging personal traits of the parties); and (b) space-time conditions to treat the issues at stake are always irrepeatable (because contexts are always changing also). Nevertheless, actual professional achievements structurally imply a degree of asymmetry—the so-called power–knowledge gap—in the course of socio-professional interaction. This asymmetry cannot be hidden by mere communication, in the short or long term; it therefore leads to the so-called "fall of trust rate" on the part of the weaker interactant (Fox, 1974).

In order to overcome the above risk and "reduce" social unpredictability, professionals—together with their clients—look opportunistically also for any sort of ready-made, pre-defined, long-term device providing certainty and security. An unrestrained exploitation of these instrumental devices, however, is precisely what jeopardises the whole *rationale* of professional action, i.e. the ability to deal with the irrepressible complexity of social dynamics. It is not by chance, therefore, that if the above is not monitored regularly and in strategic terms, the inevitable result for the individual professional (as well as for the professional group as a whole) will again be the "fall of trust rate" seen at the social, technical and political levels. In other words, sooner or later, the assessment of a power–knowledge gap based primarily on pre-defined selective arrangements rather than on contextual guidelines clashes with the functional prerequisites of a relational contracting which implies, by definition, social mutability and indeterminacy.

Professional self-regulation is, then, precisely that cluster of standard references which guides behaviour in order to avoid the "low trust spiral" inherent in the above ambiguous asymmetry and unpredictability. In this sense, professional self-regulation is actually a "container" of continual warnings "condensed" into restatements and precepts. Professional standards of living recall the fact that social complexity cannot be "reduced" at whim or by force, but have to be (and can be) "recognised" and "treated" in a certain manner. In sum, these cautions have been and are set up to "unload" generations of professionals with the risk of destroying the self-same professional system. In this respect, any attempt at scientific systematisation and formal-legal codification are misconceived expedients which, far from reducing professional risks, actually aggravate them.

(b) The "Re-embedding" Function

As is also well known, professionalism in modern western society is a means through which to organise the power/knowledge nexus in a monopolistic manner whilst treating formal knowledge and "know-how" as a means of "social engineering". This is done to foster larger constructionist techno-political projects (Larson, 1977). The more such a double organisational task is performed, the greater the impact on the social composition of society at large. Professionalism can therefore appear, at any given moment, either as the ideal-type of social mobility and progress or, alternatively, of social closure and depowerment. In any event—as Giddens notes—the overall result of the involvement of professional expertise in the construction of what has been called "modernity" has been—and still is—an increasing distantiation and differentiation of human experiences and the lifting out of social action systems from local contexts and communicational contacts. Not surprisingly—for reality is always contradictory—such a process of "dis-embedding" society from its "natural" (i.e. original) living conditions produces not only extraordinary technical achievements but also unusually high levels of social risk. Because of such a recurring contradiction, the creation and enforcement of *ad hoc* "re-embedding" mechanisms has also become unavoidable in order to recast social trustworthiness within the general evolutionary process of society as a whole. It is not by chance, therefore, that paradoxically the institutionalisation of risk is socially "moulded" by relating it to security and trust in the rationalising—discursive, rather than technical—capacity, of the same professionalism.

Seen from this perspective, professional self-regulation is a "re-embedding" device *par excellence* in modern society, for—as Giddens notes—it re-embeds professionals also! Indeed, as a loosely coupled socio-normative system, self-regulation is able to offer insights and guidelines to confront problems stemming from the two most recurrent dilemmas of professional action related to the above contradictions: the so-called "prisoner's dilemma" and the so-called "snakes and ladders game" dilemma.

It is well understood that the "prisoner's dilemma" deals with the fact that any information from a (distant) party might imply also a secret or a half-truth, so that any good decision could turn into a potential danger (risk derived by the social uncertainty about social interactions, due to social fallibility and the relativity of the human condition/knowledge). On the other hand, the "snakes and ladders game" dilemma is concerned with the fact that any incorrect move implies a halt, or even the witwdrawal, from the given "playground" (risk derived by the social insecurity about human action, due to the social unpredictability of prospective outcomes of human conditions/decisions). As can be seen, in both cases a "rational" balance between risk and trust could lead to a self-disruptive stalemate: a state of affairs in which professional self-regulation does not exist at all, for it is against "the natural order of things", i.e. movement and change.

If one now assesses lawyers' self-regulation in relation to the achievements (security) and failures (risk) of the form of positive state law *vis-à-vis* the social dynamics of modern society, one can readily see the extent to which professional standards protected and nurtured not only their century-old "legitimacy to act", but also their traditional role as boundary agents of long-standing epochal socio-institutional projects. Consequently, any attempt to transform and/or simplify the Janus-headed nature of professionalism ends, in fact, in the destruction rather than development of one of the basic pillars of western civilisation.

VI. LEGAL ETHICS: THE ANOMIC ROLE OF LATE-MODERN PROFESSIONALISM

The two functional dimensions of professional self-regulation sketched in outline above—as might already be apparent—concern either individual professionals or their wider professional group, or else specific technical, or more general social, problems. In either case what really matters is that professional self-regulation is tailored to treat any professional dilemma concerning needs or claims arising out of the institutionalisation of socio-technical arrangements which imply the dynamics and interplay between trust-risk and security-uncertainty. This fact requires further development.

Since such an interplay is based on irreconcilable structural contradictions, such as contradictions between "nature", "culture" and "civilisation", it follows that the functional dimensions of professional self-regulation cannot but be oriented toward a sort of superior and unique end: that of guaranteeing the *nomic* function of professionalism in any province of the broader social system.

Indeed, in modern western society professionalism so far has been conceived and perceived as a typical nomic agent, i.e. a proper "ordering" system for the whole of society because of the mix of competence, meritocracy, rewards and status which are embodied within it (Durkheim, 1958). The real problem with such a role, however, is that it is any longer sustainable. If one looks carefully at social dynamics, one notices that several professional groups are in fact now converting to *anomic* status (Larson, 1998). Instead of contributing to the search for solutions to basic social problems—they seem instead to follow a "perverse" and myopic logic whose meaning is totally detached from, and disinterested with, society at large.

At least two principal explanations might account for this shift. First, the fact that among the so-called "consequences of modernity", the "dark side" of the kind of "progress" fostered by professionalism is now spreading on a global scale, i.e. the so-called *Risikogesellshaft*, also known as the "risk society" (Beck, 1986). Secondly, the fact that the irreversible decline of classical political economy and the Enlightenment's socio-technics exposed the intrinsic limits of the "abstract promises of modernity", i.e. the impossibility of establishing social equity, technical rationality, political equality and so on. All in all, such major events—and the radical changes which they give rise to—have altered fundamentally the pragmatic and ideological impact of professionalism on society. So much so that it is now clear that the ideal of a 'social trustee professionalism', resting as it does on the fusion of scientific competence and civic morality (Brint, 1994), can today hardly be assessed unless new favourable structural conditions from outside the system of professions are provided. It is also increasingly uncertain whether traditional organisation-sets, i.e. the professional guild system, will survive (Krause, 1996).

Such a disconcerting trend is widespread amongst lawyers too. The amount of scientific literature now available on this topic even goes so far as to suggest that we might witness "the end of legal professions as we knew it" (Cownie, 1990). If so, new questions arise: for example, how could the academic teaching of "legal ethics" deal with the structural conditions of current professional "alteration" and what general cultural pillars are at hand for this purpose?

VII. LEGAL ETHICS: A BOUNDARY FIELDWORK

The extraordinary implications of these observations cannot be fully appreciated unless one is aware also that the above functional dimensions of professional self-regulation are maintained by official arrangements relating to the specific traits of each professional group.

The vast majority of such arrangements are not based on longstanding, tradition-oriented patterns, but rather continuously evolve according to the issues brought to the fore by current socio-political 'engineering' projects. They are produced, handled and systematically enforced by state officials (e.g. *pro-tempore* policy-makers, judges, etc.) as top-down decisionistic devices, and therefore they are, as a rule, ready-made, pre-defined, etc. Their official aim is to neutralise risk and generalise security conditions and trust relations for society at large, exactly in accordance with the dominant ideology. By so doing, they also directly (and/or indirectly) bolster certain professional standards and simplify professional interactions while simultaneously favouring, for reasons already mentioned, professional self-interest and opportunism. Taken together, however, political power, technical competence and social trust concentrated into agencies of the state greatly exceed the influence possessed by professional associations. The relationship is therefore asymmetric. Moreover, since the competition for political power always remains open this same relationship with State rulers is always uncertain. Finally, both power élites and agents of the State can use their knowledge and know-how either arbitrarily and oppressively or else in more gracious and attractive ways. Given this institutional context, it is hardly fortuitous that professional dilemmas about the contradictory mix of risk and security, certainty and uncertainty, are routinely exasperated.

Professional self-regulation deals also with these problems. On the one hand, regulation of conduct suggests how professions can escape from over restrictive, all-embracing, one-dimensional State-oriented involvements undermining the ability of professionals to "perceive" societal needs. On the other hand, such regulation reveals the optimum conditions to apply State-oriented security/trust devices without exceeding certain social limits (of convenience). The *rationale* that is at the core of such a position is clear: to assess a socially "reasonable" persistence and consistence of professional activity *vis-à-vis* the "irrational" variability of State arrangements and instability of ruling elites. Accordingly, professionalism, while performing certain social functions, historically transcends political regimes which, by contrast, typically are oriented toward continual power struggles.

As far as legal professions are concerned, the above adds up to significantly more than a mere general framework: it is a co-essential, *constitutive* part of the same process of professionalisation. And yet legal professions are, by definition, Janus-headed: as "boundary agents" between State and society, they therefore not only have to face the trust-risk dynamics of both the broader social system and the official State apparatuses, but must also couple them in a highly refined and specific way. As such a complex coupling is accomplished largely by means of official legal arrangements, professional self-regulation is therefore structurally and functionally *compelled* to signal lawyers' peculiar operational assets and strategic positioning regarding the interplay between State and society. It stresses professional independence as an essential tool guaranteeing the performance of professional standards in practice. In turn it emphasises the social importance of such independence as an inalienable social value. The social justification of both issues is the socio-legal *detachment* of its socio-technical patterns from those of any other normative domain.

Unfortunately, the above *rationale* has not always been followed consistently by legal professions. Consequently under the overwhelming pressure of the "irrational" forces of State and society dynamics the results invariably have been fairly devastating. For example, immediately following the traumatic experience of French lawyers during the French Revolution, legal professions in the west arrived at a special strategic "solution" to deal with this issue. Instead of imposing a genuine detachment they consented to the enforcement of a "reciprocity principle" linking the three relevant powers involved, i.e. that of political élites (force of command), that of legal professions (legal knowledge and know-how) and that of social dynamics (class consensus/opposition). As argued elsewhere (Olgiati, 1996), this "reciprocity principle" has indeed been tacitly signed and substantially enforced for more than one hundred and fifty years; in fact, it shaped the so-called "liberal professional model" as well as the so-called *Rechtsstaat*, i.e. the rule-of-law system (Larson, 1988; Karpik, 1995).

At present, however, notwithstanding the influence of the principle at an ideological level, the material pre-condtitions for its further development are over. In fact, at least from the 1930s onwards, almost everything has changed in the relationship linking State, society and the professions. Powerful semi-autonomous socio-legal orders now challenge the regulatory role of nation-States and, as a result, society is disciplined more by means of neo-corporatist infrastructures than by legal rules, while, in turn, professional action systems are fragmented and decomposed. These are among the reasons which explain how and why the "reciprocity principle" withered away!

Even so, what remains significant is that the "reciprocity principle", while still favouring certain institutional interests, had a traumatic impact on the inherent functioning and inner logic of the self-same professional self-regulation. On the one hand, it fostered the subsumption of the matter under the cover of the official legal system as a mere subsidiary regulatory device.

On the other hand, it also weakened professional sensibility about the epistemological *meaning* of basic professional standards. Hence, to the extent that it supported professional cynicism and self-serving protectionism, rather than the social *necessity* of professional action, above all it also eroded a patrimony of professional culture and experience which dated back over several centuries. Consequently, the *real* reference standards for professional self-regulation are now largely ignored while lawyers, having exploited the mere *utility* of that "principle", now suffer from a deep-rooted "crisis of identity". Taking this disturbing state of affairs into account, one might well consider the following question: what kind of novel normative social framework could the academic teaching of "legal ethics" reasonably refer to?

VIII. LEGAL ETHICS: A SPECIAL NETWORKING TOOL-BOX

One of the most "perverse" ideological legacies of the "reciprocity principle", set up under the cultural and normative umbrella of classical political economy, is the theorem (based on the so-called "suppletive pluralism" doctrine) that professional self-regulation can match that of the State legal system without raising significant theoretical and practical contradictions. Given the long-term disciplinary hegemony of State-centred legal positivism, this theorem has been culturally embodied to such an extent (even amongst legal professionals) that it is common knowledge that the rules of the former are "akin" to the rules of the latter and, moreover, that the "system" of professional conduct is merely the coupling of professional-oriented and State-oriented rules of professional conduct.

Fortunately, for reasons already mentioned, the epistemological, historical and scientific falsehood of such a theorem cannot be sustained any longer. If one carefully analyses the epistemological *rationale* of lawyers' professional self-regulation, i.e. contradictions and dilemmas raised by socio-legal trust/risk interplay, one realises that it is a *sui generis* and somewhat peculiar "tool-box". As said above, in the same way as any *Lebenswelt* (life-world) regulatory device, it deals with social functions in the final instance (while, by contrast, the positive law of the State deals with conflicting power relationships); on the other hand, as a specific domain tailored to treat socio-legal issues it is a true (semi-)detached *meta-system* acting in between the broader normative domains of both State and society.

In other words, lawyers' professional self-regulation is not simply a socially ascribed professional attribute inherent within any professionalised field. Nor is it an outcome stemming from the mere fact that legal professions, as with any other profession, are in practice State-backed cartels. Nor, ultimately, is it a product of mere contractual negotiations taking place between legal professions and their clients. Given its structural and functional character, it is rather a constitutive fact/value dimension to the overall evolutionary design of the given professional group, enforced by incorporation through that same group in order to make clear to society at large that it can act convincingly as a plausible (i.e. rationally settled) and socially adequate (i.e. based on primary social needs) socio-legal *institution*.

These epistemic patterns can be detected in any westernised legal profession (the ideal-typical "universal" dimension), but they need to be seen in relation to historically determined operational conditions (context-based "local" dimension). Hence, if attention turns toward an historically determined perspective one cannot fail to see that the core standards of lawyers' self-regulation transcends, as said already, any official legal arrangement of any political régime. In fact these core standards are, *de jure* and *de facto*, pre- and *extra*-State law and their socio-legal source, i.e. professionalism, is independent from, as it even pre-exists, current types of State-form. Should social needs require it, they can also drive professional conduct towards *praeter* and *contra* state law (Olgiati, 1990).

If looked at seriously from a scientific standpoint, one cannot but notice also that professional self-regulation derives its normativity not *per legem terrae*, as positive (territorial) State-law (at least since the Magna Carta) but rather, as said already, it derives from functional performances related to existential problems (Drinker, 1961). That is why it is not a true (systematic) "system", but instead more of a networking fieldwork which includes a combination of rules, principles, uses, etc., which are related to various normative, semantic and discursive factors. Together they exert general guidance in terms of flexible *Zweckprogramm* orientation, i.e. a purpose-oriented action system, rather that a strict *Konditionalprogramm* coercion, i.e. a rule-determined constraint (Febbrajo, 1985;1987). Briefly, if one evaluates this fieldwork scientifically excluding legalistic and/or doctrinal prejudices it will be seen that professional self-regulation, to use a metaphorical model drawn from ancient architecture, cannot be theoretically constructed or imagined as a part of an Egyptian pyramidal system with a *Grundnorm* at the apex in the manner that positivist legal science suggests. On the contrary, it has to be theoretically constructed or imagined as a system modelled on a Greek temple, supported by harmonious pillars whose reference points capture the horizontal and vertical social rhythms rationally "measured" throughout the space-time symbolism and material interaction of blanks and solids, light and shadows. The combination of these architectural elements bears down either on the ground (facts) or on the heavens (values) according to different ideographic devices, such as basements and trabeations, in order to shape (and conceal), by virtue of a well-refined microphysical distribution, the responsibility of its builders, while enchanting its lucky inhabitants.

Yet again, this is not a mere rhetorical device, since the metaphor is based on the most significant insights within the cultural tradition of professionalism. However it is worth remembering that this is only part of the picture. One should not forget that within the evolutionary *continuum* of contemporary legal professions, one finds, *inter alia*, three formidable obstacles which impede comprehension of the epistemic and historical core of the problem, namely, the new forms of legal pluralism, social differentiation and moral polimorphism.

As is well known, following the decline of the "principle of reciprocity" described above any attempt to reduce legal pluralism, the major and enduring "knowledge mandate" of legal professions, has not met with success. As a result these professions have been attracted by different sources of law and further destabilised by legal phenomena such as that of *interlegalité, norm erosion* and *desbordamiento del derecho*. Consequently they are now increasingly losing the ideological and performative guidelines according to which they have hitherto defined their *political loyalty*.

Along with the rise of new forms of legal pluralism, radical technological and organisational changes have also taken place within the law-and-society realm. For legal professions these changes have led to the creation of new market niches, different work structures, new social claims and so on. As a result, individual professionals as well as their wider groups increasingly have both been drawn into processes of technical specialisation, cultural differentiation and social fragmentation, right up to the very point of losing the traditional ideological and performative guidelines which define their *cultural identity*.

Last, but by no means least, alongside these major transformations one must also take into account something which is typically neglected but which is of extraordinary significance for our present concerns. I refer to the *élitist* (i.e. fragmented and stratifying) acquisition and *non-collegial* (i.e., competitive and discriminating) use of the professional power/knowledge nexus which, when applied to the large socio-institutional sociotechnics of modernity, brought social interaction to such a degree of social dis-embedment that *moral polimorphism* has become a generalised device. Hence, with the withering away of socio-institutional pre-conditions which sustained the "principle of reciprocity", even the most dedicated members of professional groups have been unable to assess which moral guidelines are truly relevant to the issue of their professionalism, for example those sustaining a shared "service ideal".

As early as the middle of the nineteenth century and prior to Durkheim in France, Rosmini in Italy perceived the potential danger of the contextual conflictual co-existence of individual (person-oriented), domestic (group-oriented) and civic (society-oriented) morals (Olgiati, 1994). A century later contemporary authors describe moral polimorphism in terms of the "division of moral labour " (Luban, 1984). This new definition, however, cannot disguise and in fact confirms the depth of the problem. Not only are traditional reference points concerning a common cultural background challenged by the intermixity of social complexity and technical specialism, but also the possibility of enhancing a single cultural mainstream have been rendered totally unrealistic, at least in so far as cultural pluralism is officially recognised as a positive issue for society at large.

If one now turns attention to the fact that, at least since the fifteenth century, lawyers' professional self-regulation has been internally divided according to two sets of standards: first, those related to the risk-trust dilemmas stemming from the *forum fori* (i.e. social interactions in courts); and secondly, those related to the dilemmas of the *forum coscientiae* (i.e. reflexive introspection concerning personal behaviour) (Ala, 1605), one can readily appreciate what kind of "geometrical" crescendo of complexities is at stake when current typologies of moral polimorphism are taken into account seriously. In the final analysis, the question which must remain open is this: what mission should the academic teaching of "legal ethics" aspire to?

IX. TOWARD AN ACADEMIC TEACHING OF "LEGAL ETHICS": WHAT IS TO BE DONE?

"What mission should the academic teaching of "legal ethics" aspire to?" is indeed the key question which ultimately must come to the fore if the teaching of academic law is serious about finding a meaningful *rationale* for contemporary, late-modern western society.

As we have seen, due to radical changes arising out of broader socio-legal dynamics, the general (cultural, institutional, technical, etc.) conditions of professional action systems remain extremely problematic at present. The quest for a new, more credible and socially adequate socio-normative framework is yet another puzzling issue. This quest derives from, but also transcends, the ever-increasing claims for "better" services, the decline of trust in professional interactions, the "withering away" of institutional arrangements, the "crisis" of identity of professional bodies, the "loss" of well-established professional attributes, the "emptiness" of formal-official credentialism and so on. Taken together, these and other variables have to such an extent undermined the functional and structural dimensions to professional self-regulation that many professionals, either as social strata or as learned expertise, are increasingly being transformed into *anomic* actors.

Consequently, all efforts at the reconstruction of a normative climate appropriate for a general re-alignment of professional values in which social, political and cultural issues are well-balanced have so far met with little success and the prospects for finding a viable solution remain somewhat dubious. On the one hand, traditional legal sanctions backed by the State have lost a great deal of their compulsory regulatory efficacy; on the other hand, socio-professional negotiations cannot appeal any more to a "service ideal" grounded on shared ethical precepts or common moral values. This is caused not merely by the unprecedented socio-graphic differentiation and specialisation characteristic of contemporary professional groups, including professional élites (a structural trend which promotes inter-professional conflicts while impeding the creation of collective professional projects). It is also a by-product of the failure of both established and new professional élites to act unequivocally as legal *honoratiores* (i.e. notables), for amongst "the consequences of modernity" other than legal pluralism, social fragmentation and moral polymorphism, one should also mention widespread socio-cultural and organisational changes within society at large, as other contributory factors which undermine professional legitimacy in its various forms.

If one now bears in mind that all of the above takes place within geo-political entities such as Europe, in which grand "social engineering" programmes of *longue dureé* are in the process of political construction, one can clearly understand the extent to which the risk-trust, security-uncertainty, dynamics of generic socio-professional performances give rise to dilemmas which can barely be contained within current cultural standards. As this state of affairs can be neither ignored nor hidden by a scientific approach to contemporary professional self-regulation, it follows that the above questions cannot but have a unique action-oriented answer and a single meaning: to advance and search for a new compatible intertwinement between the *two* irrepressible conditions of societal dynamics, i.e. knowledge and creative know-how, and social change. In other words, to identify a new normative framework which considers afresh the social necessity of the (anti-statical) *nomic* function of the professional action system.

This social function is inevitable on account of its historical necessity, and yet it cannot properly be carried forward without taking another strategic step forward, namely, the recasting of professional identity in accordance with a new alliance linking *science and nature*. In fact, only such an alliance can halt the impending global disruption caused by the outcomes of a risk-society. Without this alliance, it is axiomatic that the *rationale* of professionalism, as such, will lose any meaning for society at large (Olgiati, 1998).

But this is not all. It also implies the need for two clear commitments which, if absent, would have devastating consequences: first, the need to link professional responsibility to social claims for substantive (not merely formal) human rights enforcement mechanisms, i.e. to re-establish law's moral foundations not in an abstract way, but rather in relation to basic social needs; and therefore, secondly, also to link professional conduct to the binding principle of self-constraint, i.e. to re-establish a normative nexus between social utility and historical necessity within the same professional action. As is immediately apparent, the above factors add up to a set of inter-connected challenges for current socio-cultural and institutional arrangements. Surely, therefore, they will become a pivotal issue for the profession in the next millennium.

If the object, therefore, of an academic course on "legal ethics" within a modern western law school is to improve the level of social awareness about the prospective implications of the "is" and "ought" dimensions of lawyering a tentative suggestion usefully might be considered from the outset. The suggestion is this: to consider dealing with professional self-regulation not as doctrine, nor as a code, and not even as mere narrative (discursive formation) since each of these implies a process of selective typificisation that at best approximates to the distorting mirrors game. By way of contrast with such a "map of misreading", students should instead talk about and treat it, in the manner of the arguments of ancient Roman jurists, as a method as well as a structure of *cybernetic*, i.e. as the etymology of the Greek word indicates, not only as a particular socio-technical device, but also and above all as a socio-institutional context (i.e. as an organisational "texture") for "navigating" (controlling and driving) relevant professional issues throughout irrepressible problematic social "fluctuations".

REFERENCES

A. Abbott, *The System of Professions. An Essay on the Division of Expert Labour* (Chicago, Ill., University of Chicago Press, 1988)

A. Abbott, "Professional Ethics", 88,5, American Journal of Sociology, 1983, p. 855–885

P. Ala, Tractatus brevis de Advocato et Causidico Christiano, (Mediolani, 1605)

B.l. Arnold, F.M. Kay, "Social Capital, Violations of Trust and Vulnerability of Isolates: The Social Organization of Law Practice and Professional Self-regulation" 23 International Journal of the Sociology of Law, 1995, p. 321–346

U. Beck, *Risikogesellshaft. Auf dem Weg in eine andere Moderne* (Frankfurt-am-Main, Suhrkanp, 1986) (English Translation: Risk Society, New York, Sage, 1990)

R. Benveniste, "Expert and Sociotechnics" in A. Podgorecki, J.Alexander and R. Shields (eds.), *Social Engineering* (Ottawa, Carleton University Press, 1996)

I. Botteri, Tra onore e utile: il galateo del professionista, in Storia d'Italia, Annali 10 (Torino, Einaudi 1996), p. 721–762

P. Bourdieu, "Les juristes, gardiens de l'hypocrisie collective", in F. Chazel and J. Commaille (eds.), Normes jurdiques et regulation sociale (Paris, LDGJ, 1991)

S. Brint, In an Age of Experts (Princeton, NJ, Princeton University Press, 1994)

F. Cownie, The Reform of the Legal Profession or the End of Civilization as We Know It, in F. Patfield, R. White (eds.), The Changing Law (Leicester, Leicester University Press, 1990)

R. Cooper, S.Fox, The "Texture" of Organizing, 27 (6) Journal of Management 1990, p. 575–582

M. Drinker, Legal Ethics (New York, Columbia University Press, 1961)

E. Durkheim, Professional Ethics and Civic Morals, (New York, The Free Press of Glencoe, 1958)

A. Etzioni, A Comparative Analysys of Complex Organizations (New York, The Free Press of Glencoe, 1961)

A. Febbrajo, Struttura e funzioni delle deontologie professionali, in W. Tousjin (a cura di), Le libere professioni in Italia, Bologna, Il Mulino, 1987, p. 55–86

A. Febbrajo, L'etica dell'avvocato come progetto professionale, 3 Sociologia del diritto 1985, p. 13–33–

E. Freidson, Professional Powers. A Study on the Institutionalization of Formal Knowledge (Chicago, University of Chicago Press, 1986)

A. Fox, Beyond Contract: Work, Power and Trust Relations (London, Faber & Faber, 1974)

A. Giddens, The Consequences of Modernity (Cambridge, Polity Press, 1990)

H. Jamous and B. Pelloille, "Professions or Self-Perpetuating Systems ? Changes in the French University-Hospital System", in A. Jackson (ed.), Professions and Professionalization (Cambridge University Press, Cambridge 1970)

L. Karpik, Les avocats. Entre l'Etat, le public et le marché, XIII-XX siecle (Gallimard, Paris 1995)

E. Krause, Death of the Guilds (New Haven, Conn., Yale University Press, 1996),

D. Luban (ed.), The Good Lawyer. Lawyers' Role and Lawyers' Ethics (Totowa, Rowan & Allanheld Publ., 1984)

R. Murphy, Social Closure. The Theory of Monopolization and Exclusion (Oxford, Clarendon Press, 1988)

V. Olgiati, "L'etica professionale come ordinamento", in Saggi sull'avvocatura (Milano, Giuffré, 1990) p. 131–166

V. Olgiati, "Diritto positivo e autoregolazione professionale nei Discorsi sull'Avvocatura di Giuseppe Zanardelli", in Saggi sull'avvocatura (Milano, Giuffré, 1990) p. 95–129

V. Olgiati, "La cultura giuridica come credenziale professionale", in Saggi sull'avvocatura (Milano, Giuffré, 1990) p. 167–204

V. Olgiati, Autoregolazione e sviluppo delle professioni giuridiche, in AA.VV. Storia del diritto e teoria politica, Milano, Giuffré, 1991 p. 887–917

V. Olgiati, L'autoregolazione professionale come forma di comunicazione: accostamenti, definizioni, tendenze, Teoria Sociologica, n.3, Milano Angeli, 1994 p. 216–250

V. Olgiati, Process and Policy of Legal Professionalization in Europe. The Deconstruction of a Normative Order, in Y. Dezalay, D. Sugarman (eds.), Professional Competition and Professional Power (London, Routledge, 1995) p. 170–204

V. Olgiati, Assetto locale e posizionamento strategico: le questioni di fondo del professionalismo giuridico europeo, V. Olgiati, Le professioni giuridiche in Europa. Politiche del diritto e dinamica sociale (Urbino, QuattroVenti, 1996) p. 23–57

V. Olgiati, Self-regulation of Legal Professions in Contemporary Italy, International Journal of the Legal Profession 1997, p. 89–107

V. Olgiati, Risk, Professions and the Claim for Human Rights, in V. Olgiati, L.H. Orzack, M. Saks (eds.), Professions: Identity and Order in Comparative Perspective (Onati, IISL Onati Series, 1998)

T. Parsons, Sociological Essays (New York,The Free Press of Glencoe, 1954)

A. Paterson, Legal Ethics: Its Nature and Place in the Curriculum, in R. Cranston (ed.), Legal Ethics and Professional Responsibility (Oxford, Clarendon Press, 1995) p. 175–188

H. Popitz, Der Aufbruch zur artifiziellen Gesellschaft (Tübingen, J.C.B. Mor, 1995)

M. Sarfatti Larson, The Rise of Professionalism. A Sociological Analysis (Berkeley-Los Angeles, The University of California Press, 1977)

M. Sarfatti Larson, "The Changing Functions of Lawyers in in the Liberal State", in R. Abel and P. Lewis (ed.), Lawyers in Society, vol .3, Berkeley-los Angeles, University of California Press, 1988)

M. Sarfatti Larson, The Professions' Nomic Functions and the End of Modernity (European Yearbook for the Sociology of Law, Giuffrè, Milan, 1998 forthcoming)

Part 2

INTRODUCING LEGAL ETHICS INTO THE CURRICULUM

6

Why Canadian Law Schools Do not Teach Legal Ethics

H. W. ARTHURS*

INTRODUCTION

Central to the concept of professionalism[1] is the notion that only the initiated—those with actual professional knowledge, skills and credentials—are able to determine proper professional procedures and standards of practice. This premise, in turn, supports the proposition that professions should be self-governing or, at very least, that they should play a central role in the administration of the norms which regulate professional conduct. And from this proposition dangle several corollaries: that if members of a profession are going to be disciplined for violating professional norms, they ought to know something about them; that this knowledge ought to be acquired prior to their being admitted to practice; that institutions which are responsible for professional formation ought therefore to teach the subject; and—most controversially—that no one ought to be admitted to practise whose ethical competence has not been tested and certified. Proposals that law schools ought to teach legal ethics, then, are lodged in the deep logic of professionalism.

Conversely, debates concerning the goals, scope and methodology of instruction in legal ethics take us to the very core of debates over legal education itself. If law schools are perceived primarily as training institutions for the practice of law, one set of pedagogic conclusions follows; if they are seen as part of the larger project of liberal education and advanced research, along with other university disciplines, quite another. In the former case, legal ethics will be taught with a view to having students master the norms which govern

* Earlier versions of this paper were delivered in the Summer Seminar Series of Osgoode Hall Law School in June 1996 and to the International Working Group on the Sociology of Law at Peyresq, France, in July 1996. I am grateful to Tamara Barclay and Jeremy Dacks for their research assistance and to Stephen Traviss of the Law Society of Upper Canada for his co-operation.

[1] The very notion of professionalism is under attack: see e.g. R. Nelson, D. Trubek and R. Solomon (eds.), *Lawyers' Ideals/Lawyers' Practices: Transformation in the American Legal Profession* (Ithaca, NY, Cornell University Press, 1994).

professional practice; in the latter, legal ethics will be intellectually grounded, contextualised within the general field of applied ethics or as a part of a broad examination of relations of trust and power or as a socio-political phenomenon typical of intermediate bodies in civil society. In the former case, legal ethics will be studied from the inside out; in the latter, from the outside in.

Yet as the Cotter Report[2] showed, Canadian law schools remain largely indifferent to both versions of legal ethics. And whether as a cause or a consequence of this indifference, governing bodies of the Canadian legal profession make no serious attempt to test would-be lawyers for either moral probity or knowledge of professional ethics.

Nonetheless, from time to time, governing bodies, legal academics and editorial writers invite, exhort, even propose to require law schools to instruct their students in legal ethics. Invite, exhort, require: but then subside. These transient enthusiasms for the teaching of professional responsibility tend to be triggered by public scandals involving prominent lawyers, such as Watergate,[3] highly publicised thefts of clients' funds, or egregious behaviour by young lawyers. When such events occur, the profession naturally wants to prevent repetition of the offending conduct, but also to deflect demands for legislative intervention. The ability to show that the problem can be dealt with internally, that new recruits will be trained and vetted to ensure they meet the required ethical standard, serves this purpose admirably. However, proposals for greater academic attention to legal ethics may also proceed from deeper strategic considerations: the profession's desire to socialise its new recruits and to save them from academic agnosticism about the profession,[4] the countervailing desire of academic critics to ensure that law students do not succumb to professional cynicism when they enter practice,[5] the desire of law schools to legitimate themselves as important contributors to the project of professional formation,[6] or simply the scientific impulse to examine the normative system which purports to regulate an important group in our society.[7] However, while these strategic considerations differ and diverge, all—except

---

[2] W. B. Cotter, *Professional Responsibility Instruction in Canada: A Coordinated Curriculum for Legal Education* (Montreal, Conceptcom, 1992; prepared for the Joint National Committee on Legal Education).

[3] In 1974, the American Bar Association resolved that all ABA-approved law schools "require of all candidates for a first professional degree, instruction in the duties and responsibilities of the legal profession" (Standard 302(a)).

[4] In Canada, admission to practice requires a combination of classroom instruction—provided by the profession in most cases—and service under articles. These requirements ensure some degree of professional socialisation. They also provide an opportunity for instruction in legal ethics, formally and by example, which takes place with varying degrees of effectiveness and intensity: see Cotter, *supra* n. 2, at 2–50 ff.

[5] This was my own initial motive: see H. W. Arthurs, "The Study of the Legal Profession in the Law School" (1970) 8 *Osgoode Hall LJ* 183.

[6] Lord Chancellor's Advisory Committee on Legal Education and Conduct (ACLEC), *First Report on Legal Education and Training* (London, HMSO, 1996).

[7] See e.g. C. Reasons and D. Chappell, "Continental Capitalism and Crooked Lawyering" (1987) 26 *Crime & Social Justice* 38.

the last—share a common premise: that law schools can and should operate as the moral preceptors of the legal profession. If students are properly instructed, the argument runs, they will behave more "ethically" when they arrive in practice, although there is no clear agreement on what constitutes "ethical" behaviour. Underlying this argument is an assumption—seldom made explicit—of a cause-and-effect relationship between instruction in legal ethics and ethical behaviour in professional practice. But both the argument and the assumption are problematic.

There is in fact no demonstrated connection between instruction in legal ethics and ethical behaviour.[8] Unethical behaviour seldom results from lack of knowledge about what is right or wrong: most serious "ethical" breaches involve theft or fraud or some other criminal conduct. Rather, such behaviour results from structural influences within the profession or the larger society which shape the conduct of lawyers in particular circumstances.[9] Moreover, even if causality were demonstrated, the project might still be misconceived. Canadian law schools are in principle committed to providing a liberal education in law, not simply professional training. While familiarity with professional ethics is a legitimate expectation of those who seek admission to practice, that familiarity can and should be achieved through the articling experience and bar admission and professional training courses. Further, many Canadian law schools have a strong commitment to institutional autonomy, and tend to be wary of professional dictation in matters of curriculum and pedagogy, a reflection of their long struggle to free themselves from professional hegemony.[10] Institutional autonomy, moreover, is reinforced by the character and beliefs of many individual legal academics who chose to teach law precisely because they wished to take their distance from the profession's values and *modus operandi*. Thus, it is unrealistic to expect law schools and law professors to use their mandate to teach legal ethics so as to indoctrinate students with the official version of professional norms. And finally, few law schools and legal academics would accept that students should be tested for ethical "competence": a course in legal ethics—like a course in, say, real estate or labour law—requires only that students study the syllabus, not that they believe in it.

For all of these reasons, and others canvassed below, attempts to encourage or require instruction in legal ethics *simpliciter* have been largely unavailing,

---

[8] 30 years of intermittent teaching in this field have made me a sceptic, though not yet a cynic. My most disconcerting experience involved a student who was exposed to an ethical problem inserted in an early edition of my labour law casebook. 20 years on, my ex-student was disciplined, *inter alia*, for what the problem had specifically identified as a form of unethical advocacy.

[9] See J. Carlin, *Lawyers on their Own* (New Brunswick, Rutgers University Press, 1962) and *Lawyers' Ethics: A Survey of the New York City Bar* (New York, Russell Sage Foundation, 1966) for pioneering work in this area.

[10] A notorious—but not necessarily representative—episode in this struggle is recounted in C. I. Kyer and J. Bickenbach, *The Fiercest Debate: Cecil A. Wright, the Benchers, and Legal Education in Ontario 1923–1957* (The Osgoode Society, Ont., 1987).

and the subject barely exists as a viable pedagogic enterprise in most Canadian law schools

TEACHING LEGAL ETHICS IN CANADIAN LAW SCHOOLS

The Cotter Report,[11] showed that fourteen of twenty-one Canadian law schools claimed to offer a course in legal ethics; in fact only eight did so regularly, and in a mere three was such a course mandatory. In fact, while Cotter's data are somewhat unclear on this point, only half a dozen schools actually taught legal ethics in a separate course; in the others, legal ethics formed one topic amongst several in a broader course on legal profession. Overall, Cotter estimated, only about 25 per cent of Canadian law students are exposed to a course in which legal ethics are a significant part of the syllabus. This is particularly striking in view of the corresponding figures in the USA, where 95 per cent of the law schools offer a compulsory course in professional responsibility.[12]

Moreover, the Cotter Report shows that in about half of the law schools, legal ethics are taught by part-time lecturers—lawyers and judges—rather than full-time academics, and that the involvement of the latter was shrinking rather than expanding.[13] The Report further noted that virtually none of the full-time academics who taught legal ethics published academic articles in the field.[14] Absent the long-term commitment of academic instructors, absent adequate teaching materials,[15] absent academic analysis or critique—a point considered below—the subject clearly resides at the margins of the curriculum in most law schools. This is not to deny that, along with other courses perceived to be relevant to practice, it may nonetheless be taken quite seriously by some career-minded law students.

Finally, the Cotter Report rightly reminds us that in fact some teaching of legal ethics takes place elsewhere than in specific courses bearing the title of "legal ethics". The Report notes the "pervasive" presence of legal ethics issues in almost three hundred individual courses across the curriculum in various Canadian law schools. However, it concludes that:

[11] *Supra* n. 2. Brent Cotter, former law professor at Dalhousie University, now Deputy Attorney General of Saskatchewan, produced his report at the request of the Joint National Committee on Legal Education (representing the Federation of Law Societies and the Council of Canadian Law Deans). His research was conducted between 1987 and 1990, and the Report was published in 1990.

[12] *Supra* n. 2 at 2–20, 2–25.

[13] *Supra* n. 2 at 2–19.

[14] *Ibid.*

[15] The first self-described "student text"—an edited collection of previously published articles—appeared only in 1996: D. Buckingham, J. Bickenbach, R. Bronaugh, and B. Wilson (eds.), *Legal Ethics in Canada: Theory and Practice* (Toronto, Harcourt Brace, 1996). Unpublished teaching materials, in various stages of gestation, are in use at several law schools.

"The so-called institutional commitment of Canadian law schools to the teaching of professional responsibility pervasively is largely non-existent. Where such a commitment does exist, it has generally been unsuccessful as a teaching strategy or philosophy."[16]

Cotter also identifies legal clinics as a potentially important site of ethical instruction, notes their limitations, praises clinical teaching as "possibly the best means" of complementing systematic instruction in a dedicated ethics course, but concludes that the clinical strategy is expensive, and that "its promise has gone unfulfilled".[17]

Thus, it must be said that at many Canadian law schools few, if any, students are exposed to the subject of professional responsibility or legal ethics in anything resembling the structured and sophisticated way in which they are exposed to other bodies of substantive law and other systems of social ordering.

LEGAL ETHICS AND LEGAL SCHOLARSHIP

One of the greatest obstacles to teaching legal ethics in Canadian law schools is the almost total absence of a body of domestic scholarly literature on the subject. Cotter noted that very few legal academics conduct research or publish in the field. A recent search of the literature confirms this. Between 1985 and 1995, just over fifty publications of all kinds appeared in Canada which treated legal ethics as a primary theme. Of these, three were books: two fairly comprehensive—but intellectually unambitious—texts,[18] one a collection of previously published articles.[19] Most of the rest were either publications of governing bodies or articles by practitioners dealing with specific ethical issues or with discipline procedures. Only a dozen or so scholarly articles were published, whose perspectives ranged from the historical to the philosophical and sociological—but seldom a concern with the substance of ethical rules themselves. And while information is difficult to come by, over the past ten or twenty years only the merest handful of ongoing academic research programs have been concerned with legal ethics.[20]

Not only is the secondary literature scant at best; so too, until very recently, were primary materials—authoritative ethical codes and a corpus of ethical case law. In each Canadian province, a self-governing professional body is

---

[16] Cotter, *supra* n. 2, at 2–36.

[17] *Ibid.*, at 2–44.

[18] B. Smith, *Professional Conduct for Canadian Lawyers* (Toronto, Butterworths, 1989); G. Mackenzie, *Lawyers and Ethics: Professional Responsibility and Discipline* (Scarborough, Carswell, 1993).

[19] D. Buckingham *et al.* (eds.), *supra* n. 15.

[20] See e.g. B. Arnold and J. Hagan, "Self-Regulatory Response to Professional Misconduct within the Legal Profession", (1994) 31 *Can. Rev. Soc. & Anthrop.* 168; W. Pue, "Becoming 'Ethical': Lawyers' Professional Ethics in Early Twentieth Century Canada", (1990) 20 *Man. LJ* 227. The Westminster Institute for Ethics and Human Values, in conjunction with the Faculty of Law, University of Western Ontario, is engaged in a long-term project on legal ethics.

statutorily mandated to discipline lawyers for "professional misconduct", "conduct unbecoming a barrister and solicitor" or similarly vague language.[21] Only in the past twenty years has this vague statutory language has been supplemented in most provinces by a Code of Professional Conduct,[22] adapted from the model code of the Canadian Bar Association—a voluntary national body—and by detailed regulations concerning such matters as solicitors' accounts and trust funds. However, these Codes typically comprise statements of general principles, only slightly less vague than the legislation, and commentaries which are mostly hortatory, often contradictory and of uncertain legal import.[23] Nor is there a readily available body of decisional material which gives precision and point to the legislation, codes or commentaries. While disbarments and other serious sanctions are routinely publicised, the actual reasons for decision of discipline tribunals are not. Even in Ontario and British Columbia, leaders in this respect, only synopses of decisions are regularly reported to the profession,[24] although this situation may be changing: an on-line databank of discipline decisions has been initiated recently by a commercial firm in co-operation with the Federation of Law Societies of Canada.

On the other hand, it is questionable whether publication of reasons for decisions would advance matters very much: in many instances they do not appear to have much to do with the Code of Professional Responsibility or its provincial counterparts. For example, in 1987, the Law Society of Upper Canada (Ontario) provided its members with a *Professional Conduct Handbook*, its adaptation of the Canadian Bar's Code of Professional Responsibility. Alas: the *Handbook* does not include the Law Society's own regulations; it has not been updated in the ten years since it was issued; the most recent item in its bibliography is now twenty-five years old; and in twenty pages of end-notes it does not cite a single decision of any disciplinary tribunal or court which interprets the language of the Code or, indeed, any case, book, article or statute later than 1972.[25] In other words, Canada's

[21] In addition, in some Canadian jurisdictions, lawyers are specifically liable to suspension or disbarment if incapacitated by mental or physical disabilities or drug or alcohol abuse, and in a few are liable to be disciplined for incompetence.

[22] The CBA's first Code was adopted in 1920, and was modelled closely on a code which had been adopted by the American Bar Association in 1908. The 1920 Code—which had never been amended, litigated or authoritatively discussed for half a century—was replaced by an entirely new Code in 1974, which was itself amended in 1986.

[23] A court has held that when the Law Society adopted the Code of Professional Conduct, even though it did do so pursuant to its power to enact subordinate legislation, the provisions of the Code and its commentaries acquired a quasi-governmental character sufficient to require compliance with the Canadian Charter of Rights and Freedoms, see *Klein* v. *Law Society of Upper Canada, Dvorak* v. *Law Society of Upper Canada* (1985) 50 Ont. Rep. 118 (Div. Ct.).

[24] This practice began only in 1992 in Ontario.

[25] All of the decisions cited in the endnotes to the Code are court decisions. However, the courts play no role in professional discipline, other than by way of judicial or appellate review of decisions of professional discipline tribunals, essentially on administrative law grounds. Thus, most of the decisions cited involve the courts applying the law of contracts, torts or crime to lawyers, together with a few *obiter dicta* concerning professional conduct, some of them pronounced in nineteenth-century England.

largest legal professional governing body has not yet attempted to develop and disseminate a *corpus juris* of legal ethics which probes, refines or illustrates either the statutory provisions under which it operates or its CBA-inspired code of professional conduct. Can we really expect that if the norms of professional behaviour are so casually treated by their official authors, they will actually shape lawyers' behaviour, inform subsequent decision-making, provoke professional debate, or provide the raw materials for academic teaching and research?

This cavalier attitude to the Code and to the need to develop and disseminate a jurisprudence of ethics is somewhat surprising. After all, the essence of lawyers' knowledge, their very stock-in-trade, is the law—legislation and common law; central to their ideology is the rule of law, the notion that decisions affecting people's rights must be taken in accordance with the law. But in its own internal legal-ethical system, the profession has not developed a body of "law", in the absence of which professional discipline can be said to be conducted in accordance with the rule of law only in the most nominal sense. Or, to make the same point more pragmatically, how can the profession expect its members to develop sensitivity to ethical issues if its own Code is so carelessly presented, so casually disseminated, so badly updated, so seldom adverted to and, in effect, so rarely enforced?

This, of course, brings us back to the teaching of legal ethics. Without authoritative "legislation", without a body of case law, without descriptive materials, without an integrative, reflective or critical literature of legal ethics, we lack the raw material to give students an intellectual experience comparable to what they receive in even the most mundane substantive course. The intellectual impoverishment of the subject in turn gives rise to pedagogic problems which explain, perhaps, the penchant for using judges and practitioners, rather than academics, to teach the subject. The former are likely to bring to it what the latter lack: a talent for the anecdotal and a willingness to settle for the unproblematic. Given the difficulty of mounting proper courses in legal ethics, attention shifts to the possibilities of teaching the subject in law school clinical programmes or during the apprenticeship phase of practical training, in the context of practical encounters where experiential learning occurs. However, experiential learning requires that students place the real life problems within a framework of systemic analysis and critique[26]—the very thing, alas, which is most lacking in the scant Canadian literature on legal ethics.

Obviously, it might be possible to teach or write about legal ethics in Canada, seriously and with intellectual ambition, by drawing on the American literature. That literature is extensive and much of it is very good; but it is not necessarily pertinent for Canadian scholars and students. The structure of professional governance in Canada differs considerably from that of the dominant American models; the demography and political economy of the

---

[26] J. Hathaway, "Clinical Legal Education" (1987) 25:1 *Osgoode Hall LJ* 239.

profession, while related, exhibit important differences; our political and legal cultures, while obviously influenced by those of the United States, diverge in many respects. To reiterate a previous observation: the absence of indigenous materials creates an almost insurmountable barrier to teaching and scholarly research in legal ethics in Canadian law schools; and to editorialise: so it should.

THE ETHiCAL ECONOMY OF THE LEGAL PROFESSION

The teaching of legal ethics is deeply implicated in what I have elsewhere termed the "ethical economy" of the profession.[27] In this ethical economy, the profession's treatment of discipline reflects a tendency to allocate its scarce resources of staff time, public credibility and internal political consensus to those disciplinary problems whose resolution provides the highest returns to the profession with the least risk of adverse consequences. "Returns" in this context means the enhancement of public goodwill or professional solidarity; "risks" means the possibility of damaging either of these. This ethical economy, I argue, produces a situation in which governing bodies direct virtually all their attention to two types of behaviour: clear dishonesty (especially in regard to clients' funds), and subversion of the profession's regulatory processes.

The modest available empirical evidence supports this thesis. Only a small percentage of complaints against lawyers end up in full-scale discipline hearings. The vast majority—over 95 per cent according to one estimate[28]—are disposed of informally. The decision to deal with complaints informally involves the exercise of discretion by the prosecutorial staff of the governing body, acting within specific policy guidelines or according to tacit understandings.[29] Informal disposition can lead to apologies, admonitions and other corrective measures; however discipline such as suspensions and disbarment can only be imposed following a formal hearing.[30] The pattern of cases which survive through to formal disposition is therefore a relatively accurate guide to what the professional body perceives as providing returns worthy of the risks involved; conversely, cases which are dealt with informally are those

---

[27] H. W. Arthurs, "Climbing Kilimanjaro: Ethics for Postmodern Professionals" (1993) 6:1 *Westminster Affairs* 3, and "The Dead Parrot: Does Professional Self-Regulation Exhibit Vital Signs?" (1995) 33 *Alta. Law Rev.* 800.

[28] J. Brockman and C. McEwen, "Self-Regulation in the Legal Profession: Funnel In, Funnel Out, or Funnel Away?" [1990] *Can. J. Law & Soc.* 1.

[29] B. Arnold and J. Hagan, *supra* n. 20.

[30] In Ontario, the largest provincial bar, and the locus of most empirical research on the subject, discipline is handled by staff lawyers who dispose of cases informally, screen them and, if they are serious, send them forward for formal disposition by a committee of Benchers (the governing body). While the committee has power to impose reprimands and minor sanctions, suspension and disbarment can only be imposed by Convocation, the Benchers' plenary body, and is subject to appeal to the courts (which is rare).

regarded as either too trivial or too risky for formal disposition. Incompetence is a case in point. Virtually no lawyers are disciplined for incompetence *per se*[31] because, I would argue, the underdeveloped and contested nature of legal-professional knowledge makes proof of incompetence almost impossible in all but the most egregious cases, and because new initiatives to discipline lawyers for incompetence would create political turmoil within the profession.[32]

By contrast, where there is a high degree of consensus over ethical standards, and little risk of political repercussions, discipline is likely to be imposed. In fact, over time and, so far as evidence is available, across space, the pattern of formal discipline has been quite consistent. A pioneering study of disbarred Ontario lawyers through a twenty-year period from 1945 to 1965 revealed that 83 per cent were disbarred for misappropriation of clients' funds or other financial wrongdoing.[33] A second Ontario study, covering the period 1975–6 showed that virtually all formal discipline proceedings involved either wrongful dealings with clients' funds, fraudulent or criminal conduct or regulatory offences—principally failing to keep proper accounts or failing to respond to inquiries from the Law Society.[34] A British Columbia study of discipline proceedings against lawyers during the period 1979–89 showed that the great majority of cases sent forward for formal adjudication and sanctions—especially disbarment—were likely to involve financial wrongdoing or other conduct which is at least arguably criminal.[35] And a particularly careful study covering complaints against Ontario lawyers from 1979–86 produced similar data.[36]

The results of a small updating study undertaken in connection with this paper suggest that the position has not changed much into the mid-1990s. The great majority of lawyers who were subject to serious discipline in Ontario during this period were in fact charged with financial irregularities including fraud, misappropriation of funds and breach of trust, or with other criminal behaviour. Many of these—and all of the remaining lawyers—were charged with regulatory offences, including failure to keep proper books of account, failure to respond to inquiries from the Law Society, failure to honour undertakings given to the Society and, an arcane offence of dubious origins, being "ungovernable". While in a limited number of instances charges were laid alleging offences of a different type—such as misconduct in court, conflicts with other solicitors or failure to render diligent service to clients—in virtually all such cases, regulatory offences or financial offences were also alleged. Whether by design or by accident, this pattern of multiple charges has enabled

---

[31] B. Reiter, *Discipline as a Means of Assuring Continuing Competence* (unpublished study for the Professional Organizations Committee, Ontario, 1978).

[32] H. W. Arthurs, "A Lot of Knowledge is a Dangerous Thing: Will the Legal Profession Survive the Knowledge Explosion" (1995) 18:2 *Dalhousie LJ* 295.

[33] S. Arthurs, "Discipline in the Legal Profession in Ontario" (1970) 7 *Osgoode Hall LJ* 235.

[34] B. Reiter, *supra* n. 31, Table VII, 431.

[35] J. Brockman and C. McEwen, *supra* n. 28.

[36] B. Arnold and J. Hagan, *supra* n. 20.

the Law Society to deal with almost all serious cases efficiently, on relatively straightforward grounds, rather than having to become involved in the adjudication of difficult cases involving controversial ethical questions. This is precisely what one would expect in a regulatory system governed by principles of ethical economy.

Many provisions of the Code are seldom discussed and almost never enforced. Some of these provisions relate to the societal obligations of the profession, such as the duty "to encourage public respect for and to improve the administration of justice" and "to make legal services available to the public".[37] Others, including provisions relating to competitive practices within the profession, attract very infrequent attention; in the updating study only one out of four hundred and seventy-two charges (0.2 per cent) involved competitive practices. And, perhaps most surprising, although about 12 per cent of all charges in the study involved the failure of lawyers to serve clients diligently or to keep them informed, there was not a single straightforward charge of failure to render competent service, a specific provision of the Code.[38] There are things which might be said about these odd statistics: that societal obligations are meant not to control lawyers' behaviour but to offer symbolic reassurance to the public; that efforts to enforce limits on competition are fraught with legal and political danger; that competence is difficult to define and perhaps best dealt with by non-disciplinary strategies; that hortatory language has educational and inspirational value. Nonetheless, given that so much of the Code of Professional Conduct excites so little attention from professional bodies, one must ask whether it is worth the attention of law students.[39]

In fact, further investigation of the ethical economy yields conclusions which are potentially even more disconcerting. Those ethical rules which are enforced are enforced very unevenly. Studies have long demonstrated that serious disciplinary sanctions are directed primarily at solo practitioners or those in small partnerships.[40] The updating study confirms these findings: approximately 79 per cent of those disciplined were solo practitioners, and 16.4 per cent members of small firms. This is a considerable over-representation of solo

---

[37] Law Society of Upper Canada, *Professional Conduct Handbook*, Rules 11 and 12; Can. Bar Association, *Code of Professional Conduct*, 1987, Rules XIII and XIV.

[38] Cf. B. Reiter, *supra* n. 31.

[39] To be sure, many subjects are studied in law schools which are largely ignored by the legal practitioners and professional governing bodies—the history, philosophy, economics, sociology and institutional structure of law to name just a few. There is no reason why legal ethics could not be studied from a similar external perspective, as way of gaining insights into law's causes and consequences. But such an approach to legal ethics—as an object, rather than as a subject, of study—is hardly what proponents of teaching in this field usually have in mind. Nor is it inappropriate to expose law students to the intellectual study of practical ethics, using lawyers' behaviour as a case in point. But such exposure does not necessarily have as its objective the internalisation of the Code of Professional Conduct; indeed, it may conduce to conduct which is seriously at variance with the Code, and with the conventional practices of lawyers as well.

[40] S. Arthurs, *supra* n. 33; B. Arnold and J. Hagan, "Careers of Misconduct: The Structure of Prosecuted Professional Deviance Among Lawyers" [1992] *Am. Soc. Rev.* 771.

practitioners[41] and likely of small firms as well. The updating study also suggests that geographical location may affect exposure to discipline, with a slight over-representation of lawyers from outside the downtown core and suburbs of Toronto.[42] This is probably because within the legal profession, geography serves somewhat as a proxy for class: large corporate law firms and prestigious niche practices are concentrated in the core area of Toronto, the commercial capital of Canada and the provincial capital of Ontario, and, to a lesser degree, in Ottawa, the national capital; in addition some mid-sized firms are located in cities across the province. By contrast, lawyers in suburban locations and smaller communities are more likely to be solo practitioners or members of small firms serving a local clientele, often in routine and not particularly remunerative matters.

The unevenness of enforcement has a yet more problematic aspect. There is serious debate over the disproportionate burden of discipline which falls on solo practitioners. Are solo practitioners targeted because so much of their practice involves conveyancing, which has always presented attractive opportunities for misappropriation and fraud?[43] or because their position at the margins of the profession deprives them of collegial supports and controls? or because solo practice attracts a disproportionate share of individuals whose professional skills or personal characteristics mark them as marginal?[44] Or is there a more disturbing explanation?

Considerable evidence suggests that members of ethnic and religious minorities are over-represented in solo practice and small partnerships, as compared with elite firms.[45] More generally, it has been argued that solo practitioners comprise something of an underclass (the term is of course relative) and are vulnerable to discipline because they lack power and prestige, both within the profession[46] and within the pecking order of North American capitalism.[47] The ethical economy, then, shapes prosecutorial discretion by directing it towards the least powerful elements in the profession, but also by mobilising the full force of formal discipline proceedings against dishonesty and regulatory offences, two forms of misbehaviour which generate few controversies either within the profession or in the public mind.

To a significant extent, then, the enforcement of legal ethics can be read as an exercise in the imposition of social control by the privileged of the

[41] 24.7% of Ontario lawyers are solo practitioners: J. Hagan and F. Kay, *Gender in Practice: A Study of Lawyers' Lives* (New York, Oxford University Press, 1995), 208.

[42] Of those confronting serious disciplinary proceedings, 30% came from the core of the city and 30% from its suburbs. However, approximately 50% of the Ontario bar practises in Metropolitan Toronto.

[43] See B. Reiter, *supra* n. 31; S. Arthurs, *supra* n. 33.

[44] S. Arthurs, *supra* n. 33.

[45] See D. Stager with H. Arthurs, *Lawyers in Canada* (Toronto, University of Toronto Press, 1990); J. Hagan and F. Kay, *supra* n. 41.

[46] J. Hagan, M. Huxter and P. Parker, "Class Structure and Legal Practice: Inequality and Mobility Among Toronto Lawyers" (1988) 22:1 *Law & Soc.* 9.

[47] C. Reasons and D. Chappell, *supra* n. 7.

profession on the marginalised. However, this conclusion must be tempered by three considerations. First, especially during the late 1980s and early 1990s, lawyers in several large, prestigious firms were charged with serious offences, and were subjected to serious discipline (though it has been argued that they received relatively lenient treatment).[48] While the number is small in proportion to the total population of disbarred lawyers, it may nonetheless signal a changing trend. Secondly, the literature shows that the rising incidence of ethical violations correlates closely with declining economic conditions.[49] It is therefore hardly surprising that lawyers with the least possibility of shielding themselves from economic adversity—solo practitioners or members of small partnerships—are those most likely to succumb to temptation. Thirdly, if indeed some solo practitioners are professionally marginalised as the result of the same personal factors which predispose them to misconduct,[50] it is not surprising that solo practitioners should bear a disproportionate burden of professional discipline.

Finally, the available evidence does in fact seem to challenge the conventional assumption that instruction in legal ethics will alter behaviour. Given the failure of law schools to instruct students in legal ethics, one might expect that recent graduates would be over-represented in the ranks of those who commit serious violations. After all, young lawyers not only lack formal instruction; they have not yet had time to learn ethics by precept or personal experience. But in fact, the evidence is to the contrary. Few recent graduates become involved in serious disciplinary proceedings. In fact, almost 80 per cent of those formally disciplined had practised for eleven years or more and ethical misdemeanours are twice as common in the second decade of practice (43.5 per cent) as the first (21.6 per cent). While less than 10 per cent of these lawyers were under the age of 35, 33 per cent were between 36 and 45, and even more, 42 per cent, between 46 and 55. In other words, ethical lapses generally occur when lawyers are at the peak of their powers, but also at the point of maximum opportunity and motive to misbehave; when they have been in practice long enough to be entrusted with considerable responsibility, but also long enough to learn how to steal; and when they have had every opportunity to be exposed to ethical issues and become sensitive to ethical standards, but also when they are experiencing pressure finally to realise their life's ambitions.

CONCLUSION

In sum, to the extent that proposals for teaching legal ethics stem from a desire to improve the ethical behaviour of lawyers, the project seems to be

---

[48] See M. Crawford, "The Lang Michener Affair" (1990) 14:3 *Can. Law.* 27, B. McDougall, "The Rise and Fall of a Rainmaker" (1992) 16:7 *Can. Law.* 14.

[49] B. Arnold and J. Hagan, *supra* n. 40.

[50] S. Arthurs, *supra* n. 33.

misconceived. Most aspects of the ethical code are not taken seriously by the profession's own governing body, and greater knowledge of the whole code will hardly affect the incidence of serious discipline proceedings. The primary determinants of ethical misbehaviour appear to be structural rather than informational, and instruction in legal ethics will not affect the capacity of marginal individuals, primarily those in solo practice, to resist temptation, pressure or targeted enforcement procedures. And, finally, the low incidence of ethical problems amongst young lawyers, closest to their educational experience, suggests that instruction in this as in other matters, is wasted on the young; it is more senior lawyers, who have been in practice two or three decades, who can profit from it most.

If, then, structural factors are so influential in the administration of professional discipline, and if professional discipline is largely carried on without reference to the Code of Professional Conduct, it is surely inappropriate to teach legal ethics as if the Code were simply an authoritative and self-contained body of rules, to be taken seriously by all intending lawyers because its provisions are all applied thoughtfully and fairly to all who come under its purview.[51] It follows that if legal ethics are to be taught rigorously and honestly, this must be done within a full understanding of the context, with an appreciation of how professional discipline is actually administered and, more generally, of the profession's role in society. However, to contextualise is to subvert. To paraphrase, no one who sees food prepared or legal ethics administered is likely to maintain much of an appetite. Teaching ethics with a full awareness of how discipline is exercised will hardly reinforce professional solidarity or promote respect for the institutions and symbols of the profession, including its ethical code.

---

[51] See H. P. Glenn, "Professional Structures and Professional Ethics" (1990) 35 *McGill LJ* 425.

7

Lawyers Behaving Badly: Where Now in Legal Education for Acting Responsibly in Australia?

ANDREW GOLDSMITH* and GUY POWLES**

One of the greatest failings of the organised bar in the century since the American Bar Association was founded is that it has fought innovations. When greater competition has come to the legal profession, when no-fault systems have been adopted, when lawyers have begun to advertise—in short, when the profession has accommodated the interests of the public, it has done so only when forced to.[1]

[T]he high ethical standards of the profession . . . have been very much grounded in the close-knit professional communities represented by such institutions as the Inns of Court and local law societies. As the organizations in which law is practised become larger and more complex, as competition and instability in the market for legal services increases, and as many legal practitioners experience a growing sense of insecurity, there are real dangers that professional standards will be threatened unless counter-balancing steps are taken to reinforce ethical values.[2]

I. INTRODUCTION

The moral authority of lawyers is in crisis. In Australia, at a time when universities are producing law graduates in unprecedented numbers, the external

* This chapter is part of work done under a Large Grant from the Australia Research Council. Its assistance is gratefully acknowledged. His thanks go also to Christine Parker for reading and commenting upon an earlier draft. Portions of this chapter have appeared previously in his "Heroes or Technicians? The Moral Capacities of Tomorrow's Lawyers" (1996–7) 14 *Journal of Professional Legal Education* 1. The consent of the journal editors to use parts of this earlier chapter was much appreciated.

** Research for this chapter was assisted by work done under a Small Grant of the Australian Research Council which reviewed the ethical rules of Australian legal professional bodies and for which the research assistance of Marilyn Head is gratefully acknowledged.

[1] President Jimmy Carter, "The Law and Lawyers Serving the Ends of Justice" (speech to the Los Angeles County Bar Association, 4 May 1978) (1978) 52 *Australian Law Journal* 410 at 413.

[2] The Lord Chancellor's Advisory Committee on Legal Education and Conduct, *First Report on Legal Education and Training* (London, ACLEC, 1996), 17.

environment for the legal profession has probably never been so demanding. The impact of Federal government intervention (including the application of its competition policy to the professions), greater competition for legal work from other professions and renewed calls for greater accountability by the professions have caught the Australian legal profession largely unprepared. The unanticipated nature of many of these pressures has caused the legal profession in many instances to act reactively and defensively. It has been very much on the back foot. Strategically and tactically, the legal profession has allowed itself to be outmanœuvered on a raft of issues. Of course, it may be said that the practical significance of some of the changes produced has not altered fundamentally the lawyers' role, that lawyers continue to serve adequately the interests of their corporate and large commercial clients and that Australian law schools produce technically competent lawyers, but the profession's claims to autonomy, innovation and public spiritedness lack substance. Lawyers could be doing better.

Without question, law schools in Australia have not done enough to promulgate and promote more substantive conceptions of legal competence and professional responsibility.[3] But it would be a mistake for anyone to think that law schools operate in a vacuum in such matters.[4] Indeed, in our view, the legal profession itself has been guilty of gross dereliction of duty in both obvious and more insidious ways. The first section of this chapter will demonstrate how, in Australia, progress with attempts to raise ethical awareness amongst practitioners and students has been seriously retarded by the profession's unwillingness to articulate what practitioners consider to be the essential requirements of professional duty and ethical obligation. At a more fundamental level, professional leaders on the whole have been blind to the importance of developing strategies to address the whole question of the ethical conduct of practitioners and the public's perception of them.[5] As types and structures of legal practice diversify and professional collegiality disintegrates, inaction has caused ground to be lost which it will now be almost impossible to make up. Unless the professional bodies contribute meaningfully to thinking about how professional and ethical standards can be raised through educational processes, and are willing also to contribute resources to the enterprise, it may well be doomed. This chapter will look at the nature of the deficit and where the responsibility lies for such few remedial measures as may still be feasible.

For their part, we suggest that law schools and other professional training programmes have failed to ensure that law students are provided with a the-

---

[3] Goldsmith, "Heroes or Technicians? The Moral Capacities of Tomorrows Lawyers" (1996–7) 14 *Journal of Professional Legal Education.*

[4] See Robert Granfield, *Making Elite Lawyers: Visions of Law at Harvard and Beyond* (New York, Routledge, 1992); Andrew Goldsmith, "Warning: Law School Can Endanger Your Health!" (1995) 21 *Monash University Law Review* 272.

[5] For a recent study and account of legal professional regulation in Australia, see Christine Parker, *Lawyers' Justice, Lawyers' Domination: Regulating the Legal Profession for Access to Justice* (unpublished PhD thesis, Australian National University, Mar. 1997).

oretically as well as practically challenging education. Both are necessary, we argue, for conceptualising the professional responsibility of lawyers in terms of the goals of *public service* and *justice*. In drawing attention to the joint complicity of law schools and the profession in the moral and practical short-comings of lawyers as a group and individually, we contrast what we call the *replicative* model of professional formation with the *transformative* model as a way of developing our argument about the limitations of present approaches, the necessary scope of legal knowledge and the kinds of approaches we should be pursuing. Pedagogical approaches based upon narrow conceptions of legal competence, which fail to examine closely or crit-icise current professional conventions, misrepresent the diversity of actual and possible approaches to legal practice and stifle its future development.

We argue in this chapter that the issue of lawyers' professional responsi-bility should not disappear in the thicket of talk about competition policy, markets for professional services and efficiency gains through specialisation and law firm expansions. Professional responsibility, we suggest, requires more than plain technical capacity as lawyers and conformity to the ethical codes, statute and case law relevant to professional practice. In contrast to this *thin* conception of lawyerly competence, professional responsibility also necessitates consideration of a variety of social relationships and, in particu-lar, the actual and possible consequences of deploying various legal devices and techniques for those relationships. Education for a *thick* conception of legal professional competence, the subject of the second part of the chapter, requires the development of moral as well as practical capacities, aptitudes and abilities grounded in a realistic understanding of the range of social inter-ests influenced by law. We believe law students need to be taught and reminded that behaving well in a professional capacity requires at times the ability and willingness to act "across the grain",[6] that is, to be prepared to ignore professional conventions when they unwarrantedly ignore other perti-nent considerations and obligations.[7] Acting responsibly is not the same as behaving like moral saints[8] or mythical heroes. But it does require that lawyers become occasional, indeed if only local, heroes in their daily lives and practices.[9] Thus, the dereliction of the legal profession in Australia in

[6] On the notion of acting courageously, see Douglas Walton, *Courage: A Philosophical Investigation* (Berkeley, Calif., University of California Press, 1986).

[7] Professionals, like other members of society, occupy positions in which they are subjected to intersecting, and often conflicting, obligations by reason of their multiple "memberships" of dif-ferent social groupings (e.g. clubs, trade unions, churches, ethnic affiliations, etc.). On the impact of these memberships for responsible professional practitioners, see Larry May, *The Socially Responsive Self: Social Theory and Professional Ethics* (Chicago, Ill., University of Chicago Press, 1996).

[8] It is not at all clear that lawyers can or should be purely saintly in their professional com-mitments. See Susan Wolf, "Moral Saints" (1982) 79 *Journal of Philosophy* 419.

[9] By "local heroes", we suggest the importance of professionals acting courageously and inde-pendently in their immediate settings, rather than having to take action of mythical proportions. Inevitably, they encounter localised injustices revealed in the course of their professional lives, which their professional skills and knowledge have some potential to ameliorate or remove. On

promoting greater professional responsibility and the theoretical and strategic prospects for re-orienting legal education towards this end are the twin themes of this chapter.

II. THE PROFESSION'S DERELICTION

(a) The Demise of Traditional Legal Practice

While lawyers have always varied in their backgrounds and approaches to practice, there can be no doubt about the greater diversity of backgrounds and fragmentation of fields of practice among lawyers in recent years. The extraordinary expansion of lawyer numbers,[10] driven largely by the growth in law school numbers,[11] the consequent pressures upon the legal job market and the trend to larger law firms have taken place alongside new norms of productivity, profit-orientation and specialisation in the legal workplace.[12] There has also been increased pressure from outside the profession for greater accountability, principally through external regulation.[13] In many senses, then, the nature of the legal profession and legal practice has significantly and irrevocably changed.[14] However, despite all this movement, there is little evidence that public estimations of lawyers have improved as a consequence of these changes. Lawyers as a group are perceived to be guilty of excessive charging and general self-interest, and of showing indifference towards areas of legal need. Any public awareness of lawyers being collectively committed to altruistic public service, or of them contributing statesman-like figures to the

the importance of local moral criticism, see Michael Walzer, *Thick and Thin: Moral Argument at Home and Abroad* (Notre Dame, University of Notre Dame Press, 1994), 51.

[10] According to statistics produced by Christine Parker, there were 16,100 lawyers in practice in Australia in 1983, whereas by 1993 there were over 29,000: Parker, "An Oversupply of Law Graduates? Putting the Statistics in Context" (1993) 4 *Legal Education Review* 255, 262.

[11] The number of law schools in Australia doubled between 1987 and 1995, with yet another, University of Notre Dame, scheduled to come into operation in the near future. The Australian position stands in stark contrast with the Canadian, where there have been no new law schools created in the same period. The impact of the Australian changes on numbers of law students has been substantial, with the traditional law schools reducing their intakes only slightly, if at all. In 1994, there were nearly 22,000 law students enrolled in Australian universities, while the number of practising lawyers for Australia stood at just below 30,000: See Centre for Legal Education, *Newsletter* (July 1994).

[12] See e.g. Marc Galanter and Thomas Palay, "The Transformation of the Big Law Firm" in Robert Nelson, David Trubek and Rayman Solomon, *Lawyers' Ideals/ Lawyers Practices: Transformations in the American Legal Profession* (Ithaca, NY, Cornell University Press, 1992).

[13] Reports of the Trade Practices Commission and other federal and State government inquiries, and the legal profession's response, are discussed below. For an analysis of the changing discourse around lawyer accountability in Australia, see Christine Parker, "Converting the Lawyers: The Dynamics of Competition and Accountability Reform" (paper delivered at the Australian Sociological Association Conference, Newcastle, 1995).

[14] For an overview of changes in Australia to 1992, see David Weisbrot, *Australian Lawyers* (Sydney, Longmans,1990) and "Competition, Cooperation and Legal Change" (1993) 4 *Legal Educ. Rev.* 1.

nation's public life,[15] if either image ever had much foundation in reality, has largely dissipated.

Some changes have been widely seen as positive, however. Greater access to legal study has meant, to some extent at least, a larger and more diverse pool of potential entrants to the profession.[16] While the increasing number of women students has been the most significant change of this kind in Australia,[17] the composition of the overall profession has also changed discernibly in terms of ethnic mix and social background.[18] This is not to say that questions of equity have largely disappeared, especially in relation to indigenous persons. Nevertheless, the longstanding Anglo-Australian male middle class domination of the legal profession is a little less secure now. The composition, therefore, as well as the size and organisation of the profession is noticeably different. Inevitably, changes of all types test the foundations of the legal profession as a single organised entity. They facilitate the questioning, at least in certain sectors of the profession, of the validity or importance of particular professional doctrines and practices. Current gender-based concerns about the discriminatory effects of some work practices in large law firms is an example of the signs of growing professional dissonance.[19] A further dichotomy is that which separates the interests of the mega-firms generally from those of the rest of the profession. The recent self-consciousness by some leaders of the profession about preserving professional unity[20] is another indication that professional consensus and a shared identity are increasingly problematic. Yet we have seen little tangible evidence to suggest a real concern among the leaders of the profession about the challenges of professional legal responsibility and of its importance as a component of legal education and professional practice.

[15] This image is cherished and lamented by Anthony Kronman: see Kronman, *The Lost Lawyer: Failing Ideals of the Legal Profession* (Cambridge, Mass., Harvard/Belknap, 1993). While many Australian politicians are legally trained, their significance in parliament is commonly rated in terms of their ubiquity and verbosity, rather than by reference to any supposed public benefits from their legal training or professional background.

[16] In a recent paper, Jack Goldring has described the changes in law school admissions as "not markedly" altering the social profile of law students. While the composition now reflects far more women than before, there are fewer mature age and part-time students and the proportion coming from affluent middle class backgrounds remains similar. The representation of non-traditional groups among law students is, hardly surprisingly, greater among the newer law schools located outside the city centres: see Goldring, "A Social Profile of New Law Students in NSW and Victoria—1996" (manuscript, Nov. 1996).

[17] Women have constituted more than 50% of the LL B.intake at Monash since 1989 (statistics compiled by Peter Balmford).

[18] Weisbrot, *supra* n. 14, ch. 4.

[19] See Margaret Thornton, *Dissonance and Distrust: Women in the Legal Profession* (Melbourne, Oxford University Press, 1996).

[20] See e.g. MacCrate, *Legal Education and Professional Development—An Educational Continuum: Report of the Task Force on Law Schools and the Profession: Narrowing the Gap* (Chicago, Ill., American Bar Association, 1992), at 119, where the "survival of a single public profession" is articulated as an express desideratum. In Australia over the last 3 years, the Law Council, representing State bodies, is now pushing hard for national blueprints and models (see *infra* nn. 37–40).

(b) A Matter of Professional Myopia?

> "Stephen Giller's biting observation [is] that young lawyers lack ethical standards not because they've been poorly taught in law school but because their experience on their first job tells them nobody cares."[21]

The Australian legal profession and legal educators appear to share a weighty responsibility. For its part, the profession has failed itself, and the society which it serves, in coming too late to the realisation that the ethical development of lawyers requires strategic planning and significant input from the profession itself. Lawyers have lost ground so badly in their attempts to secure public esteem and sustain professional morale that some explanation is called for. The story must bring to mind the apparent Australian blindness to dramatic developments which unfolded on two stages overseas—namely, regulatory reform commenced in England under Prime Minister Thatcher and the campaign for professional responsibility in the United States.

Also, it would seem that, in Australia, the discovery has been made only recently that the capacity of the lawyer to handle ethical issues appropriately is not something with which one is born, nor is it likely to be acquired in brief encounters, such as might occur in short pre-admission classes on "professional standards" or in subsequent sporadic exposure in legal practice.

This is not just a matter of oversight on the part of the profession; because it has failed to ensure that a well-defined and rigorous syllabus is adequately taught to all applicants for admission to practice—although there is still no sufficiently specific requirement on that score. Rather, the deficit is more fundamental and in this sense is probably also shared by most legal educators. It has to do with their acceptance of the way in which legal ethics are characterised as a set of principles and rules intended to assist the lawyer to recognise and balance competing claims. For example, duties to client are to be correctly identified and balanced against duties to wider notions of "the court", "the profession" and "the administration of justice". The function is mechanical, the professional disciplinary bodies determine how the "balance" should be achieved, and both process and outcome are portrayed as capable of being resolved without moral challenge.

From the educator's point of view, there has been a dearth of resources for learning—not only an absence of evidence of what "lawyers in action" regard as their ethical signposts, but also a lack of institutional foundation for the examination and articulation of professional thinking on the subject. In order to appreciate the magnitude of the problem, it may be useful to look briefly at some major factors which have inhibited progress and others which have distracted the profession from achieving any clear focus on the development

---

[21] Sol Linowitz (with Martin Mayer) *The Betrayed Profession: Lawyering at the End of the Twentieth Century* (Baltimore, Mld., Johns Hopkins University Press, 1994), 131.

of legal ethics in Australia. Only with an understanding of these can realistic strategies be planned.

(c) A Fragmented and Parochial Profession

The Australian legal profession is split in two ways. The first prompts the "Australian excuse"—federalism. Like the "Australian wave" (when appearing to brush flies from the face becomes an instinctive gesture), the task of reconciling the interests of eight jurisdictions (six States and two Territories) within the Commonwealth of Australia[22] has had problems, but some more imaginary than real. For legal professional bodies largely self-made and tied to their own courts and business centres, the development of national approaches to Australian issues was hindered by lack of interest, and the tardy, reactive character of their responses for which legal professions are notorious.[23]

Secondly, the entrenched barrister/solicitor distinction encouraged the duplication of professional bodies in each jurisdiction. In Queensland, New South Wales and Victoria the persisting structural division continues to attract government attention.[24] The other jurisdictions feature informal bar associations. In taking a firmly defensive stance on the amalgamation issue, the bar associations in the eastern States have tended to see themselves as leading the fight for "independence of the profession" and as guardians of ethical standards.[25] While expressing occasional irritation, the solicitors' branches of the profession in the eastern States generally accept the convenience of structural division and, correspondingly, have concerned themselves less with the ethics of the practice of law in the adversarial system.

Apart from occasional constitutional issues over the years, Australian lawyers have not been obliged to think nationally until recently.[26] The Labour government aroused the profession's interest nationwide when it introduced federal schemes for legal aid in 1973. Then, reform of the federal family law jurisdiction, followed by dramatic extensions of the federal court system, brought more Australian lawyers onto common ground. In the 1980s, further factors contributing to raise a national consciousness included the threat of federal competition policy, evidence of reform in the United Kingdom, recognition of the usefulness of the American Bar Association lobby in the

[22] Constitutional authority for the regulation of lawyers in Australia rests with each State and Territory, and the courts in each jurisdiction. In that sense, there are 8 professions.

[23] President Jimmy Carter, *supra* n. 1.

[24] Attempts by politicians last century to fuse or amalgamate the two branches of the profession were defeated in New South Wales and Queensland and only partially successful in Victoria—where changes brought into operation this year still allow separate practice to flourish under separate representative bodies. *Legal Practice Act* 1996 (Vic.).

[25] See e.g. the Victorian Bar Council publication, *The Victorian Bar: Its Work and Organisation* (Melbourne, VBA, 1990).

[26] Australia has no constitutional bill of rights to stimulate national interest in such issues.

United States and the first of a number of inquiries into the legal profession.[27] The two national associations of Australian lawyers have only very gradually asserted themselves.[28]

The Law Council of Australia, comprising representation from the law societies of the eight jurisdictions and the bar associations of the three eastern States, has appeared not to concern itself with legal education or ethics until this decade.[29] Following a legal education conference in 1991, some Council members were moved to make submissions to Canberra on the funding of law schools.[30] The Australian Bar Association, representing the members of the eastern bars and the separate associations formed in South Australia and Western Australia, came to look at ethical rules, and produced a "model code of conduct" for Australia, but that was not until 1993 and the Association's model is still not adopted by all of its constituencies.[31]

It is worth noting that the one attempt at consultation between the profession and law schools on a national basis, the Australian Legal Education Council, formed in 1977, died seven years later when the Law Council of Australia withdrew its financial support.[32] In 1987, the year in which the American Bar Association established a Commission on Professionalism and made recommendations aimed at strengthening ethics courses at law schools,[33] a government committee's survey of Australian law graduates was published expressing dissatisfaction with the law schools' role in professional skills development, including strong concern that law schools should remedy their failure to teach professional and ethical standards.[34] The Australian legal profession has made no obvious national contribution to the issue.

Any advancement in legal ethics at a national level has ridden on the coattails of initiatives aimed at mutual recognition of qualifications within Australia,[35] uniformity of admission requirements, agreement on other ingredients of a national market for legal services[36] and the promulgation of model rules of professional conduct and practice.[37] These moves were themselves

---

[27] The New South Wales Law Reform Commission, see *infra* nn. 43 and 44.

[28] See Weisbrot, *supra* n. 14, 188–92.

[29] This contrasts with the role of the American Bar Association in accrediting law schools, where since 1974 the ABA has required instruction in "the duties and responsibilities of the legal profession".

[30] Law Council of Australia, "Quality of Higher Education: Submission to the Higher Education Council" (Canberra, Law Council, April 1992). The funding of universities is primarily a federal responsibility in Australia.

[31] Australian Bar Association, *Code of Conduct* (Canberra, ABA, 1993), and see *infra* at the text associated with n. 94.

[32] Weisbrot, *supra* n. 14, 144.

[33] *Ibid.*, 19.

[34] *Ibid.*, 132.

[35] Mutual Recognition Act 1992 (Cth).

[36] Law Council of Australia, "Blueprint for the Structure of the Legal Profession: a National Market for Legal Services" (Canberra, Law Council, July 1994).

[37] Law Council of Australia, "Model Rules of Conduct and Practice: Proposed for Adoption in Each Australian State and Territory" (Canberra, Law Council, March 1996), and see *infra* at the text associated with n. 95.

part of the broader thrust towards uniform professional standards urged by government policy-makers.[38]

Historically, control over educational requirements for admission to practice rested with the senior judges in each jurisdiction,[39] who have stipulated courses, usually leaving the law schools to determine much of the content. The government-driven moves towards uniform professional standards led to a meeting of the nominees of chief justices of all jurisdictions[40] which, in 1992, published Uniform Admission Rules incorporating the pre-admission requirement of the study of eleven "areas of knowledge", of which "professional conduct (including trust accounting)" was one. There had been no consultation with the profession or law schools at a national level as to how this area of knowledge should be taught.[41]

(d) Re-regulation, Competition and Other Distractions

The leadership of the profession has quite naturally devoted most of its attention to the very real threats to self-regulation and monopoly at the State and Territory level.[42] Failure to heed warning signals kept the profession on the back foot. In New South Wales and Victoria, where nearly three-quarters of Australia's lawyers practise, the professional bodies searched for tactics with which to fend off reformist governments, and seemed to have little energy or inclination to examine the role of ethics and professional responsibility as part of a long-term strategy to restore public confidence.

As early as 1976, the New South Wales Law Reform Commission took up terms of reference for its inquiry into the State legal profession. Proposals for major structural and disciplinary reform which appeared in 1982[43] included reference to the US experience with ethical codes and the UK Benson Commission views on written professional standards. The NSW Commission recommended the preparation of a single "code of professional conduct" which would apply to both branches of the profession.[44] It was ten years before a "Draft Code of Ethics" appeared—and then for the solicitors' branch alone.[45]

---

[38] See Independent Committee of Inquiry, *Report on National Competition Policy* (Canberra, AGPS, 1993); the Hilmer Report; and Trade Practices Commission, *Study of the Professions: Legal: Final Report* (Canberra, AGPS, Mar. 1994).

[39] In some, judges and practitioners now comprise the majority membership of councils or boards which carry out the function. The new *Legal Practice Act* 1996 (Vic.) ensures representation from all law schools on the Victorian Council of Legal Education, but also preserves the authority of judicial officers and practitioners (s. 331).

[40] The Consultative Committee of State and Territory Law Admitting Authorities.

[41] Sam Garkawe, "Admission Rules" (1996) 21 *Alternative Law Journal* (3) 109.

[42] See Christine Parker, *supra* n. 5.

[43] NSWLRC, *First Report: General Regulation* and *Second Report: Complaints, Discipline and Professional Standards* (Sydney, NSWLRC, 1982).

[44] NSWLRC, *Second Report, ibid.*, chap. 10, Recommendation 25.

[45] Law Society of NSW, "Draft Code of Ethics" (1992) 118 *Caveat* 1.

The NSW Bar developed rules for its own members.[46] In the meantime, a statute introducing reforms had been passed, and subsequently implemented by further legislation.[47] Also, a second inquiry into the NSW profession had taken place and its recommendations on the need for ethical codes had concluded:

> "Legal ethics should be about defining and encouraging the provision of proper services having regard to general concerns about candour, fairness and social responsibility."[48]

The Law Society's final "Statement of Ethics" was published in 1994,[49] in which year also a comprehensive set of rules governing solicitors' conduct and practice had been made by the Law Society and approved by the Attorney General under the changed regulatory regime.[50]

To turn to Victoria, some parallels can be seen with the NSW experience, but the Melbourne-based profession has been even less inclined to pre-empt imposed reforms. Review of the divided structure of the Victorian profession and concerns for lack of guidance in ethical matters were in the air from the early 1980s. Tapping elements of long-standing community frustration with the profession,[51] La Trobe University hosted a conference in 1982 where senior practitioners clashed publicly.[52] In the following year, the Attorney General announced a government investigation of regulatory structure and restrictive practices,[53] which was ultimately referred to the Victorian Law Reform Commission.[54]

Perhaps the clearest single indictment of the Victorian profession's failure to address the ethical dimension of its responsibilities was seen nearly fifteen years ago when a group of younger members formed a Young Lawyers' Assembly, undertook studies of ethical issues in the Australian context and produced a three-part "Code of Legal Professional Ethics" covering such

[46] This was a rather loose collection until a revised compilation appeared in 1994 , introduced by a short statement of principles to parallel the solicitors' code (NSW Bar Association, *The NSW Barristers' Rules* (Sydney, NSW Bar Association, 1994)).

[47] *Legal Profession Act* 1987 and *Legal Profession Reform Act* 1993 (NSW).

[48] NSWLRC, *Scrutiny of the Legal Profession*, Discussion Paper (Sydney, NSWLRC, May 1992), para. 4.86.

[49] Law Society of NSW, "Statement of Ethics" (Nov. 1994) *Law Soc. J* 74.

[50] Law Society of NSW, *Professional Conduct and Practice Rules* (Supplement to *Law Soc. J*, May 1994) under s. 57B *Legal Profession Act* 1987 (NSW).

[51] The barristers' and solicitors' branches had effectively frustrated the legislature's intention to fuse them (*Legal Profession Practice Act* 1891) by maintaining a *de facto* division incorporating restrictive practices which the public believed increased cost and inhibited client redress against practitioners.

[52] For example, Brian Shaw, QC, Chair of the Victorian Bar Council, declared that recommendations for change mooted by the NSW Law Reform Commission (in Discussion Paper No. 2 (1979) on Complaints, Discipline and Professional Standards) were irrelevant to the profession in Victoria: see *Reforming the Organisation of the Legal Profession: Is the Victorian Profession Prepared?* (Melbourne, La Trobe University, 1982).

[53] "Full Text of the Attorney General's Statement" (1983) 57 *Law Institute Journal* 1270.

[54] See *infra* n. 61.

matters as the duty to make legal assistance available to the community, independence of judgement, client-loyalty, conflicts of interest and competency.[55] In presenting its Code, the working party was concerned to ensure that it would serve a number of distinct purposes, namely:

> "that it is positive in its terms; that it is rooted in the law, not in professional lore or self-interest; and that it serves as a teaching tool for law students and young practitioners."[56]

The Code has been neither re-issued since nor used in Law Institute, professional training or university publications. As far as we are aware, the young lawyers' challenge to their profession has gone unheeded.[57]

Having expressed concern at mounting external pressures,[58] in 1988 the leadership of the solicitors' branch sought to test the attitude of "rank and file" membership to proposals for reform, only to receive a resounding rebuff.[59] Indeed, the eyes of Victorian practitioners were firmly blinkered at a time when the news from the United Kingdom in the wake of the Lord Chancellor's proposals was that:

> "Never in its history has the legal profession been so uncertain about its prospects, so confused about its purpose and so polarised in its views about the future."[60]

In the early 1990s, the Law Reform Commission of Victoria published assessments of the profession which were regarded by the latter as ill-informed and unjustified. When the Commission recommended the publication in Australia of a collection of information on professional conduct presented in a manner useful for law students, like the American Bar Association's Canons of Professional Conduct, which "would be a great aid to practitioners and would enhance the teaching of professional conduct to intending lawyers",[61] the Bar and the Law Institute expressed "reservations about the degree of commonality possible".[62] No such publication has appeared in Victoria.

The Victorian Bar provided to its members in 1993 a consolidated revision of rules which already reflected the impact of pressures for the reduction in

---

[55] "A Code of Legal Professional Ethics" (1983) 1 *Lawyer* (No. 3) 1; (1983) 1 *Lawyer* (No. 5) 12; and (1984) *Lawyer* (No. 8) 8. This journal of the Young Lawyers' Assembly was supported by the Law Institute for 3 years, then discontinued. .

[56] (1983) 1 *Lawyer* (No. 3) 1.

[57] The Code is, of course, used for teaching purposes in subjects dealing with ethics and the profession taught at Monash and La Trobe Universities.

[58] "Letter to Members", President of the Law Institute, 18 Nov. 1987.

[59] Proposals to separate the "disciplinary" and "solicitor-support" functions of the Law Institute and to abolish the prohibition on "fee-advertising" were both rejected by over two-thirds of solicitors in a postal referendum ("Letter to Members", President of the Law Institute, 21 Dec. 1988).

[60] Marcel Berlins, writing in the *Financial Times* and reported in (Jan. 1988) 14 *Commonwealth Law Bulletin* 293.

[61] Law Reform Commission of Victoria, *Accountability of the Profession*, Discussion Paper No 24, July 1991, 15.

[62] LRCV, *Access to the Law*, Report No 48, July 1992, 22.

scope of restrictive practices.[63] The Law Institute's contribution, which appeared in the same year, was a massive loose-leaf collection of legislation, rules and discussion, described as a "handbook" of everything a solicitor could possibly need to know.[64] Arrangements were made for a reduced version to be printed for law students, but the lack of any useful articulation of ethical principles, coupled with the chaotic treatment of a selection of ethical rulings, greatly diminished the value of the publication.[65]

The recent re-regulation imposed upon the Victorian profession in many areas, including that of conduct rules, has not come without warning. In 1994, the Attorney General appointed a Working Party to investigate the profession[66] and disseminated a paper setting out her views.[67] These included her concern that responsibility for the key rules "crucial for the protection of the interests of the public and administration of justice"[68] could no longer be left to the professional bodies alone. Over objections from those bodies, the Working Party recommended that the legislature should enact "broad principles" to govern their rules, such as "the minimum content" of the rules and "the general qualities that they must display".[69]

The resulting statute now requires[70] that the recognised professional associations which have succeeded the Law Institute and Bar Association shall have practice rules for their members in which "the general principles of professional conduct [are] reflected". The accompanying statement of principles covers the field, from duties to client (due skill and diligence, promptness, confidentiality and the avoidance of conflicts of interest, excessive charging and conduct calculated to defeat the ends of justice) to the duties of honesty, candour, fairness and courtesy to be observed in the circumstances defined in the statement—together with the wider duty to act "in a manner conducive to advancing the public interest".[71]

In effect, section 64 constitutes the Attorney General's view of what the elements of a code of legal ethics should be. By taking this initiative to

---

[63] Victorian Bar Council, *Rules of Conduct and Practice*, May 1993. Further amendments in that direction followed in 1994 with new provisions relating to chambers, "direct access", "co-advocacy" and advertising.

[64] Law Institute of Victoria, *Members' Handbook* (Melbourne, Law Book Company, 1993).

[65] LIV, *Members' Handbook: Student Edition* (Melbourne, Law Book Company, 1993). The 2nd edn. in 1995 will be the last.

[66] Having abolished the Law Reform Commission, she was free to choose the Working Party.

[67] Jan Wade, *Discussion Paper: Reforming the Legal Profession—An Agenda for Change* (Melbourne, Attorney-General's Department, June 1994).

[68] *Ibid.*, 5.

[69] Attorney General's Working Party, *Reforming the Legal Profession* (Melbourne, Justice Department, Aug. 1995), 35.

[70] *Legal Practice Act* 1996 (Vic.), s. 72.

[71] *Legal Practice Act*, s. 64. The statement embodied in the s. appears to have drawn some inspiration from the NSW Law Society's "Statement of Ethics" (*supra* n. 49), with differences in emphasis. The language used in Victoria was attacked by a practitioner for being so vague as to be meaningless (M. Rickards, "Dangerous and Woolly Concepts" (1996) 70 *Law Institute Journal* (4) 6), which demonstrates a lack of understanding of the function of a statement such as this.

Parliament in the name of the public interest (as part of the broader reform package), the Attorney has drawn attention to the profession's failure to develop its own code. In the eyes of students and others who have followed these events, it would seem that the Victorian profession has been somewhat humiliated. Further, it may have damaged the cause of ethical development in another way. By failing to agree upon and adopt common ethical propositions in consultation with other Australian professional bodies, with a national code in mind, the Law Institute and Bar of Victoria have allowed a single State government to enshrine a particular set of principles in legislation, thereby putting off, for some time, any hope of achieving nation-wide consensus on the language to be used in such a code and the relative emphasis to be accorded to each of its elements.

The attention of the Australian profession has also been diverted away from ethics in a direction which, unlike worries about regulation and competition, is not the result of obvious external pressures. Law firms have decided that their first concern must be to "lift their game". Quality of service delivery to clients, taken to its ultimate in "total quality management", is seen as the way ahead, the way out of the thickening fog of low public esteem. Practitioners seem to treat ethical decision-making negatively, as a matter of risk analysis and management. This has involved the engagement of management experts by larger firms coinciding with computerisation of major aspects of practice, leading many practitioners to put restructuring of office organisation in the name of efficiency at the top of a list of priorities on which broader ethical considerations do not appear. Of course, they point with satisfaction at how conflicts of interest can be addressed by the new technology when a computer is enlisted in aid of early recognition of client–client conflict. It is significant that Law Book Company's latest major publication in Australia on the subject of legal practice devotes its nearly three hundred pages to providing "a strategic management framework . . . that will help practices to be profitable and competitive" without any significant reference to an ethical dimension.[72]

(e) Academia's Response: Too Little Too Late

Australia's law teachers seemed uninterested, unable to respond to developments in the USA, until a remarkable collection of extracted materials and commentary appeared in 1977, offering the basis for courses on the profession, its history, sociology, regulation and ethics.[73] Necessarily, the work drew

[72] David and Charis Stein, *Legal Practice in the 90s* (Sydney, Law Book Company, 1994). There is no index entry under "ethics", and only a half page devoted to the topic. The forward to the book, interestingly, is written by Professor Fred Hilmer, an acknowledged expert and adviser to the Federal Government on matters of competition policy.

[73] Julian Disney, John Basten, Paul Redmond and Stan Ross (eds.), *Lawyers* (Sydney, Law Book Co, 1977).

heavily on US writing for its treatment of ethical issues,[74] but this alone did not explain the continuing paralysis afflicting law schools. Turning into the 1980s, only two universities offered subjects devoted to professional responsibility.[75] Empirical studies had just begun to surface.[76] Significantly, the appearance in 1982 of a challenge to the myths surrounding lawyers and judges[77] reflected public rather than academic interest in the social status, inscrutability and self-regulatory independence of the profession. The work contributed to the pre-occupation with regulation and monopoly issues which characterised thinking about the legal profession in the 1980s[78] and, in turn, led to the statute-imposed reforms of the past ten years[79].

The first, and only, national study of the discipline of law teaching expressed in 1986 no particular concern for instruction in ethics or professional responsibility.[80] Writing about teaching legal ethics began in earnest just eight years ago, and, following assessments of teaching at the NSW College of Law, it offered among its conclusions the view that the negative attitudes of teachers and students to the subject of professional responsibility, highlighted in the American literature on law schools, were similarly experienced in the Australian practical training context.[81] In the 1990s, academics began to respond to clear messages from American colleagues[82] and calls such as that made by the NSW Law Reform Commission which asserted:

---

[74] This also featured strongly in the 2nd, and last, edn., Disney *et al.* (eds.), *Lawyers* (2nd edn., Sydney, Law Book Co, 1986), in addition to the welcome inclusion of the gradually increasing body of local material.

[75] Monash University and University of New South Wales.

[76] E.g. Margaret Hetherton, *Victoria's Lawyers* (Melbourne, Victoria Law Foundation, 1978) and *Victoria's Lawyers—Second Report* (Melbourne, Victoria Law Foundation 1981); Roman Tomasic (ed.), *Understanding Lawyers: Perspectives on the Legal Professions in Australia* (Sydney, George Allen & Unwin, 1978); Peter Cashman (ed.), *Research and the Delivery of Legal Services* (Sydney, Law Faculty of University of NSW, 1981); Roman Tomasic, "Social Organization Amongst Australian Lawyers" (1983) 19 *Australia New Zealand Journal of Sociology* 447, and *The Sociology of Law* (London, Sage, 1985); Pat O'Malley, *Law, Capitalism and Democracy* (Sydney, George Allen & Unwin, 1983); and the work of the NSW Law Reform Commission (see *supra*, nn. 43 and 44). The next significant study, which did not appear for some time, was that of David Weisbrot, *supra* n. 14, in 1990. Empirical work is still rare, but see for a recent example Adrian Evans, "Professional Ethics North and South: Interest on Clients' Trust Funds and Lawyer Fraud. An Opportunity to Redeem Professionalism" (1996) 3 *International Journal of the Legal Profession* (3) 281.

[77] Michael Sexton and Laurence Maher, *The Legal Mystique: The Role of Lawyers in Australian Society* (Sydney, Angus & Robertson, 1982).

[78] As discussed in the previous section, and see J. Nieuwenhuysen and M.Williams-Wynn, *Professions in the Marketplace* (Melbourne, Melbourne University Press, 1982).

[79] Such as the comprehensive provisions of the *Legal Profession Act* 1987 (NSW), the *Legal Profession Reform Act* 1993 (NSW), the *Legal Profession Act* 1993 (Tasmania), the *Legal Practitioners Act* 1995 (Queensland) and the *Legal Practice Act* 1996 (Victoria).

[80] D. Pearce, E. Campbell and D. Harding, *Australian Law Schools: A Discipline Assessment for the Commonwealth Tertiary Education Commission* (Canberra, AGPS, 1986).

[81] Colleen Segall, "The Teaching of Professional Responsibility and Its Role in the Socialisation of Lawyers" (1989) 7 *Journal of Professional Legal Education* (1) 55.

[82] Such as Ian Johnstone and Mary Treuthart, "Doing the Right Thing: An Overview of Teaching Professional Responsibility" (1991) 41 *Journal of Legal Education* 75.

"the study of legal ethics and professional responsibility should be an integral part of any law school programme. It is only during this formative period in a lawyer's education that there is opportunity for sustained study, discussion and reflection."[83]

It is strange that, having commissioned and received a stimulating paper on the role of legal ethics,[84] the Commonwealth Senate inquiry into the cost of legal services was content in 1993 to exhort the profession to action on ethical standards without addressing its remarks also to law teachers.[85]

A phenomenon offering much scope for the raising of ethical awareness was the law school clinic located in a community legal centre. When Monash University pioneered the concept for Australia over twenty years ago, it became apparent that a clinical programme involving the supervised student–client relationship, the representation of client and community interests and classroom review was in a unique position to draw out ethical issues. Although the term "clinical" is often applied to simulation and placement programmes now mushrooming in Australia, assessments of the Monash scheme show that it is the responsibility which the student feels for the client's problem which provides the truly testing—and therefore learning—experience. Australian academics are belatedly writing,[86] setting up new courses[87] and engaging in institutional activity.[88] This leads us to inquire into the nature and extent of the Australian material available.

---

[83] NSWLRC, *Scrutiny of the Profession*, Discussion Paper (Sydney, NSWLRC, May 1992), para. 4.98.

[84] Stephen Parker, *Legal Ethics,* Discussion Paper (Canberra, Senate Standing Committee on Legal and Constitutional Affairs, Feb. 1992).

[85] Senate Standing Committee on Legal and Constitutional Affairs, *The Cost of Justice: Foundations for Reform*, Report (Canberra, the Senate, Feb. 1993).

[86] Adrian Evans, "Developing Socially Responsible Lawyers" (1990) 15 *Legal Service Bulletin* (5) 218; Susan Burns, "Teaching Legal Ethics" (1993) 4 *Legal Education Review* (1) 41; and the first Australian book devoted to the subject, Stan Ross, *Ethics in Law: Lawyers' Responsibility and Accountability in Australia* (Sydney, Butterworths 1995). This was followed closely by another first, namely G. E. Dal Pont, *Lawyers' Professional Responsibility in Australia and New Zealand* (Sydney, LBC Information Services, 1996), which presents an analysis of the law across all of the jurisdictions, with references to the statutes and rules in each.

[87] University of Wollongong, see John Goldring, "What Do We Teach: Legal Ethics or Something Else?" (1992) 10 *Journal of Professional Legal Education* (1) 83. Monash University and University of NSW have now been joined by other law schools in offering substantial stand-alone courses devoted to the subject.

[88] E.g. the Institute for Law, Ethics and Public Affairs, established by Griffith University, Queensland, in 1992, contributed to the publication of Stephen Parker and Charles Sampford (eds.), *Legal Ethics and Legal Practice: Contemporary Issues* (Oxford, Clarendon, 1995); the Centre for Legal Education, Sydney, published a newsletter, *Teaching Professional Responsibility* during the years 1993 to 1995; and the Australasian Professional Legal Education Conference held the first conference in the region devoted specifically to the topic in Auckland in 1994.

(f) Ethical Resources

On the face of it, the profession has not seen a connection between its role in the setting and maintenance of professional ethical standards and its responsibility for the guidance of succeeding generations of practitioners. To put it crudely, learning about the profession's ethics requires information on the subject from the profession itself. Teachers require resources, and one would expect the profession to provide the most definitive material and opportunities. It is, of course, characteristic of professions that they have sought to protect their internal handling of disciplinary matters and the setting of standards of conduct from external public scrutiny. In most Australian jurisdictions, secrecy surrounds the work of ethics committees and the summary hearings of disciplinary bodies, reasons are seldom given for decisions and publication of outcomes is limited and selective.[89] New legislation in Victoria will now require all hearings of the Legal Profession Tribunal (for both solicitors and barristers) to be held in public unless otherwise ordered[90] and the Tribunal must give reasons for its decisions.[91] Without express stipulation, the Act also contains ample provision for the Tribunal and the Legal Practice Board to require publication of disciplinary matters in the professional journals. To the present, court decisions on the rare appeals from tribunals have provided the only opportunities for readers of the law reports, and sometimes newspapers, to obtain insights into the fixing and enforcing of the standards of behaviour expected of lawyers.

Students of legal ethics are also handicapped (as are judges and members of disciplinary tribunals and committees and those appearing before them) by the absence or paucity of indexed collections of rulings of the tribunals and committees, or digests or other annotated sources which would enable the jurisprudence of legal ethics to be examined, much less to flourish![92]

But the enquirer, whether practitioner or student, looks naturally to the official pronouncements of the profession itself for essential information on matters of ethics. It is a tragedy that no such guidance was forthcoming in Australia until so recently. Looking back, one can appreciate how such interest as there was in teaching legal ethics was easily discouraged. Australian

---

[89] Bar associations are the most secretive. E.g. the Victorian Bar Council never identifies in its in-house journal the members against whom findings have been made or the factual basis on which the proceedings were grounded. This contrasts with recent Law Institute practice in publishing regularly in its journal all such information in relation to solicitors (some of which has been required under the *Legal Profession Practice Act* 1958 (Vic) (now repealed), s. 38ZE).

[90] *Legal Practice Act* 1996 (Vic), s. 413.

[91] *Legal Practice Act*, 1996 s. 409.

[92] A thorough search into whether specified behaviour might constitute "misconduct" would require perusal of the records of the disciplinary bodies of the 8 States and Territories, each of the 3 largest of which have 2 such bodies. By way of example, the unhelpful state of the rulings affecting Victoria's solicitors has been referred to (*supra* nn. 66 and 67). The Victorian Bar Ethics Committee rulings are not accessible for perusal.

professional bodies showed little interest in formulating even the barest statements of professional obligation. In 1983, the year in which the American Bar Association adopted its *Model Rules of Professional Conduct* (itself a major expansion of the 1969 *Model Code of Professional Responsibility*), the first "code" appeared in Australia in the form of the Western Australia Law Society's *Professional Conduct Rules*. South Australia followed in similar vein the next year,[93] but there was no further such publication in Australia until, in 1993, the Australian Bar Association approved a "model" Code of Conduct as suitable for adoption by constituent bar associations.[94] In the same year, the Victorian Bar Association produced new comprehensive *Rules of Conduct and Practice* based upon the Code, with local variations. While the Australian Bar Association Code contributed belatedly to the development of the concept of such professional codes, it further entrenched the bar's inherently "adversarial" view of the legal system and hindered the prospects of a national code for the profession as a whole. Finally, in March 1996, the Law Council of Australia promulgated its Model Rules of Professional Conduct and Practice, with the intention that the separate treatment of "advocacy rules" within the document will attract all practitioners to it.[95] The process of consideration by professional bodies is still under way.

(g) A Code for the 2000s

It has been said that the promotion by the legal profession of codes of conduct should be regarded with caution and some cynicism. During the 1970s and 1980s the thinking of Illich[96] was developed to the point where legal professional bodies in the United States could be forgiven for believing they had earned no public credit for their endeavours in this regard.[97] Similar sentiments suggesting that attempts at professional codes were merely self-serving were expressed in Australia.[98] Certainly, the dilemma remains that, while the

---

[93] Law Society of South Australia, *Professional Conduct Rules* (1984). The subsequent experiences of New South Wales and Victoria, respectively, have been outlined and the other jurisdictions have also since adopted collections of rules.

[94] See *supra* n. 31.

[95] See *supra* n. 37.

[96] Ivan Illich, *Disabling Professions* (New York, M. Boyars, 1987).

[97] E.g. Richard Abel, "Why Does the American Bar Association Promulgate Ethical Rules?" (1981) 59 *Texas Law Review* 639; John Kultgen, "The Ideological Use of Professional Codes" and Richard Wasserstrom, "Lawyers as Professionals: Some Moral Issues" in Joan Callaghan (ed.), *Ethical Issues in Professional Life* (New York, Oxford University Press, 1988); Daniel Kleinberger, "Wanted: An Ethos of Personal Responsibility—Why Codes of Ethics and Schools of Law Don't Make for Ethical Lawyers" (1989) 21 *Connecticut Law Review* 365.

[98] E.g. Barry Maley, "Professionalism and Professional Ethics" in Donald Edgar (ed.), *Social Change in Australia* (Melbourne, Cheshire, 1974); D. S. Anderson and J. Western, "The Professions: Reason and Rhetoric" in P. Boreham and others (eds.), *The Professions in Australia: A Critical Appraisal* (St Lucia, Queensland University Press, 1976); and Pat O'Malley, *Law, Capitalism and Democracy* (Sydney, George Allen & Unwin, 1983).

lawyer resists prescriptions limiting the autonomy of professional practice, the public is scornful of rules without sanctions. The answer for Australia, we believe, is twofold: it lies in redesigning the form and emphasis of ethical codes for law, in ensuring that full advantage is taken of the "code-making" process as an exercise in consultation across differing professional constituencies, and in raising awareness of ethical issues generally.

Indeed, there is today a widespread public expectation that professions will develop and conform to codes of ethics.[99] External reform proposals directed at greater accountability expressly reserve to the professions, and emphasise, their rule-making responsibilities.[100] There was once ample opportunity for the legal profession to debate the value and wisdom of ethical codes, but that is a luxury it no longer possesses.[101]

The three-level approach to code-formulation demonstrated in the American Bar Association *Model Code* merited closer examination in Australia long ago.[102] This offers the opportunity in one document to adopt (i) aspirational *canons*; (ii) *statements* and discussion of the ethical considerations involved; and (iii) *rules* of conduct with which sanctions may be associated. Skilfully crafted, a code designed in this way can dispose of objections from both practitioners and the public. What the American experience also demonstrated, of course, was that great effort and determination were required in order to achieve their goal.

A legal code of ethics for the turn of the century in this country would take account of significant shifts in the focus of legal work, diversity of styles of practice, concerns for the future of a collective professional ethos and acknowledgement of public demands for cheaper and less litigious justice. For example, the hitherto persisting preoccupation of legal ethics with the needs of the adversarial system of justice, and the trial in particular, requires reconsideration.[103] The apparent centrality of the adversarial nature of the system

---

[99] There is increasing literature on the subject which is pertinent to the case of the legal profession, such as Margaret Coady and Sidney Bloch (eds.), *Codes of Ethics and the Professions* (Melbourne, Melbourne University Press, 1996) and Noel Preston, *Understanding Ethics* (Sydney, The Federation Press, 1996).

[100] The finger was pointed directly at Australian lawyers by the Trade Practices Commission when it recommended in 1994 that joint rules of conduct (binding both barristers and solicitors) should be developed in the interests of uniformity (Recommendation 5.6) and that the ethical responsibilities of lawyers should be codified as part of their duty to promote public awareness (Recommendation 10.6): Trade Practices Commission, *Study of the Professions: Legal: Final Report* (Canberra, AGPS, Mar. 1994).

[101] Judith Lichtenberg, "What Are Codes of Ethics For?" in Coady and Bloch (eds.), *supra* n. 99, 1996, rejects more recent doubts about codes expressed by John Ladd, "The Quest for a Code of Professional Ethics: An Intellectual and Moral Confusion" in Deborah Rhode and David Luban (eds.), *Legal Ethics* (St Paul, Foundation Press, 1992).

[102] The unacknowledged Victorian Young Lawyers' Code referred to *supra* n. 55, adopted this approach.

[103] The Australian Law Reform Commission has just embarked upon a review of federal litigation, alternative dispute resolution and legal process generally aimed at reducing dramatically the adversarial nature of the administration of justice at the federal level. The initial reaction of the legal profession has been at best cool ("ALRC Issues Paper Raises Legal Hackles" (1997) 32

of justice has skewed our ethical thinking and we must now acknowledge that the centre of gravity of the lawyer's world has shifted from the courtroom to the office.[104] Further, while the broad concepts remain the same, ethical rules designed for combat will require modification when applied to civil and family disputes, and particularly to negotiation and mediation in the current "settlement-oriented" climate.

A fresh approach to the profession's stock of ethical resources would also explore how the "ethic of service" might be incorporated. An observer of ethical development within professions would have noted that the ethics of the legal profession are impoverished by the absence of a single creed or transcending aspiration. Certainly, the practice of law has had no Hippocrates to look back to. Instead, the historical association of lawyers with "Inns" and "King's Courts" established a lasting tradition of contradictory responsibilities which has sustained and continued to influence profoundly a profession of diversifying types and styles of legal practice. From one situation to the next, the ethical emphasis shifts across notions such as loyalty to the client, candour to the court, independence of judgement, confidentiality and the interests of justice. A statement of duties addressed to advocates three hundred and fifty years ago during Cromwell's Commonwealth still seems to speak to today's practitioners.[105]

In the current economic climate, which encourages re-examination of the nature of a profession in light of competition and market forces, language may be found which helps to reflect the desired distinction between profession and trade. This would involve the notion of service—or dedication to interests at stake—which goes beyond that required by legal obligation. An ethic of service would imply a level of commitment to the client and, in adversarial matters, to the court, but also, where appropriate, to such ideals as the proper administration of the law, public access to justice and the promotion of other social or community interests within the legal system. How these ideals might best be promoted within legal education ought to be a matter of general concern.

(h) Strategic Vacuum

To this point, this chapter has exposed what appears to be an absence of ideas and strategies designed to improve and preserve the ethical health of the

Australian Lawyer (5) 8). A related conference examining the future of adversarial justice took place in Brisbane in June 1997 (at the time of writing).

[104] As Stephen Parker points out, with specific suggestions for further examination which appear to have gone unheeded by the professional bodies, in the paper published 5 years ago (Parker, *Legal Ethics, supra* n. 84).

[105] Ross Cranston, "Legal Ethics and Professional Responsibility" in R. Cranston (ed.), *Legal Ethics and Professional Responsibility* (Oxford, Clarendon Press, 1995), He cites the 3 duties of advocates as "secrecy, diligence and fidelity" (6).

Australian legal profession. A certain malaise, even despair, has set in, much to the detriment of tomorrow's lawyers. Fragmentation, parochialism, short-sighted planning and the divide between profession and academia must be overcome. We now consider further the latter's share of the responsibility and what might be done to move legal ethics from the wings to the centre stage of professional practice. How we define professional responsibility and what counts as legal knowledge are central considerations, in our view.

III. PROFESSIONAL RESPONSIBILITY IN LEGAL EDUCATION

(a) Competence is Not Good Enough

There is a danger in reducing the full range and moral significance of legal practice to a range of technical competences. Responsible lawyering requires much more than simply the capacity to act in a technically proficient or competent manner. In the current market-oriented, cost-benefit and competence-based climate, there is a danger of losing sight of the ethical and social dimensions of practice. Any latter-day "Taylorisation" of legal practice (the modern equivalents of "time and motion" analysis) is clearly to sell the social significance of what lawyers do short. Ethical competence, we suggest, is more than simply *observable compliant behaviour* according to some set of minimal prohibitions or standards of performance. It also includes dispositions which are affectively as well as cognitively based.[106] As we shall argue, the capacity to *understand*, as well as to *analyse*, situations and to apply certain legal strategies in a technically competent manner are both vital to the ethical character of legal practice.

A sense of integration and balance between technical proficiency and an ethically grounded sensitivity of application is needed. How this is achieved in legal education and training programmes is vitally important. An adequate conception of professional responsibility seeks to do this. The express juxtaposition of skills with values in the recent American Bar Association-sponsored *MacCrate Report* is suggestive of one approach, and points to the crucial significance for professional education of how these terms are interpreted. McCrate identifies a number of particular legal skills: problem-solving, legal analysis and reasoning, legal research, factual investigation, communication, counselling, negotiation, litigation and ADR, and office management. However the Report also proposes certain "fundamental values": provision of competent representation, striving to promote justice, fairness and morality, striving to improve the profession, and professional self-development. These are starting points for examining practical and ethical

---

[106] We do not assume that other competences are purely behaviourally based. For a discussion of this point, see Michael Eraut, *Developing Professional Knowledge and Competence* (London, Falmer Press, 1994), especially ch. 8.

competence. MacCrate recognises the connection between skills and values in defining competence. For example, in relation to the skills necessary for competent representation, the importance of a commitment to certain ethical ideals is recognised.[107] Those practice ideals suggested are (a) attaining a level of competence in one's own field of practice; (b) maintaining a level of competence in that field; and (c) representing clients in a competent manner.[108]

Crucial to the long-term significance of formal position documents such as the *McCrate Statement of Skills and Values* will be the content given to the fundamental values listed. In the sense that skills cannot be detached from considerations of value, this debate has already started, mainly with reference to the range of skills enumerated.[109] The obvious contender here is the promotion of justice, fairness and morality. Without some elaborated curricular plans developing these ideas, it is not obvious how to interpret these exhortations, and the risk of them remaining largely platitudinous is real. It is particularly unclear the to what extent the formal adoption of these values and skills as teaching objectives by a law school or other training institution would permit deep criticism of legal institutions and practices. We would argue that a genuine commitment to the ideals of public service and the promotion of justice necessitates a more precise articulation between the teaching of ethical standards and a deepened appreciation of legal processes and institutions.[110] Interdisciplinary approaches and materials, we suggest below, clearly can play a role in developing an expanded pedagogy and scholarship of professional responsibility.[111]

Similar concerns arise with recent Canadian and British formulations of legal professional responsibility. Cotter has recently attempted in Canada to specify the scope and form of an appropriate curriculum. His definition of professional responsibility is as follows:

> "A critical understanding of:
> (a)   the legal profession, its structures, roles and responsibilities;
> (b)   the roles and responsibilities of lawyers in their provision of professional services; and
> (c)   the individual's own values and attitudes."[112]

---

[107] MacCrate, *supra* n. 20, 211.

[108] *Ibid.*, 207–9.

[109] The *MacCrate Report* has been the subject of a special symposium. See Symposium on the 21st Century Lawyer, (1994) 69(3) *Washington Law Review*. One contributor in particular has taken issue with the range of skills put forward, and with the vision of lawyering implicit in the document: see Carrie Menkel-Meadow, "Narrowing the Gap by Narrowing the Field: What's Missing from the MacCrate Report—Of Skills, Legal Science and Being a Human Being", *ibid.*, 593.

[110] On the potential to push certain professional ideals "outwards" in order to raise more fundamental issues, see Robert Gordon and William Simon, "The Redemption of Professionalism?" in Nelson, Trubek, and Solomon, *supra* n. 12.

[111] On the implications of social theory for legal practice issues, see A. Goldsmith, "An Unruly Conjunction?: Social Thought and Legal Action in Clinical Legal Education" (1993) 43 *Journal of Legal Education* 415.

[112] W. Brent Cotter, *Professional Responsibility Instruction in Canada: A Coordinated Curriculum for Legal Education* (Montreal, Federation of Law Societies of Canada, 1992), i.

Crucial to the significance of statements such as these is the meaning given to "critical" and the breadth given to the exploration of lawyers' responsibilities. Similarly open to interpretation is the expressed hope of the Lord Chancellor's Advisory Committee on Legal Education and Conduct (ACLEC) that students "be made aware of the values that legal solutions carry, and of the ethical and humanitarian dimensions of law as an instrument which affects the quality of life".[113]

Our central concern here is with the *breadth of perspective* necessary to foster an adequate level of ethical awareness and commitment among lawyers in training. The need for greater breadth of outlook on ethical matters is well-recognised by Linowitz:

> "Ethical teaching that focuses narrowly on 'professional' issues such as solicitation or conflict of interest between clients . . . tends to reinforce rather than reduce the cynicism left over from the student's other courses. Legal ethics can be understood only in the context of the relations among people. Even the most elaborate of the ethics courses deals only in passing, if at all, with the crucial decision the practicing lawyer must make: Do I want to represent this client?"[114]

Conceptions of professional responsibility need to be developed in ways that exceed, even disrupt, mainstream approaches to ethical instruction. Formal and conventional understandings of professional obligations around service delivery need to be placed in a wider context, so as to enable their close examination and criticism. Ethical development cannot take place except in an environment of discussion and questioning. The MacCrate-type approach to professional responsibility is only a very modest beginning. Curriculum development and self-conscious law school socialisation must begin to find and operationalise methods for greater professional self-awareness. Legal knowledge itself must turn outwards as well as being opened up for inspection.[115] Lawyers should not be educated simply to act like unreflective athletes.[116]

---

[113] The Lord Chancellor's Advisory Committee on Legal Education and Conduct, *First Report on Legal Education and Training* (London, ACLEC, 1996), 17.

[114] Linowitz, *supra* n. 21, 123.

[115] We refer to the processes of learning and understanding required or implied by increased scepticism towards the foundations of knowledge, including ethical knowledge. While many fear the relativism imported by postmodern social theory, a more practical response to increased uncertainty about what we know or how to act is to try and find common ground through discussion and agreement. The communicative ethics of Jurgen Habermas typically arises in discussions of this kind. These issues have been examined in the context of professional ethics and conduct by Larry May: see May, *supra* n. 7.

[116] Ronald Dworkin has used this phrase to describe Stanley Fish's theoretical account of the lawyer engaged in legal interpretation: see Dworkin , "Pragmatism, Right Answers and True Banality" in M. Brint and W. Weaver (eds.), *Pragmatism in Law and Society* (Boulder, Co., Westview, 1991), 387.

(b) Broadening the Conception of Legal Knowledge

> "The correct ethical stance will very infrequently come readily labelled. What must be done is to sensitize students to the problems that they will face in practice and to provide them with some framework so that they can resolve difficult problems."[117]

The limitations of a purely "black letter law" approach to professional education is by now fairly widely conceded. The implications of this recognition, and their pedagogical consequences, however remain largely moot. The recent quest for "post-technocratic" models of professional education has led many searchers to the door of Donald Schon,[118] and particularly to his notion of the *reflective practitioner*.[119] The principal significance of this concept is its express concern with forms of practice-related knowledge which are not readily reducible to propositional form. What is important or relevant to professional practice, in other words, cannot always be formally expressed. Thus, the "reflective practitioner's work is characterised less by the application of rules and more through interpretation of images, vignettes, and exemplars".[120] The work of Schon has excited many professional educators because of its focus upon the development of informal, on-the-job knowledge intimately connected to the completion of particular professional tasks, in contrast to the more abstract, academic knowledge usually transmitted in classrooms and lecture halls. It is therefore instinctively appealing to those professionals with a practical bent, as well to those interested in experiential learning in educational theory.

However, while making a real contribution to our understanding of professional practice, we agree that this approach needlessly downplays the contribution of formal propositional knowledge to practice. It also ignores what Jones calls *critical emancipatory reasoning*, by which is meant that knowledge (which we would argue is both empirical as well as normative) which "provides an insight into the wider ethical, social and political forces that provide the context within which professionals work".[121] It is surely obvious, and especially so in the case of inexperienced practitioners, that a background of

---

[117] Cranston, *supra* n. 105, 32.

[118] Schon, *The Reflective Practitioner* (San Francisco, Cal., Jossey-Bass, 1983) and *Educating the Reflective Practitioner: Toward a New Design for Teaching and Learning in the Professions* (San Francisco, Cal., Jossey-Bass, 1987).

[119] Philip Jones, "We're All Reflective Practitioners Now: Reflections on Professional Education" in Julian Webb and Caroline Maughan (eds.), *Teaching Lawyers' Skills* (London, Butterworths, 1996), 293.

[120] *Ibid.*, 294.

[121] *Ibid.*, 301. This concept is resonant of the work of Jurgen Habermas, whose notion of critical knowledge is premised upon what Habermas calls the knowledge-constitutive interest of emancipation: see Habermas, *Knowledge and Human Interests* (Oxford, Blackwell, 1987), 310. Goldsmith has employed this concept in thinking about forms of social knowledge relevant to a critically-informed clinical legal education: see *supra* n. 111.

formal knowledge provides a guiding framework with which to approach, and make sense of, unfamiliar aspects of professional work. In addition to providing basic concepts, frameworks of this kind offer a series of working hypotheses for relating different components of experience and skills to each other, and for making overall sense of the situation. Formal knowledge also provides vital tools for justifying one's actions as a professional to others, as well as providing legitimation for one's professional status.[122] Formal knowledge thus serves interpretive and critical, as well as narrowly instrumental, functions.

Ironically, our argument for breadth in ethically relevant professional legal education stems partly from the form of preparation common among many English barristers in particular, as well as among certain prominent American lawyers of earlier times. The practice of reading classics at Oxford, or history at Cambridge, before taking pupillage to a barrister was common at least up until World War II,[123] while Linowitz reminds us that many leaders of the early American bar were persons of considerable educational breadth.[124] While it might sound almost quaint to some, Linowitz's statement reminds us that an adequate preparation for legal practice is far more widely based than a merely technical conception of practice would require:

> "a good lawyer almost by definition should be a person of breadth, who has a grasp of what yesterday teaches us about today and tomorrow, who knows that the real meaning of words such as freedom and justice can be found only in the tapestry of history."[125]

Aside from the valuable contribution to be made by other disciplines, an insistence upon some exposure to applied moral philosophy and jurisprudence[126] points to the complementary advantages offered by an appreciation of the conceptual foundations, internal logic and internal critique of law. Similar benefits are to be derived from a grasp of the elements shared by legal thought with other areas of normative thought, including applied ethics. Building upon Linowitz's lead, we would also suggest the importance of *empirically oriented disciplines and methodologies* to the ends of understanding and evaluating legal strategies and practices.

The failure to appreciate the scale or significance of particular social phenomena with which lawyers are engaged is clearly inimical to good ethical practice. Amsterdam's classic article on clinical legal education in the twenty-first century points to the relative neglect in legal education of (what he calls) means-ends thinking, information acquisition and contingency planning.[127]

---

[122] Andrew Abbott, *The System of Profession* (Chicago, Ill., University of Chicago Press, 1988).

[123] For an account of the development of legal education in England and Wales, see William Twining, *Blackstone's Tower: The English Law School* (London, Stevens/ Sweet and Maxwell, 1994).

[124] Linowitz, *supra* n. 21, 135.

[125] *Ibid.*

[126] See e.g. Rhode, *supra*, ch. II, entitled "Traditions of Moral Reasoning".

[127] A. Amsterdam, "Clinical Legal Education—A 21st Century Perspective" (1984) 34 *Journal of Legal Education* 612, 614–15.

These skills, we suggest, form a critical foundation for ethical evaluation in any field of professional practice. Without close consideration of the context and available courses of action in a particular situation, our ethical deliberations will, assuredly, remain unworldly and abstract. In addition to the contingency associated with litigation settings, the non-adversarial roles of lawyers also operate practically in terms of *possibility,* and require *means-ends thinking* and *information acquisition.* To the extent these practical considerations are predominantly driven by instrumental thinking, they nonetheless must take sufficient account of contingency and context to require input from a variety of sources of formal knowledge.

Professional legal education therefore would benefit from turning to what Gordon and Simon call the "sociology of everyday practice settings".[128] A focus upon mundane practice is strangely lacking in most legal education courses, arising at best obliquely in discussions of "the roles and responsibilities of lawyers".[129] As Gordon and Simon put it, "professional responsibility discourse at its most ambitious talks about the good, but has little to say about the possible".[130] The advantage that sociology as well as the other empirically grounded disciplines offer is a familiarity with social contingency, and in particular with the phenomena of social diversity and social conflict.[131] By their focus upon conflict, disorder and change, these disciplines only too well appreciate the often huge gap between actuality and the ideal. By focusing upon experience and meaning, as well as examining observable behaviour, these disciplines offer *interpretive,* as well as *descriptive* and *analytical,* resources.[132] Their experimental or otherwise revisable approach to knowledge gives rise on many occasions to suggestions of ways to "narrow the gap", or otherwise to improve a particular situation. An ethical lawyer, in order to be able to act upon her moral assessments, needs to be equipped empirically and normatively in the "here and now" to take appropriate action. A firm grasp of legal doctrine or political principle is not sufficient to this task.

Another explicit objective of professional legal education should be the examination of *judgement.* The notion of judgement permits us to consider the relationship between theoretical knowledge and ethically guided action more clearly. As an important ingredient of professional practice, it also requires us to think carefully about how students might best be prepared for this task. The balancing or factoring of different, sometimes contradictory, considerations as part of the decision-making process suggests a commitment to careful comprehensive inquiry as a vital part of this process. It arguably requires something else—a degree of sympathy and compassion for the

---

[128] Gordon and Simon, *supra* n. 110, 238.

[129] See e.g. Cotter, *supra* n. 112.

[130] Gordon and Simon, *supra* n. 110, 238.

[131] Social science as well as the humanities provide a "sense of relativity" all too commonly absent from more moralistically inclined discourses: see Louis Hartz, *The Liberal Tradition in America* (New York, Harcourt Brace, 1955), 14.

[132] See Goldsmith, *supra* n. 111, 431–2.

different perspectives at stake in a particular decision. It also points to the need for a measure of detachment in order to render a balanced conclusion possible. Kronman's discussion of *practical wisdom*[133] approximates from an Aristotelian perspective what we are discussing here.

The fact that the requirements of judgement *exceed* propositional knowledge or practical know-how is brought out by Kant's decomposition of judgement into three elements: its *ethical*, *aesthetic*, and *practical* character.[134] Implicit in his analysis is the inevitable *agency* involved in exercising judgement, as well as the fact that it does not reduce completely to propositional knowledge or deductive logic. Thus, it cannot readily be taught. This ineffable quality does not mean that all efforts at education or training are useless. An empirically informed grasp of the field of legal practice is necessary, for example. In the words of Elizabeth Dvorkin, "the most effective impediment to taking responsibility is being unaware and . . . in particular a lack of awareness of the uncertainty in life".[135] Here, the importance of the "sociology of the ordinary and possible" described above becomes clear. "What is" and "what is possible", as well as "what ought to be", are necessary questions under this approach. The capacity to examine and evaluate the *consequences* of different legal actions is vital. As Judge Patricia Wald of the US Court of Appeals noted, "[W]e must consider the results of our rulings, not merely their conceptual consistency. Principled decision making does not require that we be blind to how our decisions play out in the real world."[136] Legal education for professional responsibility warrants the same commitment.

(c) Professional Formation: Replication or Transformation?

> "Man's will to profit and to be powerful have their natural and proper effect so long as they are linked with, and upheld by, his will to enter into relation. There is no evil impulse till the impulse has been separated from the being, the impulse which is bound up with, and defined by, the being is the living stuff of communal life, that which is detached is its disintegration."[137]

Given our argument concerning the historical reluctance of the Australian legal profession to view professional responsibility issues sufficiently seriously, there is an important question as to how law schools might respond in this environment. Law schools should operate as places where the aspirational

---

[133] Kronman, *supra* n. 15, ch. 2.

[134] We derive this understanding from Michel de Certeau, *The Practice of Everyday Life* (Berkeley, Calif., University of California Press, 1984), 72–6.

[135] Dvorkin, Himmelstein and Lesnick, *Becoming a Lawyer: A Humanistic Perspective on Legal Education and Professionalism* (St Paul, Minn., West Publishing, 1981), 104.

[136] Quoted in Rand Jack and Dana Crowley Jack, *Moral Vision and Professional Decisions: The Changing Values of Women and Men Lawyers* (Cambridge, Cambridge University Press, 1989), 170.

[137] Martin Buber, *I and Thou* (1937), 68.

claims of the profession (legal equality, access to law, service, etc.) and the social interests and consequences of legal practice are explored and evaluated. Law's relations with the community at large, as well as with the courts, the profession and the clients, should form part of this scholarly and pedagogical context. A necessary component of the broader contextualisation of legal practice, it has been argued, is an expanded conception of legal knowledge. In essence, this is a relational argument, one which expressly incorporates the disjunction between the interests of those in the community who cannot afford legal services and who are thereby disadvantaged in legal proceedings (the unemployed, indigenous persons, the young and the elderly, women, the homeless, migrants, etc.) and the core concerns of the legal profession, as a matter for deliberation and response in legal professional responsibility.

In suggesting ways of overcoming this disjunction, or at least of narrowing the gap to bridgeable proportions, we posit the undesirability of legal education committed to an essentially *replicative* model of professional preparation, and express our preference for a more pluralistic and dialogical approach—a *transformative* model. We develop these two models below, relying upon the key differences between each model, to outline our preferred way forward for professional legal education.

(i) The Replicative Model

This model is strongly *homosocial* in nature—that is, it seeks to reproduce members in its own image. We find this approach to professional legal education disturbing, but recognise it is one easily adopted, for obvious reasons. It is, by definition, inherently uncontroversial. Its almost "natural" character has contributed to its dominance of professional legal education. This applies to developments in Australia, but undoubtedly elsewhere as well. To *replicate* in our sense is to make a replica, a duplicate or exact copy, of something already in existence. Our opposition to this notion relates only to uncritical or unreflective applications of replication. Following Edward Levi, we believe that "the professional school which sets its course by the current practice of the profession is, in an important sense, a failure".[138] Professional education which is uncritically based upon traditional notions of education and skills in all probability no longer fits contemporary circumstances, and is therefore outmoded and objectionable. Pure replication also operates in the interests of a dominant professional group or orthodoxy, entrenching certain attitudes, values and approaches to practice at the expense of others. Other views about legal practice and professional responsibility tend to get short shrift in these circumstances. Aside from the material consequences of such entrenched dominance, it also stifles imaginative thinking about the purposes and methods of professional practice, and about the social responsibilities of lawyers.

[138] Levi, *Points of View: Talks on Education* (Chicago, Ill., University of Chicago, 1969).

In a professional education system committed to reproducing professionals uncritically, narrowly defined notions of competence become highly significant in professional ideology. A proficient practitioner need not be too concerned, if at all, by issues of choice of field, issue or clientele, for the patterns of practice, generally speaking, are well-established. Proficiency is hence evaluated in technical and strategic terms. This *performative* conception of competence lacks an obvious ethical dimension. Instead it asks of the technique and the practitioner "what works?" It emphasises the value of legal "know-how", whether that be in the form of black-letter law or practical legal skills (or both). By comparison, contextual considerations, including the different interests of the parties involved, the kinds of social consequences of particular legal strategies and broader considerations of legal ethical responsibility, get largely ignored.

The field of focus is also narrow, being confined mainly to the interests of the client and, secondarily, the minimal requirements imposed by the courts and the profession. [139] As a lawyer trained under this model, one exhibits *neutral partisanship*—an almost stoic indifference to the client's ends or interests while earnestly servicing those same ends and interests. Those interests, and the priority they receive, leave little or no scope to giving concrete attention to the wider professional aspirations of lawyers as a group. Basically, those who can afford to pay the piper get to call the tune. The indigent, not surprisingly, do not get to hear their tunes played very often, and when they do, the legal aid situation and the nature of the private bar that occasionally serves their interests mean that the tunes heard are often played by poorly-equipped one-person bands with limited repertoires.

(ii) The Transformative Model

By contrast, this model promises a more diverse repertoire for would-be lawyers in professional legal education. It does this largely by expressly adopting the aspirations of the legal profession as key organising principles for professional education. The term "transformative" is not used to suggest the virtue of ceaseless transformation for its own sake. Rather, it acknowledges and embraces the socially situated nature of legal work, recognising that not all interests get equally well served by the available models of legal service delivery, and that there are resource difficulties in supporting equally the different models in existence. It accepts that lawyers' powers extend wider than the firm, the case or the immediate client. For example, it recognises that professional legal ideologies are influential in public debates and in framing public policy. Lawyers also exert a kind of negative power to the extent they neglect areas of legal need. This relational conception of professional obligation, directed to a wider constituency, renders it vulnerable and responsible in ways unfamiliar to those

---

[139] Robert Kagan and Robert Rosen, "On the Social Significance of Large Firm Practice" (1985) 37 *Stanford Law Review* 399.

lawyers trained to focus their skills simply upon the lawyer–client relation. A sense of complexity of interests, and of the diverse nature of outcomes in professional practice, emerges as an important component of a responsible professional education. A capacity to communicate with those different interests (*dialogical*) and to understand the impact of legal provisions and actions upon persons' lives (*hermeneutical*) are crucial objectives of this approach.

Defining the professional constituency broadly promotes the possibility of a more substantive and relationally rich form of criticism. A genuine dialogue with diverse interests is bound to produce a stronger form of social accountability for professional practices. As Marion Smiley has noted, the consequences of particular practices and actions "are not simply discovered, but are instead ascribed, along with their valuation, by members of a particular community".[140] Re-defining and recognising a different "particular community" for lawyers in training, through measures such as work placements in settings of real legal need, community organising in such communities, clinical education, role-plays and admission procedures based upon substantial diversity, promise the prospect of a more broadly founded approach to legal education and professional responsibility issues. The development and integration of *knowing why* and *knowing that* forms of knowledge in their professional preparation should complement these experiential strategies, ensuring a more deliberative educational process and a more *reflective* ethical orientation. Thus, this model is transformative in two senses. It deliberately subjects its operating assumptions and methods to critical scrutiny through expanded forms of dialogue and education, ensuring that professional practice is never entirely settled or fixed. Secondly, by casting the spectrum of social interests more broadly, it inevitably commits itself to tackling the problems of differential access to legal services, and, thus, to addressing questions of a social and economic redistributive nature. It is active therefore in a social as well as professional sense.

The elements of the two models are summarised in table form below:

Two models of professional education

	Replication	Transformation
Notion of competence:	Operational	Dialogical/critical
Logic:	Strategic	Cognitive/hermeneutic
Knowledge type:	'Know-how'	'Knowing why/ that'
Object of evaluation:	Performance	Meaningful action
Criteria of evaluation:	What works?	What are you up to?
Notion of Field:	Client, profession	Community, society
Ethical orientation:	Neutral partisanship	Reflective engagement

[140] Smiley, "Pragmatic Inquiry and Social Conflict: A Critical Reconstruction of Dewey's Model of Democracy" (1990) 9 *Praxis International* 365, 375.

In summary, the transformative model presents a sketch of what we consider crucial ingredients of a professional legal education committed to a thick conception of professional responsibility. The importance of an empirically rich knowledge of law and legal circumstances has been advocated, together with a normatively informed critical analysis based upon theoretical knowledge. The value of experiential learning (e.g. through role-plays, placements, clinical programmes[141]) and more formal ethical education needs also to be appreciated and incorporated in education curricula and programmes. Much of the literature appearing in law journals dealing with the moral development of law students[142] in our view complements, but mainly from a more individualistic perspective, the kinds of legal knowledge and ethical orientations stressed in this chapter as essential for the enhancement of education for professional responsibility.

IV. CONCLUSION

Increasingly, the practice of law seems to be dictated by concerns for efficiency and profitability. Equally, in the universities, law schools and legal education are falling under the "shadow of accountancy".[143] Ethical questions, to the extent that they are recognised, too readily become narrow regulatory concerns, lawyer–client issues or matters for law firm "customer relations strategies". This is, as we have argued, a thin conception of professional responsibility indeed. Finding space or motives for self-examination and criticism on ethical issues in professional life, never easy, is even more difficult now.[144] Moving beyond lip-service to such goals, to the development and promotion of ethically aware legal education and training (a transformative model) in the face of longstanding resistance or complacency, is therefore a profound challenge. If, as legal educators or practising lawyers, we are to be involved in a broader and more substantive commitment by lawyers to professional responsibility, we need to find new ways of taking legal ethics seriously.

Our advocacy in this chapter of a broad conception of professional responsibility applies throughout the period of formal education and training of

---

[141] See Goldsmith, *supra* n. 3.

[142] This literature, while not new, continues to appear and evolve: see e.g. James Moliterno, "Legal Education, Experiential Education, and Professional Responsibility" (1996) 38 *William and Mary Law Review* 71; Steven Hartwell, "Promoting Moral Development Through Experiential Teaching" (1995) 1 *Clinical Law Review* 505; Sandra Janoff, "The Influence of Legal Education on Moral Reasoning" (1991) 76 *Minnesota Law Review* 193; Thomas Willging and Thomas Dunn, "The Moral Development of the Law Student: Theory and Data on Legal Education" (1981) 31 *Journal of Legal Education* 306; June Tapp and Felice Levine, "Legal Socialization: Strategies for an Ethical Legality" (1974) 27 *Stanford Law Review* 1.

[143] This phrase is from Roger Scruton, "Pilgrims on the Way to Extinction", a review of Michael Tanner's *Wagner* (HarperCollins): see *Times Literary Supplement*, 7 Mar. 1997.

[144] See e.g. Stein and Stein, *supra* n. 72.

lawyers and beyond. It is not simply a question for undergraduate university education in law. The profession must play its reciprocal part by establishing clearly its ethical priorities, providing moral, political and financial support for law schools, and encouraging them to take ethical questions seriously. It is for the profession to engage its membership in the development of ethical principles, and in the adoption of codes and statements which bear the imprimatur of the profession for teaching purposes. As part of the legal educators' contribution, we have advocated a critical, empirically-informed move, beyond the limited precincts of professional codes of conduct, applicable legislation and common law, to the disparate contexts in which law is practised. While it is not necessary that law students or practitioners should become legal philosophers,[145] it does suggest the importance of students having access to different vantage points and perspectives, practical as well as theoretical, on the law. Law students must come to see legal practice as socially situated, and hence as ethically complex. Technical competence is not sufficient. Together as academic lawyers and as members of the practising profession, we must work, as Barnett suggests, to protect the humanness of professional practice:

"To reduce human action to a constellation of terms such as 'performance', 'competence', 'doing' and 'skill' is not just to resort to a hopelessly crude language with which to describe serious human endeavours. In the end, it is to obliterate the humanness in human action. It is to deprive human being of *human* being."[146]

---

[145] For a personal view of how philosophy and legal education might best be combined, see Martha Nussbaum, "The Use and Abuse of Philosophy in Legal Education" (1993) 45 *Stanford Law Review* 1627.

[146] Ronald Barnett, *The Limits of Competence: Knowledge, Higher Education, and Society* (Milton Keynes, Open University Press, 1994), 178.

8

Recent Developments in the Teaching of Legal Ethics— A UK Perspective

RICHARD O'DAIR*

"Technique Without Ideals Are A Menace; Ideals Without Technique Are A Mess." Karl Llewellyn.[1]

"To be sure, there are lawyers, judges and even law professors who tell us they have no legal philosophy. In law, as in other things, we shall find that the only difference between a person without a philosophy and someone with a philosophy is that the latter knows what his philosophy is." F. Northrop.[2]

One of the most striking features of the *Report of the Lord Chancellor's Advisory Committee on Legal Education and Conduct,*[3] is its repeated insistence that one of the central goals at every stage of legal education should be to inculcate "legal values", meaning, "a commitment to the rule of law, to justice fairness and *high ethical standards*" (emphasis added).[4] In particular academic[5] law schools are invited to begin to study professional ethics, the

* This chapter was written when the writer was Visiting Research Fellow at the Keck Centre for the Study of Legal Ethics and the Legal Profession at the Stanford Law School during the academic year 1995–1996. The writer would like to acknowledge the help provided by Professor Deborah Rhode, the Director of the Keck Centre, the generous financial support provided by the Alexander Maxwell Law Scholarship Trust and the ongoing help and support of Professor Dawn Oliver, Dean and Head of Department at the Faculty of Laws, University College London.

[1] "The Adventures of Rollo" 2 University of Chicago Law School Record 3 [1952] at p 23.

[2] The Complexity of Legal Ethical Experiance (1959) at p. 6 cited by Twinning & MacCormick in "Theory in the Law Curriculum" Chapter 13 in W. Twining (ed.) Legal Theory and the Common Law (Basil Blackwell, Oxford, 1986).

[3] See The Lord Chancellor's Advisory Committee on Legal Education and Conduct consultation papers, *The Initial Stage* (HMSO, June 1994) ("the First Consultation Paper") and *The Vocational Stage and Continuing Professional Development* (HMSO, June 1995) ("the Second Consultation Paper") and its subsequent *First Report on Legal Education and Training* (HMSO, Apr. 1996) ("the Report").

[4] *Report, supra* n. 1, para. 2.4.

[5] In this chapter, the phrase "academic law teachers" is used to indicate a subset of law teachers whose principal characteristics are a preoccupation with teaching undergraduate degrees in law and with research, and an interest in abstract theoretical rather than applied knowledge. They are to be contrasted with "vocational law teachers", whose principal interest is in applied rather

implication being (rightly as we shall see) that this is something they have neglected hitherto.[6] This chapter seeks to explain why legal ethics has recently leapt to prominence and asks in effect what legal educators might hope to achieve by immersing themselves in the subject. Particular focus will be placed on the role of academic lawyers as teachers of the undergraduate degree in law and as researchers. The paper accepts ACLEC's preoccupation with the role of the undergraduate degree as an element in the legal education of future practitioners and in effect asks what academic undergraduate legal education has to offer in the ethical development of tomorrow's practitioners. It does not address directly the question (with which ACLEC was not concerned) of what legal ethics has to offer in educational terms to the undergraduate degree in law.[7] The chapter begins in section I with a description of the history of and current state of legal ethics teaching in the United Kingdom. It then moves in section II to an analysis of the reasons for recent calls for change and then deals in Section III with the prospects for the future.

I. THE CURRENT POSITION

What are legal ethics? For present purposes, I take legal ethics to be[8] the critical study of:

(i)   the legal profession, its structures roles and responsibilities—sometimes termed macro legal ethics.

(ii) the roles and responsibilities of individual lawyers in the provision of legal services together with the ethical implications of those roles—sometimes termed micro-legal ethics.

(iii) the individual's own values and standards.

This immediately distinguishes legal ethics from certain other legitimate and traditional concerns of academic lawyers, namely the question of the relationship between legal and moral/ethical reasoning and the evaluation from an ethical standpoint of the rules of substantive law.[9] Such studies focus upon

---

than theoretical knowledge. This definition expresses certain key features of the development of legal education in the UK between following the report of the Ormrod Committee in 1971 (*Report of the Committee on Legal Education* (HMSO, 1971) Cmnd. 4594). See n. 13 and following text. Morerver it also corresponds with what ACLEC seems to have in mind when it speaks about university law teachers. It does not however assume that this is a desirable picture nor that it is unchanging.

[6] Report, *supra* n. 1, para. 2.11.

[7] On this see D. R. F. O'Dair, "Ethics By the Pervasive Method—The Case of Contract", Forthcoming 17 *Legal Studies* [July 1997].

[8] See E. Chemerinsky "Pedagogy Without Purpose: An Essay on Professional Responsibility Courses and Casebooks", *Am Bar. Found Res. J* 943 [1985] and W. Brent Cotter, *Professional Responsibility Instruction in Canada: A Coordinated Curriculum for Legal Education* (Federation of Law Societies of Canada, 1992), 1–6.

[9] These aspects are, however, undoubtedly included within ACLEC's broader statements about the importance of the ethical aspects of law.

and seek to influence the decisions of judges and legislators. Legal ethics focus by contrast upon the behaviour and decisions of individual lawyers. The subject seeks to illuminate and, in so far as possible, resolve the difficulties which threaten would be lawyers' sense of vocation, regardless of whether or not they involve a threat of disciplinary sanctions. In this endeavor, the subject draws upon the resources of other disciplines particularly moral philosophy but also history, sociology, economics and theology. Thus legal ethics are best seen as being concerned with the development of engaged professionals i.e. lawyers for whom the practice of the law is not just a career, but also a source of meaning arising through commitment to a way of life having socially recognised value.[10] Looking at the matter from society's point of view, ALEC has emphasised the need to maintain:

> "the high professional and ethical standards on which our legal system and, indeed our democracy depend. . . . Forms of education and training are required that will ensure that the lawyers of tomorrow fully appreciate the essential link between law and legal practice and the preservation of fundamental democratic values."[11]

From the individual's point of view, the assumptions upon which the enterprise is based have been well put by Professor Thomas Shaffer:

> "People become lawyers for many reasons. For some it is the money; for some it is the thrill of competition and a desire for success; for others it is the status that comes from being in a profession. But the big desk, the plaques on the walls, and the things that one can purchase with a large income can only carry a person so far. We suspect that part of the reason that many lawyers are disenchanted with the practice of law is that these things are not inherently satisfying."[12]

This is not a neutral definition, for radical critics might want to present an alternative vision for the teaching of legal ethics as an exposure of the emptiness of the lawyers' pretensions to be ethical professionals.[13] However this is clearly not what ACLEC has in mind.

We can move therefore, to consider the current status of legal ethics teaching in the United Kingdom. The current picture is a consequence of artificial division between academic and professional legal education, the history of which has recently been traced by Professor Hepple.[14] With respect to

---

[10] Brainard Currie, (1969) 22 *J of Legal Ed*. 48, 59; William M. Sullivan, *Work and Integrity* (New York, Harper Business, 1995), 171.

[11] Report, *supra* n. 4, para. 1.5.

[12] Thomas L. Shaffer, *Lawyers Clients and Moral Responsibility* (West Publishing, St. Paul, Minn., 1994), 135.

[13] See generally the work of Professor Richard Abel, and especially *The Legal Profession in England and Wales* (Oxford, Basil Blackwell, 1988). Note Professor Avrom Sherr's perceptive criticism ((1990) 53 *MLR* 407, 409) that this work offers convincing evidence that lawyers' ideals have been consistently betrayed but fails to offer either an alternative vision or suggestions as to how they might be redeemed.

[14] B. A. Hepple, The Renewal of the Liberal Law Degree, 55 *CLJ* [1996] 470.

undergraduate legal education, the verdict is contained in Professor Peter Birks' comment that:

> "there is extraordinarily little knowledge in the (university) law school system about civil and criminal procedure or about all matters relating to legal practice, *including professional ethics* . . .the general neglect of the subjects assigned to the vocational phase casts a shadow over the great achievements of the university law schools in the rest of the field"[15] (emphasis added).

Professor Birks' comment is particularly apt with respect to micro-legal ethics, for when we look at published works (one of the major indices of the academic function) it is only very recently that there has begun to be any contribution.[16] Consequently, the norms of professional ethics have developed without the academic input and debate which surrounded the deliberations of the Kutak Commission in the USA.[17] It is significant that the SPTL whose members meet in specialised subject groups for scholarly discussion during the organisations annual conference got around to forming a subgroup on legal ethics and the professions only in 1994.

Following the report of the Marre Committee,[18] an independent report commissioned jointly by the Bar Council and the Law Society in 1988, vocational education at the Inns of Court School of Law and at the College of law has been revolutionised. The end product in each case was a new name (The Bar Vocational Course for barristers and the Legal Practice Course for solicitors) and more fundamentally a revolutionary skills-based approach. These courses, heavily influenced by the model of the highly acclaimed British Columbia[19] Legal Practice Training Course, have as their focus the development through practice and testing of skills such interviewing, drafting, advising, fact management and advocacy. Knowledge of and/or research into the substantive law is the prerequisite for participation in simulated practice through which the skills are developed. As far as legal ethics are concerned, the new approach has involved a short introductory course setting out the ethical framework provided by the Codes reinforced by the weaving of ethical issues into the skills exercises.

Any assessment of the new framework from the point of view of legal ethics must inevitably be mixed. The contextualising of ethical issues within simulated practice is clearly positive, making the relevance of any discussion of the issues clear to students and ensuring that developing ethical frameworks take

---

[15] P. B. H. Birks (ed.), *Reviewing Legal Education* (Oxford, OUP, 1994) ch.3 at p.20 (Birks) Cf. ACLEC, *Report, supra* n. 1, at para. 2.11.

[16] See e.g. Ross Cranston (ed.), *Legal Ethics and Professional Responsibility* (Oxford, OUP, 1995).

[17] Contrast "A Gathering of Scholars to Discuss 'Professional Responsibility and the Model Rules of Professional Conduct' " (1981) 35 *U Miami L Rev.* 639.

[18] *Report on the Future of the Legal Profession (Marre Committee)* (London, Law Society and General Council of the Bar, 1988).

[19] See Phillip Jones "A Skills Based Approach to Professional to Legal Education—An Exemplary Case", (1989) 23 *Law Teacher* 173.

account of the real world of legal practice. The Bar Vocational Course, has been greeted enthusiastically by the consumers,[20] though evaluative studies have not specifically considered ethical issues. Moreover, a 1985–6 review of the British Columbia Professional Skills Training Course, which was in many ways the model for this approach to legal education, found 83 per cent of students to be either satisfied or very satisfied with the manner in which the course dealt with professional responsibility issues.[21]

Against this optimistic appraisal we must enter two words of caution related to the quotations with which this chapter begins. The first is quite simply that students engaged in the resolution of highly contextual realistic ethical problems will inevitably bring to these tasks a set of theoretical or ideological spectacles. Ideally, the more academic stage of legal education ought to be concerned with the critical examination of these frameworks in the light of available data and alternative frameworks. As has been seen, however, the disavowal by UK academic lawyers of any interest in micro-legal ethics is likely to mean that students enter vocational education with an ethical framework which, whatever its origins, owes little to a process of critical examination in law school. In this sense, university law teachers may be failing vocational law teachers.

The second point is perhaps more controversial. In its Second Consultation Paper ACLEC expressed a concern that vocational legal education was perhaps too skills-orientated and insufficiently intellectually rigorous.[22] This observation clearly provoked strong disagreement from vocational law teachers, forcing ACLEC into a hasty retreat in its subsequent report.[23] Despite this, its seems undeniable that skills based teaching is very labour intensive and time-consuming.[24] It must follow that students are unlikely to have much time for critical reflection upon the ethical premises of the skills they are being taught and that there is therefore a danger that skills teachers will bring to their teaching implicit unexamined ethical frameworks, which will be assumed by students lacking either the time or awareness of alternatives necessary to challenge them. More generally it can be said that the skills movement draws heavily upon an Aristotelian epistemology. The ethical practitioner is one who has developed dispositions to ethical behaviour through imitation of his peers. Only after developing the necessary dispositions through practice is the practitioner in a position to give them rational exposition. The problem, as Aristotle recognised, is that one may be so well trained in bad habits as to become incapable of

---

[20] See Joanna Shapland, Valerie Johnson and Richard Wild *Studying for the Bar: The Students' Evaluation of the New Vocational Training Course at the Council of Legal Education*, (Sheffield, Institute for the Study of Legal Practice, 1988).

[21] Law Society of British Canada, *Curriculum Subcommittee Report on PLTC (Cameron Committee Report 1986)* Appendix 1, cited in Cooter, *supra* n. 8, at para. 6–33).

[22] *Second Consultation Paper, supra* n. 4, at paras. 3.10 and 5.8.

[23] See *Report, supra* n. 4, paras. 2.3 and 6.5.

[24] Consider e.g. the tight time-frame prescribed for the negotiations exercises used by the New Zealand Institute of Professional Legal Studies described in ch. 7 of W. Twining, K. Mackie and N. Gold (eds.), *Learning Lawyers' Skills* (London, Butterworths, 1989).

knowing better. If, as many think, the current *mores* of the legal profession leave much to be desired this is profoundly worrying.[25]

As an example, let us consider the approach to negotiation found in *Learning Lawyers' Skills*[26] by Professor Philip Jones, Director of the University of Sheffield Legal Practice Course and one of the leading figures in the movement towards skills based education. It is only right to say that this book has many strengths. It engages, for example, with the extensive US theoretical literature, and an attempt is made[27] to contextualise the discussion by drawing on Professor Hazel Genn's work[28] on the negotiation of settlements to personal injury actions.

However the choice between different methods of negotiating is presented almost exclusively in terms of effectiveness in achieving client goals.[29] Hence the writer emphasises empirical research "proving" that competitive negotiators are unlikely to conduct successful negotiations[30] as an argument in favour of a co-operative approach. However the only limits on party behaviour are described as being "voluntary and self-imposed"[31] for:

> "at the heart of negotiation there will always be opportunistic interaction—less than fully open motives and methods, self-interested manœuvres."[32]

Ultimately the goals of the client seem likely to be treated as decisive.[33] What one might ask is the point of paragraph 17.01 of the *Guide to Professional Conduct* providing that:

> "Solicitors must not act, whether in their professional capacity or otherwise, towards anyone in a way which is fraudulent, deceitful or otherwise contrary to their position as solicitors. Nor must solicitors use their position to take unfair advantage either for themselves or another person."[34]

What matters here is not what one thinks of the approach being recommended, for there are ethical frameworks which can be called into service in its defence,[35] some of which provide criteria for choosing between co-operative and competitive approaches to bargaining on grounds other than client choice.[36] The point is that the arguments are simply not being made

[25] See generally David Luban, "Epistemology and Moral Education" (1983) 33 *Journal of Legal Education* 636.

[26] (3rd edn., London, Blackstone Press, 1995), Philip A. Jones (ed.).

[27] *Ibid.*, 170 at para. 24.3.1.

[28] *Ibid.*

[29] *Ibid.*, 173, at para. 24.3, 177, at para. 24.4.

[30] *Ibid.*, 170, 171.

[31] *Ibid.*, 163, at para. 23.3.3.

[32] (3rd edn., London, Blackstone Press, 1995), Philip A. Jones (ed.), 177, at para. 24.4.

[33] *Ibid.*, 175 at para. 24.3.3.

[34] The Law Society, *The Guide to the Professional Conduct of Solicitors* (7th edn., London, Law Society, 1996), para. 17.01.

[35] See e.g. James J. White "Machiavelli and the Bar: Ethical Limits on Lying in Negotiations" [1980] *American Bar Foundation Res. Journal* 926.

[36] Willliam H. Simon, "Ethical Discretion in Lawyering" (1988) 101 *Harv. Law Rev.* 1083.

with the consequence that students are likely to accept the proffered framework in an undiscriminating manner. This unhelpful approach to professional ethics reaches its height at the end of chapter 27, where the author gives detailed guidance to the competitive negotiator on the use of threats, feigned displays of anger, and evasive responses to questions before concluding:

> "You should never lie and you have a professional duty to act with complete frankness and good faith consistent with you overriding duty to your client" (Solicitors Practice Rules 1990, principle 16.01.).[37]

It is true that the principle cited seems itself to be guilty of doublespeak (what if frankness is *not* in the interest of the client?). But it is nevertheless astonishing that no attempt is made to make sense of what is clearly intended to be a limit of some kind on what lawyers may legitimately do for their clients.[38]

We might sum up the current position by saying that the UK position with respect to the teaching of legal ethics represents a clear example of the unhepful disjuncture between academic and professional legal education which ACLEC is keen to end. This diagnosis is confirmed by ACLEC's proposal for a new vocational qualification, the Licentiate in Professional Legal Studies (Lic.PLS) to be obtained after a period of fifteen to eighteen weeks of study following the award of a law degree.[39] It is proposed that this should be mandatory for all prospective barristers and solicitors, but of appeal to a wider range of professional options.[40] It is significant for our purposes that the course is to be offered by institutions of higher education;[41] that it is to contain contributions from both academics and practitioners;[42] that professional ethics are suggested as a central component; and that the subject should not be confined to the study of the professional codes.[43]

II. THE SEEDS OF CHANGE

What accounts, then, for calls upon academics to enter into partnership with practitioners in the teaching of legal ethics in the United Kingdom? It seems logical enough to seek an explanation in the occupational concerns of the principal actors, namely academic law teachers and practising lawyers. As to the former, an expression of interest must be seen in the light of recent changes in the structure of higher education within the United Kingdom. On

---

[37] Para. 27.3 at 195–6. The reference in this passage seems to be erroneous. It seems likely that the intended reference was to what is now para. 19.01 of the Guide, *supra* n. 31.

[38] For a possible improvement on this see S. Maughan and J. Webb, *Legal Skills and the Lawyering Process* (London, Butterworths, 1994).

[39] Or equivalent qualification(s).

[40] See *Report*, *supra* n. 4, ch. 5.6 and 5.11–5.17.

[41] *Ibid.*, para. 5.17.

[42] *Ibid.*, para. 5.15.

[43] *Ibid.*, para. 5.13.

the one hand the government has abolished the longstanding divide between universities, traditionally associated with pure research, and the polytechnics, traditionally concerned more with teaching and applied research. Informed observers[44] view the administrative fusion decreed by the government as likely to bring about a consequential merging of cultures. Hence we might expect academics to begin to take an interest in subjects traditionally seen as vocational.

Unlike their US counterparts, who were forced to take the teaching of professional ethics more seriously by the Watergate scandal, the concerns of UK practitioners cannot be traced to a particular cataclysmic event. In retrospect, the nearest equivalent might be said to be the election in 1979 of a conservative administration committed to requiring all occupational groups to demonstrate, usually by competition in the market-place, the utility of their occupational performance. As a result the legal profession has suffered a dramatic reversal of its political fortunes. The 1979 Royal Commission of Inquiry into Legal Services[45] accepted the profession's self-portrait in classical structural functionalist terms as an occupational group which, if left free of government regulation could be trusted to serve the public interest. The profession's intrinsic motivation or sense of vocation was the ultimate guarantee of quality. How different was the spirit of the reforms introduced ten years later by the government's ground breaking Green Paper, "The Work and Organization of the Legal Profession":

> "The government believes that free competition between the providers of legal services will through the discipline of the market ensure that the public is provided with the most effective network of legal services at the most economic price."[46]

As is well known, these reforms brought about fundamental changes in the work of the legal profession. The conveyancing monopoly on which 50 per cent of solicitors' income depended[47] was abolished, provoking the response that if competition was to be allowed then solicitors would compete vigorously: restrictions on advertising were largely abolished.

More important than this fact however was the loss of trust which it represented and which was an outstanding feature of former Lord Chancellor, Lord Mackay's, seemingly endless list of reform proposals. Consider, for example, the Consultation Paper and subsequent White Paper on *Reform of the Legal Aid System*,[48] Lord Woolf's Report on *Access to Civil*

---

[44] See M. Partington, "Legal Education in the 1990s", ch. 12 of Philip Thomas (ed.), *Tomorrow's Lawyers* (Oxford, Basil Blackwell, 1992).

[45] *Report of the Royal Commission on Legal Services (Benson Report)* (1979), Cmnd. 7648.

[46] *The Work and Organisation of the Legal Profession* (1989), Cm 570, para. 1.2.

[47] Abel, *supra* n. 13 at 209, citing figures produced for the 1979 Royal Commission on Legal Services.

[48] *Legal Aid—Targeting Need* (May 1995) Cm 2854, ("The Green Paper") and *Striking the Balance—the Future of Legal Aid in England and Wales* (June 1996), Cm 3305 ("The White Paper").

Justice[49] and the White Paper on Family Law reform,[50] leading to the Family Law Act 1986. As to family law, at the heart of the new regime are first a move to no-fault divorce[51] and, secondly, the public funding and encouragement of mediation.[52] The former is based in part on the government's assumption that under the existing system of divorce many contrived but irrefutable allegations of fault are being made by lawyers anxious to expedite their clients' divorce proceedings. The latter aspect assumes that lawyers' involvement is, contrary to the professed aims[53] of the Solicitors' Family Law Association inevitably adversarial, leading to an increase in bitterness and hostility. All in all, this is not a very flattering picture of the legal profession.

A similar picture emerges from the legal aid proposals. Spiralling legal aid costs are seen as a consequence of an excessive willingness on the part of assisted persons to launch speculative litigation because of their immunity from costs in the event of failure.[54] As far as the lawyers are concerned, the government has adopted the standard economic analysis of the conflicts of interest inevitably arising between expert agents and lay principals[55]. More precisely, spiralling costs are seen as being due to the fact that under the present scheme lawyers are paid by the hour—whenever an applicant of insufficient means is certified as having a case of sufficient merit, then the State will pay for whatever work the lawyer regards as necessary for the furtherance of the client's case. Thus it is assumed that lawyers are behaving as rational maximisers of their self-interest beginning and continuing cases in their own interests and contrary to their duty to the Legal Aid Fund.[56] Out of the State's inability to trust the lawyers to restrain their litigious clients,[57] combined with an independently grounded desire to limit public expenditure, has come a potential revolution in the way publicly funded services are to be organised: in future a limited number of franchisees selected by competitive tender will operate to fixed budgets with quality assured by regular auditing by the Legal Aid Board. Again the assumed models of lawyer behaviour owe little or nothing to public-spirited professionalism. Finally, Lord Woolf's inquiry into access to the civil justice system paints a picture of a system that is excessively slow and excessively expensive, much of the blame being put on the legal professions' excessively adversarial approach

[49] *Access to Justice—Final Report* by the Rt. Hon. the Lord Woolf MR (London, Lord Chancellor's Department, HMSO, 1996).

[50] Lord Chancellor's Deparment, *Looking to the Future—Mediation and the Grounds for Divorce*, Cm 2799 (London, HMSO, 1995), at paras. 2.6–2.8 (7).

[51] Family Law Act 1986, ss. 2–9.

[52] *Ibid.*, ss. 13, 14 and 29.

[53] See the "Code of Practice of the Solicitors' Family Law Association" (1984) 14 Family Law 156.

[54] White Paper, *supra* n. 45, at paras. 4.27–4.30.

[55] "Green Paper", *supra* n. 45, at para. 3.29.

[56] *Ibid.*, paras. 1.12, 6.45.

[57] The White Paper lays greater emphasis on the irresponsibility of assisted persons, whereas the Consultation Paper focuses more clearly on the responsiblity of the lawyers.

to litigation.[58] The major solution proposed is proactive judicial case-management, the assumption being that absent the judicial policeman lawyers will inevitably exploit to their clients' advantage any opportunities allowed by the rules of court for aggressive hostile litigation.[59] Overall it is clear that the way in which the legal profession currently operates is often perceived as being an obstacle to access to justice, to be overcome either by State or market regulation or, more radically still, by making the legal profession redundant. Thus before the ink on Lord Woolf's report was dry the government had raised the jurisdictional limit on the Small Claims Court, in which no legal costs are awarded, to £3,000.[60] On May 1st 1997, the British people elected a new Labour Government. Whilst the precise details are vague it seems clear at the time of going to press that the new government will adopt at least the general direction of these reforms. At any rate, it is most unlikely that the mistrust of the legal profession on which they are based will disappear.

Within this general climate of distrust, renewed interest in the socialisation of lawyers is entirely logical. From the State's perspective, it constitutes a strategy complementary to those of regulation by the market/the State. From the profession's point of view, it is necessary to forestall these alternative strategies. The flavour of the moment can perhaps be gleaned from the case made by Peter Goldsmith QC, then Chairman of the Bar, for the adoption by the Bar of an improved complaints procedure.

> "The days of self-regulation are drawing to a close, the Treasury and Civil Service Select Committee said this month. MPs were not referring to the regulation of lawyers but they might as well have been. The signs are all too clear. Politicians attack judges for being soft on sentencing and lawyers for helping 'criminals' to get off. The National Consumer Council meanwhile proposes a government quango to tackle complaints against solicitors and barristers—a lay dominated system for which lawyers would have to pay. . . . Tonight if we want to continue to regulate our own affairs—as an independent profession should—we must show we are not prepared to shield the incompetent, the careless, the arrogant or the rude. . . . But if we reject [the new scheme], we will have no ground for complaint if the Government is persuaded to impose an expensive bureaucratic scheme in which we have little influence."[61]

III. PROSPECTS FOR THE FUTURE

At this point we need to consider what might be achieved in the United Kingdom by a stress on the importance of legal ethics at each and every stage

---

[58] *Supra* n. 49, at 2, para. 2 and 72, para. 1.

[59] *Ibid.*, ch. 6, and especially 72, para. 1.

[60] *The Times*, 8 Jan. 1996, 5. Previously the limit was £1,000.

[61] *The Times*, 21 Nov. 1995, 37. It is only fair to point out that in addition to the argument cited, the writer argued as one of two additional reasons for supporting that scheme that "it is simply right to adopt it. If a client suffers inadequate professional service, justice demands that we do something about it . . .".

of the process of legal education. This raises the broad issue of what formal educational processes can do to bring about a "commitment to the rule of law, to justice, fairness and high ethical standards".[62] It might be said for example that the cumulative effect of pre-adult learning, both formal and informal, and the impact of law office culture are likely to combine to marginalize the impact of formal legal education. This broad objection cannot be addressed in any detail here. It should be noted though that one of its central strands is the argument that in a competitive market for legal services lawyers will be forced to take any step likely to enhance their client's prospects of success, however unethical it might be, provided only that it is not forbidden by (punished as a violation of) a Code of Conduct. However, in an important article Mnookin and Gilson[63] have shown that this assumption of an inevitable race to the bottom is unfounded. Under the right market conditions a reputation for fair dealing can be in the interests of the lawyer and, in the long term, its clients. Here detailed consideration will be given (section (a)) to the contribution which might be made by academic lawyers and undergraduate courses. The next section (section (b)) considers how academic lawyers might go about realising this potential and analyses some of the difficulties which must be faced.

(a) The Academic Contribution

Our discussion of the goals of legal ethics teaching[64] contained an important implicit assumption, namely that legal ethics teaching cannot be focused on a formalistic application of the professional codes. If academics are to have an important role we need to ask why the aspiring practitioner need to know more than what the Codes say. To this question there are a number of clear answers. The first is that the current codes of ethics simply fail to address a number of very difficult issues, such as the question whether a lawyer interviewing a client should tell the client what the law is (thus providing an opportunity for perjury) before the client tells his or her story. On other issues the Codes are unclear and open-textured so that the relevant provision cannot be applied without the making of complex ethical judgements. This is preeminently the case, for example, of Solicitors Practice Rule 1 which is described in the Guide to Professional Conduct as the bedrock of ethical practice:

> "A solicitor shall not do anything in the course of practising as a solicitor, or permit another person to do anything on his or her behalf, which compromises or impairs or is likely to compromise or impair any of the following:

---

[62] *Report, supra* n. 4, at para. 2.4

[63] Ronald J. Gilson and Robert H. Mnookin, "Disputing Through Agents: Cooperation and Conflict Between Lawyers in Litigation" 94 Colombia LR 458 [1994].

[64] *Supra* text to nn. 8–12.

(a)   the solicitor's independence or integrity;

(b)   a person's freedom to instruct a solicitor of his or her choice;

(c)   the solicitor's duty to act in the best interests of the client;

(d)   the solicitor's proper standard of work;

(e)   the solicitor's duty to the Court."

Quite what this means for difficult ethical quandaries such as the decision whether to disclose in the course of negotiations material facts unknown to the other side is a question which does not admit of an easy answer but for this reason it is appropriate for discussion as part of academic legal education.

The insufficiency of the Codes has received implicit recognition with the institution by the Bar and the Law Society of "hot lines" to which lawyers may resort in case of difficulty. The confidentiality of such conversations masks their content from the scrutiny of researchers, but it seems likely that their existence makes the real norms of professional conduct a matter for negotiation between individual lawyers and the institutional ethical guide. If so it seems appropriate that intending practioners spend time considering what might be reasonable solutions to propose to the institutional guide. Academic legal education seems an ideal place for this to be done.

It could be said in response that this implies a need to reform the Codes and make them more specific. It cannot be denied that reform of the professional codes is important. Regardless of the extent to which they are actually enforced by disciplinary bodies, ethically demanding code provisions may have an important socialising effect. Moreover, code reform is an area in which academics as researchers may have much to offer. However, code reform has distinct limits as a way of raising ethical standards. For one thing, ever more detailed regulation of this kind is wont to carry the message that all ethics are simply a matter of minimalist compliance with the rules, leading to lawyers adopting a formalistic response. Since lawyers arouse considerable criticism when they interpret the substantive law in this way on their clients' behalf, this seems undesirable. Indeed, in the recent case of *Vernon* v *Bosley* (no 2)[65], the Court of Appeal clearly expressed its distaste for such an approach to ethical issues. Thorpe L. commented critically that counsel submitted that in the dilemma of decision counsel had only to look to the authorities and apply them to the cicumstances. Counsel was not to be guided by his feelings on the issue in question. I cannot accept that counsel's approach should be so strictly cerebral. There is value in instinctive and intuitive judgment[66]. In any case, a great deal of legal work is largely invisible to regulatory oversight (especially when we shift our eyes from the courtroom to the lawyer's office).[67] It therefore follows that unless lawyers view the norms of

[65]   1997 1 All Er 614

[66]   Ibid p. 653GJ.

[67]   This is particularly true e.g. of the question whether a lawyer assists his client in the commission of an illegal act when he explains the law to the client before asking for his client's story

professional life as having some ethical basis, then it is unlikely that they will be followed when contrary temptations present themselves.

If this argument for the insufficiency of code based approaches is accepted, what we can expect to achieve within the broader approach can be encapsulated within the words independence and perspective. As Northrop suggests[68], it cannot be overemphasised that law graduates will inevitably emerge from degree level legal education with a theory of legal ethics. If for three years, students are taught to explore the limits of the substantive law without any suggestion that there may be other limits on what lawyers may do for their clients, then students will be hearing the implicit message that the lawyer's job is that of the skilled technician exploiting the law to the client's best advantage[69]. Similarly, those who go on to practice will quickly find themselves being trained by more senior lawyers, each of whom will have his or her theory of legal ethics. This makes it vital that the adoption of ethical frameworks be conscious and critical. To be sure, the role of moral philosophy in the curriculum is bound to remain controversial. On the one hand, some claim that whatever the difference at an applied level between, for example, rights based and consequential ethical approaches to ethical issues, they share a common meta-ethical premise, namely that moral judgments are to be grounded in universal moral principles above and beyond those of a particular community. As one commentator has put it:

> "ethical reasoning is conceptually autonomous from more conventionally held beliefs, affording an impartial point of view from which people rise above and critically assess the ethical validity of the beliefs of their state, society, ethnic or religious or racial group."[70]

Morover, there is considerable evidence from the field of moral psychology, stemming principally from the work of Lawrence Kohlenberg, that formal educational processes are effective in developing this capacity for independent judgment: studies of American high school students demonstrate that those who go to College show considerable development in their capacity for moral judgment as compared with their peers who choose not to do so.[71] On the other hand, some have questioned whether there really is any mid-air position from which one can assess values independently of the culture and community of the assessor.[72] However, one does not have to take sides in this important meta-ethical debate in order to acknowledge the importance of law students

thereby creating an incentive for perjury: see Kenneth Mann, *Defending White Collar Crime* (New Haven, Conn., Yale University Press, 1985), at 110–111.

[68] Supra text to note 2.

[69] Carrie J. Menkel-Meadow, "Can a Law Teacher Avoid Teaching Legal Ethics?", 41 *Journal of Legal Education* 3 [1991].

[70] D. Richard, "Moral Theory, The Developmental Psychology of Ethical Autonomy and Professionalism", 31 *Journal of Legal Education* 359, 365. [1981].

[71] J. D. Rest, "Can Ethics Be Taught In Professional Schools? The Psychological Research", 1 *Ethics Easier Said than Done* 22 [1988].

[72] *See David Luban, Supra* note 25 at p. 657.

being encouraged to consider critically the norms of the legal profession. There is abundant evidence in the history of the anglo-american legal profession that at any given point, human nature being what it is, some of the norms of the profession will reflect nothing more than its own and/or its clients' self-interest: for example, the long-standing restrictions in the UK on advertising seem indefensible to modern eyes.[73] It is therefore crucial that the teaching of legal ethics be such as to encourage independent judgment and in this task moral and legal theory will clearly be a useful tool. Despite concerns that our law schools are compromising their commitment to moral and legal theory and despite evidence of undergraduate resistance to theory[74], these tools are currently more likely to be available and effective in academic law schools than at any other stage of legal education.

As to perspective, it is commonly noticed that real world objects look very different according to the perspective from which and the context in which they are viewed. So it is also with the problems of professional life. A good example perhaps is the arguments over the desirability of conditional fees. Historically, UK practitioners involved with personal injury litigation have tended to see the difficulties, particularly the incentive thereby created for unethical over-zealous representation, as insurmountable. Hence, in the United Kingdom the Bar and the Law Society were for many years opposed to conditional fees. However there is a wider perspective namely that of access to justice: the legal aid budget has stretched as far as it will go but eligibility continues to decline; private legal expenses insurance seems unattractive to the market; few can afford to fund litigation themselves. It seems undeniable that this wider perspective has led the UK legal profession to soften its opposition. And the point for present purposes of course is that one of the functions of university legal education is to develop in students a capacity for wide perspectives. Often the acquisition of more information about an ethical difficulty may lead to an ethical judgement being changed if it can be shown to be based on a false factual premise. Thus if sweeping confidentiality obligations are justified on the ground that they are necessary to engender in clients the candour necessary for effective representation, they are vulnerable to empirical demonstrations that in many cultures at different points in history professionals of all kinds have effectively represented clients without the benefit of sweeping confidentiality provisions. Consequently, the comparative perspective which is most likely to be evoked during initial stage legal education and which was ordered by ACLEC as one of the five pillars of undergraduate legal education has significant potential as a tool for ethical education. It can be seen then that in the notions of independence and perspective, there are good reasons

---

[73] For a perceptive account of this aspect of UK legal professional regulation see Abel, *supra* note 13, chapter 12.

[74] On these issues see Hilaire Barnett, "The Province of Jurisprudence Determined—Again!", *Legal Studies* 88 [1995].

to think that academic legal education has a real, indeed a vital role to play in the inculcation of legal values.

(b) The Academic Response

Thus far I have argued that the involvement of academic lawyers in teaching about and research into legal ethics has significant potential for contributing to the development of engaged professionals. Moreover despite the difficulties presented by modern economic conditions opportunities may still exist for the effective deployment of the values and attitudes thereby engendered. It remains to consider what needs to be done particularly in terms of reform of the undergraduate curriculum if this potential is to be realised.

Clinical legal education clearly has significant potential but I do not propose to consider it in detail here.[75] Not only is clinical legal education still relatively rare at the initial stage, it also has both the strengths and the weaknesses of the simulated practice which is currently such a feature of vocational legal education.[76] Therefore, even if clinical legal education were to undergo rapid development, it could only be an effective vehicle for the teaching of legal ethics if it could build upon the work already done in non-clinical courses. It is therefore appropriate to consider what might be needed in the way of non-clinical courses if ACLEC's vision is to be fulfilled.

The current programme at the Stanford Law School provides one possible model. There all students receive an introduction to the major issues of micro legal ethics and the profession's regulatory structure during their early weeks in law school. Thereafter, students are not required to take the specialist course in legal ethics but they are required to take at least one course which contains a substantial ethics component. This use of structured choice ensures that the major issues are considered in a context which is of interest to the student.[77] Finally, the school takes seriously the idea of "Ethics by the Pervasive Method"[78] which rests on the argument that ethical issues must be addressed throughout the course as they arise in substantive courses. Otherwise, the silence of teachers (other than those teaching courses which focus directly on ethics) is wont to convey the implicit message that ethics are not after all central to the practice of law. Consequently, each of the first year courses spends at least 2 of the available 24 hours of contact time on the ethical issues arising in that subject.

Making due allowance for the differences between the US position where first degrees in law are taken at the postgraduate stage and the UK position

---

[75] Deborah L. Rhode, "Ethical Perspectives on Legal Practice", 37 *Stan L Rev.* 589, 614 [1985].

[76] See Julian Webb, "Inventing the Good: A Prospectus For Clinical Education and the Teaching of Legal Ethics in England", *Law Teacher* 270 [1996].

[77] Supra notes 21–25 and following text.

[78] See Deborah L. Rhode, "Into the Valley of Ethics: Professional Responsibility and Educational Reform" [1996] 139.

where first degrees in law may be taken as an undergraduate, this model suggests a number of possibilities. In his 1993 survey of UK Law Schools[79], Professor John Wilson found that the English Legal System was widely taught being compulsory in 24 of the 34 Schools surveyed. On any view, such courses should be introducing students to the major issues of macro legal ethics. As for micro legal ethics, the main issues, though difficult to resolve, are relatively small in number focusing largely on the validity of what has come to be known as the standard conception of lawyers' ethics.[80] Consequently, it should be possible to introduce them to students within the parameters of a course on the English Legal System without creating enormous curriculum overload. With regard to specialist courses, the lure of a subject that is topical, stimulating and, in the English context, unexplored is likely to make this element of the legal ethics curriculum relatively easy to provide. Moreover, Jurisprudence courses have a great deal to offer to the business of teaching micro legal ethics, for many of the central dilemmas depend upon one's view of law and the nature of the legal system. If you really believe, for example, that the law is what officials do about disputes, then one of the classic dilemmas of legal ethics, that of whether the lawyer should manipulate the legal system in the interests of his client disappears: for ex hypothesi the just solution is whatever the system can be made to produce.[81] If this potential is to be fulfilled, jurisprudence courses must emphasize that questions about the nature of law have implications not only for how appellate judges decide difficult points of law but also for the every day working decisions of ordinary lawyers. As to ethics by the pervasive method, it is striking how many of the materials, particularly the cases commonly considered in substantive courses, simultaneously raise ethical issues. It is symptomatic of this that a recent edition of the All England Reports was almost entirely taken up with reports of two hearings in the Court of Appeal in the case of *Vernon v Bosley*[82]. The plaintiff's children had drowned when the defendant, their nanny, negligently drove their car into a river and he later claimed damages for negligence for psychiatric illness allegedly suffered as a result of having witnessed the unsuccessful rescue attempts. The first hearing concerned substantive questions as to the limits of liability in negligence for psychiatric illness. This is currently one of the most unsettled and controversial areas of English tort law and an area of enduring interest to undergraduate tort law teachers. The second hear-

---

[79] See Deborah L. Rhode, "Ethics by the Pervasive Method", 42 *Journal of Legal Education* 31 [1991].

[80] J. Wilson, "A Third Survey of University Legal Education", 13 *Legal Studies* 1 [1993].

[81] The "standard conception of lawyer's ethics" is usually thought to contain: (i) the principle of neutral partisanship requiring the lawyer do everything in his client's interests provided only that it be neither technically illlegal or a clear breach of an ethical rule and (ii) a principle of non accountability whereby the lawyer shifts to the client moral responsibility for any harm caused by conduct required by the first principle. The standard conception was first formulated in this way in the work of William H. Simon. See "The Ideology of the Advocacy System: Procedural Justice and Professional Ethics", *Wisconsin LR* [1978] 36.

[82] All ER.

ing concerned the ethical obligations of the plaintiff's lawyers upon discovering that, whilst claiming in the personal injury proceedings that he was suffering from mental illness with poor prognosis, he was simultaneously claiming (with the help of different lawyers but the same expert witness) in matrimonial proceedings that his mental health was rapidly improving in order to further his claim for custody of his children.

At first sight then, the prospects for a significant academic contribution through first degree teaching seem good. However, there are unfortunately a number of local factors which are likely to restrict the impact of undergaduate law degrees on ethics.

The major problem, in the words of Professor Cotter, is that "law teachers are committed to independence and autonomy at the cost of curriculum-wide structure",[83] and is particularly likely to manifest itself in relation to the pervasive teaching of legal ethics during substantive courses. The temptation to say that this is not my concern is particularly strong at a time when teachers are under ever-increasing pressure to publish, for the process of immersing oneself in a previously neglected area requires a investment in academic capital which is profoundly discouraged by the current system for assessing research productivity. This problem has an institutional dimension also. A wide ranging interdisciplinary approach to the teaching of legal ethics will demand of law teachers a broader knowledge and a wider range of intellectual skills than many of them received in the course of their own legal education.[84] One solution may be found in regular periods of study leave.[85] However the single most incontrovertible feature of the current landscape of higher education is the ever-growing squeeze on resources.

Finally, the historic divide between academic and practical legal studies is likely to persist for some time to come, so that an interest in legal ethics is likely to remain the interest of a committed few. Deeply ingrained attitudes cannot be changed by the reformers' prescriptive utterance. The problem also has structural features. The best way to break down the divide would be to teach an integrated four-year degree encompassing both the intellectual objectives of undergraduate legal education[86] and the skills objectives of the current vocational courses.[87] This is precisely what has been done by the University of Northumbria.[88] However, this model, however attractive, is unlikely to be widely adopted because the Treasury has indicated that it will not provide the funding for a widespread extension of law degrees from three to four years.[89] Therefore any university which seeks to follow the

---

[83] 3–17, and see n. 17 for an amusing and illustrative account.

[84] See generally ACLEC, *First Consultation Paper, supra* n. 4, at paras. 6.8–6.11.

[85] A complementary and less expensive strategy may be to enter into academic partnership with academics from other disciplines.

[86] See *First Report, supra* n. 4 at para. 4.4

[87] *Ibid.*, at 147 and 151.

[88] For a brief description see *Report, ibid* 1, at para. 2.16.

[89] *Ibid.*, at para. 3.19.

Northumbria model will impose upon students an unfunded fourth year, hence reducing its attraction in the market for undergraduate students. This disincentive to integration is likely severely to limit the effect of one of the most prominent recent developments in vocational education, namely the breakdown of the former monopoly of the Inns of Court School of Law and the College of Law as providers of the Bar Vocational Course and the Legal Practice Course. These courses may now be offered by universities. However, given the barriers to integration, these courses and their teachers are likely to remain insolated from undergraduate teachers and the undergraduate study of law.[90]

The academic–practical divide may thus continue to inhibit the contribution of academic law teachers collectively to legal ethics. A good test will perhaps be their response to the proposed "Licentiate in Professional Legal Studies".[91] On the one hand it might be embraced as an opportunity for creative partnership between academics and practitioners as ACLEC clearly hopes. Another less creative response might be to regard the course as "unacademic". Moreover the proposed stress within that course on legal ethics might be viewed as yet another reason for saying that legal ethics is "somebody else's concern".

Ultimately then, legal ethics present both possibilities and challenges for UK university law schools. There is the possibility of making a real contribution to the development, perhaps one might even say the redemption, of the professional ideal. Whether the challenges overwhelm the possibilities remains to be seen.

[90] *Report*, at para. 2.11.
[91] *Supra*, n. 39, and following text.

9

The Teaching of Legal Ethics . . . in the Tropiques*

Who cares about legal ethics in Brazil? Do Brazilian law schools really care how ethics are taught? And does the Brazilian Bar Association care? Are students interested in the study of legal ethics? Are these different interests connected to specific political agendas? Trying to answer these questions, this chapter analyses the discourses and practices of actors more closely related to the teaching of legal ethics in Brazil, i.e. the Brazilian Bar Association, legal ethics professors and their students.[1] The structure of the chapter is based on the analysis developed by Nelson and Trubek,[2] who identified four arenas of professionalism: legal education, collective action on behalf of the profession, disciplinary enforcement and the workplace. While agreeing with the authors that these arenas of professionalism are mutually influenced in a "complex and indeterminant manner",[3] pragmatic considerations require me to restrict the analysis to those arenas more closely related to the formal teaching of legal ethics, i.e. to the "multiple and conflicting ideas" produced within the collective action on behalf of the profession (the Bar Association and the Federal Council of Education)[4], and university legal education (law professors and law students)[5].

* This ch. is based on research developed in Rio de Janeiro. I am grateful to Silvia Beatriz Machado de Araújo and Cristiana Vianna Veras, who worked as research assistants, and to the Conselho Nacional de Desenvolvimento Científico e Tecnológico (CNPq), for the financial support.

[1] Raw data were collected among final year law students of the Catholic University of Rio de Janeiro (PUC-Rio) taking the mandatory course on legal ethics in 1996, and their professors. Legal documents, such as the Bar Statute and the Code of Ethics, were also analysed.

[2] R. Nelson and D. Trubek, "Arenas of Professionalism: The Professional Ideologies of Lawyers in Context", in 12. Melson *et al*, *Lawyers' Ideals/Lawyers' Practices* (Ithaca, NY, Cornell University Press, 1992).

[3] *Ibid.*, 185.

[4] Despite the legal responsibility of the Federal Council of Education for the regulation of legal education in Brazil, the current law curriculum, established in 1994, was essentially formulated by the Brazilian Bar Association.

[5] A future analysis of workplace ideas of legal ethics (as well as of the disciplinary enforcement of the Code of Ethics in Brazil) is necessary for two reasons. First, the understanding of legal education presupposes the understanding of other arenas of professionalism, as they are mutually influenced. Secondly, due to the historical role played by Brazilian legal education in

A reader familiar with Lévi-Strauss' observation that *"[l]es Tropiques sont moins exotiques que démodés"*[6] might well ask what is important about the teaching of legal ethics in Brazil. Perhaps Lévi-Strauss was wrong after all and the *tropiques* are not so *démodés*. At least, this is the point developed by a contemporary anthropologist, Paul Rabinov, astonished during a recent visit to Brazil by the coexistence of tradition, modernity and postmodernity within the same geographical and social space.[7] If this is correct—and as a Brazilian myself, I would agree with Rabinov's perception of our complexity—the terrain of legal ethics and its teaching in Brazil may also represent a meeting ground for "tradition", "modernity" and "postmodernity".[8]

I. THE BRAZILIAN BAR ASSOCIATION

Important changes relating to the teaching of legal ethics have been introduced in various Brazilian legal arenas (legal profession and law schools) throughout the 1990s. The new curriculum of law schools approved in December 1994 but not entering into force until March 1997 made, for the first time, legal ethics a mandatory course, alongside other educational requirements such as the study of sociology of law and philosophy of law.[9] The new Bar Association Statute [10] introduced (also for the first time) the Bar examination, which now includes specific questions on legal ethics.[11] Based on the Constitution of 1988, the new Bar Statute succeeded in guaranteeing the exclusive rights of audience for lawyers. And, through a new Code of Ethics,[12] the Brazilian Bar Association aims to confront ethical challenges at the end of the twentieth century.

Why these changes, and what are these challenges? The recent wave of moralisation within the political arena (beginning with the impeachment of

building the administrative elite, the socialisation of lawyers in Brazil occurs mainly at the workplace. Law schools are normally perceived by law students as a place to "obtain a diploma", and not to learn law (and, certainly, not a place to study legal ethics, which they will learn during their apprenticeship at law firms, observing legal practices and the lawyers' behaviour). For further information about legal education and legal profession in Brazil, see J. Falcão, "Lawyers in Brazil" in R. Abel and P. Lewis, *Lawyers in Society: The Civil Law World* (Berkeley, CA, University of California Press, 1988).

[6] "Tropical countries are out of fashion rather than exotic"—Lévi-Strauss, *Tristes Tropiques* (Paris, Plon, 1955) at 81.

[7] P. Rabinov, "A Modern Tour in Brazil" in S. Lash and J. Friedman, *Modernity and Identity* (Oxford, Blackwell, 1993).

[8] Despite the contemporary debate about modernity and postmodernity, these categories are quite useful for mapping a complex social reality, such as the Brazilian scene. See, *inter alia*, B. S. Santos, *Towards a New Common Sense* (New York, NY, Routledge, 1995); A. Giddens, *Modernity and Self-Identity* (Stanford, CA, Stanford University Press, 1991); M. Featherstone, *Consumer Culture and Postmodernism* (London, Sage, 1992).

[9] The former curriculum, with its more positivist approach, dates back to 1972.

[10] The new Lawyer and Bar Association Statute (July 1994) replaced the former one (1964).

[11] In fact, 4 questions out of 50, most related to formal requirements to practise law.

[12] 1994; the former Code of Ethics dates back to 1934.

President Collor, who was accused of corruption in 1991) could well have played an important role in this process. Nevertheless, the impact of national politics cannot be stressed too much on changes both in university legal education and in the legal profession. These only represent an engagement between two distinct groups (elite lawyers of the Bar Association and scholars) and, therefore, an interchange between two different discourses, which I describe as the "professional-oriented" and "political-oriented" discourses.

(a) The "Professional-Oriented" Discourse

After playing a fundamental role in the struggle against the military regime and for civil rights (in the 1970s and early 1980s) which guaranteed its social legitimation,[13] the Bar Association felt the need to develop new strategies of legitimation towards lawyers and civil society in the 1990s. Instead of the discourse based on political issues, a new discourse focusing on professional problems faced by lawyers and their clients seemed more appropriate to maintain the Bar's prestige among its professionals and within society at large. In contrast with the early 1980s, when lawyers considered that the priority of the Bar Association should be the political activity and the struggle for a legitimate government,[14] lawyers in the 1990s living in a formal democratic regime have been concerned primarily with professional interests and not with political agendas.

The first attempt of the Brazilian Bar Association to legitimise itself among its members occurred during the period of constitutional reform (the late 1980s), when lawyers were guaranteed rights of audience and legal representation, i.e. over the expanding market for legal services. Understandably the defence of the professional monopoly had a unifying effect on the profession. Acting on behalf of the profession, the Bar pacified the claims of more right-wing oriented lawyers who felt that political struggles distracted the Bar Association from its professional concerns. However, as important as resisting external competition (through the preservation of professional monopolies) was the aim of avoiding increasing competition within the profession.[15] The second stage of this legitimation strategy aimed at controlling entry to the profession, either through changes in university legal education and more direct controls over law schools, or through the vocational examination, which became the final hurdle for admission to the Bar.

At the same time, due to the increasing proliferation of lawyers over the last two decades, it was felt important to change the (negative) image of

[13] See J. Falcão, *supra* n. 5, 412, who also refers to the political role of the Brazilian Bar Association in the defence of human rights and political liberties, as well as on behalf of the redemocratisation of the country.

[14] *Ibid.*

[15] According to Joaquim Falcão, *supra* n. 5, 409, "the excess supply has generated a destructive competition among lawyers".

lawyers in Brazilian society which was affected by the rapid expansion of the commercial law school sector.[16] The Bar examination and the new Code of Ethics answered, however, an implicit demand of Brazilian society for raising lawyers' academic credentials as well as their commitment to rules of professional conduct.

There can be no doubt that these strategies of controlling the "production *of* producers" and the "production *by* producers"[17] reveal the power of self-regulation of the Bar Association.[18] Nevertheless, some questions have to be raised about the Bar Association's goals or, at least, about the effectiveness of its strategies in relation to its discourse. First, it is quite clear that the needs of society and the needs of the profession point in contradictory directions. In a society such as the Brazilian one, with low rates of litigation and poor access to justice, the monopoly of legal representation interferes with the protection of the rights of the lower social classes, obstructs access to justice, especially following the creation of small claims courts in the mid-1980s and encourages the use of other (not necessarily more democratic) informal mechanisms of dispute settlement.[19] In other words, the monopoly over legal representation does not actually guarantee lawyers the monopoly over dispute settlement since effective access to justice is denied to the majority of the Brazilian population.[20] Secondly, strategies to control the behaviour of newly qualified lawyers, especially through the approval of the new Code of Ethics, reflect the specific goals of elite lawyers rather than the demands of society or different groups within the legal profession. The Code of Ethics supports, for example, an internal hierarchy within the legal profession, which establishes lighter penalties for members who have served on the Board of Trustees of the Bar Association. Advertising, still prohibited, affects the practitioner without social capital, and not the "big guys"[21] in the profession.[22] Although the Bar Association defends an external control of the judiciary by civil society, the discipline and regulation of lawyers' conduct remain a professional monopoly. Thus, a strong professional *esprit de corps* avoids disciplinary procedures

---

[16] The democratisation of access to universities, a project established by the military regime in the late 1960s, primarily affected the structure of legal education through the creation of commercial law schools concerned more about profit than academic quality. Recent data point to the existence of 238 law schools, most of them created in the last two decades.

[17] R. Abel, *American Lawyers* (New York, NY, Oxford University Press, 1989) 112.

[18] The "moral authority" conquered during the 1970s and 1980s (J. Falcão, *supra* n. 5, 425) certainly has helped the Bar Association to assume this role.

[19] *Ibid.*

[20] *Ibid.*, 434.

[21] In 1995, 54.6% of new members of the Bar Association of Rio de Janeiro were women. But before being accused of sexism (for using the expression "guys", instead of people) allow me to recall that, despite an increase in the number of women entering law schools and the Bar, the Brazilian legal profession remains predominantly a male (and white) profession.

[22] See R. Abel, *supra* n. 17, on how American sole practitioners and small firms are more affected than large firms by the prohibition of advertising in the legal profession.

towards its peers and guarantees the imposition of light penalties when ethical violations are denounced. [23]

Not unlike its US counterparts, it seems that the Brazilian Bar Association promulgated "ethical rules more to legitimate [itself] in the eyes of the public than to engage in effective regulation".[24] The professional-oriented discourse disguises, therefore, the real concerns of this new wave of professionalism:[25] to improve the image of the Bar Association which had been damaged by the behaviour and the professional quality of lawyers graduated in commercial law schools.

(b) The "Political-Oriented" Discourse

Despite recent "professionalisation" strategies, the Brazilian Bar Association has not abandoned its political discourse in the 1990s, which is still present in its codes of practice. The Statutes of the Bar Association, for example, state that lawyers must defend the constitution, the democratic legal order, human rights, social justice, the efficient administration of justice and the progress of legal culture and legal institutions. All lawyers should be aware that law is an instrument for diminishing inequalities and guaranteeing equality. The Code of Ethics also stresses the social responsibilities of the profession: as an instrument for humanising social relations law must maintain a permanent connection with citizenship.[26]

Two factors explain the continuity of this discourse in the 1990s. First, despite the withdrawal of its political agenda, the Bar Association still wishes to be seen by Brazilian society as a paladin for the defence of human rights. Secondly, this "political-oriented" discourse was influenced mainly by critical[27] and socio-legal scholars deeply committed to the struggle for human rights during the authoritarian regime of the 1970s and early 1980s. In spite of the difference between the practices of these scholars and the Bar's strategies,[28]

---

[23] Most frequent violations of legal ethics in Brazil are: retaining judicial documents, failing to inform the clients about the case, improper conduct, and disrespect for clients and authorities: J. Falcão, *supra* n. 5, 423.

[24] See R. Abel, *supra* n. 17, 143.

[25] A. Abbott, *The System of Professions* (Chicago, IL., University of Chicago Press, 1988) 21. In his analysis of American medicine, Abbott states that its second wave of professionalisation implied the revision of its ethics and the reform of its schools, two strategies recently implemented by the Brazilian Bar Association.

[26] Code of Ethics, art. 2: "[L]awyers . . . shall defend the *democratic rule of law, citizenship, public morality, Justice* and *social peace* . . ."; art. 3: "lawyers shall be conscious that law is an instrument to *diminish inequalities in the search for fair solutions and to guarantee equality*"; Statute of the Brazilian Bar Association, art. 44: "[t]he Brazilian Bar Association shall defend the constitution, the *democratic legal order, human rights, social justice,* . . ." (emphasis added).

[27] Critical legal scholarship in Brazil was more influenced by the French movement of *critique de droit* than by the American critical legal studies movement.

[28] E.g. some of these scholars have devoted themselves to the development of paralegals, challenging the monopoly of the legal representation.

these two groups have a pragmatic interest in working together. On the one hand, scholars have the opportunity to influence law schools directly and, therefore, the opportunity to raise the social responsibility of future lawyers and to replace the positivist approaches (which have so dominated Brazilian law schools with a more humanistic perspective). On the other hand, the Bar Association is in a position to apply some of the knowledge produced during the 1980s by critical and socio-legal scholars.

Even though some political action is kept on the agenda (for example, when supporting cause lawyers), political discourse is not the main priority of the Brazilian Bar Association in the 1990s. Two examples show very clearly that, instead of promoting social values, the Bar is far more concerned about improving the professional competence of future lawyers. First, ethical questions in the Bar examination do not focus on the role of the law in a democratic regime, but rather on legal requirements to practise within the profession. Secondly, the recently approved Bar examination reinforces a positivist approach serving the demands of the private job market and ignores the humanistic perspective and public interest agenda arising out of the law schools' new curriculum.

II. THE LEGAL EDUCATION ARENA

The analysis of teaching legal ethics at the Catholic University of Rio de Janeiro (PUE-Rio), which is deeply influenced by the confessional character of catholicism, is particularly important in showing how the discourses of the Bar Association are reproduced within law schools,[29] and the students' reactions to them.

(a) Law Professors

The fact that the course on legal ethics is offered by the Department of Theology (and not by the Law School)—and that consequently professors in charge of the course have a theological background—could orient the course toward a discourse promoting social values. Yet the distinction between a "professional-oriented" and a "social-oriented" perspective can be seen when one considers the approach of professors teaching legal ethics at the Catholic University of Rio de Janeiro.[30]

---

[29] As suggested by Nelson and Trubek, *supra* n. 2, an analysis of the idea of professionalism developed by law schools should include, besides the study of courses on professional responsibility, the study of implicit messages about the law in all courses, as well as the analysis of its "hidden" curriculum. Nevertheless, this is a task going beyond the aims of the present ch.

[30] Although the distinction is not so rigid, the course taught in the morning by a full-time professor is dominated by a social-oriented approach, while the course taught in the evening by a full-time lawyer aims mainly to inculcate a professional attitude amongst the students.

(i) The "Professional-Oriented" Discourse

The first discourse, which stresses the study of the Code of Ethics, justifies its more "professional-oriented" approach with three main arguments. First, the Bar examination focuses on the Code of Ethics and, therefore, preparing students to pass the examination is important. Secondly, final-year students to whom the course is taught are not so much interested in a philosophical approach as in the technical skills which they believe may help them in professional practice. Finally, as most students already have some work experience in law firms,[31] they urgently need some practical tools to help them deal with ethical dilemmas which they begin to encounter in their professional activities. Using Denzin's analysis of American society, this approach is realist:[32] the course on legal ethics tries to offer some opportunity for law students to question the (non-ethical) practices of lawyers and law firms learned in the informal legal curriculum.

Two ethical dilemmas are explored by the professor. The first is the dilemma of defending a political opponent accused of murdering his wife. The background material for the class consists of a letter written by a famous Brazilian lawyer and politician[33] at the beginning of this century (1911), when consulted by a colleague about whether to accept the case. Rui Barbosa's answer to his colleague stressed that criminal defence work represents a guarantee of legality and justice and therefore the defence of society itself. Particularly in the criminal arena, there is no indigenous defence: it is fundamental to observe the due process of law, constitutional principles and the zealous pursuit of the truth.[34]

The second dilemma is related to the conflict between individual morality and professional responsibility. Using the film *Sworn to Silence*, directed by Peter Levin, the professor raises the problem of confidentiality in the lawyer (Sam Fischetti)–client (Vincent Cauley) relationship. The film presents the dilemma of a lawyer, appointed to represent a criminal defendant, after finding out that his client is guilty not only of murdering a teenager (the crime for which he was accused), but of murdering two other teenagers in a small American community. Should the lawyer reveal what he knows in the wider public interest or should he give priority to his commitment to his client?

---

[31] Most law students begin their apprenticeship at law firms in the third year of their studies.

[32] "Americans in the sixties and seventies were idealists; the eighties were materialists, and the nineties were realists": N. Denzin, *Images of Postmodern Society: Social Theory and Contemporary Cinema* (London, Sage, 1992) 4.

[33] R. Barbosa, *O dever do advogado* (Rio de Janeiro, Aidé Editora/Fundação Casa de Rui Barbosa, 1985).

[34] In fact, Rui Barbosa was consulted, not on account of his being a prestigious lawyer, but because he ran for the Presidency, by the same political party to which the lawyer was affiliated ("[a]s the accused is a political opponent, should I not defend him? Or, if I defend him, am I being politically disloyal?"). More than professional advice, the lawyer sought political authorisation to defend a political rival.

Despite pressures from public opinion, his own family and from the police, Sam Fischetti does not desert his client: he maintains silence until the accused himself reveals the truth. Consider the following dialogue between Sam Fischetti and Martin Cortigan, his partner:

> "*We are not in the business of Justice. We are in the business of law.* . . . *Without the law* . . . we have a house with no walls, two kids with no future, and nobody is safe. . . . If the constitution can't protect the worst of us, it can't defend the best of us. . . . Two lawyers, who are naive enough to follow the law . . . By protecting Vincent Cauley's rights under the law we protect all of us from ourselves, our friends, our neighbours. . . . *We were good lawyers. We followed the law.* . . . We are defending the Constitution of the United States, did anyone notice that? . . . There is always another lawyer to do the unpopular. This time I am the other lawyer" (emphasis added).

The message of the film is clear: lawyers are not committed to either justice or society, but to the law and to their clients' interests; the "Code of Legal Ethics we swore upon when we were admitted to the Bar" (Sam Fischetti) must be placed above the commitment to the community. But is a really good lawyer one that follows (only) the law? According to the professor, this is an individual choice: there is no ready-made solution that can be taught. Lawyers can justify any defence (either criminal or civil) based on due process (doing the "unpopular" is evidence of courage and of high commitment to the Constitution and civil rights[35]), or refuse cases based on their commitment to justice, and not to the law.

The third set of materials is the article "The Case of the Speluncean Explorers",[36] written by Lon Fuller of Harvard Law School.[37] Taking the judgment of an imaginary case (the homicide of a fellow explorer to guarantee the survival of a group in a blocked cavern while waiting for rescue) as his starting point, the author develops different legal arguments, based on different legal theories. In accordance with positivist legal theory one judge condemns the group as the law explicitly forbids homicides. Another judge, who subscribes to the idea of a *droit naturel*, defends the group on the basis that the right of self-defence cannot collide with positive law. For a third judge (arguing from contractualist theory), the cavern represented an autonomous geographical space and, therefore, the behaviour of the group could not be regulated by laws of another society. Using this material, the professor tries to raise a discussion about the responsibility of legal professionals (lawyers and judges): if any legal reasoning can be theoretically and rationally justified, decisions depend on our own values rather than on objective legal constraints.

[35] W. Simon, "Ethical Discretion in Lawyering" (1988) 101 *Harvard Law Review* 1083, defends, at least in civil cases, the ethical discretion of lawyers. He criticises both the libertarian approach (the lawyer has a ethical duty of loyalty to the client) and the regulatory approach (the lawyer has to contribute to the enforcement of the law).

[36] See also the case of *Dudley* v. *Stevens* discussed in A. W. Simpson, *Cannibalism and the Common Law* (Chicago, IL., University of Chicago Press, 1984).

[37] L. Fuller, "The Case of the Speluncean Explorers" (1949) 62 *Harvard Law Review* 612.

Instead of focusing on the public ethics of lawyers, i.e. their commitment to social values, civil rights and to justice (which could be illustrated, for example, by Milos Forman's recent film, *The People versus Larry Flynt*), this "professional-oriented" approach looks at the private ethics of lawyers' everyday activities. Of course this perspective is also important, especially in Brazil where lawyers regularly infringe both the Code of Ethics and the Criminal Code. An intelligent discussion of the "professional-oriented" approach may bring out the tensions within the legal profession[38] and call into question the strong *esprit de corps* of the Bar Association. In other words, the development of a critical approach to the Code of Ethics in the classroom may have a transformative role, especially when bearing in mind that the Catholic University prepares the elite of the legal profession. Instead of contributing to the reproduction of the legal profession's hierarchy,[39] this approach undermines and delegitimates hierarchical relations within the profession, and between lawyers and their clients.[40]

(ii) The "Social-oriented" Discourse

Doubtless this discourse is more closely related to the goals of a Catholic University where students are obliged to take as a prerequisite to the course on legal ethics a course on Christian ethics (covering the study of ideals such as freedom, solidarity, responsibility, dignity and social participation). Instead of stressing the Code of Ethics, this social approach focuses on the public ethics of lawyers, i.e. on their commitment to social justice and on the social responsibility of the profession. The course asks the following kinds of question: how might law contribute to making social relations more humane? What is the relationship between law and human rights? How should legal deontology be understood with reference to human rights?

This perspective—an implied criticism of positivism—is pursued by two complementary strategies. First, students have to read and discuss progressive theological documents written either by the Brazilian Episcopal Conference or by a leftist priest (Leonardo Boff), who abandoned the Catholic Church after being condemned to silence. Based on a Marxist Theology of Liberation, these documents develop two complementary ideas: the difference between morals and ethics, and the co-existence of structural and institutional sins. While morality is related to empirical and historical problems, ethics are seen as transcendental and, therefore, a-historical. While morality represents the values of the dominant class in each historical period, ethics represent the values

---

[38] As suggested by R. Ackerman, "Law Schools and Professional Responsibility: A Task for All Seasons" (1984) 88 *Dickinson Law Review* 202.

[39] D. Kennedy, *Legal Education and the Reproduction of Hierarchy* (Cambridge, MA., Afar, 1983).

[40] Unfortunately, by the end of the course, 55% of the students were not able to present any criticism to the Code of Ethics. Even worse, 57% were not able to point out the Code of Ethics and the Bar Statute as the main instruments governing lawyers' behaviour.

of the dominated class. Although morality represents the expression of the class struggle and oppression, a Christian should not deny the existence of social classes and accept the *status quo*. Consequently, the struggle of the poor against the social order (i.e. the social revolution) represents a struggle against sin and the devil and the only possibility of changing current oppression, poverty and cultural domination that particularly afflict Latin-American countries. Brazil, for example, simultaneously lives through a post-ethical and a pre-ethical situation: while parts of Brazilian society enjoy the benefits of capitalism and are committed with its own profits, the majority are excluded from public life.[41]

Law students are also encouraged to work in the *favelas* where the Catholic University has developed social projects since 1980. Two aims are pursued by this strategy. On the one hand, final-year law students can use their technical skills to assist poor people, teach them their rights (especially their social rights) and help the community to organise co-operatives and associations which may increase local income. On the other hand, when students participate in the project, they are able to understand the transformative role of the University, which changes reality instead of merely reproducing it. In this way students contribute to the development of citizenship in marginalised groups and are able to realise the social responsibility of the lawyer and to recognise more completely the Brazilian social reality (just entering the *favela* represents a novel experience for elite law students[42]). Students are also encouraged to visit a prison (also a new experience for most of them) in order to assist prisoners.

The legal ethics professor also tries to increase the commitment of future lawyers to the community by requiring the students to develop a research project about Brazilian society's perception of lawyers. Through empirical investigation, they are encouraged to survey not only their own social group, but also the working class (such as housekeepers, servants, doorkeepers, etc.). This exercise aims to emphasise lawyers' social responsibilities in the development of Brazilian citizenship and in the struggle for a substantive democracy. Due to low litigation rates in Brazil, students are supposed to find out after finishing their surveys that the legal conflicts of the working class are not submitted to formal dispute resolution but rather to informal mechanisms. Private lawyers and other legal professionals in the public sector, such as judges, public defenders and public attorneys, do not belong to the world of the working class, which knows neither its rights nor how best to defend them.

---

[41] Conferência Nacional dos Bispos do Brasil, *Ética: Pessoa e Sociedade* (São Paulo, Paulinas, 1993) 23.

[42] *Favelas* in Rio de Janeiro are geographically close to elite neighbourhoods. Nevertheless, despite this geographical proximity, the social distance between these two "worlds" is enormous. See B. S. Santos, "The Law of the Oppressed: The Construction and Reproduction of Legality in Pasargada" (1977) 12 *Law and Society Review* 5.

A principal objection to this approach is that it prepares students to "practise politics, not law", an argument which is also raised in the United States.[43] However, is not the law itself political? If so, courts could be seen as legitimate *loci* for the democratic struggle (especially in Brazil with the recent movement of "alternative judges" who dare to decide *contra legem* in favour of marginalised groups), and lawyers clearly need to learn about this during their time in law school.[44]

(b) Legal Ethics Students

Even more important than analysing the discourses of the Bar Association, or the approaches to teaching legal ethics is the study of law students' attitudes towards the course and their expectations of professional practice. How do law students react to the course on legal ethics? What are their attitudes towards the course? What is the impact of different discourses and approaches on their behaviour? How do they imagine the possibility of ethical behaviour inside the legal profession? This section concentrates on answers to such questions.

(i) The "Professional-Oriented" Attitude

There is no doubt that law students at the Catholic University are unrepresentative of Brazilian law students, for whom law schools generally represent either the opportunity to pursue other activities or the opportunity for social mobility.[45] Students at the Catholic University are recruited from amongst the elite of Rio de Janeiro.[46] They do not seek social prestige at the law school. Neither do they look for economic prestige. As they already have social and economic capital, they belong to the minority really interested in learning legal technical skills at law school. Most of them want to continue the legal dynasties commenced by their relatives[47]—they aspire to be lawyers, judges and public attorneys.[48]

It is quite normal, then, that students complain about the weak connections between legal ethics and the pragmatic issues lawyers face in their professional

---

[43] D. Luban, *Lawyers and Justice: An Ethical Study* (Princeton, NJ, Princeton University Press, 1988) 293.

[44] For the criticism of classical theory and pressure-group theory against a politicised law practice, see *ibid.*

[45] See J. Falcão, *supra* n. 5, 408.

[46] Data show that 81% of the students have fathers with a university degree; 57% of the students have parents with a university degree; and 73% of them live in high-class and middle-class neighbourhoods.

[47] According to the survey, 49.3% of law students at the Catholic University have relatives in the law profession.

[48] Research in progress with first-year law students at the Catholic University shows that 27.2% of the students want to be a judge; 50.7% want to enter another public career (especially as public attorneys); and 10.3% plan to work as corporate lawyers.

activities. They are neither interested in developing their social commitment nor in learning about some distant social reality. Their main interest is to succeed as a private or a corporate lawyer or to pass the examination for a career in the public sector. Furthermore, as a prerequisite for this successful career they have to answer four questions on legal ethics in the Bar Examination.[49]

In support of this point of view, 80 per cent of the students relate legal ethics to professional behaviour and, consequently, to compliance with the Code of Ethics. When asked to define ethical professional conduct, students refer to respect for both the client and their colleagues. For the majority, honesty (normally considered in opposition to corruption) is the main value of ethical behaviour within the legal profession, alongside integrity, moral balance and dignity. Consequently, most students support the study of the Code, which, according to them, needs to be more strongly enforced by the Bar Association, especially in the struggle against corruption.

(ii) The "Social-Oriented" Attitude

The case of the Catholic University contrasts with the reality reported by the American socio-legal literature, rich in the analysis of how law students are interested upon entry to law school in both public-interest law and left-oriented legal reforms.[50] Law students at the Catholic University are not interested in working for the poor. In fact, they do not know where the poor are and/or they do not want to meet them (very few students volunteer to work in the *favela*). Students have little interest in social values and they do not look for public interest jobs. They are not concerned with social reform and they do not share professional altruism in serving the disadvantaged. Moreover, since the defence of the poor is a task of public defenders, students are not encouraged to develop *pro bono* practices in order to balance their profit-oriented lawyering in the future.

Recent empirical research with first-year law students based at the Catholic University pointed out that only 2.9 per cent of the sample would be prepared to help other people (either as a cause lawyer or as a public defender). In a survey of cause lawyers, 75 per cent of the sample agreed that law students have no interest in public-interest law. As already stressed, students want either to enter private practice or pass a public examination (but not the public defender career in which both salaries and social prestige are very low).

---

[49] See *supra* n. 11.

[50] Granfield's and Stover's books are the most quoted studies on this topic: R. Granfield, *Making Elite Lawyers* (New York, NY, Routledge, 1992); R. Stover, *Making It and Breaking It: The Fate of Public Interest Commitment during Law School* (Urbana, IL., University of Illinois Press, 1989). More recently, see H. Erlanger *et al.*,"Law Student Idealism and Job Choice: Some New Data on an Old Question" (1996) 30 *Law and Society Review* 851. We are not discussing here that law students lose their initial commitment to the socialisation process of the law school, when they are urged to "think as a lawyer".

Even so, some students (16 per cent of the sample) were able to give a definition of ethics which went beyond a narrow professional meaning. For them, ethical behaviour is not just restricted to the workplace, but must be observed in every sphere of public or private life. In other words, the need to be honest (still the most important value associated with ethics), of having "good sense" (a category difficult to define) and conducting oneself according to positive values is an obligation for all human beings, whether in their professional practices or in their family life. Only 2 per cent of students linked the ethics of the legal profession to the struggle for social justice and to the social responsibility of the lawyer. One untypical respondent stated that "at the current time people do not respect each other. Money has become the most important goal. Ethics has, though, an important role to play in the resistance to *wild capitalism.*"

(iii) The "Sceptical" and the "Cynical" Attitudes

Two distinct attitudes can be identified when 68 per cent of the sample express no interest in legal ethics, and 42 per cent admit that they had taken the course simply because it was compulsory: a *sceptical attitude towards an ethical professional behaviour*, and a *cynical attitude towards a social ethical behaviour.*[51]

The *sceptical attitude* results from the anomie of Brazilian society, where rules do not exist to be obeyed. Despite the recent wave of moralisation, Brazil has not cut its links with the traditional order and established the modern rule of law. Nepotism and corruption still rule Brazilian social relationships as a legacy from the Portuguese colonial period when the attitude of "for friends, everything; for strangers, nothing; for the enemies, the law" was quite common.[52]

As with any other Brazilian, the law student is socialised in the traditional practices of Brazilian society. Law students are taught that social relations are based on the paralegal institution of *"jeitinho"*, which can be defined as a strategy of getting around anything (specially the law and rules).[53] It is not surprising, therefore, that most students *invent* (as they have informally confessed) answers when they are asked by their professor to interview the working class and analyse the social image of lawyers. Can anything else be said about the ethical attitude developed by the legal ethics course?[54] Quite openly,

[51] These categories are based on K. Economides, "Cynical Legal Studies" in J. Cooper and L. Trubek, *Educating for Justice: Social Values and Legal Education* (Brookfield, NJ, Ashgate, 1997).

[52] See R. DaMatta, *Carnivals, Rogues, and Heroes: An Interpretation of the Brazilian Dilemma* (Notre Dame, IN, University of Notre Dame Press, 1991).

[53] See K. Rosenn, "The Jeito: Brazil's Institutional Bypass of the Formal Legal System and its Developmental Implications" (1971) 19 *The American Journal of Comparative Law* 514. According to the author, the idea of *jeitinho*, which in the finest Brazilian tradition is untranslatable, but would correspond roughly to a "knack", "twist", "way" or "fix".

[54] In fact, cheating is a very common attitude among Brazilian students. Despite the competitiveness of the market, schools and universities are not competitive environments (differently, for

66 per cent of the students said that the course had no transformative effect at all on their attitudes,[55] and only 30 per cent mentioned that they had ethical principles prior to taking the course. In other words, for at least 36 per cent of the sample, the course had no effect in challenging their unethical attitudes.[56]

Although corruption and nepotism exist in most social relations in Brazil, these practices are quite strong in the legal world, as students quickly learn during their apprenticeship. At law firms, students are socialised in the informal (and, of course, illegal, if not criminal) practices every lawyer uses when dealing with either the judiciary or the police.[57] Based on their own daily experience, 63 per cent of the students recognise that lawyers are not the best role models for ethical behaviour. As there is also a pragmatic ethical rule defined not by the Code of Ethics of the Bar Association, but by lawyers themselves, students rapidly develop an attitude of indifference and apathy towards the course.[58]

Nevertheless, *the sceptical attitude* towards legal ethics is part of the *sceptical attitude* of law students towards law school itself. Students know that law schools are not the place to learn either legal ethics or the law in Brazil.[59] Due to the original goals of Brazilian law schools (essentially a school to prepare an administrative elite and not lawyers), the five years at law school are still a formal requirement needed in order to enter the profession rather than to learn the technical skills of the legal profession. The law firm, and not the law school, assumes the task of teaching future lawyers and socialising them in the professional behaviour that, of course, does not follow the principles of the Code of Ethics.

While the *sceptical attitude* is related to the perception of the impossibility of lawyers' private ethics in professional life, the *cynical attitude* is related to the absence of social commitment among law students.[60] Despite their initial reform-oriented beliefs, law students gradually become, during their studies,

example, from the USA). Cheating is a main goal of students, who know quite well that the diploma represents just a formal requisite to enter the market. Jobs depend on personal links rather than on performance at the university.

[55] Empirical research in the USA suggests that legal ethics courses have no effect on behaviour (R. Abel, *supra* n. 17).

[56] Many law students stated that ethical attitudes are learned at home, not at law school. This criticism against the course of professional responsibility is also heard in the USA from those who defend the fact that it is futile to teach moral principles for adults. Ackerman answers this criticism by saying that the main goal of the course is not to teach morality but to present professional dilemmas that students will face in their professional life (R. Ackerman, *supra* n. 38).

[57] Despite any strong legal ethics commitment, a criminal lawyer has to participate in the corrupt game of the police. There is no choice. Or there is a choice: to leave the profession.

[58] First contacts with the legal profession, during apprenticeship at law firms, tend also to produce frustration in the law student with higher commitments to ethical behaviours.

[59] Similarly, in the USA students also complain that classroom instruction does not reflect the "real world" (R. Ackerman, *supra* n. 38).

[60] The erosion of public ethics during the graduation course is quite common, not only with law students (as already mentioned), but also at medicine school (R. Granfield, *supra* n. 50).

more concerned with social and economic success as a result either of legal education methods (centred on private law) or the pressures of the job market.[61] In Brazil the tenuous initial altruism is gradually replaced by a more self-centred concern, as students learn about the lack of prestige of working for the poor. Although law students at the Catholic University do not seek social mobility, they do not want to lose their social and economic status, an inevitable consequence when opting to serve the poor.

The *cynical attitude*, however, cannot be explained simply as the consequence of the law school and/or the job market. Typical of the attitudes of the 1990s, explanations that disregard the wider context are insufficient to understand the phenomenon. We no longer live in the 1960s, a time of idealism, when politically active groups "were in love with the world they wanted to change".[62] It was similar in the 1970s and the 1980s. We live in the 1990s, with its narcissistic culture of "me first".[63] Individuals are governed by personal feelings and not by the belief in public duty.[64] All of us (or, at least, most of us) are interested mainly in our private lives, our emotions and feelings. Youth, health and sexuality have become the prime values of this "postmodern" world, which is better represented by films such as *Sex, Lies and Videotapes* (directed by Steven Soderbergh) than by *Do the Right Thing* (directed by Spike Lee).[65]

In the conservative order at the end of the millennium, there is no place for the "highest ideals of humanity, including freedom, self-respect, open dialogue, and honesty".[66] Core values in our societies are tolerance[67] rather than solidarity, and impartiality rather than equality.[68] To talk about the "good society" is to talk about the coexistence of differences, rather than the insertion of differences. The current idea of citizenship no longer implies the idea of redistribution. Civic responsibility, based on individualistic values, has replaced the ethics of redistribution. Instead of talking about social rights, we now talk about civil rights (a new type of welfare state, based on radical individualism).The democratic project is, therefore, in danger. We have developed a *touristic attitude towards life*, refusing to establish links to nations and/or social groups and geographically isolating ourselves in suburbs and shopping malls. The individualisation process is destroying communitarism and

[61] R. Granfield, *supra* n. 50; R. Abel, *supra* n. 17; R. Stover, *supra* n. 50; H. Erlanger *et al.*, *supra* n. 50; and, recently, K. Economides, *supra* n. 51.

[62] M. Berman, "Why Modernism Still Matters" in S. Lash and J. Friedman, *supra* n. 7, 43.

[63] See F. Macchiarola and J. Scanlon, "Lawyers in the Public Service and the Role of Law Schools" (1992) 19 *Fordham Urban Law Journal* 698, who recognise that the loss of community values is an attitude not restricted to law schools, but rather spread within the upper class.

[64] R. Sennet, *The Fall of Public Man* (New York, NY, Knopf, 1988).

[65] N. Denzin, *supra* n. 32, 5.

[66] *Ibid.*

[67] See J. Rawls, *Political Liberalism* (New York, NY, Columbia University Press, 1993).

[68] P. Rosanvallon, *La Nouvelle Question Sociale. Repenser l'Etat-Providence* (Paris, Seuil, 1995).

solidarity, while public debate has weakened.[69] Instead of acting, we prefer to watch others perform.[70]

Students are, though, directly affected by this narcissistic culture and by its counterpart, the consumer culture, which creates new symbols and images. A culture whose hero is the yuppy, the "selfish 'perfect consumers' and narcissistic, calculating hedonists".[71] They do not identify themselves with the *res publica*, but with their own feelings and emotions, and with their professional success, which is evaluated by social prestige and economic profit.

In this sense, students of legal ethics at the Catholic University are not only influenced by the traditional order which insists on ruling Brazilian society. They are also representatives of, let us say, the passivity of the *fin de siècle*. Of course, the simultaneous influence of the "traditional" and the "postmodern" order makes the Brazilian crisis of legal education even more serious. In the Brazilian narcissistic culture of violence there is no place for justice and law. Therefore, there is no place for projects of social change that require social co-operation and the negotiation of private interests.[72] Hope in the future no longer exists. In contrast with their parents who were able to struggle against the military regime while believing in the benefits of a democratic order, law students today have nothing left for which to fight. Nothing had substantially changed after the new democratic Constitution (1988). In short, the present time is there to be enjoyed, and law students in Brazil know it. They have historical reasons to be *cynical*.

III. CONCLUSION

Should I end with this pessimistic vision? Of course not. If each generation has its own challenges, the challenge of our generation is not to let the youth "die spiritually before they have even begun to live".[73] So, instead of being satisfied with those pessimistic analyses of this "postmodern" world, we have to look at agendas that undermine the passivity of our time. Richard Rorty, for example, defends the idea of a moral obligation of solidarity with all other human beings. The right way to take the slogan "we have obligations to human beings simply as such" is reminding ourselves that we need to expand our sense of "us" as far as we can.[74] Giddens calls for a political engagement and proposes a life-political agenda which "demands an encounter with

---

[69] C. Lash and J. Friedman, "Introduction: Subjectivity and Modernity's Other" in C. Lash and J. Friedman, *supra* n. 7.

[70] P. Stearns, *American Cool* (New York, NY, New York University Press, 1988).

[71] M. Featherstone, *supra* n. 8, 44.

[72] J. F. da Costa, "Narcisismo em Tempos Sombrios" in H. R. Fernandes (ed.), *Tempo do Desejo* (São Paulo, Brasiliense, 1988) 129–30.

[73] M. Berman, "Why Modernism Still Matters" in S. Lash and J. Friedman, *supra* n. 7.

[74] R. Rorty, *Contingency, Irony, and Solidarity* (Cambridge, MA, Cambridge University Press, 1990).

specific moral dilemmas, and forces us to raise existential issues which modernity has institutionally excluded".[75] For him, while emancipatory politics aimed to reduce exploitation, inequality and oppression, life politics aims to create morally justifiable forms of life that will promote self-actualisation in the context of global interdependence.[76] After denouncing the collapse of emancipation into regulation, Boaventura de Sousa Santos proposes to "reinvent an emancipatory map that will not turn into a new map of regulation, but also to reinvent an individual and collective subjectivity capable of using and willing to use this map".[77] Instead of a balance between regulation and emancipation, this (postmodern) project should be a "dynamic imbalance tilting towards emancipation"[78] favouring the principle of community (with its three elements, i.e. participation, solidarity and pleasure), and the principle of æsthetic-expressive rationality.

Following these optimistic voices, we do need to believe that law schools can still accomplish the role of changing students' private and public ethical attitudes. Certainly, the introduction of a mandatory course of legal ethics is not sufficient for this transformative project, as the above analysis of the Catholic University has shown. In fact, legal ethics and professional responsibility are already implicitly taught in all courses, criminal, contracts, torts, etc.[79] If we remember that the "political significance of the structure of the law school curriculum"[80] is always useful, instead of one course on legal ethics (which only confirms the small importance of legal ethics in the legal education hierarchy[81]), the whole curriculum must emphasise both the professional responsibility and the social responsibility of lawyers.[82] Students have to replace their concern for the self with a commitment to the public, and law schools have to become the *locus* for a progressive attitude.

The current *sceptical* and *cynical* attitudes of law students are not entirely their fault, but rather the fault of those who came before them. Therefore, before changing the attitudes of law students, we have to change our attitudes, including our own *sceptical* and *cynical* attitudes. We need to rediscover our own set of beliefs and values. This is really the first challenge of our generation, surely not an easy challenge either in the *tropiques* or in less *exotiques* countries. A certain dose of naïveté may help us.

---

[75] A. Giddens, *supra* n. 8.

[76] R. Rorty, *supra* n. 74, 215.

[77] B. S. Santos, *supra* n. 8, 478.

[78] *Ibid.*, 25.

[79] R. Ackerman, *supra* n. 38.

[80] D. Kennedy, "The Political Significance of the Structure of the Law School Curriculum" (1983) 14 *Seton Hall Law Review* 1.

[81] R. Ackerman, *supra* n. 38.

[82] A. Bernabe-Riefkohl, "Tomorrow's Law Schools: Globalization and Legal Education" (1995) 32 *San Diego Law Review* 137.

10

Learning and Practising Law in the South Pacific—the Ethical Dimension

RICHARD GRIMES*

I. INTRODUCTION

Lawyers occupy a unique position in society, particularly in those countries dominated by the legacy of the common law and consequently an adversarial legal system. They are called upon to advise and represent in a wide range of socially significant instances. Their role touches the very foundation of daily life: issues of social control; the regulation of domestic relationships; the implementation of personal and commercial transactions; and, increasingly, concerns of a governmental and international nature. The fact that lawyers regularly assume a pivotal position in the passage of a transaction or the resolution of a dispute, and that their clients rely on them to protect their personal and property interests, calls into question the standards by which lawyers should behave and be judged.

That lawyers should be subject to expectations as to their own ethical behaviour in the discharge of these important functions comes perhaps as no surprise, even if it has taken many years for such rules to be agreed upon and documented.[1] The ethics of legal practice are however as much concerned

* My thanks go to Mere Pulea (now Director of the Institute of Justice and Applied Legal Studies at the University of the South Pacific) for her insight and patience. Without her comments on this attempt to grapple with the cultural dimension of ethics, this contribution would have been far weaker. Thanks must also go to Mark Findlay for his detailed comments on the first draft and for his constant encouragement. His principled contribution to the development of legal education in the region has been and continues to be profound. Jennifer Corin has also greatly assisted me in marshalling thoughts and researching material. Prem Shekhar produced draft after draft, and in the end could even read my writing!

[1] Debates are at the present time still on-going on what such expectations should be, particularly in the context of legal education. See *Legal Education and Professional Development—an Educational Continuum, Report of the Task Force on Law Schools and the Profession: Narrowing the Gap* (The MacCrate Report) (ABA, Chicago, 1992), 135–221, and in particular the Statement of Fundamental Lawyering Skills and Values. The extent to which these and related values are made a pervasive part of law teaching at the University of the South Pacific are described later in the chapter.

with making lawyers accountable (even if this is largely the result of a self-regulating profession[2]) as they are with inculcating, within legal practice, a moral code of behaviour. The two are intricately linked.

But the concept of ethical legal practice cannot be discussed in a vacuum. The political, economic, professional and cultural context is central to our understanding of the way in which lawyers operate and what is, and might be, expected of them. Nowhere is this more dramatically illustrated than in the countries of the South Pacific.

This chapter attempts to discuss the learning and practice of law, and the ethical considerations arising from it, within the region broadly termed "the South Pacific". For the purposes of this work these countries fall within one or more of three main ethnic and cultural groupings: Polynesia (Fiji and east to Easter Island and north to Hawaii); Melanesia (Fiji and west to Papua New Guinea and Western Papua or Irian Jaya); and Micronesia (Kiribati and north to the Northern Marianas). Some countries within the Pacific rim (notably New Zealand) might also be included.[3]

Most of the material and references made in this chapter relate to the countries within this vast area and presently served by the University of the South Pacific (the USP).[4] All three principal ethnic groupings are represented within this sub-region.

The concept of a region must not be allowed to suggest that the South Pacific is in any way homogeneous, even if there are strong similarities between many of the languages, customs and traditions of the different jurisdictions. The sheer diversity of the "region" is awesome. In Vanuatu (the former New Hebrides—independent since 1980) it is estimated that there are over a hundred distinct indigenous languages in a country whose Melanesian population is around 150,000 (the total population is estimated at 160,000) and whose "national" language is a form of pidgin.[5]

According to Crocombe there are significant differences between Melanesia and the other two principal regional cultures, in terms of social stratification, with Polynesia and Micronesia heavily characterised by hierarchical structures of cheiftainship.[6]

While most of the countries of the South Pacific were dominated by one European power or another (and sometimes more than one) during the last 150 years, the way in which each has developed economically, politically and legally is very varied. As will be seen, Fiji, after almost a century of colonial

---

[2] Although pressure to remove the disciplinary function from the profession is noted by J. de Groot, *Producing a Competent Lawyer* (Centre for Legal Education, Sydney, 1995), 31.

[3] For a detailed account of the settling of the South Pacific and the cultural characteristics (and complex interrelationships) of the main ethnic groupings see R. Crocombe, *The South Pacific— An Introduction* (USP, 1989).

[4] These countries are: Cook Islands, Fiji, Kiribati, Marshall Islands, Nauru, Niue, Samoa, Solomon Islands, Tokelau, Tonga, Tuvalu and Vanuatu.

[5] See D. Tryon, *Bislama: An Introduction to the National Language of Vanuatu* (The Australian National University, 1987).

[6] Crocombe, n. 3 *supra*, 21

rule and almost twenty years of independence, underwent two military coups in 1987 resulting in very different political consequences from that experienced by some of its neighbours.[7]

The point that is being made is this—when considering law and ethics, the cultural differences within the region are both significant and marked. These, as will be seen, impact on the standards by which lawyers operate and shape any attempt to review those standards.

This chapter attempts to locate the debate on ethics and law within its cultural context and to look towards a realistic and responsible, but culturally sensitive, code for ethical legal practice.

Before looking in detail at the issues surrounding the learning and practice of ethics and professional responsibility in the South Pacific, first the background to legal education in the region must be understood, and this includes recent moves at the USP to design and implement a comprehensive law programme. As will be shown, this includes an undergraduate degree and moves on to cover professional practice and continuing legal education, for the USP's member countries and territories.

II. A BRIEF HISTORY OF LEGAL EDUCATION IN THE SOUTH PACIFIC

Legal representation in the countries of the South Pacific is an imported concept, coming with the colonialists at the same time as copra and sandalwood were being taken away. This is not to say that there were no "courts" or "advocates" appearing before them in pre-colonial times. The resolution of disputes often took place in the village meeting house with the views of all those present (including the protagonists) being taken by the tribal chief(s).[8] It has been said that laws were neither made nor administered but that wisdom was dispensed.[9] As property was seen as more communal than personal in character, the dispute went beyond the individual to the group.[10] Members of the family, clan or tribe were heard. This may be somewhat removed from Western notions of legal representation but, nonetheless, demonstrates that there were means of dispute resolution in existence involving spokespersons long before the colonial presence and these did not necessarily depend on weight of numbers or fighting prowess. Early forms of professionalism (particularly in Polynesia) took shape through the involvement of orators or

[7] For a valuable, if now dated, account of this and for an authoritative review of the development of law and the legal process in the South Pacific see: G. Powles, "Law, Courts and Legal Services in Pacific Societies" in G. Powles and M. Pulea, *Pacific Courses and Legal systems* (USP, 1988), 6–36.

[8] For a valuable account of dispute resolution in the Solomon Islands, both past and present see B. Gatu, "Dispute Settlement in the Solomon Islands" in G. Powles, R. Crocombe and M. Pulea Kite (eds.), *Pacific Courts and Justice* (USP, Suva, 1977), 98–101.

[9] B. Narokobi, *Lo Bilong Yumi Yet—Law and Custom in Melanesia* (USP, 1989), 24.

[10] G. Powles, "Court Systems of the South Pacific" in G. Powles, R. Crocombe and M. Pulea Kite n. 8 *supra*, 5.

talking chiefs. A professional culture emerged within the context of ethnic and legal–traditional conflicts. With such a process came shared values incorporating culturally accepted ethical standards.[11]

Traditional forms of social control and dispute resolution still form a working, if limited, alternative to centralised and imported means of adjudication. The role of the *panchayat* (for Indo-Fijians) and *bulubulu* (for indigenous Fijians) has been described elsewhere.[12] Even within the established court structure recognition is given to the role of special tribunals for resolving disputes of, and according to, tradition and custom.[13] Land rights are frequently dealt with by courts given that specific jurisdiction.

The arrival of the colonialists from the turn of the nineteenth century onwards brought a law and administration package that reflected the model used in the home country. For the main part this was a system fashioned on Britain, Westminster and the common law.[14] Upon this structure the constitutions of the bulk of South Pacific countries have since allowed for the resolution of disputes and the handling of certain cases, largely involving customary law, through specifically designated bodies.

Against this backdrop, the structure of legal education in the South Pacific has, until very recently, been heavily influenced by the British and Commonwealth. At the time of the initial writing of this chapter (May 1996) nine of the twelve countries served by the USP make it a requirement that a person must have been admitted in one of a number of specified countries, for the most part Commonwealth countries. New Zealand is the most significant of these in terms of the provision of legal education for Pacific Islanders. Two countries (Marshall Islands and Samoa) also include graduation from an accredited US law school. One (Vanuatu) specifies that, to be admitted, a person must hold a law degree from a recognised university and have two years' requisite postgraduate experience. There is no present requirement, in any of the USP countries, that a person must demonstrate competency in the laws and procedures of the South Pacific country he or she requires admission in.[15] However reviews are currently ongoing in Fiji, Solomon Islands and Vanuatu on the reform of the legislation relating to admission into practice. All of the countries of the USP region will be asked shortly to reconsider their admis-

---

[11] B. Narokobi op cit., 25–6.

[12] M. Adinkrah, *Crime, Deviance and Delinquency in Fiji* (Fiji Council of Social Services *et al.*, Suva, 1995), 3.

[13] For example the provincial and Tikina courts of Fiji which are constituted to hear disputes between indigenous Fijians (although currently these are not operating—see Ntumy *et al.* (eds.), *South Pacific Island Legal Systems* (University of Hawaii, 1993), 40—the Fijian courts sat, with success, between 1944 and 1967—see *The Beattie Commission*, 160–78); local courts in the Solomon Islands; and, the Traditional Rights Court in the Marshall Islands.

[14] For a detailed account of colonial settlement see K. Howe, *Where the Waves Fall* (University of Hawaii, 1984). For a description of the present legal and constitutional position in the South Pacific see Ntumy *et al.* (eds.), *South Pacific Islands Legal Systems, supra*.

[15] This shortcoming has been noted by the findings of the Commission of Inquiry on the Courts (*The Beattie Commission*) in Fiji , 1994, 329.

sion rules in view of the planned developments in vocational legal education at the USP.[16]

Until 1994 there was no degree level common law programme taught within the South Pacific region with the exception of the Law School of the University of Papua New Guinea (UPNG) (whose role within the region has become markedly less significant in terms of regional provision).[17] Those from the USP region's countries who wished to study law and move on to qualify as practitioners had to do so elsewhere (principally in Australia, New Zealand and the UK). Regardless of the merits of courses available abroad (and nothing here is intended to impugn them from the perspective of quality) they did not reflect the needs and cultural heritage—the diversity—that is the South Pacific. In particular, so far as these non-regional courses are concerned, where ethics and professional responsibility were included in the programme, they were focused the rules and expectations in a very different cultural context.[18]

To compound the problem, once a lawyer has qualified and is practising in a Pacific Island state, there is no continuing legal education requirement and relatively little monitoring of practice and practitioners from an ethical and professional viewpoint. This will be explored shortly.

III. THE USP LAW PROGRAMME

What changes have now taken place since the law programme at the region's principal university began, and how do these affect the ethical dimension of learning and practising law?

[16] For details of the vocational programme and the model rules that would need to be adopted to effect the goal of admission of those educated in-region see *Producing Tomorrow's Lawyers* (USP, 1995), 16–20. The Legal Practitioners Act 1997 (Fiji) effective from January 1998 empowers the newly created Board of Legal Education to approve of the educational qualifications for admission purposes. Demonstration of competency in the laws of Fiji is a post qualification requirement and must be shown within a specified period following admission.

[17] For a variety of reasons this law school is no longer a major regional provider. It did provide a significant service (especially in Solomon Islands and Vanuatu), but problems of finance, security and now the availability of the law programmme at the USP have diminished its impact. Having said that the UPNG law school continues to play an important role within that country and produces a steady flow of valuable and often unique publications, for example Jessep and Luluaki, *Principles of Family Law in Papua New Guinea* (UPNG Press, 1994).

[18] An example might assist. The Institute of Professional Legal Studies (New Zealand) is the provider of a compulsory course for would-be practitioners. A Working Party of the Council of Legal Education discussion paper—*Review of Practical Legal Training in New Zealand, 1995*—refers (at 22) to the competencies expected of the successful student. These include ethics and professional responsibility. The stated aim here is to produce lawyers who "act ethically, professionally and responsibly" with no reference to how this translates to the reality of, say, working in a multi-ethnic community. It might be fairly added that New Zealand, like other countries in the "developed world", cannot be expected to look at law and ethics from all cultural perspectives (although New Zealand does have a substantial Pacific Island community as well, of course, as an indigenous, non-white community). The point is that when the rules for admission in the South Pacific jurisdictions rely, at least until very recently, on legal education being provided out of the region, the content and focus of some of the course material may not readily translate into the cultural setting the student later comes to practise in. This applies to ethics and professional responsibility as to other issues.

In March 1992 a curriculum conference took place in Port Vila, Vanuatu, attended by academics, practitioners (private and government) advisers and members of the judiciary of the region.[19] The decision to mount a law degree had already been taken by the university. The meeting made recommendations on the content of the LL.B degree the objectives of which should be:

> "(a) to produce graduates specially qualified to participate in government service, practice, teaching or further study in the USP region;
>
> (b) to ensure that law graduates are comprehensively trained in the laws of their own country and region;
>
> (c) to establish and maintain standards which will be recognised universally."[20]

Cultural and ethical considerations, including the form and role of customary law, as well as instruction in legal skills, were seen as necessarily pervasive within the curriculum.

The meeting went on to consider post-degree professional training and the need for this further to address issues of legal ethics and professional responsibility. The recommendation of the meeting was that the LL.B programme and the professional practice course should, together, reflect the special needs and character of the region. The role of the USP in the field of research in maters of law and practice was also identified.

The extensive consultative process which underpinned, and was part of, the Port Vila curriculum workshop is ongoing. In August 1995 the discussion paper *Producing Tomorrow's Lawyers* was published. This contained a summary of the principal pedagogic issues surrounding legal education in the context of the South Pacific.[21] A number of models for regional vocational education were suggested, as was the creation of Boards of Legal Education for each jurisdiction, coupled with a region wide Council.

Again the cultural, ethical and practical considerations of educating lawyers were addressed with the ethical dimension seen as central to any vocational course.[22]

Building on the recommendations of the curriculum workshop the LL.B degree took its first students, onto a four-year programme, in February 1994. At the time of writing the degree is about to start the second semester of year three. The professional practice course is to run from February 1998 to follow the graduation of the region's first home-grown lawyers in 1997.[23]

Response to these developments by the region's countries (including Australia and New Zealand) has been very positive. The sense of, and necessity for, an in-region legal education programme are clearly recognised and

[19] For a summary of the proceedings see Law Curriculum Workshop, *Recommendations of the Law Curriculum Workshop* (USP, 1992).

[20] *Ibid.*, 1.

[21] *Producing Tomorrow's Lawyers*, n. 16 *supra*.

[22] *Ibid.*, 8.

[23] At the time of proof reading of this chapter (February 1998) the USP has now produced its first law graduate, and the Diploma in legal practice has begun. The first in-region educated lawyers are expected to gain admission in Fiji in September 1998.

supported. Quality control mechanisms, including the degree and legal practice course validation processes, have made this progress credible to those concerned. The creation of the Boards and Council of Legal Education is under way and the region's countries are at this very moment considering the modification of their own legal practice admission rules to allow for the entry into practice of students who come through the USP system.

Against this historical background what is the ethical dimension of learning and practising law in the South Pacific? So far the term "ethical" has been used in a very general sense. Although the writer was not present at the curriculum workshop it is clear from his discussions with those who did attend that this expression was intended to include issues of law and morality and the application of this to the study and practice of law. One might say much the same for references to culture and custom. These too were identified as being of great significance, but the detail of what this involves was not spelt out. With their collectively vast experience of ethical and cultural considerations in the context of the South Pacific, the participants at the workshop did not go beyond the broad concept of ethics and the role of such within a legal education programme. It seems as if there was a presumption that ethical standards were understood by all and immutable. Lawyers must be ethical. But whose standards are being talked about here and how does this translate into detail?

IV. WHOSE ETHICAL STANDARDS?

Ownership of any benchmark by which behaviour is shaped and judged depends on cultural values. These values are in turn influenced by the relative strength of competing histories and ideologies, including contemporary and ongoing histories. Within the South Pacific the answer to the question of "whose ethics?" requires examination of the juxtaposition of indigenous and colonial power and the expectations arising from both. If this were not complex enough, there is then the increasingly common imposition of international standards, largely resulting from the South Pacific states' involvement in the international community through treaties, donor aid agencies and the ever increasing significance of new technology and the information revolution.[24]

What cultural values are we talking about? Concepts of property ownership (often communal); allegiance to one's family, clan or tribe; an often rigid social hierarchy where chiefs and elders play a major role in determining what is done and how; in some cases, competing inter-ethnic values (particularly in Fiji where over 40 per cent of the nationals of the country are of Indian ethnic origin); and respect for, and long-standing dependence on, imported systems (especially legal, financial, industrial and commercial These all underpin daily life.

---

[24] These themes are explored in R. Crocombe *et al.* (eds.), *Culture and Democracy in the South Pacific* (USP, 1992) and in particular in Ati George Sokomanu, *Government in Vanuatu: The Place of Culture and Tradition*, 49.

It should not be thought that these local and imposed values are static or independent of each other. What were imposed standards (for example through the influence of Christian missionaries in the early to mid 1800s) may now appear to be very much part of the indigenous scene. In some cases there are strongly competing social and economic considerations which are reflected in a dual or multi-ethnic response to ethical standards. Fiji with its large Indo-Fijian community has a very different cultural base from which some of its own values are taken, albeit that the colonial influences have been as marked within this community as with the indigenous Fijian population.[25]

The example of Fiji, whilst certainly not necessarily representative of the South Pacific as a whole, provides some revealing examples of whose standards of ethical practice are practised, if not advocated. Following the military coups of 1987 large numbers of the legal profession left Fiji.[26] The profession is (still) dominated by Indo-Fijian practitioners. The Law Society is also predominantly Indo-Fijian. It adopted a code of ethics in 1984 based on the New Zealand code of 1980 (excluding trust accounts, of which more later).[27] The code in Fiji does not have statutory effect.[28] The Law Society of Fiji is the self-regulating arm of the profession and initiates all disciplinary investigations. Complaints against practitioners are on the increase and are reportedly not investigated with efficiency or rigour.[29] The Indo-Fijian community is also the main economic force in Fiji. The government legal service, by contrast, is dominated, particularly in the more senior positions, by indigenous Fijians, including the posts of Attorney-General and until very recently, Solicitor-General. Complaints have recently been voiced by the Law Society of Fiji and others that members of the Government legal service are appearing in court on behalf of defendants despite their position as employees and officers of the State.[30] In some instances it would appear that the people concerned may not have been in possession of a practising certificate as required by legislation.[31]

Out of legal traditions, political paradoxes and cultural expectations here emerges a unique example of a specific professional culture.

What ethical issues arise in the example given above and how far can they be traced to a cultural or ethnic origin?

The concept of accountability of the profession is certainly enshrined in legislation in Fiji. Part VIII (sections 58–75) of the Legal Practitioners' Act 1965 provided for a disciplinary procedure for barristers and solicitors.[32] The Fiji

---

[25] See Subramani *Altering Imagination* (Fiji Writers Association, 1995), 247–57.

[26] Paterson and Zorn, "Fiji", in Ntumy *et al.* (eds.), n. 13 *supra*, 71.

[27] For information on the position of the legal profession in Fiji in 1994 see *The Beattie Commission*, n. 16 *supra*, 301–22.

[28] The newly enacted Legal Practitioners Act 1997 (Fiji) now contains a schedule of Rules of Professional Conduct and Practice made under s. 101(8).

[29] *Fiji Times*, 9 Feb. 1996, 1. 73 complaints were outstanding at Jan. 1996. 7 committees were established in 1995 to investigate complaints and none had, by Jan. 1996, reported.

[30] *Fiji Times*, 3 Feb. 1996, 5.

[31] s. 79, of the then Legal Practitioners' Act 1965, Cap. 254.

[32] On admission to legal practice in Fiji a person becomes both a barrister and solicitor.

Law Society investigated any complaints against barristers and solicitors and, if it felt that a disciplinary hearing was warranted, it recommended such to the Chief Justice, who appointed a Disciplinary Committee from a list of practitioners provided by the Law Society. The Chief Justice's role was said to be little more than a formality with the investigation, from start to finish in the hands of the Law Society, a "closed shop".[33] Long delays from initial complaint to final adjudication appear common. Many cases did not reach the formal committee stage. Even the Law Society conceded in its submissions to the Beattie Commission that the complaints procedure was "an elaborate, time consuming and often . . . frustrating exercise, more so for the complainant".[34]

Although the Commission was told (April 1994) that a major overhaul of the complaints procedure was proposed, it received no details of any such proposals. This is despite the frequent attention given to the unsatisfactory situation by the national press.[35] However the recently enacted Legal Practitioners Act 1997 establishes a new and, it is to be hoped, more effective disciplinary procedure. It will be interesting to see if words and structures give rise to changes in practice and attitude.

As a cultural interloper, ultimately one can only speculate as to the reasons for such a lack of real accountability. The educational gulf between the lawyers and many of the clients cannot aid the process. As will be seen below, the private profession in Fiji displays a strong sense of business acumen. The maximisation of profit historically would appear to outstrip any sense of public duty. *Pro bono* work is, for example, uncharacteristic at the private bar, as is support for legal aid services generally.[36] Whether it is fair to label this as ethnically oriented is another matter. What can be said is that the business of law would appear to be pursued with the same commercial vigour as would be found in the market place or other retail outlets of Fiji's capital, Suva.

An interesting contrast can be found in the offices of the Fijian government's legal service. As mentioned above, the appearance in court of government law officers on behalf of private clients is not uncommon. The ethical issue here is that of conflict of interest. Whose side is the lawyer on? The court's or the client's? Who is the client in any event? Who is the lawyer accountable to? In a recent case, the Attorney-General of Fiji appeared in court on behalf of a constituent (the Attorney-General is a Member of Parliament, as well as principal legal adviser to the government). As has been pointed out elsewhere should a person in the Attorney-General's position appear privately for a client against the State of which he is the most senior representative?[37]

The Attorney-General's repost to accusations that he allowed his personal and professional lives to intermix was that it was culturally incumbent on him

---

[33] *The Beattie Commission*, n. 15 *supra*, 309

[34] *Ibid.*, 311.

[35] *Fiji Times*, 23 Oct. 1995, 3; 19 Feb. 1996, 1; 2 Mar1996, 7.

[36] See the transcript of the address by the Solicitor-General of Fiji to the Seminar on Crime Prevention and Control, Suva, March 1996, on Legal Aid in Fiji, 6.

[37] See Imrana Jalal, *Fiji Times*, 15 Feb. 1996, 20.

so to do. The client was a constituent, he was poor and the Attorney-General was available, at the time of the request, to help. The Attorney-General felt under a compellable duty to attend to the needs of this person. To what extent does the concept of conflict of interest fit with such expressed cultural expectations? Jalal points out:

> "the argument that conflict of interest and impartiality are Western concepts requires close examination. [The Attorney-General] is the Attorney-General of Fiji . . . [a]nd not just of a particular ethnic community . . . where the values of his office conflict with communal values . . . [his] commitment to the Republic ought to prevail."

and further (not without irony):

> "The dilemma is understandable: Since 1987 cultural concerns have impinged on state practice."[38]

Without prejudging the issues it should be said that the accused in the particular case was indigenous Fijian, as is the Attorney-General. The commentator cited above is not.

This incident also raises two other pertinent issues. First, the Attorney-General did not hold a practising certificate (as required by the then section 79 of the Legal Practitioners' Act 1965). Secondly, the system of Legal Aid in Fiji is extremely limited in scope and effect and there is a discernible unmet legal need.[39] The ethics of law and legal practice are inextricably bound to these matters.

In Fiji, ethical standards, as found in the practice of law, appear to be drawn from expectations that have been imported by concept (from lawyers trained outside the region), by overt reliance on another country's code of conduct, and from a set of cultural norms that may vary considerably as between different communities.

The position in other Pacific Island states may be less extreme than in Fiji, but nonetheless incorporates similar variations and tensions. For example, in a revealing account of the politicisation of culture in the Cook Islands, Ingram examines notions of democracy (based on the government of people through the work of elected representatives regardless of race, gender or class) with the social and political structures of traditional Polynesian society and the chieftain system.[40] If one substitutes the concept of parliamentary democracy (which, with the exception of Tonga, is the system operative throughout the South Pacific) for ethical standards found in the so-called developed world and cultural expectations for the hierarchical social structure, the dimension of the contrast between the two, in terms of the practice of law, is clearer. The process of decolonisation that lead to, and has accelerated since, the gaining of independence of most of the region has left behind imported value systems

---

[38] Ibid.

[39] See the transcript of the Solicitor-General's address, n. 36 *supra*, 4–7.

[40] T. Ingram, "The Culture of Politics and the Politicization of Culture in the Cook Islands" in R. Crocombe *et al.* (eds.), n. 24 *supra*, 153.

that sit alongside local cultural expectations. The two, as have been seen, are not entirely complementary. This process of decolonisation has been noted as being far from complete, especially in the economic field and also, one can add, the legal one too. This has been ascribed to a deep-rooted lack of confidence on the part of the South Pacific countries which have been too used, for too long, to over reliance on foreign values in key aspects of administrative and political life.[41]

This is not to suggest that the countries have failed to adapt the legacy of colonial rule. In Samoa the chiefly or *matai* system is still a powerful influence on the daily and political life of the country (although there have been a number of constitutional challenges to the exercise of these powers).[42]

The reality is that law, like other aspects of life in the South Pacific, does not exist in isolation. The combination of the judicial structure, the training of the profession, the involvement of a large number of expatriates and the increasing need for international interaction in issues of law have produced a set of ethical expectations, set in the context of distinctive cultures and traditions, but largely drawn from non-Pacific origins.

It is to the detail of the ethics of law and legal practice we can now turn.

V. WHAT ETHICAL STANDARDS?

The starting premise adopted here is that, whatever expectations or constraints operate in the context of law and legal practice, lawyers must be accountable. What does this mean?

The lawyer is often said to owe an obligation to three different persons or bodies: the court, the client(s) and the profession.[43] One might add to this that the practice of law is akin to the exercise of a public trust in which lawyers (practitioners and judges) are the trustees for society as a whole.[44]

In a document entitled "International Code of Ethics" and issued by the International Bar Association (a federation of national Bar Associations and Law Societies), a set of basic principles is enunciated which attempts to establish a minimum standard for lawyering practice in dealings between lawyers of different jurisdictions or activities of a lawyer in another jurisdiction.[45] This too enshrines the principle of a duty being owed to court, client and

---

[41] U. Neemia, "Decolonisation and Democracy in the South Pacific" in R. Crocombe *et al.*, n. 24 *supra*, 8.

[42] *Italia Taamale and another* v. *The Attorney-General of Western Samoa*, Court of Appeal of Western Samoa, 18 Aug. 1995 (as yet unreported).

[43] For example see *Solicitors' Practice Rules 1990*, Rule 1, cited in The Law Society, *The Guide to the Professional Conduct of Solicitors* (The Law Society, London, 1996), 1.

[44] The Rules of the Supreme Court of Illinois, Article VIII, Preamble (Chicago, Ill., 1992), 23.

[45] *International Code of Ethics* (1988 edn., IBA, London), cited in New Zealand Law Society, *Rules of Professional Conduct for Barristers and Solicitors* (New Zealand Law Society, Wellington, 1995), Appendix III, 1–5.

profession, although it makes concessions to (but does not elaborate on) the law and custom of member countries and to the detailed codes applicable in each.[46] The Code has no in-built sanction for its breach other than by report to the relevant authority in the country concerned. Other key points in the Code address civility, fairness, professional competence and conflicting interests. This latter point is prohibited in litigation and only permitted in non-contentious cases where there has been full disclosure and the clients consent. The separation of clients' money from other funds is stipulated, as is the need for proper accounting. Rule 17 deals specifically with the interests of the client and the administration of justice, both of which should not be subject to the lawyer's own business concerns.

The need for a clear set of standards and other quality control methods may arise not just because of the need for public accountability but, in some ways ironically, because of the commercial sense it may make to the lawyer.[47] A well documented and widely understood and accepted code of professional behaviour should lead to improved standards within practice, greater productivity and more control over billing and profitability. Public perceptions of lawyers will no doubt, also be affected.

So where in the South Pacific context are such rules to be found and what might they specify to serve the interests of the public, the profession and the administration of justice alike (without compromising the customs and cultural values of each jurisdiction)?

There is perhaps no better place to start than with the would-be lawyer.

A. The law student and study

In much of the common law world law is first studied at an undergraduate level, the so-called "academic" or "initial stage" of legal education.[48] This is then followed, by those who intend to pursue a legal practice career, by a vocational course and, in some cases, a period of apprenticeship.[49]

In the South Pacific, as noted above, intending law practitioners have, until 1994, had to conduct their legal studies largely out of the region. From 1998 it will be possible for these aspirants to undertake a legal practice course designed for those intending to practise in the Pacific Island States which, it is anticipated, will attract those who graduate from the USP's LL.B programme as well as possibly others.

---

[46] *International Code of Ethics*, Preamble and Rules 1 and 5.

[47] See C. Klafter and G. Walker, *Legal Practice Management and Quality Standards* (Blackstone Press, London, 1995), 14.

[48] Such a term is used by the Lord Chancellor's Advisory Committee on Legal Education and Conduct (ACLEC), Review of Legal Education, Consultation Paper, The Initial Stage, 1994, (UK), and is used to differentiate this from the postgraduate stages.

[49] A useful comparison between the different pre-admission requirements of the principal common law jurisdictions is contained in J. de Groot, n. 2 *supra*, Figure 4.2, 79, with only Canada and the states of the USA making law effectively a postgraduate course of study (i.e. non first degree).

To what extent are ethics and professional practice considerations an integral part of pre-admission legal education?

In a detailed study of the teaching of the ethics of law practice in Canada, Brent Cotter sees professional responsibility as:

"a critical understanding of:
 a) the legal profession, its structures, roles and responsibilities;
 b) the roles and responsibilities of lawyers in their provision of professional services; and
 c) the individual's own values and attitudes . . ."[50]

He looks at the design of the curriculum in law schools, and concludes that many institutions fall short of the necessary commitment to the teaching of ethics and professional practice for a variety of reasons, including poor course design, weak learning methodologies and a general lack of resources. In the context of this chapter, what is important here is the recognition that law has to be taught and learned in the context of the reality of legal practice as well as according to model ethical principles, and that both require integration within the curriculum, from law school through to post-qualification professional development.[51] Ethics are therefore a pervasive subject that cannot be usefully studied without application.

This is certainly the line that was intended to be followed at the USP. Students are introduced in Year 1 (the programme is a four-year undergraduate course) to the various legal systems and court structures of the University's twelve member States. In Years 2–4 each subject area is delivered with the concept of law and ethics as a pervasive theme, along with legal and transferable skills. These issues are designed not only to introduce students (many of whom intend to practise) to professional ethics but also to give them additional tools with which better to understand the law. In Year 1 the students also take a substantial humanities component which attempts to give cultural and historical relevance to the study of law and South Pacific societies.

The traditions, customs and practices which are an essential part of each jurisdiction are also a major part of each subject area.[52] It must be said, however, that the attention to detail found in Brent Cotter's analysis is as yet not a formal and declared part of the USP undergraduate programme.[53]

The vocational course, scheduled to run from 1998 at the USP, will further and explicitly address the ethical considerations of practice, as well as the skills fundamental to lawyering. Again both are seen, and will be delivered as, essential to and pervasive in other substantive study areas.[54]

---

[50] W. Brent Cotter, *Professional Responsibility Instruction in Canada; A Co-ordinated Curriculum for Legal Education* (Conceptcom, 1992), i.

[51] *Ibid.*, "Summary of Recommendations", iv–x.

[52] For details of the USP degree programme see *Law at USP Handbook* (USP, 1997).

[53] n. 50, *supra* in particular recommendations II–2, 3 and 4.

[54] See *Producing Tomorrow's Lawyers*, n. 16 *supra*, 8 and 10–15.

Students will, on completion of the degree in law, have a basic understanding of the role of lawyers within their own communities. This will be used as a building block for those who progress to the legal practice course. The use of clinical methods, particularly through the use of a live-client base will further enhance the understanding of professional responsibility.[55]

But the teaching and learning of ethical practices goes beyond instruction in how lawyers should behave. It goes to the very heart of learning itself. If the task of the law school is to develop understanding of not only the rules of law, but the world in which law is formed and operates, then ethics become more than just a set of standards which lawyers should follow. This sees the bringing together of professional and contextual ethics, with one informing the other.[56] Quoting ACLEC, Brownsword states:

> "All students should be required to examine the ethical principles underlying the law, and how they apply to individual cases. To understand the law, it is necessary to understand its moral quality."[57]

Learning to behave as an ethical law student is a start. It is not as if legal ethics are different in principle from ethics in any other setting, even if ethical rules in the context of legal practice have specific connotations and may take the form of rules of professional conduct.

How does this impact on law students? The following is suggested:

- turning up at seminars and tutorials—your presence impacts on others. Without you they are deprived of your contribution and it increases the pressure on the rest;
- working co-operatively—do not hog books and materials, share information, pull your weight in group work;
- leaving library facilities unspoilt for the use of others—no ripping out of articles or reports, no hiding books in some dark corner (perhaps not even in the law section!);
- individual performances are not the only indicator of progress—you will not always be on your own, work for the common good of the class;
- tolerance of others—the study of law is as much part of the real world as the law office or the social club. Prejudice on grounds of race, gender, sexual orientation, disability, age, appearance and culture has no place here as anywhere else.

Law students at the USP find this in part complementary and in part in contrast to their cultural backgrounds and expectations. Campus life is a strong

---

[55] The use of clinics is seen by Brent Cotter as an important vehicle for instruction in the ethics of practice: n. 50 *supra*, II 3 b).

[56] R. Brownsword, "Where are all the Law Schools going?", *The Law Teacher* 30 (1), 1996, 1, 8.

[57] ACLEC, n. 48 *supra*, 14, quoted *ibid*.

challenge to many.[58] Those enjoying the benefit of a state scholarship are under pressure to achieve. Their own schooling histories and family backgrounds may add to this pressure.[59] Rivalry between the predominant cultures and countries is obvious.[60] The dominance of patriarchal societies can also be, as in other cultures beyond the region, an obstacle to the ethical working practices outlined above.[61]

It is a central theme of this chapter that lawyers can, and indeed ought to, be rendered accountable for their responsibilities and actions. This may require an adjustment of the precise detail of the relevant expectations, but nonetheless the starting point is accountability. The law student is in a unique position both to study this phenomenon and to share in its application. The pressures and demands of culture are factors that must be assimilated into concepts of professional practice. They cannot be ignored, for that, rightly, may not only be unacceptable to those represented, but would be as unrealistic as it is unhelpful. At the same time however, the principle of accountability remains inviolate.

The extent to which professional legal practice is, or can be rendered, accountable, in the context of the South Pacific, can now be examined.

B. The lawyer and the client

> "A solicitor shall not do anything in the course of practising as a solicitor . . . which compromises or impairs . . . the solicitor's duty to act in the best interests of the client".[60]

> "The relationship between practitioner and client is one of confidence and trust which must never be abused."[63]

[58] Year 1 is taught at the Laucala Bay campus, Suva, Fiji. Years 2, 3 and 4 from 1997 have been based in Port Vila, Vanuatu. In both cases the students are, in the main, living away from home, some for the first time. They are surrounded by students from upwards of 20 or more distinctive cultural backgrounds.

[59] Some of the South Pacific countries have very high rates of youth suicide (see Adinkrah, n. 12 *supra*, 11 (Fiji) and Crocombe, n. 3 *supra*, 65 (Samoa)), some of which has been traced to pressures to achieve educationally.

[60] At the risk of making a gross oversimplification of this, the tensions between the assertive and vocal Polynesians and the seemingly more hesitant and reserved Melanesians is very apparent in, say, a tutorial class. The bonding of students by race and nationality is, too, powerfully evident on campus. That tensions occasionally spill over is perhaps inevitable. Rivalries also exist between particular groupings. One only has to see Fiji and Tonga play rugby against each other to realise the extent of the feeling; at least on the field.

[61] For a revealing discussion on the role of women of Fiji generally (and in relation to employment laws in particular) see A. Emberson-Bain and C. Slatter, *Labouring under the Law* (USP, Suva, 1995), 1–4.

[62] Solicitors' Practice Rules 1990, n. 43 *supra*, Rule 1.

[63] Rules of Professional Conduct for Barristers and Solicitors 1989 (3rd ed. 1995), New Zealand Law Society Rule 1.01.

"Lawyers shall never forget that they should put first not their right to compensation for their services, but the interests of their clients and the exigencies of the administration of justice."[64]

"it is necessary to work hard and be dedicated to one's profession and this in turn requires a lawyer to be a person of integrity, courtesy and sound judgement."[65]

The quotations above are taken from a variety of sources, across the so-called developed and developing world. They have one common theme—that the lawyer represents his or her client, and in doing so the client's interests are of paramount (although not always of overriding) importance.[66] There are three principal and overlapping facets to the lawyer–client relationship:

- the obligation to provide a professionally competent and confidential service;
- the duty to predict, identify and respond to conflicts of interest that may or do compromise the lawyer–client relationship;
- the requirement to account to the client and not to profit from the relationship other than to recover remuneration that is lawfully due.

How do these concepts, so often seen as fundamental to the lawyer–client relationship, translate in the world of legal practice in the South Pacific?

(i) Professional competence

The standards of professional practice in terms of the practitioner's knowledge of the substantive law and procedure, lawyering skills and managerial qualities has been widely criticised throughout the region.[67] This is not to suggest that all lawyers are to be caught by this broad sweep, but rather that there are a large variety of instances arising in practice that give major cause for concern.

The Beattie Commission's Report on the courts in Fiji devotes a substantial section to the conduct of the legal profession. In particular the Commission noted from evidence given that:

[64] International Code of Ethics, n. 46 *supra*, Rule 17.

[65] Quoted from a speech given by Sir Timoci Tuivaga, Chief Justice of Fiji, and cited in G. Powles and M. Pulea, n. 8 *supra*, 173.

[66] Under the various rules cited there are specified circumstances when a lawyer must put other interests above those of the client, for example in being truthful to the court, or when declining to act further for a client. These are the exceptions to the general rule.

[67] In his tour of 10 of the region's countries in 1995 the writer was told of concern over standards of professional competence by senior members of the judiciary, magistrates, representatives of the law societies/bar associations, politicians and members of the general public. These comments were in response to a series of interviews carried out as part of the consultative process leading to the creation of a vocational programme in law at the USP. The history of this process and the USP's vocational plans can be found in R. Grimes, "Vocational Legal Education in the South Pacific—Designing and Implementing a Programme for Progress" (*Commonwealth Law Bulletin*, 22 (3 and 4) 1996, 1193).

" (i) Many lawyers came to court almost completely unprepared . . .

(vi) Barristers disappear on holiday, on business trips or to Parliament and simply fail to turn up in Court . . .

(vii) Unpunctuality is widespread . . .

(viii) Some legal practitioners do not have current practising certificates."[68]

In a candid submission to the Commission the then Attorney-General of Fiji stated:

> "some lawyers bring legal actions with unrealistic assurances to the client. A favourite justification for this is to say that they are 'acting in the client's best interest'. For some reason this has become a licence to entertain and promote untenable causes of action . . . a cursory glance at some of the pleadings put before the courts would reveal the extent of the legal imagination in Fiji".[69]

In the same report senior members of the judiciary in Fiji, including the Chief Justice are quoted as saying:

> "It is clear to us that a large share of the blame of the fault for the continuing unsatisfactory way court processes are being managed must fall on members of the legal profession."[70]

It is difficult to see how cultural issues can mitigate against incompetence or malpractice on the part of a legal representative. As will be seen below there are many such considerations that do impact on the lawyer–client relationship, but surely a client is entitled to expect a minimum standard of service in terms of knowledge, skill and professional attitudes to the work undertaken? That the client may have a remedy under the civil law for negligence or breach of contract is of little comfort in a country where there is a limited or, in some areas, non-existent legal aid scheme and a profession where widespread unprofessionalism apparently exits.

In its recently published report on the Legal Practitioners' Act the Fiji Law Reform Commission recommends that rules be adopted to ensure that client care becomes a permanent feature of the activities of the Fiji legal profession.[71] These are, in the view of the Commission, a feature of good practice that serve both the client and the lawyer. Under such rules the client would have access to a predetermined set of information, including what complaints-handling procedure exists if the client is dissatisfied with the service given. The requirement for client care may also include details of who the person in the firm dealing with the case is, how progress in the case will be monitored and

---

[68] *The Beattie Commission*, n. 15 *supra*, 302.

[69] *Ibid.*, 305. The reader may appreciate some irony here given the allegation referred to above that the Attorney-General has recently (1996) been accused of allowing a conflict of interest to compromise his position and has been accused of appearing in court without a practising certificate (albeit with the leave of the court).

[70] *Ibid.* 306.

[71] Fiji Law Reform Commission (the Fox Commission), *Legal Practitioners' Act, Draft Report*, Oct. 1995, 20. These proposals for reform have lead to the enactment of the Legal Practitioners Act 1997 and in particular the Rules of Professional Conduct and Practice contained in the schedule to the Act. The Rules fall someway short of the recommendations contained in the Report however.

what the charges are likely to be (or how they will be computed).[72] The lawyer can expect, as a result of following such a model of good practice, to see the level of complaints reaching a full disciplinary hearing fall dramatically.[73]

(ii) Conflicts of interest

In the adversarial model the lawyer represents the client. It is, at least in litigation, one side against another, whether or not each side has a lawyer (and even if the resolution of the dispute is eventually achieved in a non-adversarial way). This, subject to professional practice rules, calls for allegiance to the client and the case.[74] In non-contentious legal work the concept of the lawyer representing the client presupposes that the lawyer is doing his or her best for the client and cannot therefore allow other influences to interfere with this goal. Both instances necessarily require the lawyer to avoid conflicts of interest. Professional practice rules, codes or notes of guidance may also make this explicit.[75] The courts too have had something to say on the existence of conflicts and the lawyers' ingenuity in trying to hold onto business in the face of such a challenge.[76]

Conflicts can arise in a variety of situations: as between the lawyer and the client; as between clients of the same lawyer; as between the lawyer and the court or other authority.

In many of the South Pacific countries and territories the concept of conflict of interest as outlined above does not fit easily into this framework. Why is this? There are several reasons suggested here:

First, there can be a social expectation that the lawyer represents, not simply the individual in the case or the transaction, but the family, clan or tribe to which the individual belongs. Nowhere is this perhaps better illustrated than in Samoa.

In Samoan society the *Fa'amatai* (social organisation of status and title) and *Aigapotopoto* (extended family) are central to daily life.[75] Through the *matai* system and the *Aiga*, social behaviour is determined and, when necessary, regulated. However it is inevitable, in a world where the old-established social order co-exits with other competing demands (the drift from village to town,

---

[72] For one model of client care see: The Law Society, *Client Care—A Guide for Solicitors* (The Law Society (England and Wales), London, 1997).

[73] In Queensland, Australia, only 4% of complaints referred by the Law Society for consideration under the complained of law firm's complaints procedure (set up under the terms of the applicable client care rule) were referred back to the Law Society as unresolved. Cited by Fiji Law Reform Commission, n. 71 *supra*, 21.

[74] Note, e.g., the rules applicable to prosecution and defence counsel as prescribed by *Rules of Professional Conduct for Barristers and Solicitors*, n. 45 *supra*, Rules 9 and 10.

[75] See *ibid.*, Rule 1.07 and *The Guide to the Professional Conduct of Solicitors*, n. 43 *supra*, Chapter 15, principles 15.01–15.06 and the relating guidance issued by the Law Society.

[76] See *Re: a firm of solicitors* [1992] 1 All ER 353.

[77] See F. T. Aiono, "The Samoan Culture and Government" in Crocombe *et al.* (eds.), n. 24 *supra*, 117.

the existence of constitutional rights (including a court structure established to preside over criminal and civil cases) and the exposure of society through visitors and the media to other sets of values) that the old ways have to take on the new. Where a family member does appear in court over, say, a property dispute (particularly land) it may be a range of interests that the lawyer is called upon to assist in. These may go beyond simply the rights of an aggrieved individual. The matter is further complicated by the fact that, as all Samoans belong to their *Agia* and one or other *matai* Samoan lawyers are part of the process. Their loyalties may be divided. The professional independence and integrity they are supposed to hold (at least if they have listened to the ethics lectures at law school in New Zealand or wherever they studied) may be tested. In other words they may have to deal with a conflict of interests.

Secondly, the cultural dimension that challenges one's view of the ethical niceties of conflicts of interest arise in a far more pragmatic setting. Take Tuvalu (the former Ellice Islands) for example. This now independent country has a population of around 10,000.[78] At the time of writing there are four lawyers in Tuvalu. One is doing postgraduate work and is out of the country. One is in government service but not in a legal practice capacity. One is the acting Attorney-General and the other is the People's Lawyer (a volunteer under an aid programme). Without suggesting any inadequacies on the part of the characters concerned (far from it; they do, in the writer's opinion, an impressive job) there is a logistical problem here. If the two sides to an action are the government and a citizen there are just enough lawyers to go round. If two or more are in dispute (and in cases concerning land rights—remember the population density) there is a serious difficulty in treading the careful line of the conflict-free. This is no light matter. Serious thought is given in the country as to how to address these practical problems. Alternative dispute resolution is an important consideration, as is careful disclosure of interests by the lawyers concerned.[79]

Tuvalu may be an extreme example, but the lack of lawyers, especially in the public sector, is a difficulty elsewhere in the region, particularly away from the capital cities and main settlements.[80]

There is, thirdly, another aspect of conflict of interest that must be mentioned. As has been seen, until the advent of the USP law programme, all aspirant lawyers had to study overseas (that is in Papua New Guinea or further

---

[78] Those interested in the history and present situation of Tuvalu, one of the most densely populated countries in the world (with an estimated density of over 1,500 per square kilometre on Funafuti, the main island atoll), see D. Stanley, *South Pacific Handbook* (Moon Publications, 1993).

[79] It should be noted that in some countries of the region, notably Solomon Islands, Tuvalu and Vanuatu (and up to 1967, Fiji) the lower subordinate courts (local or island courts) do not cater for legal representation. If cases are appealed to the higher courts then the lawyer may represent.

[80] Similar problems were reported to the writer in the Marshall Islands, Solomon Islands and Vanuatu.

afield (and mostly) in Australia and New Zealand). None of these jurisdictions, with the exception of PNG (understandably), offers the study of law and the practice of it within the specific cultural context of the Pacific Island states.[81] It is little wonder that, on return to their countries, newly qualified lawyers have to translate their learning into another context, albeit one they may be familiar with and part of. Recognising conflicts of interest has seemingly proved problematic. Cases have been reported of lawyers representing both sides in commercial transactions[82] and of advocates appearing on behalf of more than one defendant where some disagreement emerges between the parties as to their respective roles in the alleged crime.[83]

One can be cynical and suggest that the lawyers concerned are simply making the most of their earning potential. If this is the case it does not account for the fact that, when challenged, those concerned see nothing compromising about their position as practising lawyers, which suggests that the issue is simply not taken up or has become so institutionalised that it is accepted practice.[84] There is apparently no attempt to justify the action (for example by saying that there are not enough lawyers to cope with client demand). The issue of conflict, in these instances, just does not arise.[85]

The International Bar Association's Code of Ethics is helpfully explicit on the point of conflict. Rule 10 requires lawyers to give clients a candid opinion on any case, including withdrawal from a case where there is "good cause", which presumably accommodates conflicts of interests. Rules 11–17 go on to specify the detail of conflict situations and prescribe what the lawyer should and should not do, including the requirement, as has been seen, that:

> "Lawyers should *never* represent conflicting interests in litigation. In non-litigation matters lawyers should only do so after having disclosed all conflicts or possible conflicts of interest to all parties concerned and *only* with their consent".[86]

This does not directly address the cultural impact on the application of conflicts of interest. It does however offer a starting point where the lawyer must gauge for him or herself (as practitioner, judge or disciplinary panel member) what an appropriate response might be in the circumstances. This can per-

---

[81] In the case of UPNG's law programme specific and detailed reference is made to the cultural dimensions of that country: see *Faculty of Law Handbook of Courses*, 1996.

[82] In Fiji lawyers apparently regularly represent buyer and seller in conveyancing cases, as related by a member of the USP staff who was the buyer!

[83] In a criminal trial in Tonga, as reported by a senior member of the judiciary in that country.

[84] Judicial intervention in Tonga during a trial reportedly brought this response.

[85] It should be said that non-recognition of conflict is not the rule in all Pacific Island countries. According to an interview held in Suva in May 1996 with a practising lawyer from the Solomon Islands, conflicts of interest are both recognised and acted upon in the Solomons, albeit often through the creation of "Chinese walls", especially in such over-used and under-funded offices as the Public Solicitor's.

[86] *International Code of Ethics*, n. 45 *supra*, Rule 13 (emphasis added).

haps best be described as a provision that sees legal practice ethics in a culturally sensitive way.

(iii) Profiting from the client

It has long been a formal requirement in a number of countries in the so-called developed world for lawyers to account for the moneys handled by them. This ranges from the keeping of books and records to show clearly the flow and position of funds, to the need to keep separate accounts for money that belong to clients and the lawyer's own funds.[87] The purpose of these rules is to ensure that practising lawyers do manage the (often considerable) funds held by them, during the course of their work, in a manner which safeguards the client's interests and makes the process of accountability for those funds effective.

The South Pacific has been slow to develop such close regulation. Samoa has a system of trust accounts, and regulations for the operation of the rules are being drafted with the assistance of the Society of Accountants of Western Samoa.[88] The Beattie Commission notes that although rules do exist in Fiji for the keeping of such accounts, these are seldom scrutinised, as they require complaint by either the Solicitor-General or a client. The profession is not required to regulate its own affairs by, say, making it compulsory for law practices to file audited accounts on a regular basis.[89] The report recommends an annual reporting requirement.[90]

There is presently discussion in Fiji of using the interest generated by the trust accounts to fund improvements to legal practice such as the introduction of continuing legal education or the establishment of community law centres. These proposals, while representing a marked improvement on what is currently happening in terms of the provision of much-needed improvements and the destination of the interest, seem to ignore the fact that the funds derive from clients' money.[91]

Many of the points made in the section on conflicts of interest above also apply here. The concept of collective, as opposed to personal, property rights might challenge, at least in cultural terms, the principle of financial accountability. Having said that, if the client's money, or interest on it, stays in the lawyer's pocket it is hard to see how even this cultural element has relevance.

---

[87] In New Zealand the handling of client's (and other) money is governed by a number of regulations set out in the *Rules of Professional Conduct for Barristers and Solicitors*, n. 45 *supra*, chapter 5. The position in England and Wales is discussed in *The Guide to the Professional Conduct of Solicitors*, n. 43 *supra*, chapter 28.

[88] *The Beattie Commission*, n. 15 *supra*, 325.

[89] The Barristers and Solicitors (Accounts) Rules have been in effect in Fiji since 1962: *The Beattie Commission*, n. 15 *supra*, 323–6.

[90] *Ibid.*, 325. The Trust Accounts Act 1996, effective from 1/2/98, significantly tightens up procedures for legal practitioners in Fiji.

[91] A point specifically addressed by the Solicitors' Accounts Rules 1991, Rule 20 (as amended) in England and Wales. In Fiji, the Trust Accounts Act 1996 now provides for interest of trust accounts to be paid *interalia* into the legal aid fund (48%).

C. The lawyer and the court

The practising lawyer is often described as an officer of the court[92] with obligations and expectations arising as a result of this status.[93] There is a requirement for openness, honesty, civility and mutual co-operation within these respective roles, if the administration of justice is to function effectively and clients' interests are to be properly represented.

In its sometimes very frank report, the Beattie Commission identifies problems in Fiji in the relationship between the bench and the bar. Examples are cited of abusive language being used in court, of disrespect being shown to the judiciary (especially in the magistrates' court) and a general disregard for the workings of the court (particularly getting cases running on time and avoiding unnecessary delays and adjournments).[94] Quoting from the address of the President of the Tenth South Pacific Judicial Conference, held in Fiji in 1993, the report notes the "occasional but intolerable lapses on the part of lawyers" in their dealings with the courts.[95]

To deal with this and other matters, the Beattie Commission recommends that the Code of Ethics adopted by the Fiji Law Society in 1984 be revised, but interestingly makes the point that whatever such a code might say, a lawyer's ethical stance is, in the end, a matter for each practitioner to consider, viewed in the light of his or her overall professional responsibility.[96] Again it is the process of accountability that is being stressed. Where there are general rules regulating conduct and an effective system of monitoring standards, the practitioner is at risk if he or she falls short of a generally expected level of performance.

This again gives rise to cultural considerations. In some jurisdictions the size of the legal community is small. We have already seen the example of Tuvalu with only two lawyers at present providing legal services. Other states, such as the Cook Islands, Kiribati and Nauru, are in a similar, if not quite so extreme, position. The size of the practising bar is often matched by the size of the judiciary. It is inevitable that the bench and the bar have strong and intimate links. This perhaps suggests that there is an even greater need for a well understood ethical code to maintain the necessary level of integrity and independence. The close ties between the two sides of the legal community are not peculiar to the countries of the South Pacific. However where the complication arises is that in many of these states the parties before the court, as well as the advocates and judges, may well be known to all. The role of fam-

[92] See T. Mataio and N. Tangaroa, "Role of a Lawyer in Court" in Powles *et al.* (eds.), n. 8 *supra*, 91.

[93] See, for e.g., the detailed rules contained in *The Guide to the Professional Conduct of Solicitors*, n. 43 *supra*, chapter 21.

[94] *The Beattie Commission*, n. 15 *supra*, 301–2 and 315.

[95] *Ibid.*, 316.

[96] *Ibid.*, 319. The Legal Practitioners Act 1997 now contains Rules of Professional Conduct and Practice. The Law Society are currently reviewing the code of ethics (1997).

ily and title links in Samoa has already been referred to. A lawyer may well find that he or she is inextricably tied into the expectations of court, client and community alike.

An interesting point on the application of cultural issues in litigation is brought out by the former Public Defender and Secretary for Justice and Lands in the Cook Islands when they say:

> "it is a duty of a lawyer to ensure that decisions are made according to the moral and legal standards of the culture of the community. It would be unjust to apply (such standards) of the culture of New Zealand to isolated parts of Papua New Guinea."[97]

As important as the sentiment is, this perhaps confuses two separate issues. On the one hand the lawyer must, in representing the best interests of the client, bring to the court's attention anything that is relevant and applicable. In some cases this will be legal provisions (whether from the constitution, legislation, precedent or custom[98]), and in other instances it might be a customary or conventional practice, even if it is not technically part of the country's laws. The court may have considerable discretion in taking such matters into account (for example in mitigation of sentence in criminal proceedings). The other point, though, is that however unjust the application of principles of alien cultures and systems may be, if a "Western" model of legal and courtroom ethics is applied (and most lawyers to date are educated in such a context), the lawyer has little choice (and some would say a duty[99]) to follow the process regardless of effect. The fact that by culturally acceptable standards another layer of loyalty is expected further complicates the issue. One can add that these expectations may fall on judge as well as advocate.

D. The lawyer, the profession and the community

The third of the duties often ascribed to practising lawyers (after the duty to the client and the court) is the obligation to the rest of the profession.[100]

In the context of the South Pacific the ethics of legal practice in relation to other members of the profession is particularly important. Moving beyond the simple and uncontentious requirement that lawyers should behave with a

[97] T. Mataio and N. Tangaroa, n. 92 *supra*, 91–2.

[98] "Custom" is a source of law in many of the South Pacific countries—e.g. Schedule 3.3 of the Constitution of the Solomon Islands, Art. 93 of the Constitution of Vanuatu and the Custom and Adopted Laws Act 1971 of Nauru.

[99] See *Rules of Professional Conduct for Barristers and Solicitors*, n. 45 *supra*, Rule 8.01—the duty to disclose authorities that may not support a client's case if they are known to the practitioner.

[100] For an example of the formal requirement see *The Guide to the Professional Conduct of Solicitors*, n. 43 *supra*, 1 and Chapters 19 and 20. For a view of relationships between practitioners in the USA see R. Haydock *et al.*, *Lawyering—Practice and Planning* (West Publishing, St Paul, Minn., 1996).

sense of integrity and civility, to each other as well as to the client, court and third parties, some more specific issues are revealed.

The need for the profession to regulate itself has already been mentioned.[101] This has implications beyond making the profession adhere to a professional practice code (complete with effective monitoring and sanctions) and the periodic production of accounts. It addresses the way in which the profession is perceived by itself and the wider community. It challenges the profession to take responsibility for itself and to make ethics not something you have to follow for fear of disciplinary action but something that enhances your standards of work and the quality of service provided to the community.[102]

Consider the need for professional self-development. Not only do lawyers need to be competent in the laws and procedures of the country or countries in which they practise, they must be committed to maintaining and developing their expertise. The case for continuing legal education has been made in many jurisdictions and it is now compulsory in some US states, in Britain, in Hong Kong and in parts of Australia.[103] It is available and supported (though not compulsory) in other places.[104]

The case for mandatory continuing legal education is clearly made by the Fiji Law Reform Commission which recommends that a minimum level of continuing education should be a prerequisite to the renewal of a practising certificate.[105] In a recent survey of judicial training needs in the South Pacific a number of specific subject areas were identified as necessary topics for continuing education (for practitioners and members of the judiciary) including customary law, evidence and procedure, international law and legislative drafting.[106] Some respondents suggested seminars in ethics! Participation in continuing legal education demonstrates the profession's commitment to improving itself and, in consequence, its clients' position, and the workings of the administration of justice generally.

The potential for continuing legal education has not escaped the region's government law officers either. At PILOM '95[107] the meeting agreed to develop a number of initiatives to provide a regional response to continuing

[101] *The Beattie Commission*, n. 15 *supra*, 319.

[102] See C. Klafter and G. Walker, n. 47 *supra*, chapter 2 and the International Standard Quality Systems—Model for Quality Assurance in Design, Development, Production, Installation and Servicing (ISO 9001:1994) set out in Appendix 1 to that book.

[103] The Fiji Law Reform Commission, n. 71 *supra*, 33.

[104] For an interesting account of the continuing legal education need of newly qualified solicitors see J. Nelson, *A Study of the Continuing Legal Education Needs of Beginning Solicitors* (Centre for Legal Education, Sydney, 1995); and for those with substantial post-qualification experience see C. Roper, *Senior Solicitors and their Participation in Continuing Legal Education* (Centre for Legal Education, Sydney, 1995).

[105] Fiji Law Reform Commission, n. 71 *supra*, 34. The Legal Practitioners Act 1997 now makes continuing legal education mandatory (s. 7).

[106] R. Grimes and M. Findlay, *Report on the initial findings of the needs analysis and information gathering stage of a feasibility study on continuing judicial education in the South Pacific for the meeting of Chief Justices* (USP, 1995).

[107] The Pacific Islands Law Officers' Meeting, Vanuatu, Oct. 1995.

legal education needs, and as a result an intensive trial advocacy course took place in early 1996; a legislative drafting programme is scheduled for 1998.[108]

Consider also the need for insurance. Part of being accountable is ensuring that the means by which accountability is a reality are in place. There is little point in having high standards of professional practice if, on the occasion of a mistake being made, the client is unable to recover his or her losses due to the financial situation of the lawyer. Indemnity insurance has long been a feature in Britain and other jurisdictions.[109]

In the Fiji Law Reform Commission's report, a recommendation for compulsory indemnity insurance for practitioners in Fiji is made.[110] This is seen as a means of giving protection for the consumer and practitioner and, if organised within and by the profession, the costs can be kept to a minimum.

The lawyer and the profession carry a substantial responsibility to ensure that their services are available to all. The then Solicitor-General of Fiji, in his address to the Crime Prevention seminar held in Fiji in March 1996 quoted the South Australian Chief Justice who said: "If that professional assistance is denied to any citizen who reasonably needs it to assert or defend his [*sic*] legal rights, the rule of law in the society is to that extent deficient".[111]

Legal services are not like any other retail commodity. They represent the means by which access to fundamental rights is secured. Lawyers owe a duty to their profession and the general public to provide these services. It has been noted elsewhere that lawyers in Fiji have no history of supporting the legal aid system.[112] Neither is *pro bono* work characteristic. On the ground in Fiji there are no community law centres other than in the guise of much needed and valued specialist services, where legal representation is neither a central feature nor guaranteed.[113] As a matter of professional responsibility and ethics lawyers are under increasing pressure in the South Pacific to provide a service where it is needed. The problems associated with this demand involve issues of resource as well as commitment. The sheer volume of work faced by, say, the public defender in the Marshall Islands, the public solicitor in the Solomon Islands, or the people's lawyer in Tuvalu indicates the need for a strategic response from both government and the legal profession. Taking one's broader obligations seriously is as much of an ethical issue for lawyers as is the keeping of proper accounts or being appropriately dressed in court. Where lawyers have the privilege of a formal and expensive education (often a cost borne by their home countries), as in the South Pacific, those less fortunate

---

[108] By courtesy of the New Zealand Law Society and the USP respectively.

[109] Solicitors Indemnity Rules 1992, Rule 6. Since 1976 all private practitioners have had compulsory indemnity cover in England and Wales.

[110] The Fiji Law Reform Commission, n. 71 *supra*, 38–9. The Legal Practitioners Act 1997 (Fiji) now empowers the minister to introduce compulsory indemnity insurance provision for practising lawyers (s. 103).

[111] In J. Basten, "Legal Aid and Community Centres", 61 *Australian Law Journal*, 715 at 715 and cited by the Solicitor-General in the transcript of his address, n. 36 *supra*, 2.

[112] *Ibid.*, 6.

[113] For example the work of the Fiji Women's Crisis Centre.

might at least expect that the lawyers' services will be used to good effect, in the light of existing need.[114]

VI. CONCLUSION—TOWARDS A CULTURALLY SENSITIVE CODE
OF PROFESSIONAL RESPONSIBILITY

Those who learn and practise law in the South Pacific face a number of challenges. Some of these are to be found in any part of the developing world. They come from a combination of a general lack of resources (both financial and human), a lack of awareness of basic rights and entitlements and very limited access to legal services. Other demands arise in the light of the social structure and the customs and traditions so strongly evident in each of the region's various countries, and often within each country.[115] The situation is made more complex by the need for lawyers to study and practise laws and procedures that have been either inherited or adopted, often wholesale, from elsewhere.

It might be argued that as a population of new largely independent states, indigenous people have no need for laws and a legal system inherited from another cultural base. This raises valid points in terms of the future development of law and the legal process, and invites a closer examination of the needs of specific jurisdictions and their own law-making values and mechanisms. It does not however deal with the issue of what the region's countries have in place at the moment. Most, if not all, are heavily dependent upon either a British model of law, government and judiciary or derivatives (for example the north of the region, which has been subjected to a strong American influence).[116] Despite the evident presence and power of custom and culture the introduced law is still dominant and, as has been noted elsewhere, such laws are often better suited to the modern world, with its emphasis on commerce and industry and with all the international implications that has. The centralisation of government also alters the picture and the traditional ways of control and adjudication become less meaningful.[117] It is little wonder therefore that, when the ethics of law and legal practice are scrutinised, considerable difficulty is encountered in trying to make sense of what stan-

---

[114] The Legal Aid Act 1996 (Fiji) (not yet in force) will make a significant difference to legal services provision providing resourcing is made available.

[115] The reader is reminded of the power of the extended family and *matai* in Samoa and of the cultural differences between the two principal communities in Fiji. Other examples can be given, including the almost feudalistic social structure of Tonga and the linguistically and culturally divided people of Vanuatu and Papua New Guinea. For a detailed account of the decolonisation of the region and the relationship between culture on the process see Y. Ghai, "Constitution Making and Decolonisation", in Y. Ghai (ed.), *Law Government and Politics in the Pacific Island States* (USP, 1988), 1 at 39.

[116] The French-claimed territories of New Caledonia, Tahiti and Wallis and Futuna and French influence in Vanuatu are the exceptions to the imposition of a common law tradition.

[117] See R. Crocombe, "Cultural Policies in the Pacific Islands" in L. Lindstrom and G. White, *Culture—Kastom—Tradition: Developing Cultural Policy in Melanesia* (USP, 1994), 21, at 33.

dards can realistically be expected of lawyers and how far these can and ought to reflect the ethical expectations of other dominant jurisdictions.

In an interesting and seemingly unique attempt to align cultural, national and regional values with the world of change and development the three principal Melanesian states of Papua New Guinea, Solomon Islands and Vanuatu entered into an accord in 1990 entitled Agreed Principles of Co-operation in Education and Human Resource Development among Independent States in Melanesia.[118] Although this is written in very general terms it recognises the importance of culture and tradition, but in the light of the ongoing process of change in which the region's nations are unavoidably involved. It stresses the importance of education and human development and commits the signatories to a broad programme for the future that allows change to take place within the context of each country's needs. In particular a Melanesian philosophy of education is called for. One might say that such general expressions of intent are worth little until transcribed into action and that the influences of the so-called developed world are, in any event, too powerful to make such statements anything more than political rhetoric. It is suggested here that this does represent a major advance in terms of three major countries of the region addressing a framework within which culturally sensitive development can be designed and monitored. As this initiative appears to have come from those with a direct knowledge and vested interest in the outcome, it may well be better placed to succeed.

In what way is this relevant to a discussion of the ethics of legal practice? It has been said, in the context of the South Pacific, that "[t]he quality of law . . . depends on the quality of our lawyers and lawmakers"[119] and further:

> "there is more to justice than what the law prescribes. Justice entails healing of wounded feelings . . . restoration of social and economic balance . . . honour, self-respect, dignity [and] the balancing of the virtue of means against the pride of ends. Justice involves human struggle, trial and error . . . a picture of men and women doing the best they can to balance self-interest against others' interests, personal against group. . . . It expects co-operation to allow for competition and competition to allow for co-operation . . . it takes into account . . . radical change . . . as well as dogmatic adherence to well worn practices.
> . . . There is no scientific formula of justice. Techniques and approaches employed elsewhere are useful, but it is wrong to regard them as definitive solutions. . . . We have to approach our overall development from this perspective. . . . Well-meaning lawmen and women can do a lot towards that end."[120]

As exhaltative and rhetorical as these words may be, they represent perhaps the only way forward in setting an ethical benchmark by which lawyers' conduct and attitudes are shaped and, if necessary, judged. The adoption of the

---

[118] *Ibid.* Appendix 2.
[119] B. Narokobi, n. 9 *supra*, 159.
[120] *Ibid.*, 162–3.

International Code of Ethics may be one starting point.[121] The unavoidable issue is that the profession has to take the lead. It is its members that have to implement such a code and they who must be central to its making if it is to be effective.

The attraction of a set of minimum standards such as are contained in the International Code of Ethics is not, however without question. Such rules do not and cannot fully address the complexities of customs and cultures. As a standard by which to mould, and if necessary judge, lawyers in their practice of imported law (meaning both form and content) the code is valuable; it cannot however easily or perhaps usefully be translated across the cultural divide.

The value systems underpining custom in the South Pacific are engrained in virtually every aspect of legal practice, from the actions of government law officers to the functioning of the courts; from the expectations of clients to the atitudes of private practice. Such values permeate the very essence of social behaviour and can override office, position and profession.

The extent to which custom shapes the behaviour of the legal profession has not yet been properly examined. Indeed the interface between custom and law (as it operates in the formal court structures enshrined in the Pacific island states' constitutions) generally remains largely unexplored, although there have been several important and insightful accounts of the workings of the "custom courts" in the region.[122]

The only common ground in terms of ethics and professional responsibility is accountability. The involvement of lawyers in both transactions and dispute resolution calls for a means by which their role can be regulated. This regulation may be achieved by a voluntary adherence to a code of ethics or through the social pressure of family, clan and tradition.

Those dealing with lawyers have a right to expect this, whatever form the process of accountability may take.

The production of lawyers within the region, through programmes such as the law degree, the professional practice course and continuing legal education offered, through the University of the South Pacific and other organisations, in and around the region, may bolster the process of educating lawyers and the community in the ethics of legal practice. The need for continuing research on law, ethics, custom and justice in the context of the South Pacific has never been greater. It is hoped that this chapter represents a move in that direction.

---

[121] This has been adopted in a number of South Pacific countries. In the Solomon Islands it was used as a first reference point and this country is, at the time of writing, drafting its own code which will have statutory effect.

[122] See e.g. N. Warren, "A New Village Court in Papua New Guinea" in G. Powles and M. Pulea (eds.), n. 8 *supra*, 96–106.

11

Teaching Professionalism: The Issues and the Antinomies

THOMAS MORAWETZ*

What does it mean to "teach professionalism"? From one standpoint, teaching professionalism is pervasive throughout the law curriculum. If one employs a suitably broad conception of legal skills, every course essentially involves training in such skills: understanding legal doctrine, applying law, reasoning about legal policies and principles, anticipating and managing the needs of clients, litigating and seeing the larger implications of law within the context of philosophy, history and other disciplines. The acquisition of these skills marks the difference between professionals and others.

From another standpoint, professionalism cannot be taught at all, and "teaching professionalism" is an oxymoron. On this view, attributing professionalism to a lawyer is an honorific. Exhibiting professionalism is not so much a matter of deploying skills as it is a matter of deploying them in a way that reflects sound character, integrity, and respect (for oneself as well as others). Professionalism is not role-playing but role morality; as such, it refers to moral judgements about both what the actor *does* and what he *is*. The latter is not a judgement about the actor's skills but about his values and self-regard.

American legal education rejects both senses of "teaching professionalism" in favor of a third whereby professionalism *can* be taught as one academic subject among many. Virtually all American law schools offer a course variously called *Professional Responsibility*, *Legal Ethics* or *The Legal Profession*. The American Bar Association mandates that all law schools offer training in professional ethics, and most schools comply by making a discrete course on the subject mandatory.[1] The various state bar associations, moreover, require either a special examination on the subject of legal ethics, a course, or both as a requirement of bar membership.[2]

* Tapping Reeve Professor of Law and Ethics, University of Connecticut School of Law. I wish to thank my research assistant, Robert Clark, for his outstanding work on this project.

[1] This ABA requirement for accredited law schools was first mandated in 1974.

[2] Note, however, that not all states have mandatory bar membership, which remains a controversial matter in various parts of the USA. Even in those states in which one can practice law without being a member of the state or local bar, there often exists a system of registration of

For the most part these courses have the shape and feel of other subject matter courses in the law curriculum. Casebooks are widely available, as they are in such traditional subjects as contracts, property law and family law, and superficially they have the appearance and structure of casebooks in other areas. Although casebooks on legal ethics vary in many ways—level of sophistication, emphasis on theory as opposed to practice, consideration of rules governing law practice or a focus on goals—they tend to cover the same predictable syllabus of topics. These include the nature and goals of the adversary system, the meaning of zealous representation of clients, permissible trial tactics, confidentiality, and conflicts of interests (concurrent and successive). They are also likely to include client counseling, representing the public interest, the unauthorized practice of law, rules regulating fees, advertising and solicitation, and alternative dispute resolution. Most casebooks and most courses acknowledge the role of the Model Rules of Professional Conduct,[3] promulgated by the American Bar Association as a model for the codes adopted by the various state bar associations. The states codes, in turn, have all been influenced by the Model Rules (and by an earlier (1969) ABA document, the Model Code of Professional Responsibility, which the Model Rules were designed to supplant).

It is widely conceded that the intense interest shown by law schools in courses on professional responsibility, and by state bar associations in promulgating codes of conduct and giving the appearance of taking them seriously, is only twenty-five years old. This sea change in attitude is traceable to the Watergate scandal, which implicated the conduct of highly placed lawyers in the federal government and cast the profession as a whole in an unflattering light. Just as the events of Watergate are said to have inspired widespread and lasting cynicism about politics, so too they have given rise to cynicism about the conduct, ethics, and self-policing of the legal profession, an attitude the bar associations have tried to rebut.[4]

The most cynical commentators are likely to say that the proliferation of courses and the promulgation of codes are nothing more than a long-term public relations program by the profession. The truth is probably more complex and more confused. If the main goal of the continuing effort is indeed public relations, the failure to achieve it could hardly be more palpable. The public reputation of lawyers is at best equivocal and at worse very low.

---

lawyers. Jurisdiction over lawyers and enforcement of disciplinary rules are shared by judiciary and the bar in most states, and the procedures for regulation are quite variable. See C. Wolfram, *Modern Legal Ethics* (St Paul, Minn., Foundation Press, 1986), ch. 3.

[3] The Model Rules of Professional Conduct were adopted and promulgated by the ABA House of Delegates on 2 Aug. 1983. They were seen as replacing the Model Code of Professional Responsibility, which had been adopted in 1969.

[4] For a discussion of this issue, see, e.g., D. Rhode, "Why the ABA Bothers: A Functional Perspective on Professional Codes" (1981) 59 *Texas L. Rev.* 689.

Demoralization within the profession, while hard to measure, is generally thought to be growing steadily.[5]

What does all this mean for professionalism? At the very least, it means that the status and self-understanding of the profession are directly related to our understanding of professionalism in legal education. How lawyers are seen in the world at large affects how lawyers see themselves, and this in turn affects how law students and legal educators see their roles and goals. Thus, courses in professional responsibility cannot be camouflaged as mere courses on legal rules and doctrine; they have a significantly different history and different purpose from courses in any other subject. In the rest of this essay, I will look at (1) the malaise that affects the teaching of legal ethics in American law schools, (2) possible solutions to the problem, and (3) why the solutions are unlikely to be effective as long as the profession itself lacks self-definition in a context of rapid change and devolution.

I. STUDYING LEGAL ETHICS

(a) Law Teachers

Practitioners and law teachers betray their embarrassment about legal ethics with ironic detachment. They are as likely as lay persons to say, "Legal ethics, that's an oxymoron, isn't it?". For even the most thick-skinned teachers and scholars of legal ethics, the joke quickly becomes overfamiliar.

In fact, most legal academics can easily ignore the subject of legal ethics. Unlike practitioners, they are not confronted with ethical dilemmas, such as conflicts of interest and problems of confidentiality, in the context of client representation. The ethical questions they *do* face are those faced by lay persons, and they can ordinarily be resolved through tact or convention.

Thus, law teachers can (and do) often proceed in cheerful ignorance of the rules of professional conduct and of the larger issues that are implicated by professionalism—that is, unless and until they are asked to teach the course itself. That task, resisted or not even contemplated by most law teachers, often falls on visiting faculty, part-time or adjunct teachers, or the most accommodating and tractable members of the faculty. To be sure, there are exceptions, prominent teachers and scholars who build careers writing about the pedagogy and theory of professional responsibility. But they remain a small cohort and, even within their own institutions, they tend to be seen as representing a second-order and somewhat dubious specialty.

---

[5] As evidence, see A. Kronman, *The Lost Lawyer: Failing Ideals of the Legal Profession* (Cambridge, Mass., Harvard University Press, 1993) and M. A. Glendon, *A Nation Under Lawyers: How the Crisis in the Legal Profession is Transforming American Society* (New York, Farrar Straus & Giroux, 1994). Both are discussed in sect. III(c) of this essay.

In part, this attitude reflects the unarticulated persistence of the two senses of professionalism with which I began. Many observers, among them many law teachers, assume that professionalism describes the accumulated skills, capacities, and attitudes that are produced in law school and the early years of practice. Within that context, the basic rules of professional conduct define minima of acceptable conduct and should be evident to common sense and common prudence. To elevate the rules into a distinct discipline is to give undue attention to the obvious by making it problematic. This conclusion dovetails with the second sense of professionalism: if the basic rules of professional conduct are made evident in the conjunction of professional training and common sense, then the rules are fundamentally unteachable to those who lack common sense.

What are the merits of this view and attitude? To students of the professional rules, it plainly misdescribes the rules themselves. In many areas, of which conflict of interest is one good example, there are complex and often counter-intuitive legal precedents that yield a sophisticated, specialized body of doctrine. The rules governing confidentiality are also technical and have evolved through distinct and controversial changes. Much the same can be said about rules governing advertising and solicitation, fees, and trial tactics. It follows that, on a naïve interpretation, the claim that the rules of legal ethics are no more than common sense and prudence fails.

But there is a sophisticated as well as a naïve interpretation of that challenge. On this view, the rules only aspire to a degree of doctrinal interest and complexity that they do not have. It is said that the rules are intended not as guidelines but as a smokescreen behind which lawyers can do whatever they want, or at least what is most to their advantage. The rules only appear to constrain. In fact they are endlessly malleable, allowing lawyers to find or declare exceptions or reinterpretations at will. Once again, this view collapses into the indictment that self-regulation by lawyers is merely an exercise in the manipulation of public opinion.

(b) Law Students

This debate has a formative impact on the attitudes and expectations of students. It is rank understatement to say that they are unenthusiastic about courses on professional responsibility. One is tempted to say that they regard them as a necessary evil, but few would concede they are necessary.

Within the standard curriculum of American law schools, most courses in the second and third year are elective. The first year, by contrast, consists primarily of prescribed courses on common law subjects (such as torts, contracts, property law and criminal law). Quite often, the course on professional responsibility is the only mandatory course in the second or third year, the only major obstacle to specialization and/or diversification through electives.

Even if the subject matter were uncontroversial, timing alone would make the requirement unpopular.

By their second and third years, students have generally come to believe that the subject matter of professional responsibility does not justify the course requirement. Their reasons vary but are often complementary. Some observe, with justification, that the rules of professional conduct can be assimilated in a single afternoon and hardly warrant a separate course. Others point out that lawyers themselves treat the rules with irony and disrespect. (We have already seen that there is widespread cynicism both within and outside the profession about the motives and goals of self-regulation).[6] Still other students object that the aims of most courses on professionalism and professional responsibility are confused: is the intent to bring all students to a minimal level of competence and integrity to forestall malpractice, or is it to evoke idealism and a sense of public service that goes beyond the commercial and partisan aspects of legal representation?[7]

The frustrations of many students with courses on professional responsibility in American law schools are elicited by distinctive features of such courses. In the rest of this section, I will outline the main complaints. In part II, I will discuss putative solutions. Finally, in part III, I will consider the larger context of the self-understanding of the legal profession and the antinomies that characterize it.

(1) *Subject matter.* We have considered two aspects of the subject matter of a typical law school course on professional responsibility. The first is that such courses are surprisingly uniform, as reflected in the similarity of contents of most available casebooks. The second aspect is that the *core* of such courses is built around the rules of professional conduct, such issues as confidentiality, conflict of interest, the meaning of zealous representation, the implications and merits of the adversary system and so on.[8] To say that the core, agendas and syllabi of these courses are predictable is not to say that they are efficacious. Teachers are expected to build courses on legal ethics around a dauntingly thin core. The rules themselves, even if not artifacts of mere common sense, are indeed easily and briefly assimilated, and are also interpretable as malleable and insubstantial, a self-serving facade.

One way to flesh out the bones of a course on legal ethics is to use an outside discipline. Sociology is an obvious candidate, allowing students to consider, for example, how the class, gender, and race characteristics of the profession have changed and what the effects of these changes have been, or

---

[6] *Supra* n. 4.

[7] This confusion was both influenced and compounded by the Model Code of Professional Responsibility, in which various parts were labeled "disciplinary rules" and "ethical considerations". The labels notwithstanding, the so-called disciplinary rules often represented ethical ideals and the so-called ethical considerations often explained disciplinary minima.

[8] Many teachers make no secret of their disdain for the rules and use them as symptoms of concerns that, arguably, should be addressed more directly and more candidly than the rules themselves can be seen as doing.

how patterns of authority and subordination are replicated and camouflaged within the profession. History is another candidate, inviting consideration of how the nature and demands of law practice have evolved over our history. Economics plays a significant part in the story, both in the context of examining how the legal profession has been an instrument of capitalism and in the context of the economics of the profession itself, the incentive and reward structure of the profession and its effect on the professional choices of lawyers. Psychology, too, is relevant and offers a methodology for considering the role morality and partisanship of lawyers, and their effects on self-understanding and on the tensions and compromises of lawyers' lives. Finally, philosophy allows us to set the rationale and justification of the rules of professional conduct against the more ambitious and nuanced canvas of moral philosophy.[9]

In framing a course on professional responsibility, the teacher must not only consider whether and how to draw on these several outside disciplines, but she must also decide on a basic orientation. Thus, one may adopt (as the rules themselves appear to do) the definition of the lawyer as essentially a partisan or (as the cliché has it) a "gun for hire". On this view the adversary system offers the clearest picture of the limits of the lawyer's responsibilities and opportunities; she has a circumscribed and partial role to play as the agent of a client's interests and goals.

Alternatively, one may adopt the notion that the lawyer must serve "the situation", seek to achieve the best outcome for the several parties whom she is in a position to serve while keeping in mind her special obligation to her client. Accordingly, a lawyer would take seriously her role in shaping the client's perception of his interests and in working within a framework of alternative dispute resolution (alternative to the adversary system). A third possibility is that the lawyer is ultimately the servant of the public interest, and that all of his other more immediate obligations are circumscribed by that concern.[10]

Thus, the teacher of professional responsibility (or professionalism) has many options in filling out the subject matter of her course; she can choose among outside disciplines and points of view. Perhaps this demonstrates the potential richness of the subject and the opportunities such courses offer. But in practical terms it also demonstrates their potential incoherence. The sad fact is that the temptation to draw on bits and pieces of all of these ingredients is irresistible. The typical course invites students to consider in fairly close proximity the conundrums of confidentiality, the sociology of law firm

---

[9] Philosophy has probably inspired more secondary works on legal ethics than any other field in the social sciences or humanities. In addition to Kronman's *Lost Lawyer, supra* n. 5, A. Goldman, *The Moral Foundations of Professional Ethics* (Totowa, Rowman and Littlefield, 1980) and D. Luban, *Lawyers and Justice: An Ethical Study* (Princeton, NJ, Princeton University Press, 1988) have been influential.

[10] These various possibilities are discussed and evaluated in W. Simon, "Ethical Discretion in Lawyering" (1988) 101 *Harvard L. Rev.* 1083.

hierarchy, the merits of alternative dispute resolution in family law, and the psychological costs of adversarial representation. Provocative this may be; coherent it is not. And it offers a daunting challenge to the sophistication of teachers and students alike.

(2) *Class discussion.* The core of the course, consideration of the rules of professional conduct, characteristically revolves around hard questions about the lawyer's choices and responsibilities. The lawyer may, in the interest of confidentiality, be required to refrain from action that seems mandated by basic humanity. An example illustrates the problem well.

L's client has caused an accident in which P has been injured. P's doctor has determined that P's injuries are not serious. L has had P examined by her own doctor, who has determined that P, as a result of the accident, has a previously undetected condition (an aneurysm) that is life-threatening. Disclosure of this information to P would disadvantage L's client, who forbids L to give that information. L, it seems, is bound by the rules of confidentiality to keep the information secret.[11]

Other apparently hard questions may involve trial tactics, for example the strategy of making witnesses appear to be lying when the lawyer knows that they are telling the truth. Still other hard questions may involve the limits of one's obligations to clients: should one continue to represent one's client in a custody battle when one is convinced that the child would be better off if one's client did not prevail?

Provocative and interesting as they are, these "hot-button" questions are faulty triggers for class discussion. On the one hand, they are likely to polarize discussion around two simplistic approaches. One approach is to defend the adversary system and its strict rules, notwithstanding its apparent inhumanity. This approach yields two positions. An idealistic version maintains that the rules are consistent with justice even though their inhumanity is apparent and justice is not. Another version is cynical and claims that the lawyer's job is to follow rules and avoid malpractice, with matters of justice and humanity better left outside the lawyer's expertise or concern.

The second general approach is to attack the rules of the adversary system as indefensible in the light of these examples. This approach also has two forms. Some use it idealistically, with a focus on tempering rules with individuated concern for results. Others use it nihilistically, with the view that all rules are self-serving and that these are no more defensible than any alternatives.

Given this array of options, thoughtful students are likely to refrain from identifying themselves either with idealism or cynicism. They are likely to see any option as a fragile limb. Those who opt for idealism risk being seen as unrealistic or, worse, insincere. Those who choose cynicism will be accused of reinforcing the worst impulses and images of lawyers. Challenged to

---

[11] This example is drawn from the facts of *Spaulding* v. *Zimmerman*, 116 NW2d 704 (1962).

navigate between Scylla and Charybdis, students will tend toward silence. In American law schools, reticence is the normal posture of students in their second or third year. The dilemmas posed by hard questions about the rules of professional responsibility tend to reinforce it.

Moreover, these hot-button questions are faulty in a second way. They seem either too easy or too hard. Take the confidentiality question about the accident victim with the aneurysm. Questions such as "Would this be a permissible disclosure under the confidentiality rules?" and "Does this seem like a harsh result?" are insultingly easy. And the questions to which they lead ("What kinds of disclosures *should* be permitted?", "How might the adversary system be reconceived to allow lawyers to avoid such hard choices?") are unmanageably general and elusive. Discussion is likely to involve, on one hand, cataloguing the obvious applications of the rules and the predictable moral responses, or speculating windily about how one might revolutionize the system so that such dilemmas need not arise.

My conclusions may seem unjustifiably bleak. The classroom situation, as I describe it, may be seen as a challenge and opportunity for teachers and students rather than an occasion for despair. While such implications are in the eye of the beholder and there are pedagogic success stories along with the failures, the frequent result in courses on professional responsibility is frustration on the part of students and teachers. The nature of the interaction surely helps explain that response.

(c) *Course materials.* The last decade has seen a proliferation of sophisticated casebooks on legal ethics. Such prominent scholars of the field as Deborah Rhode (Stanford),[12] Geoffrey Hazard (Yale)[13] and David Luban (University of Maryland)[14]—among many others—have produced books that are widely adopted and praised. These materials set a new standard of quality. But they also leave room for debate over whether their authors have overcome the perennial obstacles that confronted their predecessors.

Authors of casebooks face an initial choice of orientation, one that reflects their inherent disposition to the adversary system and the rules of professional conduct. On one hand, they may accept and defend the adversarial model of lawyering. If so, they will explain the balance of roles and duties within the adversarial system in the light of considerations of justice, and they will use the rules to refine our understanding of these roles. On this model, the lawyer is primarily a partisan for her client; other responsibilities—to third parties, to the general public—must be seen as subordinated, even if they are not forgotten. Authors with this disposition will not criticize the adversarial legal

---

[12] D. Rhode and D. Luban, *Legal Ethics* (2nd edn.,Westbury, Foundation Press, 1995); D. Rhode, *Professional Responsibility: Ethics by the Pervasive Method* (Boston, Mass., Little Brown, 1994); D. Rhode and G. Hazard Jr., *The Legal Profession: Responsibility and Regulation* (3rd edn., Westbury, Foundation Press, edition 1994).

[13] G. Hazard Jr., S. Koniak and R. Cramton, *The Law and Ethics of Lawyering* (2nd edn., Westbury, Foundation Press, 1994), and see *supra* n. 12.

[14] *Supra* n. 12.

system as a whole, but they may well call for fine-tuning in the interest of fairer distribution of legal services or in the interest of smoothing the edges of adversarial conflict.[15]

Casebooks with this orientation are subject to endless shades of sophistication. The crudest of them simply show law students how to follow the rules to avoid malpractice. More subtle approaches explore the applications of the rules to different contexts and discuss their limitations, their malleability, and their history. Still more subtle approaches take heed of critics of the adversary system and of the practice of self-regulation and consider alternatives.

The second orientation is fundamentally critical or skeptical of the claimed central role of the adversary system as definitive of legal professionalism. Such authors will arrive at their skepticism from various starting points. Some may see the adversary system as fostering and legitimating aggression and combat as optimal modes of problem-solving and may reject that notion. Others may see the highest use of the lawyer's skills as serving the public good and the interests of general justice; they may believe that, given a choice, the lawyer must never knowingly subvert a just outcome by deferring to the needs and goals of a client. Still others, borrowing from critical legal theory, may have misgivings about using such notions as the public good and general justice, but may have even greater misgivings about lawyers serving as facilitators for powerful class interests at the expense of those who lack power. All of these positions provide a basis for questioning the prevailing adversarial model and the rules that inform it.[16]

Any observer, and *a fortiori* any casebook author, will tend to favor one of these two orientations. Either she will identify the law as a professional calling with the values of the adversary system at its core, or she will find good reasons to raise doubts about those values and will seek the nature and justification of the lawyer's role elsewhere. It is arguable that *either* kind of casebook is limited in its reach and appeal to student constitutents and other readers. One kind will seem jurisprudentially naïve in its capitulation to the ideal of the adversary system. The other will seem subversive in questioning what many practitioners consider the essence of lawyering.

The challenge of evenhandedness in the face of these options is more immediate (and more compromising) than in other subject areas. The author of a casebook on contracts or property law may have to take a stand on doctrinal issues, their justification, and their relation to public interest, but his attitude need not color and shape every aspect of his book, since his subject is not the nature of professionalism itself.

In addition to taking a stand on the adversarial character of lawyering, casebooks on legal ethics face other practical limitations. Casebooks in other

---

[15] Hazard, Koniak and Cramton, *supra* n. 13, may fairly be described as a casebook of this kind.

[16] The work of Luban and Rhode, severally and together, *supra* n. 12 and n. 14, seems to fall in this category.

areas of law tend to give pride of place to case decisions, as their name implies. This reflects both the common law tradition and the American pedagogic method of asking students to infer the law from judicial opinions. But the most interesting issues in professional responsibility are often unlitigated, and even with litigated issues, the pool of cases is thin and skewed. For example, questions about zealous representation arise in cases involving malpractice/disbarment and in appeals based on inadequate counsel. Most fine points about fidelity and zeal are not raised in these cases. This is even more true of confidentiality, violations of which rarely lead to litigation. The main exception, the only topic on which there is a robust body of cases, is conflict of interest.

As a result, so-called casebooks are heavy with extracts from books and articles. In principle, that is not a drawback. In practice, selections are often predictable and tendentious, reiterating the orientation of the author. Thus, more than with other subject matter areas, materials on legal ethics are rarely stimulating to students. On the contrary they tend to betray the (not erroneous) impression that the core materials, the interpretation of malleable rules, are thin and that speculative writings of psychologists, philosophers, economists, and sociologists used to inflate discussion suggest partial answers to questions that are never made clear.

II. PRACTICAL PEDAGOGICAL REFORMS

There are two ways to face the malaise of teaching professional responsibility. The first is to look at practical suggestions for making the course more palatable to law students. The second is to ask whether the malaise reflects deeper ills, or at least uncertainties and transitions, within the profession and practice of law itself. I shall consider the first approach briefly in this section, and the second approach in the next.

The approaches discussed in this section address issues of morale and efficacy. They are designed to alert students to the importance of considering professionalism by making courses on professional responsibility more interesting and accessible.

One idea is to enhance the classroom experience with interactive and media-based techniques. It is argued that simulations and role-playing exercises can bring the issues of professional responsibility home to students.[17] Videotapes showing such enactments and computer-based exercises in applying the rules of professional conduct are increasingly available.[18] While such

---

[17] A textbook that is structured around such training is R. Burns, T. Geraghty, and S. Lubet, *Exercises and Problems in Professional Responsibility* (National Institute for Trial Advocacy, 1994).

[18] A bibliography of such teaching materials has been prepared and promulgated by the Keck Center on Legal Ethics and the Legal Profession at Stanford Law School. The bibliography is annotated and revised periodically.

enhancements have their place, for the most part they are as useful in these courses as they are in other courses; a student might be asked to negotiate a contract or determine a hypothetical defendant's guilt. Just as one may learn something about corporations by simulating a board meeting, one may explore the ethical dimensions of preparing a client to testify.

Many pedagogical reformers argue that professional responsibility is best learned in the context of actual practice.[19] Some have suggested that students be taught legal ethics in conjunction with part-time employment in law firms. A similar idea is to give special attention to ethical concerns in in-house clinical programs. Obviously both methods, if handled deftly, have considerable merit as well as limitations. They are likely to serve only a small number of students, those with relevant employment in the first case and those enrolled in clinics. Under both suggestions, the treatment of issues is adventitious and many important questions may not arise.

A reform that has received much attention and comment over the last five years is the "pervasive method" of teaching professional responsibility.[20] The logic behind the pervasive method is impeccable. Since ethical issues come up in every aspect of practice and are relevant to every substantive subject matter area, every course in the curriculum should consider ethical questions. Under the pervasive method, every teacher would routinely discuss ethics in conjunction with the agenda of her particular courses. Such a reform addresses the universal flaw of current courses, which represent legal ethics as an add-on to the curriculum, an emetic to be administered before graduation.

The pervasive method can be used in conjunction with the standard course or in place of it. The disadvantage of the latter is similar to the disadvantage of replacing the standard course with enhanced clinical training, since in both cases many ingredients of the standard course may be lost. The degree and range of exposure a particular student has to ethical questions would depend entirely on his choices among substantive courses and on the idiosyncratic disposition of his teachers to raise ethical issues.

A deeper concern with *both* versions of the pervasive method, at least within the context of an American law school, is that different conjunctions of students and teachers will produce widely divergent experiences. Some teachers will incorporate ethical questions with enthusiasm, others grudgingly, if at all. The extent to which pursuit of the pervasive method will improve upon or undercut the relative success of the now-standard course will depend on factors nearly impossible to anticipate or monitor.

[19] See, e.g., E. Myers, "'Simple Truths about Moral Education" (1996) 45 *Am. UL Rev.* 823. The author argues that "the emphasis by the organized bar on a unitary profession with a dominant conception of practice is counterproductive" (at 825) and that "the ideal way to impart [ethical attitudes] is through a program of experiential learning" (n. 66) integrated with and differentiated through various kinds of law practice. See also L. Hellman, "The Effects of Law Office Work on the Formation of Law Students' Professional Values," Observation, Explanation, Optimization." (1991) 4 *Georgetown J of Leg. Ethics* 537.

[20] See the Rhode casebook, written to facilitate use of the pervasive method, *supra* n. 14.

A modest proposal that might obviate some of the cynicism that attends the standard course would be to move it to the first year. Doing so has several advantages. It signals to students that the questions raised are formative and relevant to the expectations students should bring to all legal problems. It situates the course among other required courses rather than singling it out as an apparent afterthought. It meets the complaint, sometimes heard from students who work as legal assistants between the first and second year or during the second year, that they are unprepared to address ethical questions in their work. And it allows students' understanding of ethical issues to evolve along with their substantive mastery of various areas of law. Moreover, students are less cynical and reticent, more optimistic and forthcoming, at the beginning of law school than in the second and third year.

The suggestions discussed in this section are all ameliorative. They treat the malaise of legal ethics courses as a problem of packaging and communication. Their assumption is that we need to make evident to students the relevance and interest of these issues, and that we can do so in a way that students will accept and even enjoy. While these suggestions are more than palliatives, they do not foreclose a deeper understanding of the malaise, one that sees the problem of teaching professional responsibility as a symptom of crises within the legal profession.

III. THE IMAGE AND SELF-IMAGE OF LAWYERS

One central purpose of a course on professional responsibility is to make fledgling lawyers examine themselves more directly and more thoroughly than they do in other contexts. One reason for the unpopularity of such courses is that such self-examination can be risky and painful and that the questions raised may yield few comfortable answers. *If* that is so, no amount of tinkering with the format and presentation of these questions is likely to erase the discomfort or the resistance.

Observers who are unsettled by aspects of the profession of law focus on several related issues. Some raise questions that have troubled observers for as long as advocacy has been a profession.[21] Other questions concern change and devolution; they reflect ways in which adherence to standards of honor and service has been eroded by economic and social changes in the profession.[22] One way of distinguishing among these issues is to look on the one hand at criticisms that emanate from outside, from observers and critics of the image and performance of lawyers, and on the other hand at lawyers' own

[21] One example is Martha Nussbaum, who draws on her background in ancient philosophy and classical litearture to illuminate the roles of lawyers, judges and other public officials. See, among other works, M. Nussbaum, *Poetic Justice: The Literary Imagination and Public Life* (Boston, Mass., Beacon Press, 1966).

[22] Eleanor Myers, *supra* n. 19, discusses these sociological aspects of law at length. See also Kronman, *supra* n. 5, and Glendon, *supra* n. 5, both discussed *infra,* sect. III(c).

self-examination and in some cases self-castigation. However one sorts these issues, they can be seen as a series of antinomies, the coexistence of incompatible but justified ideas about the nature of lawyers and lawyering.

(a) Humor and Character

The last few years have witnessed a bull market in lawyer jokes. Even if lawyers have always been the subjects of humor, most current observers agree that "lawyer jokes are unlike any other humor extant in American society, and not insignificantly, one glaring difference is their high level of aggressiveness".[23] A complementary feature is their lack of subtlety.[24] Scholars note that "they are expressions of concrete grievances specific to our society".[25]

A glance at any anthology of lawyer jokes allows us to sort them into those that merely *express* contempt (and therefore presume that the reasons hardly need to be stated) and those that suggest *reasons* for contempt.[26] The reasons generally allude to matters of character. The invariant theme is that lawyers are self-serving, at the immediate expense of clients and to the detriment of society. As Marc Galanter has observed, the implication is that lawyers are "predators and parasites".[27] Lawyers, it is suggested, will do anything, represent any cause and serve any client, without regard for moral consequences. Moreover, they will do so in ways that are covert and devious. One hallmark of their deviousness, on this account, is that they manipulate the image and rhetoric of the profession to camouflage their social harm with the appearance of selfless public service. The one consequence that matters to lawyers, it is believed, is their own success and well-being.

[23] T. Overton, "Lawyers, Light Bulbs, and Dead Snakes: The Lawyer Joke as Societal Text" (1995) 42 *UCLA L Rev.* 1069, 1074. See also R. Post, "On the Popular Image of the Lawyer: Reflections in a Dark Glass" (1987) 75 *Cal. L Rev.* 379.

[24] The appendix of the Overton article, *supra* n. 23, has many examples of lawyer jokes. Here are three:

    Q: What do you call 5,000 lawyers at the bottom of the sea?
    A: A good start.

    Q: Why did the post office have to recall its lawyer stamp?
    A: People didn't know which side to spit on.

    Q: Why does Washington have the most lawyers *per capita* and New Jersey the most toxic waste dumps?
    A: New Jersey had first choice.

[25] *Supra*, n. 23.

[26] The examples in n. 24 are of the first kind. The following jokes illustrate the second kind.

    Q: Why do so many lawyer have broken noses?
    A: From chasing parked ambulances.

    Q: What's the difference between a lawyer and gigolo?
    A: A gigolo only screws one person at a time.

[27] M. Galanter, "Predators and Parasites: Lawyer-Bashing and Civil Justice" (1994) 28 *Georgia L Rev.* 633. The title of the following relevant article speaks for itself: C. Puma, "The Missing Link: Does Lawyer-Bashing Warrant Additional Protection for Lawyers?" (1995) 19 *J Legal Prof.* 207.

Not all lawyer humor is concerned with character. A more traditional (and less censorious) preoccupation is with the tendency of lawyers to obfuscate, to be obsessed with minutiae and technicalities at the expense of more consequential concerns. Such humor draws the conclusion that lawyers are boring and disengaged.[28] Perhaps the most salient observation one can make about lawyer jokes is that there has been a sea change from the more gentle and tolerant gestures of this older vein of jokes, which treats lawyers as eccentric and irrelevant, to the now dominant themes of contempt and victimization.

Is lawyer humor mainly about the character of lawyers or about the institutions and profession of law? In other words, does it assume that the profession of law has corrupted its adherents and warped their character, or that persons of bad character have changed and corrupted a profession which can be used for good or ill? For the most part, lawyer jokes are concerned with neither causation nor redemption. Rather, they imply that both lawyers *and* the profession itself are corrupt *ab initio*, and neither is capable of salvation.

The attitudes of lawyer humor go beyond jokes. Thus, an advertisement for a television series about a firm that represents only the neediest of clients announces, "[They're OK], they hate lawyers too."[29] The advertisement takes for granted that hatred of lawyers is the norm, that *defending* the actions of lawyers is a politically and morally suspect enterprise. Only the exceptional lawyer, the lawyer as anti-lawyer, can be respected.

Is it surprising that lawyer humor is so rarely addressed or even mentioned in law schools? Surely law teachers and students do not exist in a vacuum or deny the attitudes around them. And yet they ignore the evident antinomy: the essence of lawyering is service to clients and subordination of one's own interests. The contrast between the ideal and the perceived reality could hardly be sharper, since lawyer humor affirms that lawyers do exactly the opposite of what they aver. The clear accusation is that lawyers are a paradigm of hypocrisy.

I am not concerned here with reality, with the question whether lawyers live up to their ideals or betray them, as jokes suggest. No doubt the truth is complex; some lawyers are often selfless and idealistic, while others are self-serving and duplicitous. Both extremes of the antinomy are ideal types or caricatures. I am concerned with the impact of this cultural clash on the self-awareness of law students. Courses on professionalism and professional responsibility are the most obvious context in which the antinomy can be addressed and where ideals can be spelled out, debated, and defended.

---

[28] An example, also drawn from Overton's collection, *supra* n. 23, is this:

    A hot-air balloon begins to deflate and veers off-course. Its rider is now sailing along very slowly, some three feet off the ground.

    "Where am I?" he calls to a chance passer-by. The passer-by answers, "You're in a hot air balloon, three feet off the ground, and moving north."

    "You must be a lawyer," says the rider, "because what you say is extremely articulate, totally accurate, and thoroughly useless."

[29] *TV Guide*, 1–7 Mar. 1997, advertisement for "The Practice".

(b) Dignitary Considerations

It is a short step from considering the contradiction between the message of service that law students are expected to imbibe and the message of self-service that lawyer humor conveys to considering questions of dignity and respect. The answers to the questions, What roles will I play? and What choices will I make?, are inseparable from the question, What kind of person am I?

Self-respect is almost always affected, if not determined, by the respect shown one by others. A common expectation in professional training and practice is that pursuit of a profession will not only be compatible with but will enhance respect, both self-respect and the respect of others. To be sure, this must be qualified. Most roles in contemporary society embody controversial ideals. Moreover, respect and dignity are attitudes that one earns and achieves as an individual, not rights that one acquires by practicing a profession.

These qualifications notwithstanding, one must hope that assuming a profession will not *disqualify* one for respect and undercut one's claim to dignity regardless of how one acts as a person. The prevailing attitudes toward lawyers imply just such a connection. Humor does not exist for its own sake as a matter of levity and diversion, but as a symptom of hard truths about attitudes and expectations. In thinking about professional responsibility, one cannot help asking whether becoming a lawyer does not in fact trigger such a dignitary trap.

(c) Critics Inside the Profession

Lawyers who take a defensive posture in the face of aggressively antagonistic humor and of an apparent crisis in the image of the profession may see the problem as essentially one of public relations. They may choose to interpret the symptoms as evidence of an "us against them" predicament in which the profession is misunderstood and caracatured by those outside it. However, every aspect of lawyer humor is echoed by critics within the profession. They are typically academic critics who decry the evolution of the legal profession into a "business" and the consequent corruption of professional ethics. These perceptions are not new. Recall that the events of Watergate shocked bar associations into requiring courses and examinations on professional responsibility. This response was ambiguous; while it can be read as an attempt to repair a torn public image, it can also be seen as betraying awareness of something deeply rotten in the state of the bar.

Anthony Kronman, the dean of Yale Law School, and Mary Ann Glendon, professor of law at Harvard Law School, have recently produced well-received and widely-discussed critiques of the state of the profession.[30] Kronman uses

---

[30] *Supra* n. 5.

the phrase, "the dark night of the soul",[31] to characterize a crisis in values, commitment, self-understanding, and self-confidence of contemporary law students and lawyers. He argues that we have lost "the ideal of the lawyer-statesman",[32] a professional ideal that expressed the common aspiration of nineteenth-century lawyers and was distinguished by public service and practical wisdom. The demise of this ideal is marked by an inability to see legal respresentation "in any but instrumental terms"[33] and to see the problems and goals of clients as incommensurable and therefore lacking a grounded and wise resolution. Legal training, once marked by the cultivation of practical wisdom, now stands for reductionist and relativistic thinking about lawyers as partisan tools for special interests and training in the skills of sophistical argumentation. Kronman concludes that "[t]o the ultimate question of life's meaning, it is now unthinkable that one can find even the smallest part of an answer by choosing a legal career".[34]

Glendon is also deeply critical of what she sees as the recent abandonment by lawyers of their traditional public role, a role that gave coherence to their training and meaning to their lives. She describes the legal profession as essentially a conservative social force, whereby lawyers embody the techniques and ideals of conciliation and social constraint in the larger service of preserving democracy.[35] As one critic has observed, she sees lawyers "as a moderating force against democracy's excesses"[36] and as a restraining force on social change. She sees the neglect of legal ethics as evidence of dissolution of this legal and social ideal.

Kronman and Glendon have been criticized as insensitive to new ways of conceiving and realizing social justice and as apologists for a history pervaded by hierarchy and discrimination.[37] These critics counter Kronman and Glendon's pessimism with qualified optimism. On both theoretical and practical planes, they offer critical theory and clinical education as evidence of contemporary ideals of justice and social service that can fill lawyers' lives with purpose.

Our task here is not to assess this debate but to see it as symptomatic. The familiar study of professional ethics as the study of rules of professional conduct can readily be seen as psychological avoidance and rationalization, as an effort to deny that an acute conflict of ideals is at the core of the legal pro-

---

[31] Kronman, *supra* n. 5, at 3.

[32] *Ibid.*, 11–14.

[33] *Ibid.*, 286.

[34] *Ibid.*, 370.

[35] Glendon, *supra* n. 5, especially chs. 2–4.

[36] Anon., "Book Note: A Bold Leap Backward" (1995) 108 *Harv. L Rev.* 2047.

[37] See M. Aaronson, "Dark Night of the Soul: A Review of Anthony T. Kronman's *The Lost Lawyer: Failing Ideals of the Legal Profession*" (1994) 45 *Hastings LJ* 1379; D. Wilkins, "Practical Wisdom for Practicing Lawyers: Separating Ideals from Ideology in Legal Ethics" (1994) 108 *Harv. L Rev.* 458; review of Glendon, *supra* n. 36; P. Glenn, "A Nation under Lost Lawyers: The Legal Profession at the Close of the Twentieth Century" (1996) 100 *Dick. L Rev.* 477 (introduction to a symposium on Glendon and Kronman).

fession. If the lawyer's role is more than instrumental, if justice is as central to the lawyer's thought and action as health is to that of the doctor, then it is inevitable that this antinomy of justice be addressed. Is justice achieved through the conservation of traditional practices and roles and through the practical wisdom of reconciliation, as Kronman and Glendon would have it? Or is it to be redefined through the insights of critical theory and social activism as a questioning of and confrontation with traditional beliefs and practices?

(d) The Realities of Practice

We have seen that lawyer-bashing and lawyer humor are not merely the products of ignorance, not merely the scapegoating of lawyers because of their apparent power and access to the levers of change. They are the external reflection of an internal malaise. Kronman and Glendon stand ready to explain why lawyers are sitting ducks for abuse, why they have lost the power of self-justification through the loss of ideals.

It would be seductive to see the discontent of law students as a conceptual problem, the problem of attaching ideals to the concept of professionalism. But whatever troubles the profession is not reducible to a contest between the past and the future and not curable through reconstructive nostalgia. Most law students face a more acute crisis, one that seems to put idealism in any form beyond their reach.

The recent past was, for most lawyers, a period of economic opportunity, job stability, and social mobility. Between the 1960s and the late 1980s, law firms grew exponentially in size and number and the legal profession took on unprecedented importance in managing the business and politics of the nation. These changes had their social costs, both in terms of the public image of lawyers (as reflected in lawyer humor) and in terms of constraints on lawyers' time and energy. But many lawyers knew that they had had choices, and had made their beds accordingly. In this period, talk of legal ideals and legal ethics and critiques of legal instumentalism led a marginalized life in the academy and an irrelevant one in the eyes of the profession.[38]

The current sense of crisis and ethical bankruptcy—reflected in lawyer humor, in the nostalgia of Kronman and Glendon, and in renewed attention to professionalism—is in part a response to an economic and practical crisis. Law firms have for the most part retrenched. Initial jobs and partnerships have become scarcer and less secure. Job pressures and competition have, if anything, increased. Lawyers thus find it increasingly hard to find employment or satisfaction in the jobs they have. A growing literature debates whether

---

[38] A well-regarded general study of the American legal profession in this period is R. Abel, *American Lawyers* (New York, Oxford UP, 1989).

addiction, marital strife and mental instability are epidemic among lawyers.[39] Thus, the need to look inward and find meaning in professionalism is propelled by the disappearance of outward rewards.

It is obviously perilous to generalize about trends in, and the direction of, the legal profession as a whole. Many new lawyers are able to find satisfying employment, and many are able to represent causes in which they believe. It is not hard to find lawyers whose lives and attitudes are the antithesis of what is implied in lawyer humor, nor is it hard to find lawyers who are convinced that Kronman and Glendon are dead wrong about vanishing ideals. And yet the meta-discourse about the lawyering coalesces around a sense of crisis, one that has all of the dimensions we have considered. The prevailing conviction is that even if ideals can be expressed and defended, few new lawyers have the luxury of choosing lives according to such ideals.

(e) Plato and the Sophists

There is a final antinomy that is perhaps implicit in all the others, one that echoes an argument that has been going on for more than two thousand years. It epitomizes both the disturbing essence of lawyer humor and the struggle with idealism that preoccupies legal scholars.

In *Gorgias*, Plato argues against the relativistic claim that might makes right, that the power of rhetoric defines what is right.[40] The skill of the sophists lay in persuasion. Their job was to persuade the courts that justice coincided with the interests of those they served. Plato, challenging the sophists, arguing that justice was an independent concept, to be used as a measure of the claims of the various contending parties. To serve merely the interests of one's client, to be merely a "gun for hire", is the antithesis of serving justice and the antithesis of idealism.

The deep disquiet evoked by Plato's claim has never been allayed. In particular it haunts lawyers who like to believe that they can act essentially as the agents of clients' interests and *at the same time* serve justice. In contemporary theory, lawyers' tenuous claim to doing justice is disturbed further by the suggestion of critical legal theorists that the rhetoric of justice may camouflage the pursuit of advantage and domination. Critical theorists can be seen as challenging the liberal theory of justice in much the same way as the sophists challenged Plato. In both contexts the objectivity and accessibility of the concept of justice are under seige.

---

[39] See, e.g., C. Beck, B. Sales and G. Benjamin, "Lawyer Distress: Alcohol-Related Problems and Other Psychological Concerns among a Sample of Practicing Lawyers" (1995/1996) 10 *JL & Health* 1. A response and evaluation of this study is P. Glenn, "Some Thoughts about Developing Constructive Approaches to Lawyer and Law Student Distress" (1995/1996) 10 *JL & Health* 69.

[40] Near the end of this dialogue, Socrates concludes that "rhetoric, like every other practice, is always to be used to serve the ends of justice, and for that alone": Plato, *Gorgias* (Helmbold translation, Library of Liberal Arts, 1952).

A multi-cultural society that is cynical about justice will also be cynical about lawyers. In such a society lawyers themselves will perceive a crisis in idealism. The antinomy that Plato and the sophists brought to awareness is no closer to resolution in today's value-questioning society than it was two thousand years ago.

IV. CONCLUSION

The malaise of teaching professional responsibility is over-determined. The simplest account of the problem alludes to the difficulties of making the issues in the traditional course on legal ethics cohere, of finding provocative teaching materials, and of orchestrating discussion. These concerns are manageable.

But these difficulties mask a deeper concern with whether lawyering can be seen as a principled activity and whether professionalism can be represented as more than an instrumental skill. Once we have tackled the public relations problem represented by lawyer humor and dealt with nostalgia about a possibly non-existent past, lawyers and lay observers alike will still wonder whether Plato's questions can be answered and whether legal professionals can simultaneously serve partisanship (the interests of clients) and justice. It is both the significant virtue and the curse of courses on professional responsibility that increasingly they address this dilemma directly.

Part 3

MAKING LAWYERS GOOD

12

Lawyers' Moral Reasoning and Professional Conduct, in Practice and in Education

LENY E. DE GROOT-VAN LEEUWEN*

INTRODUCTION

In the Netherlands as well as elsewhere in Europe, a wide variety of illegal practices of lawyers has been exposed in public. Parallel to this, the number of complaints (per lawyer) is steadily rising.[1] Lawyers these days are no longer depicted as crusaders of justice or enlightened upholders of the law, but as parasites feeding on the misery of others, as servants of the mafia, or as common mortals at best.[2]

In a Dutch newspaper, a lawyer stated that "[a] suspect has a right to expect that his lawyer uses every possible means to defend him". Another lawyer asserted, however, that the means that lawyers employ for the defence of their clients should be constrained by wider responsibilities, such as the duty to avoid harm to victims. Lawyers obviously hold strongly opposing views on what is proper conduct in legal practice, and express this openly in public.[3]

As a result of the problems of public image and internal contradiction, lawyers and legal academics in Europe are now intensively discussing and researching legal moral standards and how to operationalise these in complaint procedures, rules of conduct, and curricula. The present chapter is part of this "new moral wave".

* Assistant professor at Utrecht University and Nijmegen University.

[1] K. Economides, "Cynical Legal Studies" in J. Cooper and L. Trubek (eds.), *Educating for Justice: Social Values and Legal Education* (Aldershot, Dartmouth, 1997); N. Doornbos and L. E. de Groot-van Leeuwen, *Klachten op orde: De behandeling van klachten over advocaten* (Deventer, Kluwer, 1997).

[2] There may be less new under the sun than we may be inclined to think. Saint Ives (ca. 1250–1303) was declared a saint because "although being a lawyer, he did not steal from the poor" (A. Schreiner, "Heilig Moeten" in L. E. de Groot-van Leeuwen and L. H. A. J. M. Quant (eds.), *Ethiek en het Juridisch Beroep, Recht der Werkelijkheid* ('s-Gravenhage, VUGA, 1995)).

[3] E.g. during the Ars Aequi congress of October 1991: NRC. Handelsblad 19, Oct. and 5 Nov. 1991; Groene Amsterdammer, 26 Feb. 1991; and Elsevier, 31 Aug. 1991.

The chapter is based on a research project into professional ethics of lawyers, in which eighty lawyers were interviewed. A description is given of some moral dilemmas of lawyers in different contexts (e.g. large and small firms). In the interviews a distinction has been made between moral dilemmas brought forward by the lawyers themselves and predefined moral dilemmas brought forward by the researcher. The first type of dilemma has been used to arrive at a grounded classification of dilemmas. The second type has been used to study the process of coping with moral dilemmas and the domains in which moral reasoning takes place. Both types bring us to the sequence of steps involved in defining a moral problem and deciding on the appropriate action. In addition, and as a part of a course on legal ethics at the university, a questionnaire about the same subjects has been presented to approximately one hundred law students. This then serves as a basis for discussing three issues for teaching legal ethics: teaching the code, teaching the ethics of care and teaching permanently.

REAL-LIFE DILEMMAS

Current literature, largely originating from the USA and the United Kingdom, describes many ethical problems that are supposed to be connected to the practice of the legal profession.[4] Contrary to most of this literature, the present chapter will concentrate on what lawyers *themselves* perceive as moral problems in the practice of their work ("real-life dilemmas"). In the interviews, lawyers were asked if they could mention cases in which the lawyer had hesitated about what to do because of moral considerations.

Some lawyers answered in the negative. They escape from ethical reflection by phrasing all problems they may encounter in purely legalistic terms. As one lawyer said: "[t]here hardly exists any ethics in lawyering. You are allowed to go to any length in the interest of your client." Other lawyers did recognise that moral dilemmas occur, but then added that in such cases, they pass on the hot potato: "[i]f I recognize a real moral problem, I refuse to take the case. I say that I do not have time, and that it is better to go to an other attorney." At the other extreme, some lawyers answered that they were confronted with moral dilemmas "on a daily basis".

As might be expected, many different cases were brought forward.[5] One

---

[4] See, e.g., M. Davis and F. A. Elliston (eds.), *Ethics and the Legal Profession* (New York, Prometheus Books, 1986); A. T. Kronman, *The Lost Lawyer; Failing Ideals of the Legal Profession* (Cambridge, Mass., Harvard University Press, 1993); S. M. Linowitz, *The Betrayed Profession, Lawyering at the End of the Twentieth Century* (Baltimore, Mld., The Johns Hopkins University Press, 1994).

[5] Compare D. Lamb, "Ethical Dilemmas: What Australian Lawyers Say About Them" in S. Parker and C. Sampford (eds.), *Legal Ethics and Legal Practice: Contemporary Issues* (New York, Oxford University Press, 1995). In Lamb's research, 2 of the 17 lawyers reported that they had encountered no ethical problems. The other 15 lawyers reported on 80 cases of moral dilemmas. In R. Jack and D. C. Jack, *Moral Vision and Professional Decisions: The Changing Values of Women and Men Lawyers* (Cambridge, Cambridge University Press, 1989), 6 of the 36 interviewed attorneys had never encountered a moral dilemma.

lawyer, for example, told that he was asked by a doorman to defend his criminal case. The employer of this doorman, however, was also a client of the lawyer and he did not appreciate it at all that the lawyer defended the doorman. This type of dilemma, running the risk of losing a lucrative client by defending a less lucrative one, was mentioned by several other lawyers, too. One lawyer solved the problem by pointing the lucrative client at the code of conduct rule that lawyers should remain independent from clients (implying that he should defend the doorman). The other lawyers solved the problem by referring to the possibility of conflict of interest (implying that they should not take the case).

In the interviews, two kinds of conflicts of interest appear. The first is a simultaneous conflict, i.e. when a lawyer is instructed to act for two or more parties with opposing interests. The second is a successive conflict, i.e. a situation when a lawyer is instructed to act for one client against a former client. In both cases, the problem becomes more acute if the lawyer avails himself of relevant confidential information.

More often it happens that clients bring lawyers into a problematic position by trying to involve the lawyer in something immoral. One client, for instance, wanted his lawyer to argue that he should be released from his debts while at the same time the lawyer knew that the client had hidden away a large illegal sum. A lawyer indicated three reasons for not giving in to this type of request:

> "(1) 'the noble motive', simply because it is unethical, (2) the vulnerability motive: you become tangled up in all kinds of problems because you cannot tell the truth anymore, and (3) the reputational motive; you will attract more and more of these bad cases."

A second example is when clients want a lawyer to plea for something that the lawyer finds morally right but at the same time legally unachievable. As one lawyer explains:

> "This happens often in cases of legal aliens. Clients have a justified cause, but I cannot see how to make something out of this legally. Somebody for instance may want his family to join him in this country, but the legal criteria for this immigration are simply not satisfied. In such a case it is emotionally and financially attractive to go to court, to enter an appeal and so on. It is quite difficult to say to your client: 'I know what will happen so I cannot go along with you'."

Here we have seen that clients bring lawyers into two types of moral dilemmas. The first is characterised by a tension between the formal professional ethic and the personal ethic of the lawyer.[6] The second is characterised by a tension between the personal ethic of the lawyer and the public interest, as laid down in the law.

---

[6] G. J. Postema, "Moral Responsibility in Professional Ethics" in M. Davis and F. A. Elliston (eds.), *Ethics and the Legal Profession* (New York, Prometheus Books, 1986); Jack and Jack, *supra* n. 6.

However, not only do clients bring lawyers into moral dilemmas. One example is found in the following fragment from an interview:

> "Actually we lawyers have a double standard. If I see a summons of the public prosecutor and I see it contains a technical error, I have the duty to point this out to the judge and to demand the release of my client, even if I know that a man will be discharged who has done the most terrible things and is bound to do them again. What should I do? That is for me a deep ethical dilemma. I think I have no ethical obligation to point out each and every technical error; I regard that more as a professional obligation."

Later in the interview this lawyer gives another example:

> "We have sworn the oath that we will not defend a case that we cannot find justified in our conscience. Say, you have a suspect who has been detained for the alleged rape of a young child. Then you can do two things: you can ask if he really did it, or you can ask nothing and focus purely on what can be formally proven. You could tell your client, for instance, that he should never accept a DNA test because such a test can never be forced on him. The sacred 'integrity of the body' principle—you know that crap. So you and your client persistently deny all charges and the man is acquitted because of this strategy. Then do I go free? Did I act ethically? Should I really have told the suspect to always refuse the DNA test? This is the type of thing that oppress me in this profession."

Here again the lawyer experiences a tension between the duties of the profession and his responsibility towards society as a whole.

The next type of dilemma arises out of the tension between morality and the market. As one lawyer puts it:

> "We simply have to work full-speed here in order to realize the necessary turnover. We have got twenty lawyers here and they all have to make a living. You can hardly refuse a client or say that you do not take on a case. Quality suffers under this constant pressure. I think that this is a serious point. Because you are always in a hurry, sometimes you cannot do your cases as well as you know you should. Let me give you an example. Once when I was overloaded with work, one of my partners proposed to take over a certain case from me. Then I asked him if he really had the time to visit the two clients involved in this case. The clients, you should know, were put away in different houses of detention, far away from here. 'No', said my partner, 'I don't have time for that'. Then I decided not to give him the case. You cannot defend someone you have not even talked to! I think that is really unethical. This basic rule also proved right in this case. I have been away a full day to visit and talk to both these men. During the discussion I saw how happy they were with this opportunity, how much they had to say and how much inspiration I got from them for my plea in court."

This example describes a tension between the requirements of a healthy firm (and with that, the responsibilities towards the partners and employees) and the requirements of responsibility toward the client.

Morality and the market are not always opposed however. Social law firms, for instance, work for certain categories of clients for ethical motives and exclude others, such as suspects of sexual offences.[7] This also has a market dimension, as one of the lawyers explained:

> "Some cases we flatly refuse to take on; borderline cases are discussed form time to time. It is a mixture of moral dilemmas; sometimes also a political stance is involved. Often this also has a commercial aspect. Our firm happens to have a certain profile, and we want to keep it that way because we need to maintain relations with our clients."

As we saw in the foregoing, moral dilemmas can be generated by the conflicting responsibilities towards different categories such as clients, victims, the court, partners, employees and the public at large. Some problems are confined to criminal practice, such as the above examples concerning technical errors and the question whether a lawyer should accept moral limits in the defence of his client—even at the expense of the victim. Not only some problems, but also some solutions are specific to certain types of practice. Lawyers in social law firms for instance may escape the tension between market and morality by focussing on "morally acceptable" clients.

Many moral dilemmas in legal practice are generated because of the discrepancies between personal morality, professional ethic and the general public interest. Most of the dilemmas described in this section[8] can be located in this "triangle of tensions". The case of the legal alien lies on the tightrope between personal morality and general interest; the case of the technical errors lies on the tightrope between the general interest and professional ethics; the case of the hidden fortune lies on the tightrope between professional ethics and personal morality.

Two of the abovementioned cases however fall outside this triangle; they are generated by a tension between morality and the market. In the first case in this section an important client threatens to sever his relations with the firm if the lawyer chooses to do what his professional ethics may prescribe. In the case of the discussion between the two partners (which was a legal aid case in which the government pays fixed compensation per case), we encounter the ever-present temptation to cut down on the quality of the work in order to maintain profits. In other cases, the tension between morality and the market expresses itself in the temptation to bill more, or more senior, hours than are necessary or are in fact worked.

---

[7] P. H. Bakker Schut, "Iedere verdachte verdient een advocaat", NRC. *Handelsblad*, 1991.

[8] Not all ethical dilemmas mentioned in the literature were found in the interviews. Ethical dilemmas arising out of the conflicting aims of the penal system, such as the rehabilitation of the perpetrator and the protection of society (see Davis and Eliston, *supra* n. 5), for instance, are not mentioned by our lawyers.

HYPOTHETICAL DILEMMAS

In the interviews, the lawyers' responses have also been elicited with respect to a number of pre-formulated ("hypothetical") dilemmas. Two of them, translated literally from Jack and Jack (1989), are treated here. They are analysed in the same perspective as Jack and Jack's, i.e. a distinction between two types of ethics: the ethics of care and the ethics of rights.[9]

The first hypothetical case concerns divorce proceedings in which one parent wants custody over the two children. The case was worded as follows:

> "Suppose that you are an attorney in a divorce proceeding, and your client seeks custody of the two children of the marriage. In the course of your representation your client gives you a bundle of documents that inadvertently contains a letter bearing on the fitness of your client to have custody of the children. The information in the letter is not known and is not likely to become known by the other side. Without disclosure of the letter, you believe your client will win the custody battle; you are equally confident that the other party will prevail if the letter is revealed. In your own mind the information clearly makes your client a marginal parent and the other party a far superior parent."

One of the lawyers responded as if there were no moral dilemma involved in this case. Irrespective of his fitness as a parent the client gets the full effort of the lawyer:

> "In the first place I should say you are there for the person you represent. So I would do everything to legally achieve what he wants . . . If the man in this case wishes the letter not to be mentioned and if he sticks to his custody of the children, then as a lawyer you should act in accordance with the man's wishes."

Because of his interpretation of the lawyer's role, it would appear that this lawyer feels responsibility only towards (the rights of) the client. At this point of the interview the case was extended with the information that the letter contained the threat of serious bodily harm to the children. Even then the lawyer persisted in his opinion.

More numerous are the responses in which lawyers acknowledge the case as a moral dilemma. Besides their obligation to serve the interests of the client, they also feel responsibility for the children, and the circumstances then deter-

---

[9] C. Gilligan, "In A Different Voice: Women's Conception of the Self and Morality" (1981) 47 *Harvard Educational Review* 481 at 517; C. Gilligan, *In A Different Voice: Psychological Theory and Women's Development* (Cambridge Mass., Harvard University Press, 1982); J. Cheney, "Eco-Feminism and Deep Ecology" (1987) 9 *Environmental Ethics* 115 at 145; Jack and Jack, *supra* n. 6; L. Kohlberg, C. Levine, and A. Hewer, *Moral States: A. Current Formulation and a Response to Critics* (New York, Karger, 1983); A. E. Komter, *De macht van de dubbele moraal, Verschil en gelijkheid in de verhouding tussen de seksen* (Amsterdam, Van Gennep, 1990); J. Soetenhorst-de Savornin Lohman, *Doe wel en zie om. Maatschappelijke hulpverlening in relatie tot het recht* (Amsterdam/Lisse, Swets & Zeitlinger, 1990); K. Davis, "De rhetorica van het feminisme, Het Gilligan-debat opnieuw bekeken", 17 *Amsterdams Sociologisch Tijdschrift*, 4, 1991, 86 at 110.

mine which of these must prevail. Relative to the lawyer who had a strict focus on the rights of his client these lawyers have a broader, and more care-oriented, perception of the case.

The two types of ethics do not only show in the perception of the dilemma but also in the way in which lawyers decide how to deal with it. Many lawyers solve the dilemma by dropping the case. As one lawyer puts it:

> "I would say to the client: you should never have given this letter to me because now you have put me in a problematic position. I cannot convincingly defend you anymore and I must advice you to take an other attorney."

This response indicates a form of moral reasoning in terms of rights and obligations. On this view, moral obligations cease when the case is closed or dropped. On a care-oriented perspective, however, lawyers tend to consider concrete steps to protect the children, for instance by informing the Child Welfare Counsel: "[i]ndirectly I will give the court a hint that some investigation should be done". Almost all lawyers however stressed the importance of professional secrecy, e.g.: "[b]ut only over my dead body would this information be disseminated to the other party or the court."

The second hypothetical case, equivalent also to that of Jack and Jack, was as follows:

> "Suppose you are representing an accused murderer who has confessed to the crime in a way that no one, including you, has the slightest doubt that he committed the murder. Without the confession, there is no sufficient evidence to prosecute your client. A psychiatric examination and the bizarre speech and behaviour of your client convince you that he is very crazy. In fact, you are sure that you could have the confession excluded on the grounds that he was incompetent to waive his right to an attorney when given his confession. You also have every reason to believe that your client continues to be very dangerous. What would you do?"

Many lawyers are quite clear-cut in their answers, making a radical choice for their client. One response is:

> "I would certainly contest the validity of the confession. . . . It is not my duty to protect society against this man. Others will take care of that. I am only there to defend interest of the client at that moment."

This lawyer (as do many others in our sample) not only makes a choice about which of the two parties he stands for. In terms of the two ethical positions, he also works with a definition of the situation as composed of separate entities (two parties) each with its own role and rights. From this perspective a strong orientation toward the rights of the client and the professional obligations of the lawyer follows naturally. The other extreme also occurs, however:

> "Prevention for society is the crucial thing here! You should not want to keep people inside society when they should be outside. I realize this is a tough

> statement but if it is really evident I do not feel it as a moral burden. Society can-
> not but protect itself against this kind of hopeless person."

This lawyer defines the situation more in terms of society consisting of a vulnerable network of interdependencies, which people can be inside or out-side. From this image it follows that even though it is the lawyer's role to keep as many clients inside as possible, there is also an end to this responsibility. From an ethics of care perspective the responsibility for preventing harm to society can prevail, once a certain threshold (of "hopelessness") has been crossed.

In the interviews, arguments from the ethics of care perspective are often seen to compete with arguments from the ethics of rights perspective. Depending primarily on the case in hand, one perspective always prevails in the end. In the child custody case this is predominantly the care perspective, while the rights perspective carries the day in the murder case. Different domains of the law (criminal law, family law) appear to coincide with the case being treated within different moral domains. This is analogous to the find-ing of Kocken that, in the practice of the Dutch notary, notaries assume dif-ferent roles with respect to the expression of non-client interests in real estate, family and business cases.[10] This, in turn, coincides with De Groot, who states that various situations "trigger" different moral modes of reasoning.[11]

Congruent to this, a lawyer may switch from one moral perspective to the other if the character of the case shifts. In the hypothetical case of child cus-tody, lawyers often started out with a perception of the case in ethics of rights terms. If the interviewer then added that the letter contained a threat of seri-ous bodily harm to the children, many lawyers switched to a care perspective interpretation. Sometimes a lawyer volunteered to define the threshold level for this switch. One lawyer, for instance, who had stuck to the rights per-spective even after having been given the information about the content of the letter, added this point of view:

> "But if I would be convinced that the man is really up to doing such a thing, then
> I would tell the client to look for a lawyer willing to bear that responsibility."

In this way the lawyer finally extended his moral reasoning to include also care about the family's future.

PATTERNS OF MORAL REASONING

The general pattern of the lawyers' responses to events that may be morally problematic (real-life or hypothetical) may be interpreted as a pattern of six

---

[10] C. L. B. Kocken, *De hand van de notaris, Een rechtssociologisch onderzoek naar de onparti-jdigheid en invloed van de Nederlandse notaris* (Deventer, Kluwer, 1997).

[11] W. T. de Groot, *Environmental Science Theory* (Amsterdam, Elsevier Science Publ., 1992).

elements that runs from a pure rights to a care perspective. The first two are sequential decisions and the other four are alternative options within the same step.

(1) First the events have to be perceived as morally significant. In other words, they have to enter the moral domain. Lawyers who tend to keep many events outside the moral domain are those who in the interviews cannot mention significant real-life dilemmas and wish therefore to treat the hypothetical dilemmas from a strictly juridical perspective.

(2) If a case is acknowledged as morally problematic the dilemma may be shifted out of the moral domain of lawyering and into that of the judge or the public prosecutor. Thus the lawyer avoids moral problems by pointing at the division of roles in the legal system. If the problem is acknowledged as belonging to the moral domain of the lawyer the problem is analysed and some option for action is chosen. The interviews indicate that the options can be grouped as follows.

(3) The lawyers' deliberations may result in "no action" as the chosen option. One argument here can be, for instance, that according to the law no case is allowed to be left undefended.

(4) A next option is to take some "soft action", such as trying to talk the client out of an immoral idea. An argument here is the rule of conduct that the lawyer should be independent of his client.

(5) A further option is to keep one's hands clean by putting the case in the hands of another lawyer. Usually this takes place as a selection of clients, either incidentally or categorically (as we saw in the case of the legal aid advocacy). Sometimes a case is dropped at a later stage, in order to escape from a growing moral problem. This option becomes more difficult, however, the closer the case is to entering in court. By way of argument to keep one's hands clean, lawyers often refer to their oath which says they should not take on or defend a case that cannot be justified in their conscience.

(6) Finally the lawyer may decide upon more rigorous action, departing from the juridical rules and giving precedence to the protection of society or potential victims. Examples of this are found in the section on hypothetical cases. In these cases the lawyer feels morally bound to shift his role somewhat in the direction of the judge or the public prosecutor.

In this way, the hypothetical custody case may be analysed for a possible difference in inclination of men and women to treat the case from a rights or care perspective. The six categories below are again running from a pure rights perspective to a pure care perspective. In order to reflect optimally the interview answers of this case, I have collapsed the previous categories 1, 2 and 3 into one, and expanded the previous category 4 into 3, 4 and 5 below. The six categories now become:

1. To defend the client without restriction, with or without some preliminary hesitations.

2. To try to talk the client out of his or her wish, but defend the client if he or she persists.
3. To try to talk the client out of his or her wish, and advise him or her to take another attorney if he or she persists, the reason being that the conviction fails effectively to defend the client.
4. The same, but the reason being that the responsibility to protect the children weighs more heavily than the obligation to defend the client. This decision is taken after many hesitations and much soul-searching, however.
5. The same, but without the hesitations; the choice for the children is self-evident.
6. To keep the case, and use this to take action for the children, e.g. by informing the Child Welfare Counsel or defend the client in a way that can only fail.

Besides the interconnection of spheres of law and moral domains (cf. the previous section), the lawyers had a tendency to treat real-life and hypothetical cases from either a care or a rights perspective.

Table 1 shows the distribution of these response categories over fifteen male and female attorneys. It may be obvious from the table that a significant difference in male and female responses does not exist. Although the way of analysing the data differs, it is remarkable because the case had been designed by Jack and Jack to elicit gender differences, and they found these differences do indeed exist. Besides gender difference it could be surmised that characteristics such as the size of the firm, or the specialisation of the lawyer could play a role, e.g. that commercial lawyers organised in big firms should be more rights oriented. Tables 2 and 3 show the distribution of the responses over these two characteristics. As with gender, no significant differences appear.

Table 1: The Distribution of Responses between Female and Male Attorneys to the Child Custody Hypothetical Case

| | response categories | | | | | | |
	1	2	3	4	5	6	total
men	2	0	3	7	1	2	15
women	0	3	5	2	3	2	15
total	2	3	8	9	4	4	30

As a part of a course in legal ethics I teach at Utrecht University, a questionnaire about the same subjects as in the interviews with lawyers was designed. Five students on the course approached other students and asked them to fill out a questionnaire. All the respondents had entered university

Table 2: The Distribution of Responses between Small and Big Law Firms

| | response categories | | | | | | |
	1	2	3	4	5	6	total
small	1	2	5	5	2	2	17
large	1	1	3	4	2	2	13
total	2	3	8	9	4	4	30

Table 3: The Distribution of Responses between Social and Commercial Lawyers

| | response categories | | | | | | |
	1	2	3	4	5	6	total
social	0	2	3	2	3	2	12
criminal	2	0	1	1	0	0	4
commercial	0	1	2	5	1	1	10
?	0	0	2	1	0	1	4
total	2	3	8	9	4	4	30

between 1990 and 1995 and their ages varied between nineteen and twenty-six. Compared to the lawyers, the students chose far more often to protect the children. Often the care perspective was clearly worded in their written account, for example:

> "I should never be instrumental so that a bad parent gets custody over a child even if that person in my client. . . . The heart of this matter is: that the children grow up in the best possible home."

Only six of the thirty students gave opposite answers, such as:

> "I should continue backing my client. He hires me and trusts that I look after his interests." And: "If you choose this profession you must do it well, that is, act on behalf of your client."

Another difference between the answers of the students and the lawyers lies in the action they choose to protect the children. Whereas the interviewed lawyers went to complicated lengths to avoid disclosing the letter, nineteen out of the thirty students chose to reveal the letter without any ado. Two of these students added: "I do ask myself whether a good lawyer should do this. But that is the reason that I do not want to become an attorney."

Table 4 shows the distribution of the answers of the students separated by gender. The same typology has been used as the one that was found to fit best to the response of the lawyers.

In conclusion, the following can be said. Theorists of morality such as Jack and Jack (1989) have a tendency to focus on the treatment of dilemmas within

Table 4: The Distribution of Responses between Female and Male Law Students to the Child Custody Hypothetical Case

	response categories						
	1	2	3	4	5	6	total
men	4	1	0	0	2	8	15
women	2	0	0	2	0	11	15
total	6	1	0	2	2	19	30

the moral domain. In the present chapter, the "triangle of tensions" and the care/rights opposition are examples of the same focus. Before this domain is entered however, the decision has to be made to treat a matter from a moral perspective at all. This, it seems, surfaces as the tension we found between morality on the one hand, and the non-morality of the market on the other.

The results of the research indicate that the two moral perspectives of lawyers formulated by Jack and Jack can be found in the Netherlands too, but they also suggest that the two ethics are not correlated with gender.

Furthermore, lawyers usually choose radically in favour of the interest of their clients. This has limits, however, which become especially clear in the hypothetical case of the child custody. This may be due to the fact that such family affairs are a strong trigger of ethic of care responses, contrary to the hypothetical murder case, in which not real children but abstract society has to be protected. Against this background, it becomes especially sour that society has virtually disappeared from recent codes of conduct (see the next section). In the terms of Metzloff and Wilkins, the adversarial paradigm has wiped out the "officer of the court" vision.[12]

IMPLICATIONS FOR TEACHING LEGAL ETHICS

Based on the foregoing empirical results this section focuses on the role of teaching formal rules, on the need also to objectify personal ethics and the issue of lifelong learning (*éducation permanente*).

As said in the introduction to this chapter, attention to legal ethics is a recent phenomenon in universities. Most likely, therefore, the only ethics course the interviewed lawyers would have followed is the one that is part of their three-year attorney traineeship.[13] This course has a legalistic focus on

---

[12] Th. B. Metzloff and D. B. Wilkins (eds.), "Teaching Legal Ethics", *Law and Contemporary Problems*, School of Law, Duke University, vol. 58, Summer/Autumn 1995, nos. 3 & 4.

[13] See for the legal education and training in the Netherlands: J. E. Doek, "Legal Education and Training in Europe, The Netherlands", 1 International Journal of the Legal Profession, vol 2, 25 at 43; E. H. Blankenburg and F. Bruinsma, *Dutch Legal Culture* (Deventer, Kluwer, 1994).

the "written ethics" found in the law: the oath, the code of conduct and in the jurisprudence of the disciplinary committees. And indeed, as we have seen, the oath and the code are used as points of reference when lawyers are confronted with moral dilemmas. Adding another example, some lawyers during the real-life dilemmas section of the interviews said that their main concern was "to not trespass on the legal rules of the profession".

The moral quality of the codes therefore has a direct relevance to how lawyers make decisions. As stated elsewhere,[14] throughout Western Europe and the United States one finds that the self-perception of the legal profession is shifting toward that of any other consultancy business, in which demand-driven, entrepreneurial behaviour is encouraged.[15] Some authors consider this shift a positive one.[16] Others, however, see it as negative, pointing, *inter alia*, to the loss of aspirational norms and the obligation also to include the public interest in lawyers' considerations.[17] The most recent versions of the Dutch code of conduct do not counterbalance this trend toward the evaporation of wider-than-client obligations from the profession. The code is entirely organised around the relationship between lawyer and client, not lawyer and society or third parties. The same holds true for the disciplinary system.[18]

Because of the fact that the code plays a central role in lawyers' decisions, it is obviously relevant to teach it, though of course typically late in the curriculum (for students who have decided to become an attorney) or as part of the attorney traineeship.[19] Both teachers and students need to be quite aware of the lack of wider-than-client norms in the code, however, and seek to compensate for this, e.g., by taking up cases that are obviously ethical cases where the code is silent.

The ideology of the legal profession is set fully in the ethics of a rights perspective: the balancing of the scales of justice, the adjudication between competing claims, the administration of guilt, and so on. Yet, as we saw in the preceding sections, the ethics of care play a significant role in legal practice

---

[14] L. E. De Groot-van Leeuwen, "The Lawyer Poised between Client and Society" in J. Cooper and L. Trubek (eds.), *Educating for Justice: Social Values and Legal Education* (Aldershot, Dartmouth, 1997).

[15] A. Paterson, "Legal Ethics: Its Nature and Place in the Curriculum" in R. Cranston, *Legal Ethics and Professional Responsibility* (Oxford, Clarendon Press, 1995); R. L. Solomon, "Five Crises or One: The Concept of Legal Professionalism, 1925–1960" in R. L. Nelson, D. M. Trubek and R. L. Solomon (eds.), *Lawyers' Ideals/Lawyers' Practices, Transformations in the American Legal Profession* (Ithaca, NY, Cornell University Press, 1992).

[16] R. A. Posner, *Overcoming Law* (Cambridge, Mass., Harvard University Press, 1995).

[17] Kronman, *supra* n. 5; Linowitz, *supra* n. 5.

[18] N. Doornbos and L. E. de Groot-van Leeuwen, *supra* n. 2.

[19] Another educational perspective on the code is to use its history and the accompanying debates as a tool to discuss more essential, underlying ethical issues, as done, for instance by Metzloff (Th. B. Metzloff, "Seeing the Trees within the Forest: Contextualized Ethics Courses as a Strategy for Teaching Legal Ethics" in Th. B. Metzloff and D. B. Wilkins (eds.), "Teaching Legal Ethics", *Law and Contemporary Problems*, vol. 58 nos. 3 & 4, 1995). Then, of course, teaching the code is not confined to later years: see also Box 1.

too.[20] This as such can only be applauded. The risk, however, is that due to the much higher official status of the rights perspective in the profession, the care perspective becomes associated with personal (non-professional) matters and is left untrained, un-objectified.

In teaching legal ethics, therefore, the ethics of care need to be taught too. Students should be supported to articulate and objectify their (non-gendered) ethics of care intuitions, paying attention to those ethics' vision of the self and the world, their conceptualisation of moral problems as failures of response, their contextualising ("storytelling") way of reasoning, their aims of future-oriented re-establishment of relationships, their risk of reacting on real others only and neglecting more abstract principles, and so on. Since these principles are relevant for all legal occupations, they could be taken up early in the curriculum.

In the previous section, the large difference found between student and lawyer responses to the custody dilemma draws attention to the deep and rapid impact of socialisation into the legal profession. Confining legal ethics education to either the early or the later years of the curriculum would imply that students are left to their own devices either during the strongly formative first years or during the period in which most of their routines are set and morality is easily lost in the action. One way or another, teaching legal ethics has to be part of lifelong learning (an *"éducation permanente"*) and continuing professional development. One issue typically important for later years of the curriculum is to support the students' moral awareness against the tendency to silence moral dilemmas by conceptualising them in purely technical-legal terms (cf. the previous section).

For this continuing education to be successful, norms require not only the right articulation but also effective internalisation. Teaching, therefore, must be combined with experiential depth. This draws attention to the innovative, relatively "post-modern" ways of teaching legal ethics, such as the dramatic stories in Spaeth *et al.*, the clinical experience and biographic narratives found in Bundy, the analysis of Portia found in Menkel-Meadow and the participatory learning found in Paterson.[21] In addition my own method of involving students in researching the ethics of fellow students (see Box 1) may be seen in this light.

[20] Not only attorneys and students, but also notaries (see Kocken, *supra* n. 11) and judges (see L. E. de Groot-van Leeuwen, "The Equilibrium Elite: Composition and Position of the Dutch Judiciary", *The Netherlands' Journal of Social Sciences*, vol. 28, no. 2, 1992; L. E. de Groot-van Leeuwen, *De rechterlijke macht in Nederland. Samenstelling en denkbeelden van de zittende en staande magistratuur* (Arnhem, Gouda Quint, 1991)).

[21] See E. B. Spaeth, Jr., J. G. Perry and P. B. Wachs, "Teaching Legal Ethics: Exploring the Continuum" and S. McG. Bundy, "Ethics Education in the First Year: An Experiment" (both in Metzloff and Wilkins, *supra* n. 12); C. Menkel-Meadow, "Portia Redux: Another Look at Gender, Feminism and Legal Ethics" in S. Parker and C. Sampford (eds.) (Oxford, Clarendon Press, 1995); Paterson, *supra* n. 15. For a general *entrée* to the postmodern curriculum, see W. G. Wraga, "Toward a Curriculum Theory for the New Century: Essay Review of Patrick Slatterny, Curriculum Development in the Postmodern Era", *Curriculum Studies*, 28, no. 4, 463 at 474.

Box 1:
Course on Professional Ethics, Utrecht University

Most of the students are in the second and third years of the 4-year legal education at the university.
Part I and Part II of the course take equal time.

Part I: seminars
— Personal integrity and the professional ethics
— Socialization and the internalization of norms
— The oath of attorneys: lawyering between business and profession
— Notaries and business lawyers: lawyering between business and administration
— Judges and public prosecutors: lawyering between profession and administration
— The bar's code of conduct: complaints and the disciplinary system

Part II: research exercise
— design of the questionnaire on ethical issues
— training on approaching respondents and data gathering
— data gathering: filling out the questionnaire with co-students
— analysis of the data
— writing a brief report

13

Feminist Perspectives on Legal Ethics

DEBORAH L. RHODE

When commenting on the first women's admission to Harvard Law School in 1950, the then Dean Erwin Griswold reassured anxious alums that this development was not "very important or very significant". "Most of us", he noted, "have seen women from time to time in our lives and have managed to survive the shock. I think we can take it, and I doubt that it will change the character of the School or even its atmosphere to any detectable extent."[1] Such assumptions remain common. In one representative survey, fewer than half of the male attorneys (compared with three-quarters of females) believed that women's entry would have major consequences for the profession.[2]

Such perceptions are not without irony. For centuries, women were excluded from the professions on the assumption that they were different. Yet after their admission, the assumption typically was that they were the same. Women, as Virginia Woolf noted, were expected to join the procession of educated men, not to question its direction.[3]

That expectation has come under increasing scrutiny. In the legal profession, as in other contexts, feminists are demanding that institutions change to accommodate women rather than the converse. Yet the changes that are necessary raise broader issues, not just about the role of women but also about professional roles. A true commitment to gender equality requires that values traditionally associated with women *be valued* in professional life. That in turn implies a fundamental restructuring of legal education and legal ethics.

This chapter charts the directions that such a process might take. Like any exploration of feminist perspectives, it needs to begin with some working

[1] Erwin Griswold, "Developments at the Law School" [1950] *Harvard Law School Year Book* 10. This chapter draws on previously published work including Rhode, "Gender and Professional Roles" (1994) 63 *Fordham Law Review* 39; Rhode, "Missing Questions: Feminist Perspectives on Legal Education" (1993) 45 *Stanford Law Review* 1547; Rhode, "Ethics by the Pervasive Method" (1992) 42 *Journal of Legal Education* 31; and Rhode, "Whistling Vivaldi: Legal Education and the Politics of Progress" (1997) 23 *New York University Review of Law and Social Change* 217.

[2] Bill Winter, "Survey: Women Lawyers Work Harder, Are Paid Less, But They're Happy" (1983) 69 *American Bar Association Journal* 1384, 1388.

[3] Virginia Woolf, *Three Guineas* (New York, Harcourt Brace & Co., 1938), 62–3.

definition of feminism. But any effort to supply such a definition bumps up against a threshold problem. The term feminism encompasses an increasingly diverse body of work that does not easily fit under any single organising framework. Yet although feminists differ strongly on many dimensions, they generally share certain basic commitments. At the substantive level, feminism presupposes a commitment to equality between the sexes. At the method-ological level, it implies a commitment to gender as a focus of analysis and to approaches that reflect women's perspectives and concerns.

These commitments, however, also reveal a central paradox. Feminism's authority rests on its claim to speak from women's experience. But that very experience demands attention to the diversity in women's circumstances. There is no "generic woman".[4] Gender is always mediated by other forces that structure identity, such as race, ethnicity, class and sexual orientation. Recognition of this diversity complicates the search for theoretical coherence and political cohesion.

Yet if this paradox cannot be escaped, at least it can be reformulated. The factors that divide women also can also enrich analysis and build coalitions. Any ethical framework adequate to challenge gender inequality must similarly challenge the other structures of subordination with which gender intersects. Such a framework rests not on some single standpoint of woman, but on affinities and alliances among women, and on principles that can be shared by men.

I. THE STRUCTURE OF LEGAL EDUCATION

(a) Gender Bias

Although feminists have developed a cottage industry of critiques concerning legal education, the very existence of that enterprise should also remind us of our substantial progress. In a recent book on the crisis of professionalism, Sol Linowitz recalls that his law school class during the 1950s had only two women. Neither he nor his classmates questioned the skewed ratio, although they did feel somewhat uncomfortable when the women were around. And, Linowitz ruefully acknowledges, "it never occurred to us to wonder whether *they* felt uncomfortable."[5] So too, when I graduated from law school some two decades ago, gender was not a topic of polite conversation. I had no courses from a woman professor, and none that focused on "women's issues".

In today's law schools, much has changed but much has remained the same. Women are present, but not yet equal. Issues of particular concern to women are not effectively addressed. And the values traditionally associated with women are not adequately reflected in the educational culture.

[4] Elizabeth V. Spellman, *Inessential Woman* (Boston, Mass., Beacon Press, 1988) 187.
[5] Sol Linowitz with Martin Mayer, *The Betrayed Profession* (New York, Scribners, 1994), 6.

Much of the problem stems from denial that there is, in fact, a problem. To many observers of legal education, gender inequality seems like an issue long since resolved. Women now constitute almost 45 per cent of American law school students and 30 per cent of law school faculties.[6] Because women seem well represented on both sides of the podium, we lose sight of where they are missing.

The absences are in predictable places. In law school, as in life, women are over-represented at the bottom and under-represented at the top. In the United States, fewer than 20 per cent of tenured faculty and fewer than 10 per cent of law school deans are women.[7] The under-representation of women of colour is even more pronounced, and they fare worse in the hiring and pro-motion processes than similarly qualified men.[8]

Women's absence in positions of authority often reinforces negative stereo-types and impairs other women's confidence and comfort levels.[9] The lack of female tenured faculty and upper level administrators diminishes students' access to mentors, role models and decision-makers who are sensitive to gender-related concerns.[10]

Such patterns contribute to women students' disadvantage and discontent in many law schools. Comprehensive data on American legal education indi-cate that female students perform less well than males given predictions based on their test scores and college performance. Women also are less likely to be in the upper half of the class, and gender gaps widen if race and ethnicity are taken into account.[11] At some surveyed law schools, female students are under-represented among top honours graduates and in key leadership posi-tions such as editors of law reviews.[12]

[6] Richard A. White, data summary from the *Directory of Law Teachers*, personal correspon-dence, Jan., 1997: "American Bar Association Commission on Women in the Profession", *Basic Facts from Women in the Law: A Look at the Numbers* (Chicago, Ill., American Bar Association Commission on Women in the Profession, 1995), 4.

[7] Association of American Law Schools, *Meeting the Challenges of Diversity in an Academic Democracy* (Washington, DC, Association of American Law Schools, 1995); American Bar Association, *supra* n. 6; White, *supra* n. 6.

[8] Deborah Merrit and Barbara F. Reskin, "The Double Minority: Empirical Evidence of a Double Standard in Law School Hiring of Minority Women" (1992) 65 *Southern California Law Review* 2299; Richard A White, "Summary and Comments on Preliminary Report on a Study of the Promotion and Retention of New Law School Faculty Hired in 1990 and 1991" (unpublished memorandum, 1996).

[9] See Robin J. Ely, "The Power in Demography: Women's Social Constructions of Gender Identity at Work" (1995) 38 *Academy of Management Journal* 589, 594–6, 604–18.

[10] See *Law School Outreach Project of the Chicago Bar Association Alliance for Women, Women Students' Experience of Gender Bias in Chicago Area Law Schools: A Step Toward Bias Free Jurisprudence* (Chicago, Ill., Chicago Bar Association, 1995), 51–2; Ely, *supra* n. 9; Anita Allen, "On Being a Role Model" (1990) 6 *Berkeley Women's Law Journal* 22.

[11] Linda F. Wightman, *Women in Legal Education: A Comparison of the Law School Performance and Law School Experiences of Women and Men* (Washington, DC, Law School Admission Council, l996), 26.

[12] Lani Guinier, Michelle Fine and Jane Balin, "Becoming Gentlemen: Women's Experiences at One Ivy League Law School" (l994) 143 *University of Pennsylvania Law Review* 1. However, women's academic performance is not lower than men's at all American law schools. See "The

What accounts for such patterns is subject to debate, but it is clear that gender bias plays a significant role. A wide range of recent reports on women's educational experience do not make for cheery reading.[13] Conduct that in isolation often has been dismissed as trivial or aberrant assumes greater significance when viewed as part of broader patterns.

Gender bias among faculty has taken a variety of forms. Some professors have been more likely to call on male than female students and to provide more positive reinforcement, both verbal and non-verbal, for men's participation.[14] Other faculty have made comments that devalue women. A Yale torts professor wondered whether there was any such thing as the "reasonable woman".[15]

Many law school curricula have implicitly marginalised women by failing to address gender-related issues or feminist perspectives in class. One survey by a Chicago bar association found that none of the area's law schools incorporated such material into the traditional curriculum. The coverage that did occur often looked like an afterthought: a brief digression from the "real" subject.[16] Issues of particular concern to women of colour are noticeable largely for their absence.[17] Some faculty decline to include topics of obvious substantive importance, like acquaintance rape, because the issues appear too politically or emotionally freighted for "rational" discussion.[18]

Even more disturbing is the tendency of some faculty and students to dismiss concerns about gender bias in the classroom. For example, when one law school published guidelines suggesting that faculty use sex neutral language, a male professor responded by changing all "man" endings to "person, as in 'Doberperson Pincher' ".[19] Women who raise gender-related concerns often have been ridiculed for "over-reaction" and "over-emotionalism", and have acquired labels like "feminazi", "dyke" or "manhater".[20]

To many (usually male) observers, such incidents seem relatively harmless. But the cumulative effect of such incidents should not be discounted. They

Top 35 Law Schools for Women," *The National Jurist*, Oct. l995; Lorraine Dutsky, *Still Unequal* (New York, Crown Publisher, l996), 39. For a general account, see the American Bar Association Commission on Women in the Profession, "Elusive Equality: The Experiences of Women in Legal Education" (Chicago, Ill., American Bar Association Commission on Women in the Profession, l996), 5.

[13] See sources cited in *supra* nn. 8–12.

[14] Guinier, Fine and Balin *supra* n. 12; Robert Granfield, "Contextualizing the Different Voice: Women, Occupational Goals and Legal Education" (l994) 16 *Law and Policy* 1, 11–13.

[15] Dutsky, *supra* n. 12, 22.

[16] Law School Outreach Project, *supra* n. 10, vi, 53.

[17] Kimberle Crenshaw, "Forward: Toward a Race Conscious Pedagogy in Legal Education", *National Black Law Journal* (1989).

[18] Law School Outreach Project, *supra* n. 10, 55; Dutsky, *supra* n. 12, 39. The problem is long standing. See Karen B. Czapansky and Jane B. Singer, "Women in the Law School: It's Time for More Change" (1988) 7 *Journal of Law and Inequality* 135; Nancy Erickson, "Final Report: 'Sex Bias in the Teaching of Criminal Law' " (1990) 42 *Rutgers Law Review* 309.

[19] Law School Outreach Project, *supra* n. 10, 27.

[20] Law School Outreach Project, *supra* n. 10, vii, 35; Guinier, Fine and Balin, *supra* n. 12; Law School Outreach Project, *supra* n. 10, 35; Dutsky, *supra* n. 12, 28.

serve to undermine women's sense of comfort, credibility and competence, which can adversely affect performance.[21] Studies finding that women students' self-esteem drops during law school are especially worrisome in light of research linking self confidence with academic achievement.[22]

(b) Educational Methods

For many women, the problems in legal education extend beyond obvious patterns of bias and under-representation. A related concern involves the structure of classroom pedagogy. Values that traditionally have been of central importance to women—care, connection, context—are not the values that have been central to law school teaching. The authoritarian, abstract and competitive framework that dominates legal education ill serves the needs of many of its constituents.

In theory, law school's heavy reliance on quasi-socratic dialogue in large classes fosters rigorous analysis and careful preparation. In practice, however, it often pre-empts both. As experts in educational theory note, high levels of control over students' speech undermines development of independent reasoning skills.[23] The professor dominates the dialogue, invites the class to "guess what I'm thinking?" and then finds the response inevitably lacking.

The hyper-competitive ethos of many classrooms also tends to undermine self-esteem and discourage less confident or assertive students from involvement.[24] Because women often have been socialised to avoid self promotion, they are particularly likely to remain silent. A wide variety of studies find that female students participate less in conventional law school classrooms and experience greater frustration with socratic methods.[25] From their perspective, the search for knowledge too often becomes a scramble for status, in which

[21] Claude M. Steele, "A Threat in the Air: How Stereotypes Shape the Intellectual Identities and Performance of Women and African Americans", *American Psychologist* (forthcoming).

[22] Wightman, *supra* n. 11, 75; Guinier, Fine and Balin, *supra* n. 12; for the linkage between self-esteem and achievement, see Steele, *supra* n. 21; Myra Sadker and David Sadker, *Failing at Fairness* (New York, Scribners, 1994).

[23] Joseph M. Notterman and Henry N. Drewry, *Psychology and Education: Parallel and Interactive Approaches* (New York, Plenum Press, 1993), 189; E. Hayes (ed.), *Effective Teaching Styles* (San Francisco, Cal., Jossey Bass, 1989), 30–59.

[24] Notterman and Drewry, *supra* n. 23, 189; Frances Maher, "Classroom Pedagogy and the New Scholarship on Women" in Margo Culley and Catherine Portuges (eds.), *Gendered Subjects: The Dynamics of Feminist Teaching*, 29 (Boston, Mass., Routledge and Kegan Paul, 1985), 29; Stephanie M. Wildman, "The Question of Silence: Techniques to Ensure Full Class Participation" (1988) 38 *Journal of Legal Education* 147.

[25] Guinier, Fine and Balin, *supra* n. 12; Suzanne Homer and Lois Schwartz, "Admitted But Not Accepted: Outsiders Take an Inside Look at Law School" (1989–90) 5 *Berkeley Women's Law Journal* 1; Catherine Weiss and Louise Melling, "The Legal Education of Twenty Women" (1988) 40 *Stanford Law Review* 1299; *Ohio Supreme Court and Bar Association Joint Task Force on Gender Fairness* (Columbus, Ohio, Ohio Bar Association, 1995), 24; see Susan H. Williams, "Remarks: Legal Education, Feminist Epistemology and the Socratic Method" (1993) 45 *Stanford Law Review* 1571.

participants vie with each other to impress rather than inform.[26] That process runs counter to basic feminist insights, which value learning through empathy and collaborative interchange.[27]

Traditional classroom approaches also fail to develop abilities that are highly important but too often lacking in young attorneys. Over-emphasis on doctrinal analysis teaches law at the expense of lawyering. Students get the functional equivalent of "geology without the rocks . . . dry arid logic divorced from society".[28] Such a focus neglects the interpersonal, co-operative and problem-solving skills that are central to effective professional practice.

Legal education teaches little about dealing with people who are "different", or who face situations of stress. The cost of this neglect is borne by those least able to absorb it. Many matters on which individuals seek assistance are not exclusively legal problems; "they are deep human problems in which the law is enmeshed".[29] Lawyers trained only to respond to legal issues may end up talking past the concerns that are most central to the client. Of course, a law school cannot teach attorneys to be therapists, but it can foster skills of empathetic counselling. As one expert puts it, "[i]s dealing with the emotionally insensitive . . . lawyer beneath the dignity or beyond the competence of legal education?"[30] One hopes that question is rhetorical.

Yet conventional classroom approaches often compound rather than address these insensitivities. Legal education models hierarchies that may compromise performance in other contexts. Relationships between partners and associates, lawyers and clients, and professionals and support staff frequently replicate the overbearing dynamics reinforced in classroom settings. Students who internalise authoritarian norms may lose opportunities to connect their skills with real human needs. And, in feminists' view, those needs occupy too low a priority in legal education.

(c) Legal Ethics in Legal Education

A related problem involves the marginalisation of legal ethics in legal education, and the tendency of many faculty to consider professional responsibility someone else's responsibility. US Supreme Court Justice Ruth Bader Ginsburg has made precisely that point in recounting a student's initial encounter with

---

[26] See Rhode, "Missing Questions", *supra* n. 1, 1559.

[27] See Mary Field Belenky, Blythe McVicker Clinchy, Nancy Rule Goldberger and Jill Mattuck Tarule, *Women's Ways of Knowing* (New York, Basic Books, Inc., 1986), 112–29; Wildman, *supra* n. 24.

[28] Lawrence Friedman, quoted in Paul Wice, *Judges and Lawyers: The Human Side of Justice* (New York, Harper Collins, 1991), 16.

[29] Gary S. Goodpaster, "The Human Arts of Lawyering: Interviewing and Counseling" (1975) 27 *Journal of Legal Education* 5, 9.

[30] Austin Sarat, "Lawyers and Clients: Putting Professional Service on the Agenda of Legal Education" (1991) 41 *Journal of Legal Education* 43, 53.

legal ethics. The professor in a first year course was explaining a lawyer's tactic that left the student "bothered and bewildered". "But what about ethics?" the student asked. "Ethics", the professor frostily informed him, "is taught in the second year".[31]

That anecdote describes the dominant experience in legal education. Most American law schools relegate professional responsibility to a single required course, frequently taught to "vacant seats and vacant minds".[32] In the United Kingdom, the subject arises mainly in post-graduate skills training.[33]

The failure to make professional responsibility more central to professional education ill serves values of care, connection and context that are central to feminist analysis. The ethical questions missing from our curricula are missed opportunities to enlarge students' capacities for reflective judgement and for understanding the effects of professional norms on human relationships.

All too often, ethics courses replay in pronounced form the inadequacies of legal education in general. Most approaches are excessively doctrinal. By focusing on bar codes as vehicles for statutory analysis, these courses collapse legal ethics and ethical rules.[34] Traditional professional responsibility instruction offers too little theory and too little practice. It is too uninformed by theoretical frameworks in related fields, such as philosophy, psychology, sociology and economics. And it is too far removed from the actual context of lawyering and the human costs of inadequate ethical standards.

More fundamentally, the failure to treat professional responsibility issues as they arise throughout the curricula marginalises their importance. Moral responsibility is a central part of legal practice and needs to occupy an equally central place in legal education. Yet courses and casebooks outside the field of professional responsibility rarely address ethical issues in any detail. My own survey of over a hundred leading texts in the early 1990s found that the median amount of ethics coverage was less than 2 per cent of total pages.[35]

Faculty who decline, implicitly or explicitly, to discuss ethical matters as they arise in each substantive area encourage future practioners to do the same. Professional priorities are apparent in subtexts as well as texts. Every educational institution teaches some form of ethics by the pervasive method, and pervasive silence speaks louder than formal policies or commencement platitudes.

That is not to overstate the effects of ethics education. We are not, of course, likely to alter in a few classroom hours what students absorb over long

---

[31] Justice Ruth Bader Ginsburg, "Supreme Court Pronouncements on the Conduct of Lawyers", Keynote Address at the Hofstra University Law School Conference on Legal Ethics: The Core Issues (10 Mar. 1996).

[32] Dale C. Moss, "Out of Balance: Why Can't Law Schools Teach Ethics?", *Student Lawyer*, Oct. 1991, at 19.

[33] Richard O'Dair, "Recent Developments in the Teaching of Legal Ethics—a UK Perspective", *supra*, this volume.

[34] William H. Simon, "The Trouble with Legal Ethics" (1991) 41 *Journal of Legal Education* 65, 65–6.

[35] See Rhode, "Ethics", *supra* n. 1.

periods from family, friends, schools, churches and popular media. As sceptics have often noted, certain core values are matters like "politeness on subways . . . or fidelity in marriage", which cannot be acquired through course assignments in professional schools.[36] Moreover a wide variety of clinical and empirical studies make clear that ethical conduct is highly situational and that the pressures of practice often dwarf other influences.[37]

For feminists committed to contextual analysis, that insight is unsurprising and somewhat beside the point. Educators' influence may be limited, but that is not an argument for declining to exercise it. Moreover, ethical values are by no means as fixed as opponents of pervasive ethics education contend. Recent psychological studies indicate that people's basic strategies for dealing with moral issues can change significantly during early adulthood.[38] Interactive educational approaches can increase individuals' skills in ethical analysis and their awareness of the situational pressures that skew judgment. Over a hundred studies evaluating ethics courses have found that well designed curricula can significantly improve capacities for moral reasoning.[39]

So, too, not all professional responsibility issues involve matters of pre-existing moral conviction. Some ethics questions turn on bar regulatory standards that students will not have encountered before law school. Even on more value-laden issues, professional standards sometimes depart from what personal moral intuitions might dictate. Future practitioners need to know where the bar draws the line before they are in positions to cross one. And, since some of these individuals will ultimately influence where future lines are drawn, their legal education should provide background in the competing policy considerations at issue.

Moreover, despite the importance of situational pressures, psychological research generally finds some modest relationship between moral judgement and moral behaviour.[40] How individuals evaluate the consequences of their

---

[36] Eric Schnapper, "The Myth of Legal Ethics", *American Bar Association Journal*, Feb. 1978, 202, 205.

[37] A vast array of research documents the variability of moral conduct in response to stress, competition, authority, peer influence, financial incentives and time pressure. See the studies summarised in Rhode, *Professional Responsibility: Ethics by the Pervasive Method* (New York, Aspen, 1998, 2nd ed.), 6–7, and "Ethics", *supra* n. 1 at 44–6.

[38] James R. Rest, "Can Ethics be Taught in Professional Schools? The Psychological Research" in *Ethics: Easier Said Than Done*, Winter 1988, 22, 23–4; James R. Rest, Muriel Bebeau and Joseph Volker, " An Overview of the Psychology of Morality" in James R. Rest *et al.* (eds.), *Moral Development; Advances in Research and Theory* (New York, Praeger, 1986), 3, 14.

[39] See sources cited in n. 38 and Rhode, "Ethics", *supra* n. 1, 44–6; James S. Leming, "Curricular Effectiveness in Moral Values Education: A Review of the Research" (1981) 10 *Journal of Moral Education* 147.

[40] Walter Mischel and Harriet N. Mischel, "A Cognitive Social-Learning Approach to Morality and Self-Regulation" in Thomas Likona (ed.), *Moral Development and Behavior: Theory, Research, and Social Issues* (New York, Holt, Rinehart and Winston, 1976), 84, 101–7; Albert Bandura, "Social Cognitive Theory of Moral Thought and Action" in William M. Kurtines and Jacob L. Gewirtz (eds.), 1 *Handbook of Moral Behavior and Development* (1991), 45, 53; Augusto Blasi, "Bridging Moral Cognition and Moral Action: A Critical Review of the Literature" (1980) 88 *Psychology Bulletin* 1.

conduct often affects it, and education can shape these evaluative processes. Law school courses can also increase awareness of ways that economic incentives, peer pressures, structures of authority and diffusion of responsibility affect decision-making. Most lawyers who have taken legal ethics courses have given them some credit for helping to resolve ethical issues in practice, and generally favour maintaining or expanding ethics coverage in law schools.[41]

Although legal education cannot fully simulate or insulate individuals from the pressures of practice, it can provide a setting to explore their causes and the regulatory structure best able to address them. And if, as many feminists argue, current professional standards do not adequately serve the public interest, then legal education must help to lay foundations for change.

(d) Alternative Frameworks

We do not lack for alternatives. Feminists remind us what is necessary. We need more strategies that can prevent gender bias, create supportive learning environments, foster effective interpersonal skills and encourage reflective ethical decision-making. To that end, legal educators should consider a broad range of proposals. One possibility is to allocate specific responsibility for identifying and addressing gender-related concerns. Law schools also can do more to promote effective classroom teaching and curricular integration projects. Such projects should include legal ethics as well as topics of particular concern to women and minority students.

These strategies will emerge only if we also rearrange educational reward structures. Equal opportunity and professional responsibility must become central priorities, not just in theory but in practice.

II. PROFESSIONAL ETHICS IN PROFESSIONAL PRACTICE

To many observers, feminist critiques of professional ethics do not seem distinctively feminist. Rather they parallel and overlap perspectives that build on other premises. Yet such continuities should come as no surprise. The values traditionally associated with women are not solely women's values. They also play an important part in other traditions from which critics of professional norms have drawn, such as humanism, Kantian moral theory and Judeo-Christian ethics.

Feminism can, however, offer a new constituency and a new urgency for transformative visions. What drives feminists' critiques is the dissatisfaction and disadvantage that women experience under traditional professional

[41] Frances K. Zemans and Victor G. Rosenblum, *The Making of a Public Profession* (Chicago, Ill., American Bar Foundation, 1981), 176–7.

structures. What gives those critiques broader force is the universality of their underlying values—equality, empathy, care and co-operation. Those values demand a fundamental rethinking of professional role morality, lawyer–client relationships, the distribution of legal services and the structure of legal workplaces.

(a) Professional Roles

Conventional understandings of the lawyer's role illustrate what is lost under prevailing conceptions of legal ethics. In general, attorneys are expected to represent a client zealously within the bounds of the law regardless of their own views concerning the justness of the cause. Although lawyers may not assist fraudulent, harassing or illegal conduct, they are given wide latitude to protect clients' interests at the expense of broader societal concerns. For example, under the American bar's ethical codes, attorneys may present evidence that they reasonably believe to be inaccurate or misleading as long as they do not know it to be false; they may withhold material information in civil cases that the other side fails to discover; they may invoke technical defences to defeat rightful claims; and they may remain silent about a client's prior wrongful conduct even when disclosure would prevent substantial financial harm or physical risk to innocent parties.[42]

The rationale for this partisan role rests on two primary lines of argument. The first invokes utilitarian, instrumental reasoning. It assumes that the most effective way to achieve justice is through the competitive clash of two zealous adversaries, whose effectiveness depends on candid relationships with clients. In this view, an adversarial system will function fairly only if individuals have full confidence in the loyalty and confidentiality of their advocates.

From feminists' standpoint, this conventional justification for the partisanship role is too abstract and contextual to yield morally satisfying outcomes. The assumption that truth or fairness necessarily results from adversarial clashes is neither self-evident nor supported by empirical evidence. It is not the way most professions or most legal systems pursue knowledge.[43] Moreover the adversarial paradigm presupposes a fair contest between combatants with roughly equal resources, capacities and incentives. Such equality is all too infrequent in a social order that tolerates vast disparities in wealth,

[42] See American Bar Association Code of Professional Responsibility, DR 7–101; EC 7–1; DR 4–101; American Bar Association, *Model Rules of Professional Conduct*, Rule 1.2; for an overview, see Deborah L. Rhode and David Luban, *Legal Ethics* (Westbury, New York, Foundation Press, 1995), 221–56; Marvin Frankel, *Partisan Justice* (1980); Deborah L. Rhode, "Institutionalizing Ethics" (1994) 44 *Case Western Law Review* 665, 667–76.

[43] Marvin Frankel, "The Search for Truth: An Umpireal View" (1975) 123 *University of Pennsylvania Law Review* 1031, 1036–7; Luban, *Lawyers and Justice* (1988), 67–103.

renders most legal proceedings enormously expensive and allocates civil legal assistance largely through market mechanisms.[44]

In response to such criticisms, defenders of partisan norms rely on a second, rights-based justification. From this perspective, respect for clients' individual autonomy implies respect for their legal entitlements and requires undivided loyalty from their legal advisors. By absolving attorneys from accountability for their clients' acts, the traditional advocacy role encourages representation of those most vulnerable to public prejudice and State oppression. The promise of non-judgmental advocacy also encourages legal consultation by those most in need of ethical counselling.[45]

Feminists join other critics in raising two central objections to this rights-based defence of neutral partisanship. The first is that it collapses legal and moral entitlements. It assumes that society benefits by allowing clients to pursue whatever objectives the law permits. Yet some conduct that is antithetical to the public interest in general or to subordinate groups in particular may remain legal. For example, prohibitions may appear too difficult or costly to enforce, or decision-makers may be uninformed, overworked or vulnerable to interest-group pressures. In such contexts, lawyers may have no particular moral expertise, but they at least have a more disinterested perspective than clients on the ethical dimensions of legal practices. For attorneys to accept moral responsibility is not necessarily to impose it. Except where lawyers are the "last in town" (or the functional equivalent), their refusal of the partisan role does not preempt representation. It simply requires clients to rethink their actions or to accept the costs of finding alternative counsel.[46]

A second problem with rights-based justifications for partisanship is that they fail to explain why the rights of clients should trump those of all other individuals whose interests are inadequately represented. For feminists, that failure is most apparent when it exacerbates inequalities or threatens the welfare of especially vulnerable third parties, such as children in divorce cases or consumers of hazardous products. In such circumstances, partisanship on behalf of organisational profits inadequately serves values of individual autonomy. Case histories of the Dalkon shield and asbestos litigation, as well as less politicised financial scandals, illustrate the human misery and social costs that can accompany unqualified advocacy.[47]

---

[44] Marc Galanter, "Why the Haves Come Out Ahead: Speculations on the Limits of Legal Change" (1974) 9 *Law and Society Review* 95; Rhode, *supra* n. 42.

[45] Stephen Pepper, "The Lawyer's Amoral Ethical Role: A Defense, A Problem, and Some Possibilities" [1986] *American Bar Foundation Research Journal* 613. For a critical perspective, see Rhode, *supra* n. 42.

[46] David Luban, *Lawyers and Justice*, (Princeton, New Jersey, Princeton University Press, 1988), 166–74; Rhode, "Ethical Perspectives on Legal Practice" (1985) 37 *Stanford Law Review* 589, 621–6.

[47] Paul Brodeur, *Outrageous Misconduct: The Asbestos Industry on Trial* (New York, Pantheon Books, 1985); Susan Perry and Jim Dawson, *Nightmare: Women and the Dalkon Shield* (New York, MacMillan, 1985); "OPM Leasong Sources, Inc." in Phillip Heymann and Lance Liebman, (eds.), *The Social Responsibilities of Lawyers* (Westbury, New York, Foundation Press,

Finally, the submersion of self into role carries a price not only for the public in general, but for lawyers in particular. As moral philosopher Gerald Postema notes, "when professional action is estranged from ordinary moral experience, the lawyer's sensitivity to the moral costs in both ordinary and extraordinary situations tends to atrophy".[48] This detachment of personal and professional ethics threatens lawyers' ability both to provide effective representation and to retain a coherent moral identity.

From most feminists' perspective, a preferable alternative is to break down the boundary between individual values and institutional roles. In essence, lawyers should accept direct moral accountability for their professional acts. Attorneys' decision-making should not depend on a reflexive retreat into role; rather, it should consider how the purposes of that role can best be served within a particular context. In some instances, those purposes will call for deference to collectively determined legal requirements and ethical rules. But such deference will be justifiable only if the rules themselves allow room to take account of all the morally relevant factors in a given situation.

So, for example, lawyers should not evaluate the rationale for zealous partisanship by reference to some abstract model of an equal adversarial contest before a neutral tribunal. Instead, they should consider a realistic social and economic landscape in which legal rights and resources may be unevenly distributed, applicable laws may be unjustly skewed, and the vast majority of cases will settle without ever reaching an impartial decision-maker.[49] Lawyers' ethical codes should encourage such contextual judgements. They should also widen lawyers' care, concern and responsibility for non-clients whose interests are inadequately represented.

(b) Lawyer–Client Relationships

Feminists' second line of challenge to conventional professional structures involves their power dynamics. Lawyer–client relationships frequently display patterns of dominance that ill serve broader societal interests.

The hierarchical dynamics reinforced by legal education are replicated in later workplace relationships. Authoritarian, paternalistic interactions between lawyers and clients often obscure the needs that prompted professional consultation in the first instance. One study involving low-income legal aid clients found that lawyers frequently interrupted and attempted to control the topic in over 90 per cent of their comments.[50] Such conversational

1988) 184; Susan Koniak, "When Courts Refuse to Frame the Law and Others Frame it to Their Will" (1993) 66 *University of Southern California Law Review* 1075; Rhode, *supra* n. 42.

[48] Gerald J. Postema, "Moral Responsibility in Professional Ethics" (1980) 55 *New York University Law Review* 63.

[49] See Luban, *supra* n. 46; Gerald J. Postema, "Moral Responsibility", *supra* n. 48; Rhode, *supra* n. 42.

[50] Carl J. Hosticka, "We Don't Care What Happened, We Only Care About What Is Going to Happen, Lawyer–Client Negotiations of Reality" (1979) 26 *Social Problems* 599.

patterns prevent clients from assessing and asserting their own best interests. Empirical research consistently indicates that individuals who actively partic- ipate in decision-making do better and have greater satisfaction than those who do not.[51]

The adverse effects of professional dominance are compounded by other status inequalities such as class, race, ethnicity and gender. The most egre- gious cases of manipulating, circumventing or simply overlooking client objec- tives involve subordinate groups. Women's experiences in divorce proceedings offer a case in point. Legal aid lawyers frequently have refused to handle such proceedings on the ground that they present no pressing need or important law reform issues, even though clients give high priority to these cases.[52]

Even for middle- and upper-income parties, a mismatch persists between what many women seek and what many attorneys supply. Empirical studies reveal participants occupied with "two different divorces": lawyers with the financial and legal consequences of separation, and clients with the social and emotional ones.[53] Attorneys receive little training in how to respond to indi- viduals in stress, and often end up talking past the concerns that are most central to the parties. The problem is apparent in many dialogues recorded in recent research on divorce practice. For example:

> "*Client*: There was harassment and verbal degradation. No interest at all in my furthering my education. None whatsoever. . . . Just constant harassment from him.
> *Lawyer*: Mmn uh.
> *Client*: . . . I could lock myself in the bathroom and he would break in. . . . There was no escaping him, short of getting in a car and driving away. But then he would stand outside in the driveway and yell, anyhow. The man was not well.
> *Lawyer*: Okay. Now how about any courses you took?"[54]

Clients are like performers playing before bored, but dutiful legal audiences; lawyers do not "interrupt the aria but [they do not] applaud much either for fear of an encore".[55] As a result, the process becomes for many clients "at best a distraction and at worst an additional trauma".[56] While lawyers cannot sub- stitute for trained therapists, neither can they function effectively as legal advi- sors without adequate skills in empathetic listening.

---

[51] Judith A. Hall, Debra L. Royer, and Nancy R. Katz, "Metanalysis of Correlates of Provider Behavior in Medical Encounters" (1988) 26 *Medical Care*, 657; Douglas Rosenthal, *Lawyer and Client: Who's in Charge* (New York, Russell Sage, 1978).

[52] National Center on Women and Family Law, "Challenges Facing Legal Services in the 1990s" (1988) 4); Richard Abel, "Law Without Politics: Legal Aid Under Advanced Capitalism" (1985) 32 *University of California Law Review* 474, 608.

[53] Austin Sarat and William Felstiner, "Law and Social Relations: Vocabularies of Motive in Lawyer–Client Interaction" (1988) 22 *Law and Society Review* 737, 746.

[54] *Ibid.*, 750.

[55] *Ibid.*

[56] Sarat, *supra* n. 30.

(c) Access to Legal Services

A third area of feminist concern involves access to legal assistance. Current practice norms encourage unduly expensive assistance for individuals who can afford it and tolerate inadequate representation for those who cannot. The situation persists in part because the bar's financial interest lies more in maximising fees than in addressing need. That is not to imply that attorneys are driven only by economic concerns; overbilling and litigiousness are fuelled by a complex set of structural, psychological and financial pressures. All professionals have a natural desire to believe in their own effectiveness and to leave no stone unturned, especially if they can charge by the stone.[57] By contrast, where the costs of effective representation exceed what clients or legal service programmes can subsidise, the tendency is to revise expectations for assistance in accordance with financial realities.[58]

Feminist approaches offer no simple solutions to these problems. But a commitment to equal opportunity and a concern for subordinate groups demands that access-related issues become a more central priority. A feminist understanding of professional responsibilities implies a fundamental redistribution of professional services.

One obstacle to that effort involves lawyers' control over their own monopoly. Traditionally, the legal profession has asserted inherent authority to define the practice of law, to limit that practice to lawyers and thus to preempt competition from other competent providers. Repeatedly, bar leaders have insisted that consumers suffer from unqualified lay assistance, and that the "fight to stop it is the public's fight".[59] If so, the public has been curiously unsupportive of the war effort. On the relatively few occasions when consumers' opinions have been solicited, they have endorsed greater access to legal services provided by non-lawyers.[60]

Such services could help address this nation's vast array of unmet legal concerns, particularly those concentrated among women and other subordinate

[57] Rhode, "Ethical Perspectives" *supra* n. 46, 635, and "Institutionalizing Ethics" *supra* n. 42, 679; see Eliot Freidson, *Profession of Medicine* (New York, Dodd, Mead, 1972), 257–8.

[58] Thus, overburdened and underpaid criminal defence lawyers often will "cool a client out" and influence decisions in favour of a quick guilty plea rather than extended proceedings. See Albert Alshuler, "Personal Failure, Institutional Failure and the Sixth Amendment" (1986) 14 *New York University Review of Law and Social Change* 149; Stephen J. Schulhofer, "Plea Bargaining as Disaster" (1992) 101 *Yale Law Journal* 1079, 1088.

[59] American Bar Association, *National Conference on the Unauthorized Practice of Law* (Chicago, Ill., American Bar Center, 1962),101 (remarks of former ABA President John Satterfield, quoting Iowa Supreme Court).

[60] In one survey, over 80% of respondents agreed that "many things that lawyers handle—for example, tax matters or estate planning . . . can be done as well and less expensively by non-lawyers": Barbara A. Curran, *The Legal Needs of the Public: The Final Report of a National Survey* (Chicago, Ill., American Bar Foundation, 1977), 231. For other examples, see Deborah L. Rhode, "The Delivery of Legal Services by Nonlawyers" (1990) 4 *Georgetown Journal of Legal Ethics* 209, 214; Deborah L. Rhode, "Professionalism in Perspective: Alternative Approaches to Nonlawyer Practice" (1996) 22 *New York University Review of Law and Social Change* 701.

groups. Research focusing on low-income populations estimates that services are unavailable for three-quarters of their reported needs.[61] Middle-income consumers also lack affordable assistance for matters that carry special importance for women, such as those involving divorce and domestic violence.[62] Many of these unmet legal needs involve relatively routine, specialised services for which professional education is neither necessary nor sufficient. Graduating from law schools and passing bar exams provide no assurance of expertise in matters such as uncontested divorces, bankruptcy filings, welfare claims or protective orders against domestic violence. In many jurisdictions here and abroad, non-lawyers provide services in these areas with no apparent adverse affects.[63]

Relaxing the professional monopoly over legal services also could encourage reforms that would decrease the need for such services in the first instance. Reducing lawyers' financial stakes in cumbersome proceedings could reduce the obstacles to procedural simplification and innovation. Such initiatives might include citizen advice bureaux, court-affiliated ombudspersons, self-help services, no-fault insurance programmes and various alternative dispute resolution procedures. These approaches have the potential to serve values that are central to feminist agendas. Such initiatives can decrease the costs and acrimony associated with traditional adversarial processes, explore root causes of disputes as well as their legal symptoms, and draw on skills of non-legal experts with experience in facilitating relationships.

This is not to suggest that all forms of delegalisation or alternative dispute resolution are socially desirable. Rather, as feminists often emphasise, what is needed is contextual analysis. In some circumstances, informal mediation between individuals with unequal bargaining power can reinforce inequality and encourage weaker parties to negotiate rights that should be non-negotiable. Divorcing wives may trade property rights to avoid custody fights or battered spouses may agree to stop "nagging" in exchange for their partners' promises to refrain from assaults.[64] Informal processes oriented toward private settlements may also undervalue society's interest in having publicly

---

[61] American Bar Association, Consortium on Legal Services and the Public, *Legal Needs and Civil Justice* (Chicago, Ill., American Bar Association, 1994).

[62] *Ibid.* For domestic violence, see "Developments in the Law—Legal Responses to Domestic Violence" (1993) 106 *Harvard Law Review* 1498, 1525–6. For other family cases, see National Center on Women and Family Law, *Challenges Facing Legal Services in the 1990s* (New York: National Center on Women and Family Law, 1988), 4, n. 6; Gender Bias Study Commission, Supreme Judicial Court of Massachusetts, *Report of the Gender Bias Study of the Supreme Judicial Court* (Boston, Mass., Supreme Judicial Court of Massachusetts, 1989), 21.

[63] See Rhode, "Delivery", *supra* n. 60, 215; Rhode, "Professionalism", *supra* n. 60, 85–90; John Merryman and David Clark, *Comparative Law: Western European and Latin American Legal Systems* (Charlottesville, Virginia, Michie Company, 1978), 456–7; Michael Zander, *Legal Services for the Community* (London, Temple Smith, 1978), 329–35.

[64] Lisa G. Lerman, "Mediation of Wife Abuse Cases: The Adverse Impact of Informal Dispute Resolution on Women" (1984) 7 *Harvard Women's Law Journal* 57, 75; Trina Grillo, "The Mediation Alternative: Process Dangers for Women" (1991) 100 *Yale Law Journal*, 1545.

accountable officials apply collectively determined standards.[65] How best to structure the delivery of professional services cannot be resolved in the abstract. Rather, that question requires a more particularised analysis of the legal needs, social context and power relationships at issue.

The priorities underlying judicial administration and subsidized legal services also require rethinking. The reason was well illustrated in testimony before a California gender bias commission. As one prominent state judge noted, she had recently spent ten days presiding over a civil jury trial involving a $100,000 dispute between two companies. During a ten-day period in family court, she had a docket of thirty to forty custody and abuse cases per day, which involved the wellbeing of 1000 children.[66] Such disparities are by no means unique to California.[67] Nor are resource problems confined to the judicial system. Legal aid and court sponsored services are shockingly underfunded for family-related needs.[68]

Although the shape of necessary reforms is beyond the scope of this chapter, the general direction of feminist concern is clear. Society must spend more, and spend more wisely, in areas such as domestic violence, child support enforcement, custody disputes and child abuse and neglect. If we are truly committed to "family values", we need a better match between our legal structures and resource priorities.

(d) Professional Workplaces and Professional Priorities

Finally, feminists are concerned about workplace issues that implicate professional values and priorities. In America over the last decade, about two-thirds of the states and many bar associations have established commissions on gender bias or the status of women and minorities in the legal profession.[69] These groups have published research and recommendations on a wide range of matters including glass ceilings on advancement opportunities, sexually harassing and demeaning treatment and work/family conflicts.[70]

For most of these issues, the appropriate directions for change are self-evident. The same values of gender equality and mutual respect that underpin

---

[65] Owen Fiss, "Against Settlement" (1984) 93 *Yale Law Journal* 1073.

[66] "How Gender Bias Creeps Into Courts" (Editorial Writers' Desk), *Los Angeles Times*, 27 Nov. 1990.

[67] See Lois Foner, *Money and Justice: Who Owns the Courts* (New York, Norton, 1984), 109; Harriet Chang, "Sexism Pervades State's Courts, Committee Says", *San Francisco Chronicle*, 4 May 1990, at 1.

[68] Gender Bias Study Commission, *supra* n. 62; National Center on Women and Family Law, *supra* n. 62, 3–4.

[69] Kathleen L. Soll, "Gender Bias Task Forces: Have They Fulfilled Their Mandate and Recommendations for Change" (1993) 2 *Review Law and Women's Studies* 633, 634, 638.

[70] American Bar Association, Commission on Women in the Profession, *Unfinished Business: Overcoming the Sisyphis Factor* (Chicago, Ill., American Bar Association, 1995); Cynthia Fuchs Epstein *et al.*, "Glass Ceilings and Open Doors: Women's Advancement in the Legal Profession" (1995) 64 *Fordham Law Review* 291.

a feminist vision of professional roles should also inform the structure of professional workplaces.

A bar truly committed to equal opportunity must institutionalise that principle through more flexible working hours, more supportive organisational cultures and more effective bias prevention programmes. Lawyers have long been leaders in the struggles for social justice among many disadvantaged groups. The challenge remaining is to confront problems in their own profession and to translate rhetorical commitments into daily priorities.

14

Conduct, Ethics and Experience in Vocational Legal Education: Opportunities Missed

JULIAN WEBB

I. INTRODUCTION

Some twenty-five years ago, one writer came to the not wholly unexpected conclusion that:

> "studies showed that graduating law students without any experience in practice demonstrated a higher standard of ethical or public responsibility than lawyers actually in practice."[1]

Over one year ago, the Lord Chancellor's Advisory Committee on Legal Education and Conduct (ACLEC) noted that:

> "there are real dangers that professional standards will be threatened unless counter-balancing steps are taken to reinforce ethical values."[2]

Given that ACLEC's apparent answer lies in educational reform, the juxtaposition of these two views is less than reassuring. Therein, I suggest, lies the key ethical challenge: can we teach ethics in a way that really might make a difference to how lawyers behave in practice? I intend to explore this question chiefly in the context of the vocational law courses as delivered in England and Wales.[3]

---

[1] J. R. Peden, "The Role of Practical Legal Training in Legal Education: American and Australian Experience" (1972) 22 *Journal of Legal Education* 503 at 517.

[2] ACLEC, *First Report on Legal Education and Training* (London, ACLEC, 1996), para. 1.19 (hereafter "*First Report*").

[3] As a biographical point, I should say that my perspective is that of a partial outsider. I see myself first and foremost as an "academic" rather than "vocational" law teacher, though I have been involved in skills teaching on the LPC since its inception and I am sympathetic (within limits) to the case for greater integration between the academic and vocational. I have not taught "professional conduct" on the vocational courses, but do teach "professional ethics" on an LLB clinical simulation.

This chapter draws in part on some small-scale original research using both documentary and empirical evidence. The main documentary sources are the texts used on the courses and statements from the professional bodies prescribing the curricula and standards for vocational training in England and Wales. Qualitative data were also obtained from eight semi-structured interviews with staff responsible for co-ordinating professional conduct teaching at provider institutions.[4] Institutions were selected purposively to reflect a range of providers with reference to the institutional type, size of cohort and experience of course delivery, and incorporated both "multi-site"[5] and single-site providers. The aims of the fieldwork were primarily descriptive: to explore the processes of professional conduct teaching, rather than its efficacy or ethos, and thus to provide a snapshot of current practice and developments from the teacher's perspective.

In the first two parts of this chapter I will establish a context for and basic description of the framework and processes of vocational education and training, including the teaching of "professional conduct", as it is called, on these courses. The next two sections will take a step back to look more reflectively at the aims and objectives of professional conduct and ethics teaching, before using these ideas to critique more particularly the present approach of the English courses. The chapter closes by considering the ethical strengths and weaknesses of ACLEC's proposals for reform and proposing some remedies of its own.

II. VOCATIONAL LEGAL EDUCATION IN ENGLAND AND WALES[6]

The current model of vocational training in England and Wales builds substantially on the Commonwealth system of professional education which evolved chiefly out of training developments in Canada and Australia.[7] However, once we move beyond such bare generalities, the existence of a divided legal profession, each with its own system of vocational training, has meant that some dissimilarities in the training regimes for barristers and solicitors remain.

---

[4] 3 were with (prospective) providers of the new Bar Vocational Course, 5 with Legal Practice Course providers. My particular thanks are owed to these anonymous contributors. They should not, of course, be held responsible for the ends to which I have put the information they so generously provided.

[5] I use this term to denote both co-operative (e.g. the joint Bar Course for the Wales and Western Circuit mounted by my own institution and the University of Wales, Cardiff) and "franchise" arrangements (e.g. the delivery of Nottingham Trent University's Legal Practice Course at Bournemouth University), and genuine single institution, multiple site operations, such as the College of Law.

[6] See Richard O'Dair's contribution for a brief description and analysis of the wider structures of English legal education.

[7] Christopher Roper, "The Legal Practice Courses—Theoretical Frameworks and Models" (1988) 6 *Journal of Professional Legal Education* 77.

(a) Training for the Bar

The present training regime was established in 1989 with the launch of the Bar Vocational Course (BVC) at the Inns of Court School of Law (ICSL) in London. Until recently, this was the only course for those wishing to practise at the Bar in England and Wales, and, at its peak, it has had over 1,000 students per cohort. The Bar Council has now validated six[8] other institutions, in addition to the Inns of Court School of Law, to run the BVC from September 1997. The basic structural model for the "new" devolved BVC remains the ICSL course.[9]

The BVC is taught over one academic year (about thirty teaching weeks) full-time.[10] It is heavily skills-oriented, with some 60 per cent of the course devoted to skills training in advocacy, opinion writing and drafting, negotiation, conferencing (client interviewing), legal research and fact management. The main substantive elements of the course are Evidence, Civil Litigation, Criminal Litigation and Sentencing, Professional Conduct, and Remedies. Students are also expected to acquire an outline knowledge of EC law, Revenue, Accounts, Business Associations and Social Security law, and to take two specialist (substantive) options in the final term of the course.

The focus of the teaching is generally on active and integrated forms of learning skills and content, with a significant emphasis on small group work with sets of up to twelve students. A Practical Training Exercise Programme, which requires students to work through a number of case studies across the skills and knowledge areas, is also an important part of the learning process on the BVC.

(b) Solicitors' Training

The present scheme of vocational education for solicitors was introduced in 1993. This consists of two training courses: the Legal Practice Course (LPC) which may be completed full-time over one academic year or part-time over two years,[11] and the Professional Skills Course (PSC), which is studied part-time during the period of supervised practice (the training contract) which follows completion of the LPC.

---

[8] Two of these institutions are validated as joint providers.

[9] This section draws chiefly on Susan Blake, "Legal Skills Training Comes of Age?" in APLEC, *Skills Development for Tomorrow's Lawyers: Needs and Strategies. Conference Papers* (St Leonards, NSW, Australasian Professional Legal Education Council, 1996), i, 413 and the General Council of the Bar Validation Steering Committee document, *Bar Vocational Course: Course Specification Guidelines* (September 1995).

[10] The Inns of Court School of Law will offer the first part-time BVC from Sept. 1997.

[11] One (4-year) exempting degree has been established, by the University of Northumbria at Newcastle. Subsequent restrictions on State funding of new 4-year law degrees have so far discouraged other institutions from following.

The LPC is validated by the Law Society's Legal Practice Course Board. At present twenty-seven public and private sector providers are authorised to run the course in a total of thirty-one locations.[12] The majority of providers are drawn from the post-1992 universities (the former polytechnics), though the largest single provider remains the Law Society's own College of Law.

As presently constituted, the LPC involves a combination of compulsory, pervasive and elective subjects, and skills. The compulsory areas are Conveyancing; Wills, Probate and Administration; Business Law and Practice, and Litigation. There are three specific pervasives: Professional Conduct (and Financial Services); European Law; and Revenue, which are integrated into the teaching of the compulsory areas. The skills element is made up of the so-called DRAIN skills—drafting, legal research, advocacy, interviewing and negotiation. These are taught through an initial foundation course, and sub-sequently integrated into activities and workshops in the substantive courses. In addition students are required to choose two electives, which are taught in the final term(s) of the LPC. The range of electives varies from provider to provider.

Like the BVC, the LPC has required a marked shift away from the didac-ticism of the earlier vocational courses, though relative to the BVC, the cur-riculum as a whole is still biased more towards the transmission of substantive and procedural law, rather than skills.

As a consequence of a course review completed in October 1996,[13] the knowledge base and structure of the course have been revised, with the changes to take effect from September 1997. The revised LPC is much less ori-ented towards the traditional general practitioner—reflecting both the increas-ing fragmentation of the profession and the role of the City/large commercial firms as major providers of training contracts. This change is most marked in respect of the "downgrading" of Wills and Probate (which is no longer a major substantive subject) and the expansion of the Business Law and Practice element, which will now take up as much of the core teaching as Conveyancing and Litigation combined. The substantive content of the foun-dation course is increased, but negotiation has been made an optional rather than compulsory skill, so that the DRAIN skills are now, presumably, ARID.[14] The existing pervasives are retained *plus* Accounts, and there are now three, rather than two, electives. From the point of view of this chapter, however, the most interesting feature of the review has been its almost total silence so far as the teaching of professional conduct is concerned.[15]

[12] Figures based on The Law Society, *A Guide to Legal Practice Courses 1997/98.*

[13] See the LPC Review Group Report, "Review of the Operation of the Legal Practice Course" Oct. 1996, *mimeo*; also version 4 of the Legal Practice Course, *Written Standards*, Dec. 1996.

[14] My thanks to Phil Jones for this particular piece of irony.

[15] This may in part reflect the reasonably high levels of satisfaction with professional conduct teaching reported by trainees and employers alike—see Joy Hillyer, *The Future of Vocational Legal Education and the Legal Practice Course* (London, The College of Law, 1996); Scott Slorach. *The Legal Practice Course: Benefits in Practice* (Nottingham, Nottingham Law School Ltd, 1996).

The second element of solicitors' vocational training, the PSC, was also introduced as part of the new training regime. It is intended to build on the foundations of the LPC and support the knowledge demands and skills requirements of the office. The PSC (at the time of writing) contains five modules: personal work management; accounts; advocacy; investment business and professional conduct, though, as noted, accounts is now being brought forward to the LPC stage. Course delivery is normally staggered throughout the period of the training contract, the theory being that the PSC should thereby provide some degree of "in-service" training in which students have an opportunity to reflect on and ground their experience. However, a fast-track PSC option also exists, which enables trainees to work through all the modules in one block, often before the training contract has begun, thereby probably negating any likely benefits of integration.

III. CONDUCT AT THE VOCATIONAL STAGE: MATERIALS, METHODS AND ASSESSMENT

A common feature of both the BVC and LPC has been their efforts to move beyond the discrete "building blocks" (contract, tort, etc.) approach still common at the initial stage and to adopt a more integrated approach in which substantive law, procedure and skills are acquired in tandem through exercises and problem-based workshops. It is an approach that extends, to a degree, to the teaching and assessing of professional conduct.

(a) Primary Teaching Materials

Both BVC and LPC commonly make use of course manuals. For the BVC there is a substantial volume specifically on professional conduct,[16] containing text, exercises and the complete Code of Conduct for the Bar. The various LPCs, which are relatively free to select their own materials, have no direct equivalent to this, though there is one commercially published LPC manual on the pervasive subjects which devotes ninety-eight pages to commentary on professional conduct issues.[17] In some institutions this is a required course text; in others it is merely recommended or optional. All LPCs supply students with copies of the Law Society's *Guide to the Professional Conduct of Solicitors*[18]—nearly seven hundred pages of statutory rules, regulations, guidance and notes, which together define the professional

---

[16] Inns of Court School of Law, *Professional Conduct* (London, Blackstone Press, 1996), published annually.

[17] Frances Silverman, "Professional Conduct" in Bramley *et al.*, *LPC Pervasive Topics* (Bristol, Jordans, 1996), published annually.

[18] (7th edn., London, The Law Society, 1996).

responsibility of solicitors. Specific conduct issues are also considered *in situ* in both BVC and LPC manuals supporting the substantive topics and skills, though the extent and quality of discussion in these is variable. Other texts and materials tend to be devised independently for each course by its course team.

(b) Teaching Methods

The BVC as presently taught at the ICSL provides three lectures and three tutorials specifically on conduct as part of its foundation programme. The tutorials are based on three sets of eight problems published in the manual. They are all relatively short hypotheticals, reflecting the type of problems neophyte lawyers are likely to meet in the early years of practice. On the existing course these sessions are all taught by senior members of the practising Bar.[19] In addition, conduct issues are also incorporated into the practical training exercises, and to some extent in the optional subjects.[20] This pattern will not necessarily be replicated by all the new providers. One new provider I contacted, for example, anticipated a purely lecture-based delivery in the foundation course, only thereafter integrating conduct into practical exercises and workshops, whereas another was, at the time, looking to make learning about ethics more integrated and more student-centred than on the "old" BVC.

While it is even harder to generalise about LPC approaches, the pattern is not that dissimilar. The teaching hours given over to conduct vary, and may be significantly fewer than the initial loading on the (current) BVC. Students on the LPC courses I examined receive between three and six hours' teaching specifically on professional conduct during their introductory or foundation course. The teaching format also varies. For example, one institution offers two hours of lectures followed by a three hour workshop (with fifteen to sixteen students) on conduct issues; another provides three two hour sessions involving a combination of lectures and problem-solving group exercises. Another uses five hours in the foundation course to work through case studies and some short answer questions. In addition, students are normally required to follow up conduct issues during the foundation course by various mechanisms, for example, by integrating conduct issues in skills exercises, or completing take-home "paper" problems on professional conduct.

---

[19] It is a requirement for all the new BVC courses that barristers in practice are directly involved in teaching and assessing professional conduct, so as to ensure that the course providers have access to "current professional expertise": see General Council of the Bar Validation Steering Committee, *Application Procedure to be Validated to Offer the Bar Vocational Course* (Sept. 1995), Annex 1.

[20] Though, as one of my interviewees indicated, coverage in this latter context is left very much to the teachers concerned.

Following the foundation, conduct is required to pervade the course. Providers appear to take the principle of pervasiveness seriously. All those I interviewed indicated that conduct issues were integrated into the majority of exercises and workshops, certainly in respect of the compulsory subjects. As with the BVC, there is no general requirement that conduct is addressed in all the optional subjects, with the result that the approach at this stage tends to be more *laissez-faire*.

Professional conduct on the PSC appears commonly to be taught *via* a one day lecture-based course. The only published research to address training on the PSC notes some dissatisfaction with this element among trainees, both because the apparent (lack of) emphasis was thought to smack of tokenism and because, in some cases, it was seen simply as duplicating work already done on the LPC.[21]

(c) Assessment

The pervasive approach extends also to assessment. Observance of ethical standards is incorporated into the assessment of substantive knowledge areas and skills, though the precise manner of incorporation varies.

On the LPC, although conduct is largely taught and assessed in the context of the substantive courses, students must, at some point, be assessed "competent" (i.e. on a pass/fail basis), specifically in professional conduct. In effect this means that the conduct element of a problem in, say, conveyancing or business will be *separately* assessed to enable students to show that they have achieved competence (or not) in professional conduct. This does not prevent conduct also being assessed "indirectly" as an integral part of a question or exercise within a compulsory, elective or skills area—either in coursework or examination. In these settings, students do not necessarily have to "pass" the conduct element to achieve an overall pass standard in the substantive subject. However, the LPC Board does make specific provision that students who make a "serious error"[22] of conduct in a skills assessment should fail that assessment. Institutions again handle the assessment of conduct rather differently; most of the providers I contacted assess it through examinations—or, more commonly, assess it *as a pervasive* in one of the compulsory subject examinations, while integrating it into the assessment of the other subjects. One institution stood out from this pattern by assessing conduct pervasively through one piece of coursework in each of the compulsory subjects.

In the BVC, conduct is assessed pervasively throughout the course: "the criteria for every assessment should incorporate a requirement for the proper

[21] Tamara Goriely and Tom Williams, *The Impact of the New Training Scheme: Report on a Qualitative Study* (London, The Law Society, 1996), 86, 92–3.
[22] There is no formal definition of this term, so that it is a matter for the judgement of assessors at the time.

observance of ethical standards."[23] This is a different form of pervasiveness from the LPC, in that there appears from the criteria to be no separate requirement to establish competence in professional conduct *per se*.

Student performance in professional conduct assessments was not seen as especially problematic by my respondents. In all institutions failure rates for conduct were consistent with other parts of the course. Two LPC providers did specifically comment that students were generally not good at recognising conduct issues *in situ*, which suggests that conduct errors might generally have had some depressing effect on marks in the substantive subjects. One multi-site provider offered an interesting gloss to the effect that, while the proportion of failures in conduct was not out of line, there was evidence from their statistics of a positive correlation between failure in the compulsory subjects and failure in professional conduct as a pervasive subject.

IV. THE CONDUCT OBJECTIVES OF THE LPC/BVC.

Both courses take as their starting point a set of written outcomes or objectives laid down by the professional bodies. These are prescribed for all courses. Though each institution will have some discretion in interpreting the standards, validation and course monitoring procedures (including regular external review by representatives of the professional bodies), serve to ensure not just minimum levels of uniformity and compliance, but also some possibility for the dissemination of best practice.

In the BVC professional conduct is defined as a "knowledge area", with the following prescribed outcomes:[24]

"A student should be able to
  (a) identify issues of professional conduct and ethics which appear in given situations likely to arise in a barrister's practice;
  (b) identify the provisions of the Code of Conduct of the Bar of England and Wales which apply in such situations;
  (c) identify means of regulating relationships with other people to be in practice: opponents and colleagues; the tribunal/judiciary; instructing solicitors; clients (both lay and expert); court clerks;
  (d) reconcile the different duties owed to a professional client, lay client, the court, the legal aid fund;
  (e) follow the spirit of the Code in situations where there is no provision which is directly applicable;
  (f) choose the course of action which is consistent with the provisions and principles of that Code."

For the LPC, the written standards for professional conduct state:[25]

---

[23] *Course Specification Guidelines, supra* n. 9, para. 2.2.2 A(5).
[24] See *ibid.* (1995), Appendix 1.
[25] *Supra* n. 13.

"Students must by the end of the course be familiar with those areas of substantive law (e.g. negligence and fiduciary duties) and the professional conduct rules which deal with the conduct of fee earning work of a type likely to be encountered by trainees befog admission. This will include in particular:

   i.   retainer;

   ii. fees—written professional standards on information as to costs and the basis of charging;

  iii. client care—Rule 15 of the Practice Rules;

  iv. conflicts of interest—in contentious and non-contentious work including particularly Rule 6;

   v. confidentiality;

  vi. bad professional work and negligence;

 vii. the solicitor and the court

viii. professional undertakings."

In addition the LPC requires students to have an outline knowledge of the organisation of the solicitors' profession, of the conduct principles governing the obtaining of clients and of relations with lawyers and other professionals.

In analysing these objectives, we can identify a number of common themes which I shall call knowledge acquisition, professional competence and ethical awareness.

(a) Knowledge Acquisition

The dominant impression left by both statements, but particularly the LPC written standards, is of an overriding concern with substantive knowledge and the codes of conduct.[26] Not surprisingly, this is clearly reflected in the course materials and the attitudes of those teaching the courses.

At the same time, it was clear from comments made that teachers did not simply view professional conduct as identical to other substantive law subjects. Qualitative differences exist by virtue of the more open-textured character of conduct rules relative to conventional forms of "legislation", and which generate a need in hard cases to operate in terms of a "spirit of the Code".[27] Both LPC and BVC teachers seek to reflect this in at least some of the exercises set.

(b) Professional Competence

Knowledge acquisition is of course also a key component in achieving a baseline competence. In the words of one LPC tutor, "students must be conscious

---

[26] Though the LPC Written Standards for conduct need to be read in the context of the Written Standards for the DRAIN skills and the specified aims of the course. These are generic statements of skills and attributes underpinning professional competence. None of them refers overtly to professional conduct, though several could be taken to imply "conduct competence".

[27] Cf. ICSL, *supra* n. 16, 1–2.

that there is a set of rules to be followed". Tutors thus stress the importance of covering enough of the area, and especially of the "day-to-day" conduct problems (for example, the conduct implications of acting for borrower and lender in a conveyancing transaction, or of receiving a client's admission of wrongdoing) to ensure that students are "safe" to commence pupillage or training contracts. To that extent, teachers of professional conduct seem to see their role partly as one of "risk management". However, there was also clear evidence from the research that tutors were seeking to give students a more contextually sophisticated picture than this perhaps suggests. There was almost universal recognition among respondents of the multi-dimensional nature of "conduct competence". Competence is not just about knowing the conduct rules and associated substantive law; it is about developing an approach to legal problem-solving that is conduct-aware. This means that students are expected to handle "conduct dilemmas" in an appropriate way, both in terms of their use of legal knowledge and skills and their sense of what some respondents simply summarised as "professionalism": the values they brought to the task, their management of inter- (and intra-)professional and lay relationships, etc. In this way the courses, it was felt, could move beyond the minimalism of risk management towards a recognition and encouragement of best practice. The pervasive approach adopted by the LPC and BVC was clearly seen as fundamental to this endeavour.

(c) Ethical Awareness

The point has frequently been made by commentators that professional conduct and professional ethics are not one and the same thing, and to suggest they are involves a crude ethical reductionism:

> "formal codes of ethics never aimed at capturing the full network of understandings that lawyers observe in their dealings . . . they merely set forth a small body of fairly obvious minimal duties with which lawyers must comply on pain of discipline or disbarment. Where ethical problems of genuine complexity are concerned, official codes offer little guidance. They are often least helpful where most needed."[28]

On the English professional courses, teachers appear to take a fairly pragmatic view of their role. The aim of the courses is first and foremost to teach professional conduct, not ethics. As one of my respondents put it, "I avoid saying the word ethics, it is about the rules". Another, similarly, argued, "ethical problems may provoke a discussion, but the students need to know what the rules are . . .". There is certainly no question that conduct and ethics are being elided by default, but equally there is no pretence that the vocational courses

---

[28] Mary Ann Glendon, "Legal Ethics—Worlds in Collision", *First Things,* No. 41 (Mar. 1994), 21 at 26.

are deeply concerned with ethics in the wider sense. Having said that, teachers were clearly conscious of that wider dimension and engaged in some attempts to at least raise awareness of underlying issues and the limitations of a codified ethics. Students also, on the whole, were viewed as receptive to and interested in the ethical dimension when it did emerge. It is perhaps significant to note that this process seems far more overt on the BVC, where both the course manual and the written standards stress at some length the wider ethical context of "professional responsibility".[29] At least one of the BVC providers felt that this ethical sense was fundamental to the BVC, requiring the development of "an ethos to the whole course that there is a 'right' way to behave". About half of the tutors I spoke to expressed some concern or frustration that the opportunity to develop the "feel" for ethics was so limited. The time constraints on professional conduct was a recurrent theme, but particularly in this context. As one LPC teacher commented: "there is no real opportunity to discuss ethics as opposed to conduct".

Certainly, the breadth of professional conduct issues on these courses is considerable. If we take the LPC manual as a guide, it includes in its ninety-eight pages sections on practising certificates, indemnity insurance requirements, fees, disciplinary procedures, and so on. Only about a quarter of the total relates to what might be called the "core ethics" as opposed to more general matters of professional regulation.[30] In teaching terms, relatively little time can be spent on these core principles, even though it is here that the greatest potential to explore true ethical dilemmas exists.

As a final point it is worth noting that three out of the five LPC tutors approached thought that the recent review would have some negative consequences for conduct teaching. In one case it was anticipated that there might be a net reduction of hours given over to conduct teaching in the foundation course, while in two others it was anticipated that there would be some transfer of conduct teaching hours from the foundation to the core subjects. Two of these three providers also commented that the foundation would change qualitatively with, as one suggested, "more chalk and talk and less case studies".

V. THE POSSIBILITIES FOR LEGAL ETHICS COURSES

Having explored the technicalities of teaching professional conduct on the English vocational courses, we can begin to consider more critically the nature of professional conduct and ethics teaching, by identifying what it could set out to achieve and how it might achieve it.

[29] *Supra* n. 16, chap. 4.

[30] Governing lawyer–client relations, duties to the court, conflicts of interest, confidentiality, and relations with third parties: see Alison Crawley and Christopher Bramall, "Professional Rules, Codes and Principles Affecting Solicitors" in R. Cranston (ed.), *Legal Ethics and Professional Responsibility* (Oxford, Clarendon Press, 1995), who similarly distinguish core ethics from "mere regulation".

It is inevitably difficult to generalise about the aims and objectives of such courses. Nevertheless, it seems reasonable to suggest that, at a minimum, they tend to be built around one or more of the following primary objectives:[31]

- To introduce students to their professional responsibilities and to the ethical standards demanded of a competent practitioner;
- To enable students to consider their attitudes and values about the legal profession;
- To enable students to engage in appropriate ethical reasoning and to select "professional" courses of action.
- To provide students with an understanding of the nature of the legal process and lawyers' role within it.

In practice the last of these is more commonly expected of academic or integrated systems of education and training. Certainly in England it is not a central feature of vocational training. This in itself may be problematic. Relatively few university law schools have advanced courses in legal system or process, and there are few texts which attempt to explore the "institutional" or "system" ethics. There is thus little opportunity for students at present to reflect on the ways in which "the moral validity of lawyers' conduct is intertwined with the moral validity of the system".[32]

Assuming that the remaining objectives might be appropriate for vocational legal education, to try to achieve all these objectives in the same course is simply not feasible. As Alan Paterson points out and the vocational courses demonstrate, underlying any question of what to teach is the "multi-layered" character of professional responsibility.[33] Even if we adopt a fairly doctrinaire approach, our subject sounds not just in the rules of professional conduct, but in agency and fiduciary law, negligence, evidence and procedure, and so on, and has implications for skills training.[34] Anything more sophisticated and we, as teachers, begin to face potential problems, not just of subject overload, but of domain competence. To enable, for example, students to know and use the codes of conduct is a substantially different kind of activity from enabling them to engage in formal ethical reasoning, and will require significantly different approaches to teaching and learning, and a more multi-disciplinary understanding on the part of the teachers. We begin to wade into the murky depths of moral philosophy, the sociology of the professions, developmental

---

[31] Cf. Ian Johnstone and Mary Patricia Treuthart, "Doing the Right Thing: An Overview of Teaching Professional Responsibility" (1991) 41 *Journal of Legal Education* 75; Susan Burns, "Teaching Legal Ethics" (1993) 4 *Legal Education Review* 141; Alan Paterson, "Legal Ethics: Its Nature and Place in the Curriculum" in Cranston (ed.), *supra* n. 30.

[32] Johnstone and Treuthart, *supra* n. 31, 78.

[33] *Supra* n. 31, 181.

[34] Cf. the comments by Richard O'Dair in this collection; see also e.g., Stephen Ellman, "Lawyers and Clients" (1987) 34 *UCLA Law Review* 717; James J. White, "Machiavelli and the Bar: Ethical Limitations on Lying in Negotiation" [1980] *American Bar Foundation Research Journal* 921.

psychology and possibly enough other "-ologies" to scare the living daylights out of many law teachers.

So how might we decide the balance? I suggest it will tend to depend on whereabouts the designer locates her course along a continuum from what we might call the "instrumental" to the "developmental" (see Figure 1). Let me explain.

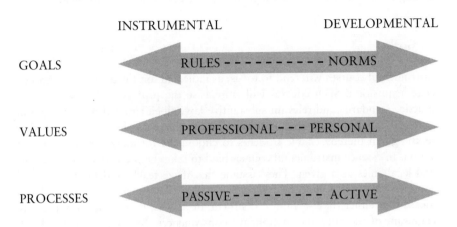

Fig. 1 *The ethics continuum*

Put simply, what I would term an instrumental approach treats ethics and conduct, often by default,[35] as another substantive area of law. It emphasises the rules of professional conduct as the subject of analysis, and course outcomes are defined primarily in terms of knowledge and understanding of the conduct rules. By contrast, a developmental approach emphasises the importance of enabling individual moral growth as a basis for fostering ethical understanding and behaviour. What we actually mean by "moral growth" is something of a loaded question, to which I shall return, but in essence the focus of such teaching is on cognitive and affective processes: on how students think and feel about ethical issues. A developmental approach is not antithetical to the teaching of professional conduct *per se*, but it does recognise more explicitly the importance of individualised professional judgement in ethical decision-making.[36]

---

[35] Because "[t]he Code of Professional Responsibility is often taught as though it were the Federal Rules of Civil Procedure. . . namely, by lawyers unskilled in moral reasoning": Joram Graf Huber and Bernard H. Baumrin, "The Moral Obligations of Lawyers" (1988) I *Canadian Journal of Law & Jurisprudence* 105 at 115.

[36] Though it can legitimately be criticised for underplaying other cultural and organisational constraints on professional action: cf. John P. Heinz and Edward Laumann, "The Legal Profession: Client Interests, Professional Roles and Social Hierarchies" (1978) 76 *Michigan Law Review* 1111.

The distinction between the instrumental and developmental is something of an ideal type, but nevertheless, I suggest, it usefully highlights some of the different approaches one might adopt to teaching professional ethics. Moreover, at the extremes, the differences are quite fundamental. This is particularly so in respect of what I would identify as the three main component parts of the learning experience: its goals, values and processes.

Though these are closely interdependent, let us consider each of them in turn.

(a) Goals

Instrumental courses will tend to focus, as indicated, on the demands of knowledge acquisition. Such courses will emphasise the professional conduct rules, practice standards and relevant substantive law, albeit situated in some kind of practical context, rather than just taught in the abstract. The assumption is that teaching can thereby enable students to choose the formally correct course of action. In essence instrumental courses tend to take the predictive power of formal legal rules as a given. They assume that if we teach students the rules of conduct, they will know the boundaries which they must not cross, and this means that either they will not cross them, or at least that, if they do, they are cognisant of the potential disciplinary consequences. By contrast, more developmental and cognitivist approaches emphasise that "ethical training is, foremost, learning about oneself".[37] Outcomes are likely to be defined more in terms of moral processes (how one reaches the decision) or of personal understanding and normative judgement ("what *ought* I to do?").[38]

The difference in focus is fundamental. Codes in a developmental model can play only a restricted role, because cognitivism teaches that ethical conduct is ultimately a matter of personal capacity and motivation for "virtue".[39] It is generated from the "inside out". Codes of conduct, in contrast, seek to impose virtue from the "outside in". This is not to say codes are worthless; they serve to universalise standards and to emphasise the particular consequences of certain courses of action, but at the cost of limiting the personal responsibility of the professional to think and act as a moral agent.

This view is reinforced by a significant and growing body of psychological research into moral development processes which suggests that teaching needs to acknowledge the multi-dimensional *process* of being ethical. Rest and Narvaez,[40] for example, argue that we need to take account of four compo-

---

[37] Ronald M. Pipkin, "Law School Instruction in Professional Responsibility: A Curricular Paradox" (1979) *American Bar Foundation Research Journal* 247 at 275.

[38] Julian Webb, "Inventing the Good: A Prospectus for Clinical Education and the Teaching of Legal Ethics in England and Wales" (1996) 30 *Law Teacher* 270 at 282–3.

[39] See e.g., Angus James Dawson, "Professional Codes of Practice and Ethical Conduct" (1994) 11 *Journal of Applied Philosophy* 145.

[40] *Moral Development in the Professions: Psychology and Applied Ethics* (Hillsdale, NJ, Lawrence Erlbaum Associates, 1994).

nents to moral behaviour if we are to understand how people make moral decisions and carry them through into action. These components are:[41]

- *Moral sensitivity:* this is a cognitive/affective component. It describes our ability to recognise an ethical problem and to understand the consequences of courses of action for ourselves and others. It therefore has what we might call "empathic" as well as knowledge characteristics.
- *Moral judgment:* this describes our ability to select the morally most appropriate or justifiable course of action. In most psychological models this element addresses appropriateness according to the structure and development of reasoning, rather than its values or outcome[42]—in itself, perhaps, a questionable value judgement!
- *Moral motivation:* concerns our capacity to prioritise moral over other (e.g. organisational) values—i.e. to see that certain courses of action ought to be privileged over others because they are ethically 'correct'.
- *Moral character:* describes our capacity to ensure that we "do the right thing", that we are not sidetracked from the ethical course of action by other pressures, or a lack of ego strength—what we might think of as "moral fibre".

What I think this model usefully does is to emphasise that failure to act ethically may be the result of a "moral failure" at any of these four stages—a failure of recognition, of judgement, motivation or character. It suggests therefore that, as teachers, we ought to be developing goals of teaching and learning relevant to a student's capacity to think and act through each of these stages. Simply knowing the conduct rules is clearly not enough. Although some such knowledge is necessary to avoid the basic failures of recognition that might arise under a more "intuitive"[43] approach to ethics, knowing the rules does not guarantee that lawyers will treat potential ethical problems as problems of professional conduct. Indeed, reliance on formal conduct rules can become a mechanism for taking the moral decision out of certain problems. Rules, in effect, replace conscience.[44]

---

[41] *Ibid.,* 23–4.

[42] This is most apparent in Lawrence Kohlberg's "stage theory" of moral development which charts development progressively from an egocentric "pre-moral" phase to, ultimately, a position of rational autonomy—see, e.g., Kohlberg, "Moral Stages and Moralization" in Lickona (ed.), *Moral Development and Behavior* (New York, Holt, Rhinehart & Winston, 1976); cf. Owen Flanagan, *Varieties of Moral Personality: Ethics and Psychological Realism* (Cambridge, Mass., Harvard UP, 1991) 181–95. For discussions of Kohlbergian moral development in legal education, see, e.g., Webb, *supra* n. 38, 279–81 and the sources cited there.

[43] Paterson, *supra* n. 31, 176–7.

[44] Cf. the "Larry Smith" interview in Rand Jack and Dana Crowley Jack, *Moral Vision and Professional Decisions* (Cambridge, Cambridge UP 1989), 57–8; also Leny de Groot-van Leeuwen in this collection.

(b) Values

The whole territory of values[45] is, inevitably, problematic and yet it must equally inevitably underpin any deeper consideration of law and legal ethics. This fact has been acknowledged *inter alia* by a number of reports on legal education.[46] However, in recent years, only one, the American *MacCrate Report*, has sought to itemise what it saw as the "fundamental values" of the legal profession, *viz.* to provide competent representation; to promote justice, fairness and morality; to strive to improve the profession; and to develop one-self.[47] Of course, here is not an appropriate place for any detailed critique of *MacCrate*—indeed this task has already been undertaken by more qualified commentators than me. Suffice it to say that such statements in the end emphasise just how difficult it is to convey anything meaningful about under-lying professional values, not least because there is a marked lack of consen-sus about what (beyond the level of broadest generality) those values are in theory, let alone practice. This difficulty is likely to be aggravated in ethical systems such as the English one, where the written ethics are found in what are essentially disciplinary, as opposed to aspirational, codes.[48] As a result, at the most extreme, instrumental ethics courses may seek to avoid any direct engagement with the issue of professional values. More commonly, perhaps, there is a tendency for teachers of such courses to defer to an unexplored and intuitive model of professionalism that is present in notions of "best practice" or in the repetition of vague platitudes about the lawyer's responsibility to behave honourably and with integrity.[49] Both these positions are understand-able. However, in neither case is the student lawyer enabled thereby to underpin her knowledge of the codes with any kind of internalised ethical norms.[50]

[45] I am conscious that the use of the term itself opens a whole definitional can of worms. Suffice it to say that for my purposes here "values" are simply higher-order reasons for acting in a particular way. I take it as given that they are intersubjective and, to some degree, socially con-structed.

[46] See e.g. the ACLEC *First Report*, para. 2.4; also the Submission of the Australian Law Deans in the Pearce Report, *Australian Law Schools: A Discipline Assessment for the Commonwealth Tertiary Education Commission* (Canberra, AGPS, 1987), and, more specifically, Brent Cotter's *Professional Responsibility Instruction in Canada* (Quebec, Conceptcom, 1992).

[47] See *Legal Education and Professional Development—An Educational Continuum: Narrowing the Gap* (Chicago, Ill., American Bar Association, 1992), 140 for a summary statement.

[48] That is, a code which defines minimum standards below which practitioners should not fall if they are to escape sanctions, rather than the higher standards to which all practitioners should aspire: see Charles Sampford with Christine Parker, "Legal Regulation, Ethical Standard Setting, and Institutional Design" in S. Parker and C. Sampford (eds.), *Legal Ethics and Legal Practice: Contemporary Issues* (Oxford, Clarendon Press, 1995), 14–15.

[49] Cf. Lord Denning MR in *Rondel* v. *Worsley* [1966] 3 WLR 950 at 962, an advocate "must accept the brief and do all he honourably can on behalf of his client".

[50] Sampford e.g. calls for commitment to a "critical morality in which individuals can debate, discuss and criticize majority views, internalizing their own values and acting on them"; *supra* n. 48, 16.

Although, as noted above, values do not apparently figure in some psychologically grounded developmental approaches either, this is misleading.[51]

Most developmental approaches, in law at least, seem sympathetic to the Aristotelian position for legal ethics advanced by Anthony Kronman: that questions of ethics reduce to individual and professional norms about living a virtuous life as a lawyer.[52] This emphasis on a personally integrated vision of the lawyer's role supposes ethics teaching is to teach not just the rules but to habituate (so far as it can) students to think and act ethically. We need to teach the rules, for sure, but if we are to encourage moral motivation and commitment we also need to provide an environment in which personal and professional values can be discussed, tested, integrated and internalised. In this way students can begin to invest professional ethics with their own *personal meaning*[53] as a sense of what is possible as well as permissible. This leads, of course, into the next question: how is it done?

(c) Learning Processes

As the American experience shows, many instrumental courses adopt a relatively traditional approach to learning which treats professional ethics as another substantive law subject, relying heavily on lecture-based teaching and rote learning of the codes.[54]

Traditional teaching mechanisms, used appropriately, have their place, but, as is widely recognised, too much emphasis on tutor-led methods of instruction can encourage passivity and a surface as opposed to deep approach to learning.[55] If, as research suggests in other professional fields,[56] extensive exposure to courses which are highly tutor-dependent and knowledge-intensive not only limits (or at best does not enhance) moral reasoning, *and*

---

[51] See Laurence Thomas's critique of Kohlberg in "Morality and Psychological Development" in P. Singer (ed.), *A Companion to Ethics* (Oxford, Blackwell, 1991), 466–70. Cf. William Perry's model, also influential in moral education, which accepts the centrality of some commitment to a moral position: see *Forms of Intellectual and Ethical Development in the College Years* (New York, Holt Rhinehart & Winston, 1970), notably at 136.

[52] "Living in the Law" (1987) 54 *University of Chicago Law Review* 835; cf. also David Luban, "Epistemology and Moral Education" (1983) 33 *Journal of Legal Education* 636.

[53] My position here follows Wittgenstein in arguing that rules cannot be understood outside the context of their application.

[54] Cf. Deborah Rhode, "Ethics by the Pervasive Method" (1992) 42 *Journal of Legal Education* 31 at 39–41; William Simon, "The Trouble With Legal Ethics" (1991) 41 *Journal of Legal Education* 65 at 66.

[55] Diana Tribe, "How Students Learn" in J. Webb and C. Maughan (eds.), *Teaching Lawyers' Skills* (London, Butterworths, 1996).

[56] Cf. in medical education the studies cited by Stephen A. Goldman and Jack Arbuthnot, "Teaching Medical Ethics: The Cognitive-Developmental Approach" (1979) 5 *Journal of Medical Ethics* 170 at 171; also D. J. Self *et al.*, "The Moral Development of Medical Students: A Pilot Study of the Possible Influence of Medical Education" (1993) 27 *Medical Education* 26; and more generally Carl Onion and Peter Slade, "Depth of Information Processing and Memory for Medical Facts" (1995) 17 *Medical Teacher* 307.

generates perhaps only limited recall of the conduct rules, then such courses arguably fall short even of the basic aims of creating reasonably competent professionals.

Developmental approaches, by definition, require a strong emphasis on active learning methods. This, I suggest, does not just mean an emphasis on participative and small-group teaching. Students need to be presented with learning situations which enable them to question their assumptions about their roles as a lawyer and to confront situations both where they must face potential (internal) conflicts between personal and professional ethics and (external) constraints on their capacity to act "morally". The use of experiential methods—hypothetical or live dilemmas, role plays and simulations—and of genuine Socratic dialogue in group work are each central to effective developmental learning.[57]

This now gives us some more critical basis for reviewing the limitations of the English vocational approach.

VI. THE LIMITS OF VOCATIONALISM

It will be apparent that, according to my typology, the English vocational courses are located more at the instrumental end of the continuum. This is not, I suggest, indicative of any failure to meet the objectives of those courses; rather it is a feature of their institutional design. This can be illustrated by reference to three significant and problematic features of the English approach to professional ethics

(a) Wrong Time, Wrong Subject?

Perhaps the most fundamental failure of the English system at present is that it offers too little, too late. Students commencing the vocational courses do so with little, if any, grounding in ethics in either their micro or macro form.[58] The effect of this should not be under-emphasised. Students approaching professional ethics do so essentially from a codified, conduct, perspective. This treats as given, and largely uncontested, a particular problem-frame and thereby overlooks the extent to which "the definition of the problem sets the answer".[59]

---

[57] See Webb, *supra* n. 38, at 282–3; cf. James E. Molliterno, "Professional Preparedness: A Comparative Study of Law Graduates" Perceived Readiness for Professional Ethics Issues" (1996) 58 *Law & Contemporary Problems* 259.

[58] See O'Dair's chapter in this collection.

[59] Carol Gilligan in E. Dubois, M. Dunlap, C. Gilligan, C. MacKinnon and C. Menkel-Meadow, "Feminist Discourse, Moral Values, and the Law—A Conversation" (1985) 34 *Buffalo Law Review* 11 at 47.

My point is not only that, as Richard O'Dair suggests, there is a strong argument that academic law teachers have failed their vocational counterparts, but also that this failure is exacerbated by the overall design of the codes, and (perhaps consequently) of the courses which teach them.

By their adoption of detailed rules, written in technical, legalistic language, the codes not only make professional conduct a difficult topic for students, they potentially encourage reliance on, at worst, a crude and unreflective compliance, or, at best, a legalistic sophistry. In either case, it is "the spirit of the code" that is likely to be left behind, never mind more generalised standards and values.[60] This is not to say that legalism is automatically an inappropriate response to conduct problems. Many conduct problems are *regulatory* rather than *ethical* and so warrant a regulatory interpretation. What is inappropriate is a failure to recognise that the distinction exists and to treat ethical problems as merely regulatory, or *vice versa*. This is a danger of the present courses because, first, that distinction is not well sustained by the codes themselves, and, secondly, there has been no attempt as yet to produce a systematising text on the English codes which offers any framework of general principles.[61] In these circumstances teachers face an uphill struggle to teach anything beyond the rules.

(b) W(h)ither the Reflective Practitioner?

There seems to me to be a clear linkage between developmental approaches to ethics and emergent "post-technocratic" models of professional education.[62]

Such models emphasise the extent to which professional practice is grounded in the ability to deal reflectively and creatively with problems which have characteristics that are complex, unique or uncertain. The source of such uniqueness and complexity is as likely to be a value-conflict or role uncertainty inherent in the problem, as any factual or legal doubts.

Reflection in this sense is shorthand for both deliberative and metacognitive processes.[63] It is deliberative insofar as it involves an attempt to understand new situations by utilising our prior practical and theoretical knowledge of the domain. It is metacognitive in that it also describes the way in which

---

[60] Cf. the loss of what Glendon, *supra* n. 28, calls "the language of moral suasion" from the American Bar Association's Model Rules following the reforms of 1983.

[61] Cf. Edmund D. Pellegrino, "The Metamorphosis of Medical Ethics: A 30 Year Retrospective" (1993) 269 *Journal of the American Medical Association* 1158 at 1159–60 on the influence of Beauchamp and Childress, *Principles of Biomedical Ethics*, on the teaching of medical ethics.

[62] See Philip Jones, "We're All Reflective Practitioners Now: Reflections on Professional Education" in Webb and Maughan, *supra* n. 55, for an excellent critical review of the key literature.

[63] *Ibid.*, 303–4; Michael Eraut, *Developing Professional Knowledge and Competence* (London and Washington, DC, Falmer Press, 1994), 145–6, 155–6.

individuals think about their own thinking—the engagement in reflective analysis which informs our decisions about what to do and what to think next. Bernard Williams[64] argues that such a reflective capacity serves to create in the practitioner an "engaged moral faculty"—a continuing state of moral unease in which she is encouraged to consider the moral implications of her actions.

The role of a post-technocratic professional ethics course is therefore to encourage that habit of reflection. This clearly is not an easy task, especially, as one of my respondents pointed out, with novice practitioners, who will have often have little in the way of past experience on which to reflect deliberatively. Reflection also demands, I would suggest, a commitment of time and resources. We cannot simply ask students to reflect. They need to be assisted in that process in terms of both the learning experiences to which they are exposed and training in the techniques associated with self-evaluation and personal development. This is most likely to be achieved through the use of active and experiential learning methods, though engaging in action by itself will not make students into reflective practitioners; they also need the space to articulate their reflection and to experiment with alternative theories and courses of action.[65] Experience elsewhere suggests that exposure to realistic, or (even better) real, transaction-based problems rather than hypothetical exercises and vignettes provide far stronger learning experiences.[66] It is not easy to build this into courses that already have a substantial loading of skills and substantive knowledge,[67] and almost certainly would demand a radical restructuring of the vocational courses.

(c) The Contradiction of Pervasiveness

The pervasive approach itself, I suggest, also constitutes another problematic for the vocational courses. Pervasiveness was adopted because conduct is important; by making it pervade the course and requiring students to jump through professional conduct hoops in skills areas and substantive subjects, the message that conduct cannot be ignored should, in theory, get across. Agreed; but the English pervasive approach perhaps also under-emphasises conduct because it is not sufficiently separate *and* pervasive. Some conduct rules (such as the conflict rules in conveyancing transactions) are so subject-

---

[64] "Professional Morality and Its Dispositions" in D. Luban (ed.), *The Good Lawyer* (Totowa NJ, Rowman & Allanheld, 1984), 259.

[65] See e.g. J. Macfarlane, N. Gold, B. Davies and M. Littlewood, "Designing New Legal Practice Courses: The Hong Kong Plan" (1992) 26 *Law Teacher* 84 at 100–1.

[66] Moliterno, *supra* n. 57; David A. Cruickshank, "Problem-Based Learning in Legal Education" in Webb & Maughan, *supra* n.55.

[67] Indeed, there is some evidence that skills training on the LPC is itself not developed in a way that enables reflection—Peter Kilpin, "Skills Teaching on the Legal Practice Courses" in Webb and Maughan, *supra* n. 55, 251, 256–8.

specific that they can be safely left to the substantive subject. They make most sense in that context, but that is less true of the more multi-dimensional rules governing, say, client confidentiality and privilege, which may become unduly fragmented by a subject-specific approach. And it is even less true of those general principles which ought to encompass the "spirit of the code".

One rationale of the foundation courses has been that they provide that separate element in which these general principles can be established. They acknowledge that, "giving the pieces of legal ethics a home everywhere . . . deprives its core concepts of a home anywhere".[68]

But are these courses adequate? Given the descriptive aims of the fieldwork, this point was not pursued directly with the teachers interviewed. My own suspicion is that they are too brief and possibly too early to encourage deep or systematic study. This is not to say that teaching ethics in the foundation is a bad idea: it can usefully orientate students to the subject and has a symbolic value in emphasising their importance. However, it is interesting to contrast the English with the US pervasive approach, where there appears to be some movement towards combining substantial (usually semester-long) free-standing ethics courses with pervasive ethics teaching.[69] It is also noteworthy that two of the five LPC respondents volunteered the view that a more substantial, free-standing, professional conduct course was needed. Given the continuing pressure from the profession, especially on the LPC, to maintain a high level of substantive law teaching, such a change would not be easy to achieve within the existing framework.

VII. OPPORTUNITIES MISSED?

The reforms of 1989 and 1993 were undoubtedly significant developments and, evidence suggests, have improved the vocational training of lawyers in England and Wales. But with hindsight I would suggest that they were informed by a restricted model of competence which emphasises substantive knowledge and only a limited range of skills, organised around the DRAIN/ARID typologies. The formal tendency to treat conduct as a knowledge attribute underplays the extent to which "behaving ethically" should itself be treated as a far more complex and skilled process. This tendency is unlikely to be mitigated by the pervasive approach adopted in the English courses, since that serves probably as much to dilute as to reinforce the importance of professional conduct and ethics. Consequently, despite some

[68] Stephen Bundy, "Ethics Education in the First Year: An Experiment" (1995) 58 *Law and Contemporary Problems* 19 at 28.

[69] See e.g. David T. Link, "The Pervasive Method of Ethics Teaching" (1989) 39 *Journal of Legal Education* 485; Carrie Menkel-Meadow and Richard H. Sander, "The 'Infusion' Method at UCLA: Teaching Ethics Pervasively" (1995) 58 *Law and Contemporary Problems* 129; Deborah L. Rhode, *supra* n. 54, and "Into the Valley of Ethics: Professional Responsibility and Educational Reform" (1995) 58 *Law and Contemporary Problems* 139.

qualitative differences between BVC and LPC, I suggest vocational ethics teaching is grounded in what I have elsewhere called a weak pervasive model[70] which focuses too instrumentally on the teaching of professional conduct. I suggest such courses will do little to diminish the pragmatic, risk-management, response to ethical issues that dominates the world of practice.

This kind of criticism appears implicit also in the position adopted by the Lord Chancellor's Advisory Committee in its *First Report,* which doubted whether:

> "the present approach. . . is sufficient to meet the complex ethical issues that lawyers are likely to face in modern practice. Professional ethics and conduct should certainly form a central part in the extended education that we hope intending solicitors and barristers will receive in future. Students must be made aware of the values that legal solutions carry, and of the ethical and humanitarian dimensions of law as an instrument which affects the quality of life."[71]

ACLEC's own proposals offer an "integrated" response to the problem: a greater emphasis on legal ethics and values at the initial stage of legal education; a core course on the principles of professional legal ethics within a new, common intermediate award, the Licentiate in Professional Legal Studies; and a pervasive approach to professional conduct in the revised LPC/BVC. I have to say that I share much of Richard O'Dair's scepticism about ACLEC's chances of achieving a meaningful consensus on these reforms from the range of academic and professional interest groups involved. Nevertheless, let us evaluate what is on offer.

(a) Structure

What ACLEC seems to have in mind is a progressive particularisation of the ethical focus of legal education.

At the initial stage, the implication seems to be that students are to focus primarily on the general system ethics: the values implicit in the legal system and in substantive areas such as Criminal Law and Tort. These might be supported by options in jurisprudence and moral philosophy, with perhaps some sociology of law and of the legal professions, and possibly by clinical options.

At the Licentiate stage, ACLEC offers a framework, but relatively little detail or prescription. Broadly, it proposes that the course should constitute an "intellectually rigorous" programme built around common transferable skills and values, with an emphasis on integrated learning. The *Report* offers one indicative example which suggests a programme of four or five modules, focusing on professional responsibility, dispute resolution, accounts and two substantive options. The professional responsibility module specifically

---

[70] Webb, *supra* n. 38, 292.
[71] *First Report,* para. 1.19.

addresses "general principles, with projects in civil and criminal procedure and evidence".[72] The possibility of some in-course practical experience through short work placements is also mooted. The whole course should be of fifteen to eighteen weeks duration, and may be followed by a first (six month) period of in-service training under a General Training Agreement (GTA).

ACLEC's proposals for the LPC/BVC also restrict it to a fifteen to eighteen week period, with the net result that the Licentiate and LPC/BVC would continue to operate within the established thirty to thirty-six week time frame of the established vocational courses. Again, the substantive detail is not fully developed, but the general principle is that each course should focus, through a general core, on the reserved or primary areas of work undertaken by each branch of the profession, with specialist options in addition. Both courses would seek to develop lawyering skills beyond the level expected of the Licentiate, while work on the professional conduct rules would be expected to pervade all aspects of the course.

From the ethics perspective, the overall logic of what is proposed is hard to fault. The approach offered is much more structured than what has gone before, and recognises the need to commit more time and resources to the ethical preparation of future professionals. Its emphasis on progression is consistent with a shift along the continuum towards a more developmental approach, though quite *how* developmental is left to the detail of course design. However, as I shall explain, I have reservations about the form and substance of some of what is on offer, and I would ultimately question whether ACLEC has itself missed the opportunity to follow its own logic to a conclusion.

(b) Educational Coherence

A central feature of the ACLEC Report has been the attempt to make the process of legal education and training more flexible, particularly through the provision of multiple entry and exit points to the process. From the point of view of access, this is commendable, though not without some dangers. From the perspective of coherence and comprehensibility, the benefits are rather more debatable. The Licentiate is intended as a free-standing intermediate qualification which would qualify lawyers for careers other than the traditional legal professions. As I have argued elsewhere, I have some doubts about the market value of such a qualification,[73] but let us just focus on the "professional responsibility" dimension.

---

[72] *Ibid.*, para. 5.14.
[73] See "Post-Fordism and the Reformation of Liberal Legal Education" in F. Cownie (ed.), *The Law School: Global Issues, Local Questions* (forthcoming).

If the course is to service a range of careers—including perhaps a nascent new breed of paralegals with the Licentiate qualification—should we teach a more generic form of professional responsibility? To be sure there are some interesting analogies waiting to be made. Different occupational groups do face some common problems—say of confidentiality or conflicts of interest, and there probably are things that lawyers could learn from the comparison. But there are obviously limits: others do not necessarily treat our ethical dilemmas as problems of ethics and, where they do, the contexts and outcomes may be very different. Even if, as is more realistic, we take a more restrictive view of the likely career paths of our students, just how far are the ethical responsibilities of qualified lawyers and these new paralegals to be treated as equivalent? The point is that the ethical problems of certain kinds of lawyers may be sufficiently distinctive to reduce knowledge transfer if we move too far down the path of generality. This may even be a problem, perhaps not so much in respect of the division between solicitors and barristers, between those engaged in contentious and non-contentious work.

If transfer is one problem, retention may be another. For example, a student might do the Licentiate, then work for six months, then do the LPC. Will the value of the "principles" approach developed on the first course be sustained until entry to the second? This might be arguable if the work is under a GTA; but what if the student is taking six months, or even a year, out doing something else, because it will actually earn her enough to pay her way through the LPC? Just what should the shelf-life of the Licentiate be?

(c) More and Better?

History tells us that more certainly does not necessarily equal better. In the United States the Stanley Commission's[74] attempt to redeem professionalism involved a call for more training in professional responsibility, without giving much indication of what was required. Perhaps it is not surprising, then, that this call was answered largely quantitatively by the law schools. As Gordon and Simon note, "[the report's] influence will more likely frustrate than advance the more ethically ambitious interpretations of the professionalism project".[75] In the *First Report* also much is left to the discretion of course designers. This is perhaps a pity. As the old saying has it "the devil lies in the detail" and I for one would have been interested to see a stronger lead, consistent with the emphasis on professional values and on active learning elsewhere in the *Report*.

[74] ABA Commission on Professionalism, ". . . . *In the Spirit of Public Service": A Blueprint for the Rekindling of Lawyer Professionalism* (Chicago, Ill., American Bar Foundation, 1986).

[75] "The Redemption of Professionalism" in R. L. Nelson, D. M. Trubek and R. L. Solomon (eds.), *Lawyers' Ideals/Lawyers' Practices* (Ithaca, NY, Cornell UP, 1992), 236, though cf. Bryant Garth and Joanne Martin, "Law Schools and the Construction of Competence" (1993) 43 *Journal of Legal Education* 469 at 502–3, which offers a more optimistic assessment.

(d) Integrating Work and Learning

A more developmental approach at the vocational stage is not guaranteed by itself to produce more morally responsible practitioners, even though there is some evidence of a modest correlation between "improvements" in moral judgement and moral behaviour.[76]

The real challenge is whether any such changes can survive the impact of entry into the working environment and the pressures that involves. The evidence from research is that workplace experiences are a stronger determinant of professional behaviour than education.[77] I suggest, however, that, as some of the more recent scholarship on social and cognitive development suggests, the basic problem is not as simple as work versus learning; rather it is that we cannot separate the context from our thinking and doing.[78] The situation we are in does not just influence our behaviour, it is part of it. If we are to change the behaviour we might need to do more to influence the context. This point of view has not been adequately addressed by ACLEC, and it suggests that perhaps we need to look at a more radical solution than ACLEC has proposed.

VIII. A WAY FORWARD?

The key issue seems to be how can we achieve closer integration of education and workplace training, particularly to give students the opportunity to reflect on practical workplace experience in the educational environment? This is unlikely to be achievable *via* the optional 'thick sandwich' model of Licentiate, GTA and LPC/BVC envisaged by ACLEC, and any alternative block-release model is likely to come up against funding difficulties (amongst other things).

A rather different option which perhaps comes close enough to the ideal has been advanced in very broad outline by Avrom Sherr.[79] It utilises one variation on the ACLEC model of an integrated Masters in Professional Legal Studies (MPLS). As Sherr envisages this, it would be a course of approximately eighteen months' duration, combining Licentiate, GTA, LPC/BVC and wholly replacing the remaining training contract/pupillage.[80]

---

[76] See e.g., Walter Mischel and Harriet N. Mischel, "A Cognitive Social-Learning Approach to Morality and Self-Regulation" in Lickona (ed.), *supra* n. 42.

[77] Lawrence K. Hellman, "The Effects of Law Office Work on the Formation of Law Students' Professional Values" (1991) 4 *Georgetown Journal of Legal Ethics* 537 at 616, and the general studies cited by Rhode, *supra* n. 69, at 44–8.

[78] Cf. Barbara Rogoff, *Apprenticeship in Thinking* (New York, Oxford University Press, 1990).

[79] "Vocational Education and Training—A Critique" in ACLEC, *First Report on Legal Education and Training: Report of the Proceedings of the Conference Held on 8 July 1996* (London, ACLEC, 1996), 35 at 44; I hope Professor Sherr will excuse my hijacking his idea.

[80] Though Sherr is silent on this, I suggest there might be a case for maintaining a period of, say, 6 months' restricted practice, requiring some additional CPD and office supervision, so that

The key to this course is reliance on a substantial element of clinical simulation.[81] Along with many others, I also take the view that clinic provides potentially the best environment for teaching practice, and specifically professional ethics, in a relatively realistic but manageable fashion.[82]

Clinical learning could be supported by some of the traditional and experiential teaching and learning methods of the existing courses. But more developmental and reflective techniques, which are already well established in business and professional education—such as mentoring of trainees, problem-based learning, the use of learning logs and action plans, etc.—could and should also be introduced.[83] In terms of professional ethics, the course should combine both a free-standing "foundation" course emphasising the general principles of professional legal ethics with a pervasive clinical experience across the range of substantive areas which would enable students to work through the stages identified by Rest and Narvaez. I would also argue that there might be a case for maintaining some degree of separate ethics tuition beyond the "foundation"—possibly in a workshop format in which students could be encouraged to discuss in greater depth and to integrate ethical issues experienced in the substantive courses. Properly implemented, such a programme has, I propose, a better chance of bridging the gap between law school and practice than the existing courses.

The profession also needs to consider the role of continuing professional development (CPD) in professional conduct and ethics. Little CPD for solicitors focuses specifically on issues of conduct and ethics. The Bar has recently made it a requirement that barristers take a minimum of four hours' CPD on professional conduct in the first three years of practice, which is some acknowledgment that the area has some special status. There seems to be no logical reason why a similar requirement should not apply to solicitors.[84] It is worth noting that ACLEC, in its recent *Second Report,* has come to a similar conclusion, and has called on the professions to prescribe CPD in professional ethics for all practitioners in their first three years of practice.[85] Perhaps a little less expected is the suggestion that the professions should issue guidance on appropriate CPD on conduct issues *beyond* the initial three years. This is accompanied by what the profession will surely see as a thinly veiled threat:

the newly qualified practitioner does not immediately find herself facing the uncontrolled pressures of a fully fledged assistant solicitor or junior barrister: cf. P. K. Cooper, "Training Solicitors: The Expectations of the Profession" (1985) 3(1) *Journal of Professional Legal Education* 57.

[81] Sherr uses the phrase "fully simulated clinical course", *supra* n. 79. My own view is that considerations of cost and scale would make the live client clinical model unrealisable in this context.

[82] Webb, *supra* n. 38; also Rhode, *supra* n. 69; Luban, *supra* n. 52.

[83] Cf. Cruickshank, *supra* n. 66; Mike Maughan, "A Capability Approach to Assessing Skills on the LPC" in Webb and Maughan (eds.), *supra* n. 55.

[84] It is interesting that 3 out of the 5 LPC teachers I interviewed volunteered their support for requiring professional conduct CPD in the first 3 years following the PSC.

[85] *Continuing Professional Development for Solicitors and Barristers: A Second Report on Legal Education and Training* (London, ACLEC, July 1997), para. 2.33.

you should monitor the extent to which your guidance is followed, and if it is ignored by too many practitioners, you should be ready to extend compulsion beyond the three years.[86]

But just as for the earlier stages of training, more is not necessarily better—especially if it is imposed by compulsion. If the developmental model is to be sustained then it will demand forms of CPD that are more innovative and challenging than much of what exists at present.[87] Provided a more developmental approach is instilled through the early years, then, in theory, this should be achievable using many of the mechanisms already considered.

IX. CONCLUSION: TOWARDS LIFELONG ETHICAL LEARNING?

A key theme of the ACLEC *First* and *Second Reports*, and of much of the recent literature on higher and professional education, has been the need to instill habits of lifelong learning. Lifelong learning demands that we enable students and practitioners to become self-motivating and intellectually independent and self-reflective individuals. As ACLEC acknowledges, these habits need to be instilled at the initial and vocational stages to a greater degree than at present. While, as I have sought to show, there is much in the recent ACLEC *Report* that is supportive of that aim, more could be done at the vocational stage to increase both the depth and ethical realism of the learning experience, and to provide students with the conceptual tools to become more reflective practitioners. A revised MPLS offers one model whereby this might be achieved. But it would not by itself provide a sufficient, continuing, basis for development through the early years of practice. Hence the call in this chapter for a greater focus on new forms of CPD to support the learning of professional conduct and ethics.

More fundamentally, if we are to change the context of professional behaviour, I suggest education is not enough. I return again to the codes of conduct. We also need to think about their form and content. This is obviously a far larger topic than I can do justice to here, but I will briefly offer three related suggestions. First, that, particularly in the context of the core ethics, there needs to be a greater recognition of general principles that are capable of speaking to an increasingly fragmented profession. Secondly, there is a case for developing a stronger moral and less regulatory language. Thirdly, there may be grounds for giving practitioners more autonomy and discretion in some areas so that it becomes less easy, or less necessary, to use the codes defensively.

Such changes are not insubstantial, nor are they uncontroversial. They probably still fall well short of an answer to the current crisis of professionalism, but they might just constitute the start we need to face up to the ethical challenges of the twenty-first century.

---

[86] *Ibid.*

[87] Cf. *First Report*, para. 6.29. ACLEC's *Second Report* is essentially silent on matters of delivery.

15

The Politics of Decontextualized Knowledge: Bringing Context into Ethics Instruction in Law School*

ROBERT GRANFIELD

I. INTRODUCTION

There are two theoretical propositions that enjoy prominent standing within educational sociology. The first adduces the general principle that curricular knowledge in its various forms is social, existing not in some independent ethereal realm but, rather, constructed within a complex of political, cultural and ideological presuppositions. This proposition asserts that the knowledge constructed within schools is generally arbitrary, a point that was not lost on Herbert Spencer when he asked the question "[W]hat knowledge is of most worth?" Curricular knowledge typically answers Spencer's query by reifying concepts, principles and epistemological rationales disseminable as common sensical "official knowledge" under a rubric of objectivity, neutrality and naturalness.[1] Official knowledge, however, always involves a complex process of selection before it gets to be declared legitimate. Schools disseminate a particular common sense selected from a broad range of alternative possibilities.

A second related proposition that has spawned important research in educational sociology is the principle of institutional embeddedness. This principle declares that neither educational institutions themselves nor the complex activity within them can be understood independently of their relationship to social structures and dynamics occurring outside schools. For instance, no schooling process can be considered separate from the economic foundations of society, divisions based on differences in race, class and

* An earlier version of this chapter was presented at Stanford Law School, November, 1994. Data for this chapter were collected during a Keck Fellowship at Harvard Law School. Special thanks to David Wilkins and the Program on Legal Profession.

[1] M. Apple, *Official Knowledge*, 1993 (arguing that "educational policy and practice are the results of struggles by powerful groups and social movements to make their knowledge legitimate, to defend or increase their patterns of social mobility, and to increase their power in the larger social arena").

gender, labor markets, social movements or cultural traditions within which educational institutions are embedded.[2] Schooling is best understood only in relation to the ongoing social life that exists beyond a school's tangible but immensely permeable borders. Schools, including professional schools, are not isolated institutions, but are situated within a particular social, economic, political and cultural context that inescapably affects the practices of teachers and the experiences of students.[3]

I wish to employ these propositions in order to explore the experience of being schooled in law and the related implications associated with legal practice. By grounding legal education and student experiences within these general propositions, I want to argue that the transformation of law student ideologies in law school is a response to both internal conditions prevalent within law school curriculum and culture as well as the social and professional life existing outside law schools. In addressing the newly constructed identities law students assume during law school, it is not enough simply to attend to the law school curriculum independently of external social conditions. Student identities emerge through the adoption of ideologies acquired in school that connect to lived experience, but also in relation to the social patterns and movements occurring within society over time. Thus, I wish to explore how student identities, particularly their occupational decisions and ideologies concerning ethical practice, emerge within an embedded context of internal and external realities.

II. LEGAL EDUCATION AND DECONTEXTUALIZATION

Almost since their development in the late 1800s, American law schools have been embroiled in vociferous debates over the form and content of legal pedagogy. Legal education has represented ideologically contested terrain ever since the days of Langdell.[4] The institutionalization of Langdell's scientific method was not easily won.[5] In his 1978 book on the clash of professional

---

[2] See, generally, P. Bourdieu and J. C. Passerson, *Reproduction in Education, Society and Culture*, 1977 (arguing that schooling is intimately connected with family background); P. Willis, *Learning to Labor*, 1977 (arguing that working class boys accept working class jobs because of cultural values supporting masculinity); P. Cookson and C. Persell, *Preparing for Power*, 1982 (arguing that preparatory school education prepares students to assume high-status positions in society).

[3] My previous work on the socialization of Harvard law students offers detailed analysis of how the context of legal education affects student decisions about legal practice. See R. Granfield, *Making Elite Lawyers*, 1992.

[4] Christopher Columbus Langdell is considered to be the founder of the modern law school pedagogy.

[5] Langdell believed that law was a science in which objective standards were to be discovered in law school. According to Langdell:

"Law, considered as a science, consists of certain principles or doctrines. To have a mastery of these as to be able to apply them with constant facility and certainty to the ever-tangled

cultures, Walter Johnson captures the pedagogical wars waged over the definition of legal education. As Johnson writes:

> "By 1900 the sources of agreed upon principles of justice and fairness had become objects of disagreement. The older generation of lawyers, trained in the nineteenth century but completing their careers as eminent practitioners in the twentieth century, would continue to rely upon broad moral principles as the basis for justice. Case lawyers, especially those who were taught in the major universities, would, in contrast, rely upon a narrow scientific historicism for their sources of justice."[6]

The struggle over the form, content and purpose of a law school education has continued into the twentieth century.[7]

Legal education continues to be contested terrain. It has become almost a cliché to criticize law schools for failing adequately to prepare law students for the contingencies which they must face as lawyers. Many in the legal profession bemoan what they see as the loss of traditional doctrinal pedagogy in law school. From this perspective, law schools are said to be experiencing declining standards by failing to teach practical skills, techniques of doctrinal analysis and ethical standards and virtues.[8] Some legal educators stand accused of practicing impractical scholarship and pedagogy.[9] Others have criticized law schools for their recent trends of urging narratives that stress the historical uniqueness of legal cases, pedagogies that import abstract theory to expose the assorted latent values that hide beneath the surface of legal doctrine, or pedagogies that give voice to subordinated perspectives.[10]

A completely different critique has criticized legal education for being too far removed from the actual context of legal practice. Upon graduation, the typical law school student has had negligible client contact and has learned

---

skein of human affairs is what constitutes a true lawyer; and hence to acquire that mastery should be the business of every earnest student of law."
See Granfield, *supra* n. 3 (citing Langdell).

[6] W. Johnson, *Schooled Lawyers: A Study in the Clash of Professional Culture*, 1978, 118.

[7] See generally, T. Koenig and M. Rustad, "The Challenge to Hierarchy in Legal Education: Suffolk and the Night School Movement", (1985) 7 *Research in Law, Deviance and Social Control* 189 (arguing that the night school movement was opposed by elite law schools like Harvard). See also R. Stevens, *Law School: Legal Education in America from the 1850's to the 1980's*, 1993.

[8] Perhaps the most turgid critique of the failure of law schools to educate graduates to deal with complex legal realities is A. Kronman, *The Lost Lawyer: Failing Ideals of the Legal Profession*, 1993. Kronman cites the "decline" of law school instruction for failing to promote the character traits of deliberative wisdom and public-spiritedness that are associated with the "lawyer-statesman". For a review of Kronman, see A. Alfieri, "Denaturalizing the Lawyer-Statesman" (1995) 93 *Mich. L. Rev.* 1204.

[9] For a general discussion of this critique of legal education, see H. Edwards, "The Growing Disjunction Between Legal Education and the Legal Profession" (1992) 91 *Mich. L. Rev.* 34.

[10] See L. Alexander, "What We Do, and Why We Do It" (1885) 45 *Stan. L. Rev.* Alexander is particularly forceful in his opposition to multicultural perspectives in legal education, such as those advocated by critical race theorists (arguing that "there is one movement in legal education that we should vigorously resist, and that is the movement that goes beyond deemphasizing formality toward multicultural balkinization of the law itself") at 1902.

law in the absence of actual clients. These neophyte lawyers will, perhaps for the first time, come into direct contact with the messy world of legal practice complete with clients, corporate entities, other miscellaneous interested communities, families, governmental regulations and regulators, colleagues and partners, opposing counsel and a host of other assorted players. For many young lawyers, these initial practice experiences can be emotionally and intellectually overwhelming.

Austin Sarat, for instance, writes that law students "have learned little about encountering people in situations of stress and fashioning solutions to their problems in ways that are responsive to the human as well as legal dimensions of the problems".[11] For the greater part of their three years, law students study and debate law as if it were an isolated social institution independent of the complex, often ambiguous social contexts within which it is located and the "sunken theoretical and empirical suppositions of lawyers practices".[12] As if this were not enough, rarely will any of these graduates have more than a shred of accurate information concerning legal practice nor will they have been made privy to reflective analyses about the social contradictions of lawyering in a way that would allow for more informed decisions regarding their professional lives.

These two pedagogical paradigms, the traditional doctrinal approach and the social contextual approach, are engaged in what sometimes is a bitter struggle over the control of legal education. I want to suggest that it is only through a contextual pedagogy, one that takes seriously the intricate connections between what is taught and the context of practice including social inequality, organizational hierarchy, gender and racial discrimination, and economic pressures, that questions of professionalization and ethics can be addressed in meaningful ways that will ultimately have the greatest value for law students.[13]

The dominant paradigm within law school pedagogy cultivates professional identities that divorce students from the social context of law by teaching that legal doctrine is neutral, rational, and objective, and that lawyers constitute an ethical community of autonomous experts who contribute to the maintenance of social order.[14] This conventional view of lawyering assumes that professionals are independent specialists who "stand above or apart from the competing social, economic, and political bases of power in the society" and therefore play "a mediating or integrative role serving to draw disparate ele-

---

[11] A. Sarat, "Lawyers and Clients: Putting Professional Service on the Agenda of Legal Education" (1991) 41 *Journal of Legal Education* 43.

[12] R. Gordon, "Lawyers, Scholars, and the 'Middle Ground' " (1993) 91 *Mich. L. Rev.* 2075, 2098.

[13] See Eleanor Myers, " 'Simple Truths' About Moral Education" (1996)45 *Am. U. L. Rev.* 823, 824 (arguing that "if our educational efforts are to make a contribution to the revival of professionalism, our teaching should be informed by an appreciation for the dominant role that the culture and values of the workplace have on the way that lawyers behave professionally").

[14] See Granfield, *supra* n. 3.

ments together, to resolve conflicts among them, and thus to preserve or enhance the functioning of the society".[15] Rarely, however, are these professional ideals themselves, the associated ideology of professionalism and professionalizing pedagogies within law school subjected to critical inspection.

In contrast to this conventional view, perhaps a more revealing analysis of professional legal ideals and practices, and the pedagogy that produces them, would depict them as constructed realities possessing largely unexamined normative assumptions. Curricular knowledge is after all selected knowledge; it does not invent itself.[16] From this perspective, the curricular knowledge, the ideologies law students and lawyers develop and place into action, as well as the institutional structures that give rise to practical wisdom among professionals need to be theorized and empirically researched. It was this general perspective that was the driving theoretical force behind my work on legal education.[17]

Law schools, like other educational institutions, are characterized by a "symbolic violence" that constructs norms, values and cultural dispositions that social actors, for the most part, willingly accept.[18] The knowledge and dispositions that emerge are not elements of a false consciousness, but rather become part of a new common sense that is fundamentally consistent with the predominance of a market-based understanding of social relations and a particular form of democratic life that is elitist, as opposed to participatory. Law schools monopolize the "juridical field" of legitimate knowledge and teach law as natural and neutral.[19] The juridical field presented through legal education is characterized by a norm of perspectivelessness in which students are taught that "it is possible to create, weigh and evaluate rules and arguments in ways that neither reflect nor privilege any particular perspective of the world".[20]

The world views and visions of law and practice are constituted through the symbolic boundaries contained within legal education. The symbolic boundaries contained within any professional group, such as the legal profession, represent powerful forces in the construction of professional identity.[21] The fact that there is considerable pedagogical similarity across the diverse

[15] J. Heinz, "The Power of Lawyers" (1983) 17 *Ga. L. Rev.* 891.

[16] Apple, *supra* n. 1.

[17] Granfield, *supra* n. 3.

[18] See Bourdieu and Passeron, *supra* n. 2 (arguing that "all pedagogic action is, objectively, symbolic violence insofar as it is the imposition of a cultural arbitrary by an arbitrary power").

[19] P. Bourdieu, "The Force of Law: Toward a Sociology of the Juridical Field" (1987) 38 *Hastings L. J.* 805.

[20] K. Crenshaw, "Forward: Toward a Race-Conscious Pedagogy in Legal Education" (1989) 11 *National Black LJ* 1, 3,.

[21] See, generally, E. Freidson, *Professional Power* (1986) (arguing that occupational groups seek to elevate their position in society by claiming professional status). See also M. Larson, *The Rise of Professionalism* (1977) (arguing that professions engage in "collective mobility projects" as a way of establishing monopolies in order to control the allocation of professional services). For a discussion of Larson's work on collective mobility projects as it relates to the American legal profession, see R. Abel, *American Lawyers*, 1989.

spectrum of American law schools demonstrates the power these symbolic boundaries have in the reproduction of professional social roles.[22] Boundaries dramatize professional order by establishing the cognitive, normative and educational requirements, i.e. symbols of cultural capital, that are necessary to attain a privileged status in society.[23] The construction of these boundaries, as well as law schools' lockstep pursuit of prestige symbols, has produced a virtual educational hegemony which has undermined laudable goals of equal distribution of legal services.[24] Law students who challenge the institutionalized, dominant common sense within legal education complete with its proclivity toward gamesmanship and ideological boundaries, have often earned vociferous attacks from some law professors and peers.[25]

Among contemporary social theorists, Pierre Bourdieu is perhaps the most instructive in light of this discussion. Writing and conducting research in France during the 1960s, Bourdieu was primarily concerned with the lack of success working class students experienced in higher education. In his attempts to work out a theory of this problematic, Bourdieu developed the concept he refers to as the "habitus". Bourdieu employs this concept to explain the relationship between constructed visions of the world and the proclivity of social actors to contribute to the maintenance of external structures in pursuing their own subjective ends. The habitus is defined abstractly as the system of internalized dispositions that mediates between social structures and practical activity, being shaped by the former and regulating the latter.

The habitus of legal practitioners might be described as the principle producing practices that are "strongly patterned by tradition, education and the daily experiences of legal custom and professional usage".[26] Because lawyers share similar educational trajectories they "share forms of habitus characterized by internal resemblances within the group—habitual, patterned ways of understanding, judging, arguing, and acting—that arise from their position as members of a specific social field, playing a particular social game".[27] These learned but deeply internalized structures of behavior tend to cause the group's practices and its sense of identity to remain stable over time. It is through the mediation of the habitus that the categories and boundaries of

---

[22] See W. S. Van Alstyne, J. Julin and L. Barnett, *The Goals and Mission of Law Schools* 1992 (arguing that law schools model themselves after the "prestige image" of elite institutions). For a review of this thesis, see R. Granfield, "The Goals and Mission of Law Schools" (1993) 17 *Legal Stud. Forum* 1.

[23] R. Granfield, "Constituting Professional Boundaries in Law School: Reactions of Students and Implications for Teachers" (1994) 4 *S. Cal. Rev. of L. and Wom. Stud.* 1 (arguing that law students narrow their perspectives in law school).

[24] Granfield, *supra* n. 22, at 114 (arguing that "the lockstep pace with which law schools chase prestige symbols reproduces a hegemony within legal education that is ultimately detrimental to the production and distribution of legal services").

[25] Granfield, *supra* n. 3.

[26] R. Terdiman, "Translator's Introduction" (1987) 38 *Hastings LJ* 805, 807.

[27] R. Coombe, "Room for Manoeuvre: Toward a Theory of Practice in Critical Legal Studies" (1989) 14 *Law & Soc. Inq.* 69, 104.

perception "incline agents to accept the social world as it is, take it for granted, rather than rebel against it, to counterpose to it different, even antagonistic possibilities".[28]

Bourdieu's theory is not unlike the indeterminacy arguments posed by critical legal scholars, postmodern legal feminists and critical race theorists who maintain that identities are constructed through legal discourse in ways that subordinate historically marginalized groups by privileging ahistorical and acontextual perceptions of law. The legal knowledge as taught in law school is, in a sense, arbitrary. Legal knowledge separates what is thinkable from what is unthinkable; what is practical from what is impractical. It defines what is important and attempts to distinguish it from the trivial. It is bounded, institutionalized social practice that confers meaning upon deeds. Law school teaches an ordinary religion, the assumed ground rules of society as Kennedy calls them, that privileges perspectivelessness, toughmindedness, instrumentality, skepticism, cynicism and individualism.[29] As Gerald Lopez has written:

> "Legal education conceives of and treats people, their traditions, their experience, and their institutions as essentially fungible. It declares, at least tacitly, that two people are, how they live, how they struggle, how they survive, how they interact with others, how others interact with them, and how they relate to conventional government and corporate power need not be taken into account in any sustained and serious way in training lawyers. Generic legal education teaches law students to approach practice as if all people and all social life were homogenous."[30]

The absence of social context and perspective in legal education, however, fails to alert attorneys to the dangers of "higher immoralities", a term C. Wright Mills used to describe the institutionalized immorality and organized irresponsibility associated with American capitalism.[31] It also fails adequately to prepare students to deal with questions of community interest, inequality and the related contradictions of practice. Too little of what goes into law school today bears any relationship to either actual legal practice or the lives of those who utilize legal services. Perhaps the greatest disjuncture between law school and practice exists within the separation of law from the actual social contexts in which law, lawyers, their clients and their communities are embedded.

---

[28] P. Bourdieu, "The Social Space and the Genesis of Groups" (1985) 14 *Theory & Society* 723, 728.

[29] R. Campton, "The Ordinary Religion of the Law School Classroom" (1978) 29 *J. Legal Educ.* 247. See also D. Kennedy, *Sexy Dressing: Essays on the Power and Politics of Cultural Identity* 1993 (arguing that legal discourse provide the legal rules for social legitimation).

[30] G. Lopez, "Training Future Lawyers to Work with the Politically and Socially Subordinated: Anti-Generic Legal Education" (1989) 91 *W Va. L Rev.* 305, 307.

[31] C. Wright Mills, *The Power Elite* (1951) (arguing that the powerful, through their domination of the law and other social institutions, can behave immorally without fear of sanction).

During law school, students learn that the social context of a case is irrelevant and distracting. The dominant message conveyed throughout the process of legal education is that students should become toughminded, hyper-rational and insensitive to issues beyond the interests of their client. The law school experience encourages students to perceive the world with detached cynicism. Legal issues are reduced to the level of gross manipulation and gamesmanship. Non-legalistic views of justice are often critiqued as being naïve and simplistic. As a result, students become adept advocates, trained to ignore the social implications of the position being advanced. For example, plant closings are isolated from the devastating effects on people's lives, criminal law is removed from the racist and classist assumptions embedded within its construction and application and legal practice itself is reified in such a way that it is all but completely removed from the actual vagaries of practice. Jerome Auerbach was correct when he said that the legal mind is one that "can think of something that is inextricably connected to something else without thinking about what it is connected to".[32] Law schools are quite adept at teaching this skill.

Even ethics courses, which became mandatory in the wake of Watergate,[33] frequently ignore social contexts by often adopting conventional principles of legal pedagogy. They also tend to compartmentalize ethics and isolate these concerns from other areas of law.[34] De-contextualized instruction in ethics makes students "vulnerable in professional responsibility discussions both to myths fueled by their own fears and hopes and to the authority of the teacher".[35] De-contextualized legal education accords too little attention to how "the market and organizational structures, career patterns, professional self-images, firm cultures, financial pressures, patronage networks and power-hierarchies condition how lawyers see their jobs, self-interest, loyalties, obligations, and develop practical moralities, and how these conceptions play out in their work".[36]

Surveys have shown that students regard ethics courses as inferior to those that teach legal skills.[37] For the most part, such courses are perceived as the

---

[32] J. Auerbach, "What Has the Teaching of Law to do with Justice?" (1978) 53 *NYU L. Rev.* 42.

[33] See R. Abel, "Why Does the American Bar Association Promulgate Ethical Rules?" (1981) 59 *Texas L. Rev.* 639.

[34] See C. Croft, "Reconceptualizing American Legal Professionalism: A Proposal for a Deliberative Moral Community" (1992) 67 *NYU L. Rev.* 1256, 1339 (arguing that "by 'fencing off' [law school ethical] discourse with a limited credit, delayed enrollment course, providing precious little time for extending discussions beyond the uninspiring rules of the Model Code and Model Rules, legal education effectively insulates discussions of legal professional standards from the rest of the law school curriculum").

[35] R. Gordon and W. Simon, "The Redemption of Professionalism?" in R. Nelson, D. Trubek and R. Solomon (eds.), *Lawyers' Ideals/Lawyers' Practices: Transformations in the American Legal Profession* (1992), 240.

[36] Gordon, *supra* n. 12, at 2088.

[37] R. Pipkin, "Law School Instruction in Professional Responsibility: A Curricular Paradox" (1979) 2 *ABF Res. J.* 247.

"dog of the law school curriculum" in which students learn the rules without a foundation to challenge their premises and to explore their limitation.[38] By merely teaching standards and failing to explore the actual problems lawyers face across differentiated practices, ethics courses lose their potential value. Ethics, like law itself, become mechanized and instrumentalized in a way that, according to the critical theorist Max Horkheimer, "takes on a kind of materiality and blindness" which undermines the development of any broader vision of social life.[39]

One reason for the low regard for ethics courses is that students correctly see that the lessons have little to do with the social contradictions lawyers confront in their daily practice. In law school, ethics are often reduced to narrow rules that define the practices that the legal profession deems problematic. In such courses, students generally lack the opportunity to engage in critical self-reflection and are left to develop various cognitive dissonance reducing strategies to deal with the contradictions and conflicts they experience.[40] Law students frequently deal with the contradictions of lawyering, particularly as it relates to law's inherent perspectivelessness and acontextuality, by engaging in such ideological work as claiming to be committed to *pro bono*, believing they will refuse morally uncomfortable cases, or by seeing their work as neutral.[41]

For the most part, the canons of ethical responsibility reinforce assumptions of individualism, competence, autonomy and neutrality that law students experience in other courses. Ethical dilemmas are redefined in terms of occupational malfeasance such as conflicts of interest, impropriety or courtroom conduct as opposed to larger normative questions regarding morality, power or community. Such issues are considered to fall outside the purview of most legal ethics courses, and outside the realm of legal practice itself. Ethical lessons in law school fail to stimulate reflective understanding of the ways that professional norms shape human relationships.[42] Who one represents and what is at stake are less an issue than how that representation is carried out. In this way, legal ethics, like legal education generally, co-opts students' pre-law moral codes.

---

[38] D. Rhode, "Missing Questions: Feminist Perspectives on Legal Education" (1993) 45 *Stan. L. Rev.* 1547, 1561.

[39] M. Horkheimer, *Eclipse of Reason*, 1947 (arguing that formalization of reason "becomes a fetish, a magic entity that is accepted rather than intellectually experienced").

[40] See R. Granfield and T. Koenig, "The Fate of Elite Idealism: Accommodation and Ideological Work at Harvard Law School" (1992) 39 *Social Problems* 4 (arguing that law students experience psychological conflict over their career decisions).

[41] *Ibid.* (arguing that law students use several strategies to resolve the conflicts they experience).

[42] Rhode, *supra* n. 37.

III. CONTEXTUALIZING ETHICS IN LEGAL PRACTICE

The dearth of social context limits the usefulness and potential of legal ethics courses. Follow-up interviews I have conducted with several original participants in my book reveal that they almost uniformly felt that their ethics training in law school bore little resemblance to the issues they were confronting as practicing attorneys.[43] Only three of the forty respondents characterized their ethics course as valuable preparation for legal practice.[44] The vast majority reported that their ethics course merely provided them with formalistic instruction about the rules of professional responsibility that were largely silent on the fundamental contradictions inherent in their practice.

Many respondents criticised their courses in legal ethics for severing cases from the social, political, and organizational contexts in which they were embedded. They argued that the model rules taught in law school had little bearing on their daily activities as lawyers. One woman who was working at a large law firm explained that:

> "I don't think ethics classes did much at all. My ethics class was really a study of the model rules and the model codes. It was about conflicts of interest and that kind of thing but it didn't teach you at all about the kinds of issues that really come up. . . . I don't think it really trains you to know what to do or to feel strongly one way or the other."

Several respondents complained that the ethics cases presented to them in law school were too nebulous to provide much guidance. Even some public inter-

[43] Data for this chapter were collected as part of a longitudinal study of the professional lives of elite lawyers: see Granfield, *supra* n. 3. Forty Harvard Law School graduates who had been interviewed extensively as students were selected for in-depth follow-up interviews. This stratified sample was selected in order to ensure gender and racial diversity. Almost one-half of the interviewees were women and nearly one-quarter were minorities. This sample included attorneys working in a wide variety of professional settings in order to evaluate the relevance of ethics teaching to varying organizational contexts. Lawyers in this study were employed in such diverse settings as large law firms, in-house counsel, public interest practice, public defender, federal, state and local governments and boutique law firms. Extensive interviews were conducted to determine whether the ethical guidance that they received in law school had proven valuable and to examine what moral conflicts, if any, they were experiencing in their legal careers.

The average length of time since these lawyers had graduated from law school was 4 years. No respondent refused to be interviewed. Most expressed considerable interest in continuing to participate in the study. In-depth, tape-recorded interviews lasting approximately two hours were conducted with all 40 respondents, demonstrating their willingness to explore complex issues. A semi-structured interview guide that focused on the respondent's career path, work-related pressures, experiences with discrimination, the extent of respondent's preparation for legal work and ethical problems and dilemmas was utilized. This semi-structured format was used in order to elicit open-ended narratives from respondents. All interviews were conducted during a Keck Fellowship the author had at Harvard Law School.

[44] It should be noted that all these law students graduated from law school in the late 1980s, before many of the recent curricular efforts to improve ethical training. There have been significant changes in the teaching of legal ethics at Harvard Law School and elsewhere since this time. Many course now include context-based content: see (1995) 58 *Law and Contemporary Problems* 3/4 (reviewing several attempts to reform ethics education in law school).

est lawyers experienced this problem. One legal aid lawyer found her legal ethics course to be of little assistance, "because the rules of ethics are only attached to the worst cases or are too vague. They don't frankly come up a lot in the practice of law." The cases she had studied bore little relevance to the issues that arise in criminal defense:

> "The kinds of ethical problems that come up for me are questions about how to treat clients or problems with opposing counsel. Like how invasive do you get in a client's life to find out what's going on, how much you help them solve only the problems they bring to you and how much you have an obligation to get into their face and identify a problem they don't want to admit to. This could be everything from a women being battered to the person being an alcoholic. Courses on ethics are pretty silent on these things."

The rules of professional responsibility are theoretically universal, but in fact offer little guidance to help resolve the complex problems that poverty lawyers confront in their daily practices. What lawyers give to indigent clients by way of redeeming their community and what they sometimes take from them like dignity and self-determination is not typically explored.

Because courses in legal ethics emphasize individual rights even at the expense of community wellbeing, as Mary Ann Glendon argues, "our rights talk, in its absoluteness, promotes unrealistic expectations, heightens social conflict, and inhibits dialogue that might lead towards consensus, accommodation, or at least the discovery of common ground. In its silence concerning responsibilities, it seems to condone acceptance of the benefits of living in a democratic social welfare state, without excepting the corresponding civic and personal obligations."[45] Legal ethics classes generally ignore such communitarian concerns, preferring instead to focus on professional standards of responsibility. Yet these issues frequently arise in legal practice. One lawyer explained the dilemma of defending a drug dealer who was being evicted from his apartment:

> "No one in the community wants this person in the apartment anymore. It gets pretty heated because you get feedback from the community, and I often agree with them. People who sell drugs are bad for a community. No one tells you in the ethics class what to do in such cases. What is your duty to the client as it relates to the community. The model is totally based on the lawyer and the client, and you put the client first. There's not a lot of room in the model for the person who's also thinking about the community."

Nothing in the code of professional ethics satisfactorily addressed this type of dilemma. As she explained, in the absence of any relevant, contextual education, "[m]ostly, I fly by the seat of my pants". How a public interest lawyer works with indigenous and often subordinated communities is not typically considered the province of ethics.

---

[45] M. Glendon, *Rights Talk: The Impoverishment of Political Discourse*, 1991, 14.

Even those practicing in the large urban law firms report that their ethical training did not apply to the personal conflicts they experienced as advocates. One respondent who worked for a prestigious Washington-based law firm explained the shortcomings of his ethics course:

> "It didn't deal with the kinds of things I saw in practice. I don't think people in law school know or understand these issues. [As ethics are currently taught in law school], it's simply not a conflict of interest to represent the tobacco industry. As the profession defines ethical problems, there's no ethical problem with representing the tobacco institute. The kind of slimy ethics thing that I didn't run into is what they talk about in law school."

For many, it was ethical issues ignored by the code of professional conduct that troubled them as practitioners. One lawyer explained that the ethical code taught to her on the job is more relevant to her practice than the model code:

> "It's interesting because a lot of emphasis in the ethics course is about conflict of interest. When you work in a big firm, there's basically so much conflict of interest that there are whole departments that screen for conflicts of interest so it's never really a problem. What I would like to see is something like Professional Responsibility and Legal Culture. They could cover stuff like the glass ceiling, bureaucracy and hierarchy in the law firm. I think students really need to be given the opportunity to discuss practice issues and [courses should] bring in people to present these issues. I remember when I was in law school I didn't know anything about being a lawyer."

Sociologists have frequently noted the importance of social roles in defining behavior. Erving Goffman, for instance, defines a role as consisting of the activity the incumbent would engage in were he to act solely in terms of the normative demands upon someone in his position. Thus, all roles, including occupational ones, have moralities and boundaries that impose normative demands upon those occupying them. The morality associated with any particular role frequently distances that person from other salient roles[46] as well as the common morality prevalent in society.[47] This role morality draws occupationally-based boundaries that give professionals the privilege of freedom from being judged by many of the normative standards applied to the public as well as exonerate a person from the moral demands of that role.

Ethical dilemmas arise when the morality of one role conflicts with the morality of another role. For these lawyers the moral ambiguity produced by this dissonance was often substantial. However, in their interviews, the respondents reported that the actual conflicts they experienced rarely had

---

[46] S. Stryker and R. Serpe, "Commitment, Identity Salience, and Role Behavior: Theory and Research Example" [1982] *Personality, Roles and Social Behavior* 199 (arguing that individuals possess multiple roles, but some are more salient than others).

[47] D. Luban, *Lawyers and Justice: An Ethical Study* (1988) (arguing that lawyers rely on the principle of "nonaccountability" which states that lawyers are not the conscience of their clients. This norm protects lawyers from moral culpabilty).

much to do with the standard conception of professional ethics. Even when the code directly addressed a moral issue, professional standards often failed to resolve the conflicts. In practice, though, such questions are often not so easily dismissed. For example, when asked about how he handles the personal contradictions of representing toxic dumpers, one fourth year large law firm associate commented, "I just close my eyes and do it".

The role morality espoused by the code of professional ethics, actually desensitized many young lawyers to the moral dilemmas posed in the contradictions they experienced. By focusing on the technical correctness of their work, these attorneys overcame their moral qualms. They held to the letter of the code, believing that technical compliance absolved them of any blame. As one large law firm associate explained:

"We represented a client in a plant closing case that was opposed by the community. That one made me think a lot because I grew up in [a poor community] which used to have a heavy manufacturing base and everyone worked in the mills. I watched the plants close and watched the parents of friends get laid off and watched the community go down hill from there. I recognize that was very possible in this case. While I'm representing the company, I recognize the community interests also. Intellectually, though, it's easy to see that the basis for the community's law suit has no merit. . . . I guess what I ended up doing was concentrating on the legal issues because that was really all that I had control over."

This lawyer resolved the dramatic contradiction associated with his practice by practicing a subtle "banality of evil"[48] in which his actions, as harmful as they might be, are transformed into a value-neutral technical task.

Another large law firm lawyer explains how the ideology of advocacy helps reduce his ethical ambivalence:

"We had a case where a company wanted to develop a hazardous waste incinerator in a poor area. What we did was perfectly legal. We bought the land from the owners. We told them we were developing an industrial park, which was semi-true. But, this case went against my general convictions about environmental issues, particularly putting something like this in a poor area where people can't or won't resist. But I convinced myself that there's always another side. By the time I was done, I thought our client was closer to the right side of things than the townspeople. The stuff has to go somewhere. I tended to accept what the client was saying about all the precautions they would take."

The established moral boundaries of the legal profession requires this lawyer to advocate a position which he originally opposed. Nothing in the model rules encourages him to examine his clients' intentions or to insure the interests of the community. In the words of one female lawyer, "nothing in the rules tells you how much to question what your own client tells you as true".

---

[48] H. Arendt, *Eichmann in Jerusalem: A Report on the Banality of Evil.*(1963) (arguing that professionals used rationalizations to turn the slaughter of European Jews into a value-neutral technical task).

As long as rules of the legal process are not violated, the client's goals are not the attorney's concern. In the words of one respondent, "I used to care about how the things I did as a lawyer affected people, but I don't find myself asking these questions anymore". As another respondent explained, "whenever I feel uncomfortable about a case, I just make sure that everything I do is ethical and on the up-and-up".

These young attorneys strategically used role differentiation and role morality to avoid their ethical dilemmas. They dealt with moral ambiguity by relying on professional ethics rather than personal codes. As long as their behavior breaks none of the canons of professional responsibility, they are absolved of guilt. For example, a lawyer may find her client personally distasteful, but still owe that client zealous defense.

Several respondents reported resolving ethical reservations by viewing litigation as a game and ignoring the social consequences. As one large firm associate explained:

> "I buy into the game metaphor, it's very important to me. It helps me define my role. When I construct arguments with my boss, you never say that I'm not going to make that argument because it's not fair or because I don't believe in it. The only question you ask is it good enough to make in terms of its success."

Ironically, the extreme examples of malfeasance presented in their professional responsibility class is occasionally used to minimize many of the moral ambiguities in the respondents' practice. One justified an ethically questionable case by saying that "I wouldn't have worked on the Pinto case. The cases I work on aren't nearly as bad." Another respondent who was defending a client who had bilked the government out of tens of millions of dollars had no ethical qualms because "at least I'm not hurting people". Helping people to keep large sums of money that the attorney does not think they are really entitled to becomes neutral because "it is only rich organizations who are fighting over these issues. Everything that I do is pretty neutral."

Another lawyer minimized the moral ambiguity of representing interests she disapproved of by ignoring the social context:

> "The closest I really came to a case that was difficult for me was that one of my clients was a tobacco company. In law school I swore I'd never work on a tobacco case. But what I was doing was helping the president who was an investor in this electric company. It wasn't like I was representing him to do tobacco stuff."

The fact that it was tobacco profits which were being used to dominate other firms was thus effectively neutralized.

Defining ethics as a "due process" question rather than working toward a just outcome allowed respondents to justify their behavior. Morality is seen as not violating any laws. Respondents frequently reported that they faced no moral dilemmas because they had not been asked to engage in illegal or unethical acts.

Also, loyalty to their work group replaces individual responsibility for many activities. It is natural that a group of individuals working long hours together in an attempt to win a case would become close friends, but in these bonds lie potential moral pitfalls. Many respondents stated that no one they worked with compromised ethical principles. Several charged that attorneys in other parts of their firm had suspect ethics, but insisted that no one in their team would ever bend the rules too far. They often argued that opposing attorneys behaved unethically, placing the respondents' team at a tactical disadvantage.

This partisan perspective sometimes kept them from recognizing questionable activities performed by their own work group. A black attorney ignored the social implications of drafting documents which would result in foreclosure against large numbers of minority homeowners by thinking of her actions as "neutral" and as merely "pushing paper". A strong sense of teamwork and group loyalty prevented her from seeing the case as anything other than a game in which her cleverness was valued. Now that she has left the firm to begin her own practice in a poor community near Boston, this individual has completely redefined her experience and marvels that she did not recognize that she was supporting the interests of power.

> "I didn't think about the imbalance of power at the firm. It was mostly one person with money against another person with money. Even when it started getting involved with bank stuff, I didn't see an imbalance of power. But now, being on the other side, I see what that meant. I was assisting banks who didn't want to comply with community reinvestment laws."

Coming to see the client as a victim was another mechanism which helped reduce stress. It was very common for respondents to identify with clients for whom they had expressed antipathy during their law school interviews. For example, one long time advocate of tenants' rights found herself assigned to defend developers and landlords. She explained that:

> "I wanted to be involved in developing affordable housing. I really believe in subsidized housing. But as a lawyer, I work for a firm that represents towns. I'm representing a town that is trying to do everything it can to stop subsidized housing. You owe a duty of representation. I went out and looked at the site and could see why they had a lot of concerns about the project. However, I think I'd rather be on the other side."

By the logic of cognitive dissonance, strain is reduced by coming to believe that you and your team are in the right.

Ironically, these young lawyers were employing tactics to handle the contradictions associated with lawyering they had developed in law school just a few years earlier.[49] Although recognizing that context was relevant to cases,

---

[49] Granfield and Koenig, *supra* n. 42.

many strived to remove themselves from the broader questions of power, inequality and community.

IV. CONCLUSION

The young lawyers in the study did not receive sufficient guidance in law school for the complex moral dilemmas which they now confront. In general, their law school ethics course stressed occupational malfeasance such as conflicts of interest, impropriety or courtroom misconduct. Broader questions regarding morality, power, organizational context, team loyalty or community responsibilities were rarely, if ever, explored. Such issues are all too often considered outside the purview of instruction in professional ethics. However, as these lawyers reveal, these are the most salient issues young lawyers confront in practice. Ironically, these may not be the interests that law students have while they are studying ethics and preparing for the bar. As Robert Gordon has observed, "the minute that a teacher launches a discussion of theory, policy, ethics, or social context that is not immediately and closely tied to resolving a case situation, most students tune out and put down their pens".[50]

However, these young lawyers would have benefited from more explorations in law school of real-world situations, or from a comparison with other ethical frameworks, or even from the experiences of other practicing lawyers experiencing similar problems. Whatever pedagogical strategy is used in teaching ethics, it is important that discussions of legal ethics not be divorced from their real-world contexts. Because of the enormous complexity of these contexts, it is no doubt too much to ask for a single course to fill such a broad mandate. Broader ethical issues need to be integrated into the whole curriculum in a pervasive manner rather than ghettoized into a single professional responsibility course.[51] As the legal profession contemplates reforms in legal education and ethics, it would do well to pay attention to the institutionalized contexts of professional practice.

[50] Gordon, *supra* n. 12 at 2108.
[51] D. Rhode, "Ethics by the Pervasive Methods" (1992) 42 *Journal of Legal Education* 31.

16

Educating Lawyers to be Ethical Advisers

C. SAMPFORD and S. BLENCOWE

I. INTRODUCTION

The subject of this chapter was first suggested in 1993 when Griffith University was designing its Masters in Law. In consulting the local profession as to what was lacking in the LLM courses then available, we were jolted when a senior partner of one of Australia's largest and most successful law firms suggested that lawyers should be taught ethics—not so much for themselves but for their clients. Her view was that clients needed more than just legal advice. They needed, and were increasingly seeking, "whole of business" advice. They had gone beyond asking lawyers for the legal consequences of potential decisions and accountants for the financial consequences. Some of them were asking: "what do you think I should do?". In her view, lawyers should be the professionals to whom clients should naturally turn for such advice—and should be educated accordingly.

This is a tantalising suggestion because it is so contrary to the received image of law as the most amoral of professions—yet so suggestive of what a nobler role for lawyers might entail.

In this chapter we examine the arguments against the capacity and appropriateness of lawyers as sources of ethical advice and suggest that these arguments are based upon a number of flawed assumptions about the nature of law, ethics, legal practice and the lawyer–client relationship. We will consider the reasons why it might be in the interests of clients to receive a richer mix of ethics in their legal advice, citing a number of case studies. The implications of these changes for the role of lawyers and the ways in which legal education might be modified to equip them more effectively for this role are considered next. We will conclude by considering how lawyers might convince clients of the need for ethical advice and the legal profession's ability to provide it.

II. KNEEJERK AND BEYOND — THE CASE AGAINST LAWYERS
GIVING ETHICAL ADVICE

(a) The Ethical Incompetence of Lawyers

The grand jury of public opinion would have us believe that lawyers are the
last people to whom clients should turn for ethical advice — from the myriad
of (often very funny) anti-lawyer jokes to the higher points of English literature. Luban cites Macauley's indictment that a lawyer "with a wig on his
head, and a band round his neck [will] do for a guinea that, without those
appendages, he would think it wicked and infamous to do for an empire".[1]
Shakespeare's Wat Tyler simply passes sentence and urges his followers to
"kill all the lawyers".

Less savagely, some would argue that lawyers lack the competence to offer
advice beyond the strictly legal. They are not, with very few exceptions, professional philosophers or astute business people.[2] Thus Morris argues that:

> "[I]t is not . . . clear that someone who wanted moral or political advice would
> or should seek it from a lawyer. There is no reason to believe that lawyers have
> special moral or political expertise. In fact, general public opinion would proba-
> bly suggest the contrary."[3]

This argument supports the need for the better education of young lawyers,
but does not establish that lawyers lack the potential to offer valuable advice
on the social and business consequences of a client's proposed course of conduct.

We do not seek to contradict the popular disenchantment with past legal
practice. Legal education has generally failed adequately to equip lawyers to
go beyond a discussion of legal consequences to broader social and ethical
consequences. However, the assumption that lawyers should not offer ethical
advice (even if they could do so with confidence) rests upon a very limited
understanding of the role lawyers can, and in some cases do, play in advising
clients. As the case studies in this chapter indicate, the clients of lawyers who
confine themselves to aggressive interpretations of law and procedure may
suffer very badly. As Lake quips, "good advice is rarely as short-sighted and
narrowly drawn as helping Scrooge fire his employees on Christmas Eve".[4]

---

[1] D. Luban, *Lawyers and Justice: An Ethical Study* (Princeton, NJ, Princeton University Press,
1994), xxi.

[2] I. Ramsay, "Ethical Perspectives on the Practice of Business Law", *Law Society Journal*, June
1995, 60 at 62.

[3] J. Morris, "Power and Responsibility Among Lawyers and Clients: Comment on Ellmann's
Lawyers and Clients" (1995) 9 *Georgetown Journal of Legal Ethics* 781 at 808.

[4] P. F. Lake, "Make Lawyers, Not Lethal Sheep" (1992) 42 *Journal of Legal Education* 271 at
272.

(b) The Subjectivity of Ethics

A related justification for leaving questions of ethics, justice and morality for the philosophers is that these concepts are sometimes seen as inherently subjective and unstable.[5] What may be abhorrent and socially unacceptable behaviour to some people may be perfectly legitimate in the eyes of others, particularly where there is no law prohibiting the conduct; or the relevant law is seldom enforced, provides no effective sanction or a good lawyer can find a way around it. However, as both Ramsay and Haskell point out, there is a broad consensus amongst philosophers and even lawyers regarding the basic elements of moral action: doing good, avoiding harm to others, keeping promises and telling the truth, amongst others.[6] Simon argues that within the legal profession these basic norms have observable regularity and are mutually meaningful to those who refer to and engage in them.[7]

Disagreements at the margin, especially involving moral dilemmas and clashes between important principles, should not disguise the fact that most ethical philosophers, indeed most rational people, will agree on the correct behaviour in most everyday situations. Despite the different bases of ethical theories, there is convergence on many real life issues. Lawyers who think that the law allows their clients to do what the vast majority of ordinary citizens believe to be unethical are the ones who have given the profession a bad name. As we shall see in this chapter, it may be bad advice as well.

(c) Overdrawn Contrasts between Law and Ethics

These arguments are based on assumptions about the differences between law and ethics. Ethics are not as subjective as is suggested nor is law as clear as these criticisms would suggest. In recent years legal theory has emphasised the indeterminate nature of rules and the inability of laws to regulate all aspects of human affairs.[8] Indeed legal theory mirrors ethical theory in ranging through, but generally avoiding, the two extremes of "one right answer" and complete indeterminacy. The margins of indeterminacy are very broad and both law and ethics are subject to bouts of scepticism. However, the strength and consistency of our moral conclusions belie the shaky theoretical foundations of our moral arguments. Similarly, legal theory is more controversial than the relevant law in the vast majority of what were once called "easy

---

[5] Ramsay, *supra* n. 2 at 62.

[6] *Ibid*; P. G. Haskell, "Teaching Moral Analysis in Law School" (1991) 66 *Notre Dame Law Review* 1025 at 1031.

[7] W. Simon, "Ethical Discretion in Lawyering" (1988) 101 *Harvard Law Review* 1083 at 1120.

[8] See R. Tur, "An Introduction to Lawyers' Ethics" (1992) 10 *Journal of Professional Legal Education* 217.

cases" (in most legal disputes, the majority of lawyers will be able to predict with reasonable accuracy the relevant law).

This should not surprise. Both law and ethics involve the application of values to human action. They involve general rules subject to varying formulations, conflicts and uncertainties in interpretation. The logical, ontological and moral status of both legal and ethical rules is subject to a number of controversial and conflicting theories. There are differences — of which the most important is the establishment of legal hierarchies for both the making and interpreting of law. These in turn produce texts which are expected to have legitimate as well as persuasive authority, whereas the texts produced by ethical philosophers have to rely purely on their capacity to persuade (and the interests of audiences).

Yet this important distinction does not undermine the continuity and links between law and ethics. Law provides a forum through which differences over values can formally be debated and through which attempts are made to reach tentative solutions. Despite its highly formalised manner, law is, in effect, a continuation of ethical debate by other means.[9] Although justice, ethics and common values are the language in which debate over legislation or the common law is fought, the battles are not concluded with the passage of legislation or judicial decisions at final appeal. Such decisions involve significant compromises and lawyers rarely completely succeed in either articulating the values that drive the decisions or in expressing them in language that can apply to the infinite variety of human experience. Accordingly, competing values lie at the heart of the interpretations of authoritative texts by courts, citizens and lawyers.

This intertwining of law and ethics in both the formulation and interpretation of law makes it possible for law and ethics to be mutually supportive. According to Warren CJ:

> Law floats in a sea of ethics. Not only does law presuppose ethical commitment; it presupposes the existence of a broad area of human conduct controlled only by ethical norms and not subject to Law at all.[10]

Simon sees so-called moral options as competing legal values.[11] Not all of ethics is incorporated into law. Some ethical concepts are too general to be effectively encompassed by laws. For example, it may not be cost-effective or efficient to enforce some norms as laws if we adopt Mill's harm principle that

---

[9] This is not to say that law is only about values. We do not wish to convey that law is not about power. Indeed, I have previously sought to adapt Clausewitz's immortal dictum that "war is a continuation of politics by other means" to say the "law is a continuation of politics by other means". See M. Howard, *Clausewitz* (Oxford, Oxford University Press, 1983), 34. Like all complex institutions, law reflects much that occurs in society. In the case of ethics and value debate, this is the most proximate medium through which other social forces influence law.

[10] R. Murphy, "Defining and Practising Business Ethics" in K. Woldring (ed.), *Business Ethics in Australia and New Zealand: Essays and Cases* (Melbourne, Nelson, 1996), 46.

[11] According to Simon, this reflects the fact that the ethical conflict arises within legal culture itself: Simon, *supra* n. 7, 1114.

laws should not enforce morality where no harm is done to others. Laws tend to respond to temporary ethical issues rather than lead them,[12] and ethical behaviours and cultures cannot generally be created by law.[13]

For these and other reasons, law and ethics are not identical. However, at their best they are mutually supportive, with ethical principles providing the principled justification for legal rules and offering valuable interpretive tools for legal rules as well as the basis for a supportive ethical culture.[14]

The similarities between law and ethics lead to similarities in the nature of legal and ethical argument and advice. Both involve imprecise general rules in need of interpretation that are applied to complex real life situations. Unsurprisingly, this has led to an interest by ethicists in both common law modes of reasoning and the jurisprudence that attempts to explain the nature of such reasoning.[15] The applicability of legal reasoning to applied ethics underlines the potential of lawyers as ethical advisers.

Even if lawyers attempt to provide only good legal advice, it will not be without ethical content. Explaining the law and the possible interpretations of it that a court might take necessarily involves an explanation of the ethical values that are likely to inform those interpretations. A lawyer who pretends that the law operates, for the court, in an ethical vacuum is misleading his or her client.

Good legal practice depends upon the making of complex judgements about a variety of matters not strictly related to the law. As Eberle points out, the lawyer applying a body of technical rules to practical business problems must exercise "a capacity for sound judgment and practical wisdom, a process of imagination, careful deliberation, and intuitive comprehension".[16] These skills can be and are harnessed to offer advice that goes beyond the black letter of the law to the psychological, social, public relations, monetary and business consequences of a particular transaction or course of conduct. Indeed, those lawyers who possess such skills may be almost uniquely suited to the role of ethical adviser.

(d) The Imperatives of Modern Practice

Several attributes of legal practice are said to limit the potential of individual lawyers to raise ethical issues with clients: the self-interest of lawyers,

[12] Murphy, *supra* n. 10, 46.

[13] J. F. Dalton, "Boardroom Ethics" in Woldring, *supra* n. 10, 179.

[14] C. Sampford and D. Wood, "The Future of Business Ethics" (1992) 1 *Griffith Law Review* 56; P. Finn, "Commerce, the Common Law and Morality" (1989) 17 *Melbourne University Law Review* 87; and The Hon. Sir Gerard Brennan, "Commercial Law and Morality" (1989) 17 *Melbourne University Law Review* 100.

[15] C. Sampford, "Law, Ethics and Institutional Design: Finding Philosophy, Displacing Ideology" (inaugural professorial lecture) (1994) 3 *Griffith Law Review* 1.

[16] E. J. Eberle, "Three Foundations of Legal Ethics: Autonomy, Community, and Morality" (1993) 7 *Georgetown Journal of Legal Ethics* 89 at 123.

institutional and market pressures and the financial dependence of large law firms on corporate clients.[17] Nelson argues that the institutional pressures of large firm practice and the competition to attract clients in a contracting market for legal services means that lawyers are more likely to further the client's self-interest than engage in discussion about the ethical implications of a proposed legal strategy.[18] Wilkins considers that "[l]ike other self-interested actors, lawyers frequently overestimate their own abilities and privilege their own interests".[19] According to Langevoort, lawyers cope with the pressures of daily practice and the need to achieve market-place success through the use of heuristics, mental shortcuts and blind spots (making positive assessments of clients and ignoring evidence to the contrary).[20]

It is easy to see the nature of modern legal practice as hostile to the exercise of moral judgement and ethical persuasion. The income and reputation of individual lawyers and their firms may be substantially dependent on keeping clients through furthering their short-term interests. One of the major reasons for the general malaise affecting so many lawyers is said to be the feeling that they are employed to be no more than mere "tools of their clients", possessing no "duty to tell the client that he's wrong".[21] This sense of powerlessness is reinforced by the structuring of work within large firms, with little personal interaction with clients (except for senior partners) and the handling of various aspects of the client's problem by discrete, specialised departments.[22]

However, the tension between "doing good and doing well" may well be exaggerated.[23] It is too simple to see lawyers as the pawns of greedy corporate clients, as slaves to their firms' time sheets and driven solely by a market-driven legal culture. Such images give too little credit to the power and independence of lawyers and understate the client's respect for the expertise of lawyers (why else would they pay hundreds of dollars per hour for their services?) and the importance of ethics. It also assumes strong distinctions between business, legal and ethical advice.

---

[17] See G. C. Hazard, "Ethical Opportunity in the Practice of Law" (1990) 27 *San Diego Law Review* 127; R. Nelson, "Symposium on the Law Firm as a Social Institution" (1985) 37 *Stanford Law Review* 503; and D. Arron, *Running from the Law: Why Good Lawyers are Getting Out of the Legal Profession* (Berkeley, Ten Speed Press, 1991).

[18] Nelson, *supra* n. 17, 537–9.

[19] D. B. Wilkins, "Practical Wisdom for Practicing Lawyers: Separating Ideals from Ideology in Legal Ethics" (1994) 108 *Harvard Law Review* 458 at 470.

[20] D. C. Langevoort, "Where Were the Lawyers? A Behavioural Inquiry into Lawyers' Responsibility for Clients' Fraud" (1993) 46 *Vanderbilt Law Review* 75.

[21] Arron, *supra* n. 17, 46 (interview with "Kate").

[22] See P. Joy, "What We Talk About When We Talk About Professionalism: A Review of *Lawyers' Ideals/Lawyers' Practices: Transformations in the American Legal Profession*" (1994) 7 *Georgetown Journal of Legal Ethics* 987 at 1007. However, most lawyers in Nelson's survey felt they had ample opportunity to give non-legal advice to clients, irrespective of the size of their firm: Nelson, *supra* n. 17, 532.

[23] Wilkins, *supra* n. 19, 472.

The powers of a lawyer include the power to define what the law is and how it applies to client conduct and relationships.[24] Felstiner and Sarat argue that in any lawyer–client relationship no party dominates the other. Rather, the relationship is characterised by a process of negotiation in which power is constantly shifting and is never exclusively in the possession of either the lawyer or the client.[25] The relationship is one of shared interest, co-operation and mutual benefit. Lawyer–client relationships are not zero-sum games. Co-operation and respect are important and clients generally recognise the advantages of resolving and, better still, avoiding disputes.

Furthermore, lawyers do not so much simply object to a client's proposal on philosophical or public-policy grounds as use a number of strategies to bring the client around to their way of thinking. Nelson observes that the lawyer's evaluation of legal options itself shapes client behaviour by suggesting what is possible and able to be accomplished legally.[26] Levin lists the practical strategies used by lawyers to dissuade clients from particular courses of conduct, including limiting the duration of discussion, controlling the direction of dialogue and warning of the possibility of legal sanctions and other adverse social or business consequences.[27]

The rules of professional conduct, the risk of malpractice litigation and the threat of externally imposed sanctions also affect the nature of advice given to clients, ensuring that considerations other than the short-term interests of clients are taken into account. Model Rule 2.1 of the American Bar Association states that "a lawyer may refer not only to law but to other considerations such as moral, economic, social and political factors, that may be relevant to the client's situation".[28] Although the rule does not oblige lawyers to provide such advice to clients, the Comment to the Rule acknowledges the potential benefit of broad advice:

> Advice couched in narrowly legal terms may be of little value to a client, especially where practical considerations, such as costs or effects on other people, are predominant. Purely technical legal advice, therefore, can sometimes be inadequate. It is proper for a lawyer to refer to relevant moral and ethical

[24] Hazard, *supra* n. 17, 132.

[25] W. Felstiner and A. Sarat, "Enactments of Power: Negotiating Reality and Responsibility in Lawyer–Client Interactions" (1992) 77 *Cornell Law Review* 1447.

[26] Nelson, *supra* n. 17, 548. Also see W. Bradley Wendel, "Lawyers and Butlers: The *Remains of Amoral Ethics*" (1995) 9 *Georgetown Journal of Legal Ethics* 161 at 173.

[27] L. C. Levin, "Testing the Radical Experiment: A Study of Lawyer Response to Clients who Intend to Harm Others" (1994) 47 *Rutgers Law Review* 81 at 123–6.

[28] United States American Bar Association Model Rules of Professional Conduct (1983). See S. Ross, *Ethics In Law: Lawyers' Responsibility and Accounting in Australia* (Sydney, Butterworths, 1995), 173–4. There is no equivalent in Australia. However, Ross notes that the Family Law Act 1975 (Cth) , s. 17 and Family Law Regulations, s. 19, require lawyers to declare that they have given their client a copy of a prescribed document, informing the client of "the legal and possible social effects of the proposed proceedings" and the counselling and welfare facilities available. *Ibid.*, 174.

considerations . . . [that] impinge upon most legal questions and may decisively influence how the law will be applied.[29]

There is an increasing possibility that a failure to provide the client with broad advice may amount to negligence or a breach of fiduciary duty.[30] For example, taxation authorities now expect a lawyer's advice to conform with government policy and the standards expressed in taxation legislation, which Philipps sees as effectively "conscript[ing] the lawyer as part of the government's enforcement mechanism".[31]

In isolation, such external requirements might only intensify the potential conflicting demands on lawyers. Fortunately, there are some hopeful signs that modern legal practice includes some developments favourable to the giving of ethical advice by lawyers. The emphasis is shifting from a model of pure technical expertise to an understanding of the nature of the client's business. Major clients like to deal with a single partner who will bring in other experts as necessary. This generates the possibilities of inter-personal relationships in which lawyers can understand clients and their business needs and can be trusted in their advice. Finally, the greater emphasis lawyers now give to preventive action in areas where the law is uncertain is based upon a conception of lawyering that emphasises the avoidance of questionable behaviour rather than promotion of clients' short-term self-interests.

These developments are breaking down the distinctions between business and legal advice and between legal and ethical advice. They also shift attention from the immediate needs of the client in a particular matter to long-term interests. Although there may be apparent conflicts between short-term interests and ethical action, conflicts between long-term self-interest and ethical action are extremely rare. Some might even be tempted to see a necessary connection because, in the long run, we are all dead and must either face the judgement of an ethics-conscious deity or our own judgement of whether the life we are about to depart from is one of which we can be proud (in one sense, our inability to "take it with us" means that only those good works which outlast us can constitute a long run that outlives us). However, we do not attempt to *equate* ethics with long-term self-interest. Because of the vagaries of the future predictions and the varieties of interests any "self" may have, what is in the long-term self-interest is not susceptible to certainty.

---

[29] Ross, *ibid.*, 174.

[30] P. S. Menell, "Legal Advising on Corporate Structure in the New Era of Environmental Liability" [1990] *Columbia Business Law Review* 399; T. Greenwood "Ethics and Avoidance Advice", *Law Institute Journal*, August 1991, 724.

[31] J. T. Philipps, "It's Not Easy Being Easy: Advising Tax Return Positions" (1993) 50 *Washington and Lee Law Review* 589 at 621. For an Australian perspective, see Greenwood, *ibid.*; "Ethics and Avoidance Advice", Law Institute Journal, August 1991, 724; and G. S. Cooper, R. L. Deutsch and R. E. Krever, *Income Taxation: Commentary and Materials* (Sydney, Law Book Company, 1993), ch. 24. An Australian tax adviser may be subject to a variety of sanctions for unethical conduct, including criminal liability under the Crimes Act 1914 (Cth), the Taxation Administration Act 1953 (Cth) and the Crimes (Taxation Offences) Act 1980. See Cooper *et al*, *ibid*, 24–16 to 24–21.

However, ethical behaviour is rarely against long-term self-interest. It is a safe choice. It is also generally simpler—honest people do not have to remember the particular lies they have told different people; fair dealers do not have to watch out for revengeful victims, and those who try to live by the spirit of the law are unlikely to be pursued by officials who are determined to get them next time. Those who try to defeat the purpose of the law may find that their luck runs out as their overly clever lawyers find that the judge neither agrees with their interpretation of the law nor has sympathy for the client who has sought maximum advantage from it.

(e) The Proper Role of Lawyers

Another argument that lawyers should not give ethical advice rests upon a common view of the proper function of the lawyer, variously called the libertarian, client advocate or amoral model.[32] According to this model, lawyers should set aside their own or community conceptions of ethical behaviour from their dealings with clients. Bradley Wendel describes lawyers who engage in such role-differentiated behaviour as "Teflon professionals—none of their client's slime sticks to them".[33] The lawyer is simply there to maximise the client's interests, using whatever means, so long as those means are within the letter of the law (if not its intent), including the laws and rules of professional conduct.

The client advocate role may have been based on the idea that justice is best served by a rigorous competition for the truth. It sits well with liberal economic theories relying on competitive amoral markets in which self-interested behaviour by clients and their lawyers will result in overall gains for the community.[34] It centres on obligations to the client arising from the conception of the lawyer as a zealous advocate[35] and prefers relations based upon contract and economic interest over relations based upon duties to institutional and higher ideals.

[32] The chief proponents of this view are Fried and Pepper. See S. L. Pepper, "The Lawyer's Amoral Ethical Role: A Defence, A Problem, and Some Possibilities" [1986] *American Bar Foundation Research Journal* 613; C. Fried, "The Lawyer as Friend: The Moral Foundations of the Lawyer–Client Relation" (1976) 85 *Yale Law Journal* 1060; and R. A. Wasserstrom, "Lawyers as Professionals: Some Moral Issues" in P. Y. Windt *et al.*, *Ethical Issues in the Professions* (NJ, Prentice Hall, 1989), 88.

[33] Bradley Wendel, *supra* n. 26, 165. See J. Allegretti, "Shooting Elephants, Serving Clients: An Essay on George Orwell and the Lawyer–Client Relationship" (1993) 27 *Creighton Law Review* 1.

[34] R. Gordon, "Corporate Law Practice as a Public Calling" (1990) 49 *Maryland Law Review* 225 at 258; Bradley Wendel, *supra* n. 26, at 176. This assumption ignores the reality of inequality of bargaining power and resources between the opposing sides and of social barriers such as race, gender and class.

[35] N. Cahn, "Forward: Responsible Lawyers" (1995) 63 *George Washington Law Review* 921 at 926 notes that the term "zealous" is itself ambiguous: a lawyer can be zealous both by putting the client's interests first, and by putting the lawyer's own interests above those of the client.

The flaws in this view are many. It marginalises the lawyer's duty as an officer of the court. It is based upon a paradigm of individual clients rather than large organisations.[36] It is also founded on the paradigm of the criminal defence lawyer's valiant defence against the State's attempts to deprive the underdog of his liberty. Both paradigms paint a distorted picture of the reality of much legal work—the pursuit and defence of complex civil litigation and the creation of long-term legal devices (corporations and trusts) and business relationships.[37]

> We find it hard to accept that the role of lawyers is to ensure that their clients can prosper despite acting in a way that the majority see as unethical and contrary to values of justice and ethics underlying the law. Even if success is achieved in using the law in this way, large corporations are dependent on their success on much larger issues. An unsympathetic legislature may seek to change the laws that are misused and in any case will not take kindly to corporate representations. Even more fundamentally, as Pitt and Groskaufmanis point out: the litigator's syndrome overlooks the crucial fact that the preservation of a company's credibility—and perhaps even its survival, in the marketplace—often will turn on the company's capacity to tell the truth, admit fault, and make amends.[38]

Of course, once litigation is joined, the client has a strong interest in avoiding adverse findings. However, it could be argued that litigation frequently arises because long-term ethical advice to clients has been deficient or nonexistent, a fact that seems to be ignored in much of the literature that supports the amoral role of the lawyer.[39] As noted above, this literature relies on arguments that presume a separation between ethical and legal advice and that law is not itself "a source of moral limits".[40]

Marqulies warns of potentially undesirable consequences for the legal profession if the amoral role of the lawyer is abandoned. Lawyers may have to provide ethical advice at no cost because clients will not wish to pay for it and lawyers could leave the profession after feeling the effects of additional (uncompensated) ethical responsibilities.[41] Although it may be true that some clients will have to be persuaded that it is in their best interests to consider ethical issues, it is unlikely that they will refuse to pay for such advice, particularly as so much of legal advice is inevitably bound up with the ethical values which are required to explain and interpret the law. It would be highly

---

[36] J. Leubsdorf, "Essay: Pluralising the Client–Lawyer Relationship" (1992) 77 *Cornell Law Review* 825.

[37] P. L. Rizzo, "Morals for Home, Morals for Office: The Double Ethical Life of a Civil Litigator" (1991) 35 *Catholic Lawyer* 79 at 82, 90.

[38] H. L. Pitt and K. A. Groskaufmanis, "When Bad Things Happen to Good Companies: A Crisis Management Primer" (1994) 15 *Cardozo Law Review* 951 at 967.

[39] Cahn, *supra* n. 35, 926 at n. 22.

[40] Pepper, *supra* n. 32 at 626.

[41] P. Marqulies, "Who Are You to Tell Me That? Attorney-Client Deliberation Regarding Non-legal Issues and the Interests of Non-clients" (1990) 68 *North Carolina Law Review* 213 at 246 n. 118.

artificial (if not impossible) for a lawyer to offer advice to a client with the proviso that only technical advice is included within the services to be paid for. Furthermore, we have seen that lawyers are changing careers because they are *disillusioned* with the amoral role. Finally, the decision to refrain from providing ethical advice is itself a moral choice. As Bradley Wendel observes:

> Lawyers *qua* professionals cannot avoid asking moral questions merely because they are difficult to answer. Lawyers routinely confront moral quandaries as persons undifferentiated by role, and probably do not believe that moral argumentation is worthless in the context of their own private morality. In addition, the decision to become an amoral actor is a moral judgment, and must be justified in moral terms. Attempting to justify one's nonaccountability requires a rather sophisticated argument that belies the contention that one is not capable of making ethical judgments. Lawyers do not accept radical moral scepticism. Lawyers assume that ordinary citizens can make ethical judgments, such as whether they are dealing fairly and in good faith, or exercising due care.[42]

This challenges the assumptions on which the client advocate role is based: that the lawyer's duty to the client can be distinguished and separated from his or her duty as an officer of the court and obligations as an individual moral citizen *and* that the client is solely interested in monetary gain. These presumptive images of a schizophrenic lawyer and a sociopathic client are at the heart of the client advocate model's rejection of the lawyer's giving of ethical advice. The lawyer's duty becomes a matter of advancing and defending the selfish interests of the "bad man".

(f) Advising Holmes' "Bad Man"

This immediately raises Oliver Wendel Holmes' "bad man"—one of the most evocative images of modern jurisprudence.[43] The bad man was not concerned with ethics or principle but with "what the courts would do, in fact". In the client advocate model, the lawyer should not judge or preach but advise what actions would avoid the court's wrath.

But let us consider the best advice that would be given to a bad man. If lawyers want to know what the court will do, in fact, they have to consider the values that will be used to interpret the law and make sense of it (not to mention the values that the judge will bring to bear in imposing sentences or awarding damages should the client lose). This does not mean that those values need be adopted by either lawyer or client. It is possible to treat them as mere facts about the beliefs of others—important in explaining and predicting behaviour. However, such detached observation and prediction is no easy task. Judges do not generally have the time, the inclination or the training

---

[42] Bradley Wendel, *supra* n. 26, 177–8.
[43] See M. D. A. Freeman (ed.), *Lloyd's Introduction to Jurisprudence* (London, Sweet and Maxwell, 1994), 670–6.

systematically to consider their values or articulate them. The values judges bring to bear are to be found embedded in their judgments and then only to the extent that they are necessary for the case at hand. Those values are, in any case, likely to vary substantially from judge to judge and be subject to development through exposure to different cases, life experiences and changing community opinion.[44]

Rather than try to stay fully detached and second-guess the values particular judges will bring to bear, the lawyer will find it easier to seek an approximate understanding of those values, adopt them and use them to interpret the law and advise the client how to act. Both lawyer and client will find it much easier to adopt the values which underlie and justify the law than to stand outside them and attempt to keep just outside the range of actions which courts will penalise. The prediction game is time-consuming and unreliable. The more precisely the lawyer and client try to judge what the courts will do, the more often they will lose—and the less sympathy the court will have for their breaches. On the other hand, someone who is trying to follow the values underlying the law is far less likely to fall foul of it and will be treated far more leniently, by official and judge alike, if their action inadvertently strays into that which the law, as interpreted by the judge, prohibits.

Thus we find the great irony. The best advice of the lawyer to the "bad man" is to attempt to be "good" according to the lawyer's best understanding of the values underlying the law. The most efficient behaviour is generally that in compliance with the law and its principled justification.

Of course, individuals are free agents and may have principled disagreements with the values the lawyer sees as informing the law. The underlying rationale of the client advocate model is to protect client autonomy. However, the necessary protection for independent moral judgement is rarely relevant in the case of large corporate clients. In any case, if the values underlying the law are enunciated, it is easier for the client to identify that the law has different standards from his or her own and then to decide whether to defy the law as a matter of principle. Where clients' values are in line with a controversial interpretation of the law, they can be advised of this fact and tailor their actions accordingly, knowing that they run the risk of losing in court.

The best legal advice to bad men, good men and principled rebels highlights the underlying ethical values (and any conflicts within or among them) of the law. This makes compliance easier for the majority who wish to comply and makes principled opposition easier for those who are genuinely offended by the values the law seems to espouse.

---

[44] E.g., many Australian judges' attitudes towards Australia's indigenous people would have been affected by growing public awareness of past injustices. See *Mabo* v. *Queensland (No 2)* (1992) 175 CLR 1; and *Wik Peoples* v. *Queensland* (1997) 141 ALR 129.

III. WHY CLIENTS NEED ETHICAL ADVICE FROM LAWYERS

Far from suggesting that lawyers are inappropriate dispensers of ethical advice, the nature of law, the nature of practice and the role of the lawyer all indicate that lawyers need to be able to advise on ethics merely to give good legal advice.

A striking illustration of why clients need ethical advice from lawyers comes from the Federal Sentencing Guidelines in the United States.[45] Since 1991, federal judges have been required to take into account an organisation's "culpability" when imposing fines on companies whose primary purpose was not to engage in criminal activity. A firm can reduce its culpability score and escape with a significantly reduced penalty if it can satisfy certain requirements. The most important requirement is that prior to the conduct occurring, compliance standards and procedures were in place that were reasonably capable of reducing criminal conduct. Furthermore, a senior employee (who will often be an in-house lawyer) must have been made responsible for managing the compliance programme. The existence of a written code of conduct will not be sufficient to prove that the company had diligently sought to prevent and detect criminal conduct. Rather, the company must have undertaken active monitoring and auditing of its operations to ensure that they complied with the purposes of legislation, provided mechanisms for employees to report breaches in confidence and educated all employees about the policies and procedures in place.[46]

Of course, courts will tend to take these matters into account irrespective of the existence of explicit sentencing guidelines. Courts are increasingly embracing a purposive interpretation of legislation, particularly in relation to the environment, public safety, health, privacy and the conduct of corporations overseas.[47] Judges inevitably bring values such as justice and good faith to the interpretation of the law, and are often influenced by the concept of corporate social responsibility, "the notion that corporations [and their employees] have an obligation to constituent groups in society other than stockholders".[48]

However, clients and lawyers should not confine their discussion of ethical issues to the imponderable values a judge may apply in determining the validity of the client's actions, should the matter get to court. Rather, a proper

[45] United States Sentencing Commission Guidelines, 52 Fed. Reg. 44, 675 (1987). See P. E. Fiorelli, "Guideline Amendments Dramatically Change the Structure of Organizational Fines" (1991) 35 *Catholic Lawyer* 181.

[46] *Ibid*, 189–91.

[47] See D. L. Rhode, "Ethics by the Pervasive Method" (1992) 42 *Journal of Legal Education* 31 at 38; T. Donaldson, "Moral Minimums for Multinationals" in W. M. Hoffman and R. E. Fredrick (eds.), *Business Ethics: Readings and Cases in Corporate Morality* (New York, McGraw-Hill, 1990), ch. 12; and T. Donaldson, *The Ethics of International Business* (New York, Oxford University Press, 1989).

[48] M. Cash Mathews, *Strategic Intervention in Organizations: Resolving Ethical Dilemmas* (California, Sage Library of Social Research, 1988), 28.

consideration of ethical considerations requires both lawyers and clients to bring their own values into conversations about the law and then to attempt to live by them.

(a) Australian Case Studies

In Australia, the reputation of a major mining corporation has been badly scarred by its willingness to operate in another country in ways unacceptable at home and then to engage in questionable tactics to avoid paying compensation. In June 1996, BHP Limited finally agreed to an out-of-court settlement of a class action brought by landowners affected by the company's joint venture mining operations in the western highlands of Papua New Guinea. Since 1984, following the collapse of the original tailings dam, all the waste from the mine had simply been dumped into the Ok Tedi and Fly river systems, with devastating environmental consequences. The tailings had washed downstream, settling on the lower reaches of the river. The resultant silt build-up had killed fish and also destroyed trees and market gardens.

During the two-year legal battle, BHP embarked on a massive publicity campaign to convince the Australian public that it was doing everything possible to find a cost-effective solution acceptable to all parties. For example, half page advertisements appeared in major metropolitan newspapers captioned "BHP and Ok Tedi: Are you sure you are getting the full picture on Ok Tedi?" and "BHP: Answers for Our Global Future".[49] However, BHP's public relations campaign was not helped by the finding by Justice Cummins that the company was in contempt of court for its role in drafting legislation before the PNG parliament. The legislation would have restricted landowners' ability to access courts of a foreign jurisdiction, thus placing an immediate halt to the litigation in Victoria. It would also have made it a criminal offence for land holders to seek further compensation through the courts once they accepted a settlement package from BHP. It seemed more than merely coincidental that an earlier agreement between the PNG Government (itself a shareholder in the mine) and BHP, dealing with the subject of compensation, contained penalty clauses mirroring those in the proposed legislation. Although Justice Cummins was reversed on appeal,[50] the damage had been done. BHP's experience indicates that a "legal win" (the avoidance of formal legal sanctions) may be truly pyrrhic in terms of a corporation's standing in the community.

The former chief executive of BHP publicly admitted that BHP and its lawyers in particular had been "more inclined to listen (so we could) argue the point than to understand what the broader community had got to say

---

[49] The *Australian*, 4 Oct. 1995, 3.
[50] *BHP* v. *Dagi* (1996) 2 VR 117.

about our standard of behaviour".[51] He concluded that management's failure to ensure that "there was proper understanding (in the legal team) of all the values necessary" had played a critical part in BHP's loss of standing in the Australian community.[52] One newspaper editorial noted that the Australian public now thought of the company as the "Ugly Australian", contrary to BHP's advertising image of itself as the "Big Australian".[53] The "win at all costs" mentality of BHP's legal advisers and their willingness to condone, if not participate in, ethically problematic behaviour played a major role in this public relations disaster. No advertising campaign could remedy the negative publicity.

By contrast, an Australian biscuit manufacturer's response to a recent extortion threat provides an example of the benefits of ethical behaviour for companies. Arnott's Biscuits Ltd quickly responded to a threat by an anonymous letter writer to contaminate its biscuits with enough poison to kill a young child by recalling its products from approximately 2,500 supermarkets and shops in two states and then destroying the 800 truckloads of biscuits which had been stockpiled.[54] The biscuits were off the shelves for two weeks, costing the company a million dollars a day at a time when it faced intense competition in the food sector and declining profits.[55] The company was also forced to stand down hundreds of employees.

However, the early signs are that Arnott's placing of the safety of its consumers above immediate financial considerations has paid off in terms of minimising long-term damage to the company's market position. Arnott's managing director held daily media conferences and the company put together a team comprised of senior executives, including the head of its legal division, to oversee the company's response to the crisis, which included the provision of a telephone call-in service for concerned customers and retailers. Arnott's prompt and public reaction to the extortion crisis and its well-planned crisis-management strategy has clearly earned it the respect of the media, investors and the broader Australian community.[56] In the not so long-term, it also advanced that company's interests.

---

[51] "BHP Visits the School of Hard Knocks", *Weekend Australian*, 15–16 June 1996, 54. Following the Ok Tedi saga, BHP appointed a senior executive in each division of its operations, responsible for ensuring that the company's values and performance in such areas as the environment and safety reflected and stayed abreast of public expectations.

[52] *Ibid.*

[53] Editorial, *Australian*, 28 Sept. 1995, 10.

[54] "Biscuits Back on Shelves", *Age*, 26 Feb. 1997.

[55] "Arnotts Gears Up for Big Climb Back", *Age*, 15 Feb. 1997.

[56] "Arnott's Agenda", *Age*, 22 Feb. 1997. Arnott's response seems to have been modelled on that of Johnson and Johnson to the Tylenol scare in the USA over 15 years ago. See Pitt and Groskaufmanis, *supra* n. 38 at 951.

IV. ALTERNATIVE MODELS OF LAWYERING

If the artificial dichotomies between law and ethics are rejected, it becomes relatively easy to locate the giving of ethical advice within the lawyer's over-all duty to his or her client. However, this will require an alternate model of lawyering to the simple client advocate model discussed above. In so doing it will need to avoid the mistaken dichotomies between legal and business advice; the short-term and long-term consequences of action; the lawyer's duty to the court and duty to the client; and the lawyer's duty as a moral citizen and as an advocate.

In helping to rethink the lawyer's role, Eberle lays down three foundations: the 'autonomy foundation' (client advocate role of lawyer); the "community foundation" (lawyer's obligations to the broader community, including the courts); and the "morality foundation" (the lawyer's and client's duty to use ethical means to achieve ethical ends).[57] He observes that lawyers tend to give only secondary consideration to community and moral interests, despite the fact that:

> Interests relevant to clients involve duties to themselves in achieving their rights under the law, duties to community arising from their connections and sense of belonging to others, including lawyers and our system of law, and duties to conscience as given content by fundamental moral norms.[58]

Critics of the narrow client advocate role have embraced alternative models of lawyering that require the lawyer to establish a moral dialogue with his or her client to give more weight to these community and moral interests. The moral dialogue approach is based on the assumption that not only is it often in the client's interests to receive ethical advice, it is also the lawyer's duty to consider ethical issues (whether the client wishes to or not) and that the lawyer has an interest in the outcome as an independent moral actor and member of the community. However, these various duties should not be viewed as mutually exclusive. Rather, they should complement each other to achieve a result that "empower[s] clients to achieve autonomy in an ethical manner within the context of a just community".[59] An example of this approach is the lawyer who suggests realistic structural solutions to environmental or occupational health and safety problems instead of encouraging clients to evade their legal and moral responsibilities.[60]

Proponents of the moral dialogue school differ in the weight they give to each type of interest and the degree of autonomy they allow the client to exercise. Under Simon's model, the lawyer should assess the relative merits of the

---

[57] Eberle, *supra* n. 16 at 91. Also see R. W. Painter, "The Moral Interdependence of Corporate Lawyers and Their Clients" (1994) 67 *Southern California Law Review* 507.

[58] *Ibid*, at 97.

[59] *Ibid*, at 125.

[60] Gordon, *supra* n. 34, and Menell, *supra* n. 30.

client's interests and the interests of others and then attempt to resolve the competing claims, taking "those actions that, considering the relevant circumstances of the particular case, seem most likely to promote justice".[61] He argues that it is legitimate to give this degree of discretionary judgement to a lawyer because, amongst other things, any increase in the lawyer's capacity to frustrate client goals is balanced by a reduction in the lawyer's capacity to frustrate goals of third parties and the public.[62]

However, others point to the risk of paternalism or domination of the client inherent in this model. Heller suggests that after providing the client with a "full picture" of the law, its purposes and the possible consequences of the client's preferred course of conduct, the lawyer should allow the client to be the final decision-maker.[63] Heller argues that the lawyer should privilege the client's views even if this requires the lawyer to exploit either a legal loophole or a lack of legal regulation in the area, or to argue for an interpretation of the law that does not accord with the lawyer's.[64] Although the client-centred approach recognises that, from the client's perspective, the lawyer is employed to act as his or her agent (one of the many roles of the lawyer) it overestimates the extent to which lawyers can dominate clients, particularly where the client is a corporation.[65] As Morris notes, not all clients can be classified as "frightened and uninitiated".[66] In fact, the economic power of clients often poses a significant barrier to lawyers' ability to retain ethical autonomy from their clients.[67]

A more moderate approach is taken by Margulies, who sets out a list of factors to guide lawyers in the exercise of their discretion to undertake ethical counselling.[68] These factors include morality (the action or decision may harm others, involve lying or misleading, violate the equality norm or be one that the client would not wish for everyone in society); psychology (the action or decision may engender guilt or regret, perhaps the client should be advised to seek the services of a mental health professional); and policy (unintended consequences and net cost to society). He argues that the lawyer should have a duty to advise the client to modify his or her position when the factors in

---

[61] Simon, *supra* n. 7, at 1090.

[62] *Ibid*, at 1127.

[63] J. Heller, "Legal Counselling in the Administrative State: How to Let the Client Decide" (1994) 103 *Yale Law Journal* 2503 at 2504; S. Ellmann, "Lawyers and Clients" (1986) *UCLA Law Review* 717 embraces a similar approach.

[64] *Ibid*, at 2518.

[65] Thus Hazard argues that "[a] lawyer is an agent, not a principal. Having taken on a client, a lawyer is not free to pursue the client's objectives only to the extent that the lawyer may see fit. The lawyer has to go forward to the point that the client sees fit, within the limits of the law": Hazard, *supra*, n. 17, 135.

[66] Morris, *supra* n. 3 at 783.

[67] Hazard, *supra* n. 17 at 136.

[68] P. Margulies, *supra*, n. 41, 221–2.

his list are present, and a right to withdraw altogether if the client is not convinced of the lawyer's advice. Margulies' proviso is that the client's interests must not be "immediately and irrevocably" prejudiced by this latter action.[69] However, even if the lawyer is "the last lawyer in town", a refusal to assist the client is unlikely to affect the interests of justice unless the client's *rights* (as opposed to the client's ability to manipulate the law to suit its own business interests) are at stake. As even Fried acknowledges, the last lawyer in town should not feel morally obliged to help the finance company repossess a widow's refrigerator.[70]

There is much merit in these views. However, there is a common strand which emphasises conflicts between client interest and ethical action. As we argued above, long-term self-interest is strongly correlated to ethics. Most clients want to be ethical, they want to "be able to sleep with themselves at night". The divorce of legal and ethical advice seems to operate on the assumption that clients are sociopaths. On this view, the lawyer assumes a duty to act as if clients' interests are to be pursued whatever values inform the law. This mirrors an unfortunate assumption by some company directors that they have a similar duty with respect to their shareholders, as if they really were sociopathic warriors for stockholder interests.

However, as suggested above, the best legal advice highlights the underlying ethical values (and any conflicts within or among them) to make compliance easier for the majority who wish to comply and makes principled opposition easier for those who are genuinely offended by the values the law seems to espouse. In so doing, the best legal advice assists clients to integrate rather than separate their roles as corporate executive and moral citizen. Sampford has previously suggested the way to resolve and integrate the roles of lawyers and business executives with their values as citizens and human beings.[71] The individual lawyer should seek to justify his activity as a lawyer on the basis of the benefits it provides to the society as a whole. Such justifications emphasise the importance of ensuring advice to, and representation of, individual citizens and the organisations to which they belong. Such justifications are based on human rights and the rule of law. Such justifications tend to unify rather than dichotomise the lawyer's various duties as a lawyer, a professional, a citizen and an officer of the court. Similarly, corporations and their executives need to justify their activity on the basis of the benefits it brings to society as a whole rather than to their shareholders in particular— through increasing the economic output of society and the benefits that this

---

[69] *Ibid.*

[70] Fried, *supra*, n. 32, 1056–7.

[71] C. Sampford, "Law, Institutions and the Public Private Divide" (1991) 20 *Federal Law Review* 185. This has been developed in C. Sampford and D. Wood (eds.), *Business, Ethics and the Law* (Sydney, Federation Press, 1993); and C. Sampford and S. Parker (eds.), *Legal Ethics and Legal Practice* (Oxford, Oxford University Press, 1995).

brings to all citizens, whether or not they are shareholders in their or any other corporation.

(a) Role of the In-house Lawyer

Most of the above models are based on outside lawyers advising clients. However, in-house lawyers have a particularly important role to play in giving whole business advice, particularly as their relationship with their employers (as "clients") and their method of lawyering is likely to be distinctive. As the above case studies indicate, in-house lawyers who provide broad advice are more likely to serve the interests of the corporation and ensure its long-term survival in the market-place. Mackie notes that in-house lawyers must observe how '"public policy considerations" enter case law and legislation; of how narrow commercial goals have long-term repercussions in community perceptions of business and in business liabilities.[72] They must see that the consequences of a proposed course of action for the company's external relations with customers, suppliers, competitors and the government and its internal relations with employees and shareholders are at least as important as legal ramifications.

Accordingly, one of the in-house lawyer's most important roles is to promote corporate compliance with legislation and to predict possible developments in the law. This requires a consideration of broad moral and ethical issues and the potential future reaction to current corporate practices.

The in-house lawyer can play a vital role in helping to institutionalise ethics within a corporation by counselling employees at all levels, influencing the decision-making of senior management and "creat[ing] the facts of the client situation rather than react[ing] to the situation imposed by the client".[73] In a large corporation, the in-house lawyer who successfully combines a preventive role with a counselling role has the potential to combat the risk, identified by Solomon, that "ethics will degenerate into a set of abstract rules rather than remain a living community of interpersonal relations . . . compromised (or reinterpreted) under the pressures of the corporate hierarchy".[74]

However, the important role that in-house lawyers can play in framing ethical corporate policy and changing the behaviour of both employees and management needs to be balanced against the risk of the lawyer also succumbing to "the pressures of the corporate hierarchy". Aibel notes that it requires considerable strength of character to give advice that conflicts with accepted management practices, particularly if such advice places at risk the

---

[72] K. J. Mackie, *Lawyers in Business: And the Law Business* (Basingstoke, MacMillan, 1989), 185.

[73] *Ibid*, 98.

[74] R. C. Solomon, *The New World of Business: Ethics and Free Enterprise in the Global 1990s* (Maryland, Rowman and Littlefield, 1994), 114.

lawyer's career path within the company.[75] On the other hand, if the lawyer does not provide such advice, the reputation of both the company and its lawyers may be adversely affected. Corporations which do not admit different values and opinions are not only impoverished but are less adaptable to change—especially when confronted by laws informed by different values from those of management. As Murphy notes, corporations cannot justify their existence to the community if they do not adhere to broad social values, even if this adherence is largely for customer-relations or profit-maximisation purposes.[76]

Nonetheless, the in-house lawyer is even more clearly a candidate for a moral adviser to business people than the outside lawyer. He is more than a "friend", as Fried would see him. He is part of the family. As a good employee, he has the long-term interests of the company to look to and has no pecuniary interest in expensive protracted adversarial litigation.

V. ETHICAL EDUCATION OF LAWYERS

So far, we have set out the needs of clients for ethical advice, the strong relationship between ethical advice and good legal advice, the particular suitability of lawyers to provide such advice and the models of lawyering that emphasise that suitability. However, we have also acknowledged that many lawyers are not equipped for this role, highlighting the importance of developing legal education so to equip them. Fortunately, most of the changes that are necessary to make lawyers effective ethical advisers are already occurring for other reasons in some of the more progressive law schools and are advocated by major reports into legal education.[77] What is needed is a reinforcement and, in some cases, extension of these changes to attitudes and curricula.

(a) Avoiding Mistaken Assumptions

The first change to legal education is to ensure that educators do not suffer from the same mistaken assumptions against lawyers giving ethical advice identified above. Law should not be seen as divorced from ethics. Legal advice

---

[75] H. J. Aibel, "Corporate Counsel and Business Ethics: A Personal Review" (1994) 59 *Missouri Law Review* 427, 431.

[76] Murphy, *supra* n. 10, 44. See B. Kaye, "The Real Issue in Business Ethics? Institutional Ethics and the Free Market" (1994) 19 *Australian Journal of Management* 121 at 131.

[77] D. Pearce, E. Campbell and D. Harding, *Australian Law Schools: A Discipline Assessment for the Commonwealth Tertiary Education Commission* (Canberra, Australian Government Publishing Service, 1987); C. McInnis and S. Marginson, *Australian Law Schools After the 1987 Pearce Report* (Canberra, Australian Government Publishing Service, 1994); and Lord Chancellor's Advisory Committee on Legal Education and Conduct, *First Report on Legal Education and Training* (London, Lord Chancellor's Advisory Committee on Legal Education and Conduct, 1996).

should not be divorced from ethical advice or general business advice. Duties to court and clients should not be separated from each other or from the students' ethics and values as moral citizens. Clients should not be seen as sociopaths nor lawyers as moral schizophrenics. Instead, the role of ethical values in forming the law and interpreting it should be emphasised. This is not a difficult message to sell to young academics—it merely needs to be emphasised that this is not a matter of individual moral musings but a central element to law. This is not to say that values should be the only factors external to the legal texts which are studied and emphasised. The role of history, culture, power, economics and other disciplines in the development and interpretation of the law is important for all law schools. However, values are generally the medium, the mechanism, through which other forces affect the law. The examination of values will remedy a weakness of theories which seek to demonstrate the relationship between the content of laws and the interests of powerful social groupings but do not convincingly indicate how the one affects the other.

Law schools should reverse the idea of separating law and students' sense of morality, though making them appreciate that the morality is contestable and is, indeed, the stuff of legal debates. As Shaffer observes, for far too long legal educators have followed Llewellyn's advice "to treat ethics, social policy, and their students' sense of justice as 'woozy thinking' ".[78]

Attempts should be made to identify the moral conflicts in law and in legal practice. Matasar identifies some of the most important reasons for integrating the teaching of law with the teaching of ethics:

> First, exploring the various contexts in which ethical questions underlie . . . decisions exposes the moral dimension of everyday lawyering. Seeing that dimension helps us to understand better the consequences of our decisions and allows us to balance client, personal, and societal interests. Second, examining whether some of our solutions to ethical problems are culturally contingent, whether some problems have only one right answer, and whether we have correctly perceived our problems reveals a range of ethical dilemmas and solutions that makes morality and doctrine functions of each other, not separate matters. Delimiting dilemmas and solutions shows that morally and technically sound lawyering often merge. Third, studying ethics and doctrine together allows us to confront directly the difficult questions lawyers face. Fourth, understanding that all players in the legal system—clients, lawyers, judges (and even students and teachers)—are moral actors who must take responsibility for their decisions suggests that we must all share the pain of ethical practice.[79]

Open discussion of the ethical issues involved in key areas of law and of the potentially competing values involved should be encouraged in all subjects. If the law is taught as involving certain clashes of values, then it will not

[78] T. L. Shaffer, "On Lying for Clients" (1996) 71 *Notre Dame Law Review* 195 at 196.
[79] R. A. Matasar, "Teaching Ethics in Civil Procedure Courses" (1989) 39 *Journal of Legal Education* 587 at 588.

only serve to assist students to understand legal doctrine and argument,[80] it will assist them in anticipating and understanding future changes and in advising clients of the law and of what to do under it.

(b) Curriculum Changes

These changes of attitude need to be supported by, and reflected in, the curriculum. As with other elements of theory, this does not involve merely adding an optional or even a compulsory subject to an otherwise unchanged curriculum.[81] It involves building ethics into the core of the curriculum. Like other elements of theory, we would argue that this is best done by a three-pronged strategy.

First, students should be introduced to ethics in the first year and given the tools to analyse ethical problems. The ethics taught should not be limited to legal ethics but should include general issues of ethics of relevance to ordinary moral citizens so that students may think through their own moral positions and assist clients to do so.

Secondly, ethical issues should be incorporated within a proportion of the problems discussed in every subject of the degree.[82] Nothing should seem more natural than that ethical issues are raised by law and that clients will need to be advised of them. This should also counter the possibility of the unethical character of an end result being obscured by fascination with legal techniques.

Thirdly, students need to revisit ethics towards the end of their legal education to think again more generally about the relationship between law and ethics and to engage in some deep reflection on their own values. This is the approach taken in some thoroughgoing reforms to the curriculum in existing law schools[83] and in some new law schools such as Griffith.[84]

In corporate law courses, students need to be introduced to the ethical dimension of corporate behaviour and the institutional dimensions of corporate ethics. We do not want to compound the mistake of separating law and ethics by the mistake of seeing ethical problems and solutions as merely indi-

---

[80] See C. Sampford and D. Wood, "Legal Theory and Legal Education—the Next Step" (1989) 1 *Legal Education Review* 107.

[81] C. Sampford and D. Wood, "Theoretical Dimensions of Legal Education—a Response to Pearce" (1988) 62 *Australian Law Journal* 32.

[82] This is sometimes referred to as the "pervasive" method. See Rhode, *supra* n. 47. However, it is best linked to specific core subjects for reasons given in C. Sampford and D. Wood, *supra* n. 81; and C. Sampford, "Rethinking the Core Curriculum" (1989) 12 *Adelaide Law Review* 38.

[83] D. T. Link, "The Pervasive Method of Teaching Ethics" (1989) 39 *Journal of Legal Education* 485 discusses curriculum changes at Notre Dame Law School.

[84] The curriculum is available from the Griffith law school and has been published in C. Sampford, "Reflections of a Foundation Dean—the Griffith Experience" (1996) 26 *Queensland Law Society Journal* 227.

vidual concerns. By showing them how many ethical problems arise from institutional weaknesses that subject staff to ethical dilemmas or ethical temptations, they will not only learn much of use in advising corporate clients but also understand more generally the institutional dimensions of most organisational ethics.

Change should not be limited to the first degree stage (LLB or JD). Subjects in Master's degrees could be of great interest to members of the profession. Ethics should also play a significant role in continuing legal education, once the profession is convinced of its utility in advising clients.

(c) Other Measures

To support these attitudinal and curriculum changes, it is highly desirable that law schools encourage research into ethical issues concerning a wide spectrum of law subjects (preferably in conjunction with ethically attuned lawyers in the profession) and to generate materials and cases. Both assist in "pervasive" teaching of ethics and in increasing academic awareness of, and sensitivity to, ethical issues.

In developing and selling the new curricula to the profession, academics should seek out the ethically attuned members of the profession. The profession does not appreciate being preached to. Yet academics who are used to deriding the crassness of the profession may be pleasantly surprised at the significant minority of ethically aware practitioners who will welcome academic allies—as we should appreciate professional ones.

VI. SELLING ETHICAL RISK MANAGEMENT TO CLIENTS

Although introducing ethics into the law course is valuable in its own right, the aim of educating and encouraging lawyers to be ethical advisers counts for nothing if clients are not interested in receiving the advice. Likewise, if lawyers do not believe that clients are interested in receiving advice, they will be reluctant to embrace the educational opportunities. Given the negative attitudes of many to the ethical credentials of lawyers, this requires more thought than a change in letterhead.

Increasing client awareness of the value of ethical advice will often be incremental—adding on to existing service. Lawyers may do any one or more of the following:

- incorporate ethical dimensions in more effective explanation of the law (especially in major litigation involving significant value questions);
- add ethical advice to the legal advice they are otherwise asked to give;
- incorporate ethics into compliance regimes that lawyers are increasingly being called upon to establish within corporations to protect them

against large potential liabilities imposed by government regulation or trade practices law;

- incorporate ethical elements when asked for broad-based, whole of business advice or when the clients asks "what should I do?"; and
- when clients find themselves in messy and difficult litigation, especially through the unethical behaviour of their staff or business associates, lawyers may be able to offer to suggest ways of avoiding similar problems in the future.

There is also scope for a pro-active marketing of ethical services to clients. Large law firms are now used to promoting their capacities to clients in a number of ways and contexts, such as in:

- tendering for work;
- advertising directed at particular clients or in the form of general information about services the firm offers;
- newsletters and client briefings on current developments within the firm's areas of expertise; and
- promotional activities such as sponsorship of public events and in media coverage of the firm's activities.

The range of services of use to clients that could be packaged and offered by these means could include the following:

(i) Ethics Management Advice

This entails advice on the various means of incorporating sound ethical practice into a client's management processes and includes:

- providing awareness seminars for senior staff;
- advising on the role of a code of conduct;
- advising on suitable structures and processes for promoting ethics for new and existing staff; and
- advising on dealing with ethical issues as they arise.

(ii) An Ethics Audit

This is a process for examining the ethical issues facing the organisation, their current means of resolution and the needs of the organisation for ethics development.

(iii) Assistance in drafting or re-drafting a Code of Conduct for the organisation

This includes:

- advice and/or training sessions on developing codes of conduct;

- generation of internal case studies to focus code development on real problems;
- consultation with staff; and
- follow-up training to increase staff understanding of the code's purpose, meaning and effect.

(iv) Ethics Education for Staff

This includes:

- induction training,
- training of trainers, and
- ethics awareness sessions.

(v) Ethics Maintenance

This includes:

- provision of ongoing advice on the operation of ethical programmes and sustaining the ethical performance of the organisation;
- monitoring code awareness and effectiveness;
- provision of confidential advice on ethical issues as they arise.

In all of this, law firms might emphasise both the positive advantage of improving the ethics of a client's organisation as well as the potential damage caused by not taking ethical considerations into account.

A firm which successfully decided to offer ethical advice would establish a marketing edge over others. Not only would the firm be meeting an important client need, its clients' public image would benefit from being seen to be advised by the "ethics firm". Other firms would need to compete to maintain their own clients and to avoid being branded one of the "no ethics" firms. This competition would generate expectations within the business community that at least some lawyers were suitable persons to whom they might turn for ethical advice. The increasing expectation would be met with increasing provision in what is potentially a virtuous circle (or rather a virtuous spiral). Even if the spiral does not reach its full felicific potential, it would mean that at least some lawyers were offering ethical advice and assisting themselves and their firms to create a more noble profession.

VII. CONCLUSIONS

In this chapter, we have considered the tantalising suggestion that lawyers should be the natural profession to whom clients should turn for ethical advice. We went beyond the knee-jerk responses based on oxymoronic lawyer jokes to consider the arguments against lawyers taking such a role. We argued that the case against lawyers giving ethical advice is based upon a number of flawed assumptions about the nature of law, ethics, legal practice and the essence of the lawyer–client relationship.

Rather than seeing law and ethics as opposites sides of an institutional chasm, they share much in common. Both law and ethics involve the application of values to human action, with law providing a forum in which differences over values can be formally debated. They are not identical, but they can be mutually supportive.

Although some attributes of modern legal practice may seem to limit the potential of individual lawyers to raise ethical issues with clients, other aspects are highly positive. Not only does the best legal advice have ethical content (if only to reflect the ethical values that will affect the decision-maker), but it is in the interests of clients to receive a richer mix of ethics in their legal advice, as the above case studies indicate.

If the artificial dichotomies between law and ethics are rejected, it becomes relatively easy to locate the giving of ethical advice within the lawyer's overall duty to his or her client. However, this will require an alternate model of lawyering to that of zealous advocacy.

This is not to say that lawyers can simply adjust their shingles. Legal education has been infected with the same erroneous attitudes to law and ethics that lead many to reject an ethical role for lawyers. Clients should not be seen as sociopaths or moral schizophrenics and law schools should reverse the idea of separating students from their own sense of morality. Educational reform must tackle those attitudes head on and make supportive curriculum changes. Law firms will have to sell ethical risk management to their clients through a pro-active, though incremental approach. However, there are benefits to clients and law firms if the latter are seen as ethical. Such benefits open the possibility of a profession which lives up to its high ideals.

The jokes about lawyers that support a knee-jerk response to the idea of lawyers as ethical advisers represents real elements of lawyering. However, the natural linking of ethical and legal advice provides some signposts towards the best and most noble ideals of the profession and its academic members. These are ideals worthwhile instilling in students as well as their future employers, partners and clients.

17

Legal Ethics in Europe

AVROM SHERR

1. INTRODUCTION

This chapter reflects a study of the state of legal ethical rules in four countries across Europe. It represents the first fruits of an exercise funded by the European University Institute in Florence which brought together on two occasions legal ethicists from six countries. The initial intentions of the project were: to provide an opportunity for scholarly exchange in this field; to build up an initial picture of the major recent and current issues relating to legal ethics within each jurisdiction; to draw from this the beginnings of a comparative understanding of legal ethics across Europe; and to gain a higher level analysis of legal ethics and of ethical issues than would be available from within the context of a single jurisdiction. The background for such objectives was the overall European Union desire to provide a harmonisation of law and legal professionals across Europe.

The group considered legal ethics to be of interest in themselves, in terms of self-regulation, in the picture that changes in ethics provides, in the different approaches between civil and common law countries, in terms of control of entry into the profession and in the symbols they provide of professional life.

1. Legal ethics are intrinsically important because they provide a particular view of both law and lawyers. Since legal ethics regulate and constrain the activities of legal professionals it is important to note how such constraint is organised and accepted in different jurisdictions by those who themselves apply the law to others. Not only is the nature of such regulations of interest, but also the lack or abundance of them. Similarly relevant is whether such rules are in general obeyed and what procedures, systems and tribunals are available for policing and judging the conduct of lawyers affected by such rules.

2. The level of self regulation was also studied. By tradition, professionals regulate themselves. Some would say this remains a defining characteristic of professionalism. But increasingly there is a lay involvement in professional discipline, and in some parts of the world, an increasing societal or governmental influence which removes ultimate power from the legal profession to regulate itself.

3. The nature of recent changes in ethical rules also provides insight. In a sense, conduct rules act as a barometer of change within the market for legal services, of professional attitudes to their work, of the decline of altruism in the professions and in general the deprofessionalisation of legal work. Changes in the level of competition in the market for legal services, new players in this market, and renegotiations among professional bodies for areas of "turf", all lead on to changes in conduct rules which reflect the new state of the market.

4. Apart from the intrinsic importance of the details of the rules themselves and how much they tell the observer about the legal profession, the legal services market and the culture of law, the context of such rules is a deciding influence. In the European context there is a clear division between civil law and common law countries and the different approaches that each might have to rules of conduct and the business of professional discipline. Is the level of understanding of conduct issues similar in both legal families? Could harmonisation of Europe be progressed through the harmonisation of conduct rules? Does the draft code of the *Barreaux* of Europe[1] provide any clear guidance within each jurisdiction to take such approaches forward? These are all issues of increasing importance.

5. Openness of the professions and especially equality of opportunity on entry into the legal profession is an indicator of a more democratic society and of a legal system dedicated to fairness. The ethical rules will often be at the heart of regulation regarding entry, qualification and practice as professionals; although in many countries such issues will be enshrined in statute rather than professional regulation. The *rites de passage* are important indicators of the social construction of the profession, such as the eating of dinners in the Inns of Court as a part of the process of qualifying as an English barrister, until recently.

6. Methods for control of numbers entering the profession are worthy of study in themselves, but are also symbolic of the social exclusion which professions adopt. In Scotland and Northern Ireland, young barristers have been allowed to take cases from a library desk, rather than having to find a tenancy in chambers as in England and Wales, which acts as an artificial barrier to entry, so carefully guarded by the existing members of the profession.

7. Court dress can also be a major symbol of turf and status warfare between branches of the profession. In England and Wales, solicitors can apply for Higher Court rights of audience like the barristers who have previously held this monopoly. But, only barristers may still wear the wigs which maintain a clear visual separation between the two branches.

8. In Germany, a spouse, even if divorced, may not be admitted to the same court, nor an applicant who is related to the judge at that court to the third

---

[1] CCBE "Joint Draft Code of Ethics".

degree (i.e. including grandparents, uncles and aunts and their offspring, and in-laws to the second degree—parents, brothers, sisters and their offspring). In Scotland, by contrast, the small inbred bar (Faculty of Advocates) is replete with sons and daughters of judges who not infrequently appear before their parents, and have on occasion appeared on opposite sides in front of their fathers. All of these symbols reflect parochially meaningful allusions to control, status and exclusiveness of the profession or different parts of it. Conduct rules provide a rich seam of such symbolism, couched within ancient traditions of ancient professions.

This chapter brings together some of the initial output of this project based on a common template. It was intended that each country should provide similar information from which further synthesis and analysis might proceed. Not only do countries and legal jurisdictions differ but so also do their legal philosophies and their scholars and writers. The end product does not quite provide an equal structure or content from each participant. Nevertheless, a picture emerges from which much can be gained in both individual and overall perspectives.

Initially authors were asked to keep to the following structure:

1. Information from each jurisdiction should relate principally to the legal profession which is "most relevant in socio-legal terms". This will often be the profession with the largest group of lawyers within that jurisdiction. This does not mean that "groups" of lawyers or "legal professions" should be ignored even in the initial analysis if they provide interest or are of importance, but in order to begin somewhere most attention should be paid to the most "relevant" or the largest legal profession in each jurisdiction. The initial jurisdictions were as follows:

Leny de Groot-van Leeuwen	—	The Netherlands
Luis Diez-Picazo*	—	Spain
Vittorio Olgiati*	—	Italy
Alan Paterson	—	Scotland
Ulrike Schultz	—	Germany
Avrom Sherr	—	England and Wales

* (Unfortunately Professor Diez-Picazo's schedule did not allow for full involvement in this stage of the project, though his helpful comments were of use throughout. Professor Olgiati's report does not sufficiently conform to the structure for easy comparison and therefore is not reported here.)

2. The entry conditions or "generational rites de passage" (Olgiati) to the profession should be specified. This should not be detailed plans of the full scheme of education and training, but more an analytical comment on how open the profession is, who act as the gate-keepers, what specialisms exist and what conditions are necessary for these, what numbers are applying and what numbers get into the professions and perhaps some comment on gender, ethnicity etc. of successful applicants over unsuccessful—all of this

to be viewed from an "ethics" perspective, rather than a legal education perspective.

3. A short description of the level of self-governance, self-administration and self-judging that occurs within the profession in relation to the setting of rules and assessing their breach. What level of third party regulation and lay involvement exists?

4. Some basic statistics showing the numbers of complaints, number of complaints per lawyer, number of hearings, numbers of sanctions and number of serious sanctions, perhaps compared with other professions such as medicine in that jurisdiction.

5. A statement of the three major issues (currently or recently) under discussion for legal ethics in that jurisdiction.

6. Some comment, or a more detailed analysis, of the situation regarding some particular issues in each jurisdiction: specialisation, conflicts of interest, sole-practitioners.

7. Some assessment of the current position, and trend, regarding a move from "professionalism" to "business enterprise" in that profession.

8. Some assessment of "the gap" between the rules and reality. This would have to be intuitive only at the beginning unless something more concrete can be provided.

9. Some piece of "jurisprudence" i.e. a case, preferably in English showing how a major issue of legal ethics has been dealt with by the courts in that jurisdiction.

10. Some hypothetical, or hypotheticals, allowing each jurisdiction to comment on how the case would be handled there. This might involve the selection of a mainstream case (such as conflict of interest). Each writer would discuss what course the complaint would normally run, and who would do what at what stages.

It was also agreed that "we should initially aim mainly for the concrete, the specific and the basic".

In the first national reports of the project[2] the individual items do not actually conform in total to this structure but, where there is conformity, a level of comparison becomes more possible between the different jurisdictions. An overview of issues, approaches, levels of complaints, conflicts, levels of competition and deprofessionalisation begins to appear.

2. WHAT ARE LEGAL ETHICS?

An issue which underlies all discussions of legal ethics and is beginning to have some effect at the regulatory and educational levels is much more fundamental and questions the nature of legal ethics in principle.

[2] See *International Journal of the Legal Profession*, Special Issue 1/2/97.

A positivist or "black letter law" view would detail legal ethics as simply the regulations passed under some sort of statutory framework which are called "principles of conduct" or "legal ethics". If an issue is covered in those regulations then it is a matter of legal ethics and if it is not so covered it will not be a matter of legal ethics. There are clearly a number of difficulties even in the face of the regulations with this sort of approach. Some codes of conduct are quite short and may be written in a vague, exhortatory fashion, rather like a statute or code in a civil law country. In other jurisdictions a legal profession might decide to spell out the details, so far as is possible, of regulations going to some 600 or 700 pages. It is likely to be the case that similar ethical issues arise in each of those jurisdictions, but the regulations drafting policy is simply different. It is even possible that the regulatory approach is similar even though the mode of regulation is different.

In such widely differing systems it is also possible that the distinctions between a common law approach and a civil law approach to legal reasoning also become clear. Hence, legal ethical regulation may be seen as simply another set of rules to circumvent. This places legal ethics in the same context as all other laws, which they are not. In some civil jurisdictions a further distinction is made between statute, "deontology" (the Code of Conduct) and ethics (moral rules).

As legal professions themselves develop, they need different rules to govern the way in which they work. Government or society may also dictate changes in approach or rules. It has been suggested by moral historians that morality was simply another way in which one class exerted influence over another. In terms of early legal ethics writings, Carlin's work on Sole Practitioners seems to suggest that this was at least true for the rules of ethics in Chicago.[3] Large and wealthy firms of lawyers dictated to small lawyers who worked for the poor how they could, and could not, do their business. The lawyers who ran professional organisations and policed the conduct book usually came from one class and those who were affected by the rules, came from another. Indeed a brief survey of the rules of "etiquette" existing in 1974 for solicitors in England and Wales (the year this writer qualified—published as "*A Guide to the Professional Conduct of Solicitors*", 1974, 229 pages) shows a set of rules which are largely about how solicitors should react to each other (no competition), how solicitors should react to barristers (treat other professionals with respect) and how solicitors should react to the court. There is little about how to deal with clients.

Although all areas have grown, the current Guide (7th Edition, 1996) has a staggering 745 pages and many of the elements of the new "conduct" rules deal mainly with safeguarding the client through rules of "competence".

In England and Wales the Courts and Legal Services Act 1990 attempted to bring about an atmosphere of competition in legal services which attempted

---

[3] Carlin, Jerome, *Lawyers On Their Own* (Republished 1994, Austin & Winfield Inc, Maryland).

to deregulate the "industry" in such a way that people who were not qualified as lawyers might be able to qualify as being licensed in a small specialism of law. Deregulation brought with it a multitude of regulations for the new licensees to achieve a particular level of competence in order to safeguard the public. But if the new more limited professionals were to be covered by these rules, they also had to be shown to cover the fully qualified solicitors as well.

In addition the enormous growth in the numbers entering the profession in the late 1980's brought a more heterogenous group of young lawyers on stream. Coming from somewhat wider backgrounds there was a feeling that they were not policed, as previous generations may have been, by the class system. If the government were to encourage or introduce competition into the legal services industry then there had to be some means of ensuring quality. The idea of a social contract which enabled lawyers and other professionals to have high status relied on lawyers' altruism and the inherent quality of their work.[4] The effect of competition might be to undermine the altruism and to lower the quality of work to a level the profession could get away with in the market place, not what it would be proud of in the committee rooms. If law was to become a "business" then a more fully articulated code of conduct was essential. Common law lawyers were highly adept at seeing loopholes in the law, finding ways of getting around the letter of the law on behalf of their clients and ignoring its spirit. This could not be the case for the rules of ethical conduct of the profession itself.

This takes the discussion onto a more general discourse which seems to erupt periodically, at least in Common Law jurisdictions, which questions the nature of "legal ethics". Would it not be better, suggest the purists, to call the lawyers "Code of Conduct" what it is rather than attempting to dignify it with the title of an area of moral philosophy? Legal ethics, it is said, are not really about moral behaviour, in the same way that laws are not necessarily about moral behaviour but more about economic, social and political power among a ruling or governing elite. The issue has some amusement value, especially where non-lawyers consider "legal ethics" to be an oxymoron, (and especially in America where the jokes about lawyers' grasping behaviour and immorality are rife).

But sometimes an issue is raised which goes to the crux of this division between "conduct" and "ethics". An interesting example of this which has become important in the United States and is now receiving some attention in the UK is the issue of mandatory *pro-bono* legal work.[5] Beginning with Nixon's administration, money for the Legal Services Corporation has been diminished and large numbers of people who need legal services cannot afford them or obtain them. Many Bar Associations in different states have

---

[4] See Paterson *infra.* n. 9.

[5] Jollife, D., "Mandatory Pro-Bono work for Lawyers: Professional Responsibility or Legal Enslavement?", Institute of Advanced Legal Studies Seminar, 18th March 1996.

attempted to service this problem in some small way through mandatory hours of providing free legal advice or assistance in order to maintain a license as an attorney in that state. Such rules are made by the Supreme Court of each state and two states have been prominent in pushing for a mandatory number of hours. There are all sorts of exemptions and ways in which people who work in large firms can organise for someone else to do the work for them. But the real question is why lawyers should be placed in this position, as opposed to doctors, accountants, architects or butchers, bakers and candlestick makers. One might suggest on the style of Rodell,[6] that lawyers actually create the legal problems themselves that affect people and therefore should have an obligation to help out those who are poor and cannot afford legal services that are necessary to solve those problems. Apart from this notion, the only real justification for the suggestion that lawyers should operate mandatory *pro-bono*, as opposed to voluntary *pro-bono*, is that they should have an altruistic, higher morality or ethical behaviour.

This then is a discreet example of an issue which provides a dividing line between a proper code of conduct and a question of higher morality. Apparently in New York State research was carried out to plumb the depths of unmet legal need and that research suggested that there were some three million issues per year that needed to be dealt with by lawyers which were not receiving that treatment. In New York the chief judge of the State Supreme Court was the most vocal proponent of mandatory *pro-bono*.[7]

There was a great deal of opposition from among the lawyers. The source of the Chief Justice's argument was the moral high ground and he was advocating that lawyers be mandated to provide this service on grounds of superior morality. Unfortunately, when he was found to be involved in some issue of moral turpitude, the force of his arguments relating to *pro-bono* collapsed and so did the issue itself.[8] In Florida it was a group of senior partners in larger firms who were pushing the issue of mandatory *pro-bono* and the reaction from the profession was so strong that it has been relaxed there as well. This particular issue therefore seems to suggest that lawyers' codes of conduct and laws of morality are rather different exercises.[9]

It will be seen that such issues are crucial in any future definition of the principles of ethical legal conduct. The battleground over mandatory *pro-bono* work and whether this form of regulation should appear as part of the conduct rules, exemplifies the distinction between moral behaviour and legal ethics. Similarly, proper understanding of this issue has a major effect on the purpose of teaching of legal ethics at all stages of legal education.[10] If what is really intended when a Report such as the ACLEC Report refers to teaching

---

[6] "Woe unto you Lawyers" Rodell, F.19.
[7] Jolliffe, *Supra*, n. 5.
[8] id.
[9] id.
[10] See comments within ACLEC's *First Report* on Legal Education mentioned above.

lawyers to be more conscious of ethics, is that they should in general behave more ethically and more morally towards their work and their clients, irrespective of what the conduct rules state, then what is required is something very different from a simple knowledge element of what those conduct rules contain.[11]

In the United States it has been essential for some time for all university law courses intending to qualify students for the profession to include a compulsory course on "legal profession". Such courses vary considerably, but they largely teach and examine their students on the statutory and conduct basis for legal rules. All of this is quite different from the intentions of Chief Justice Warren Burger, when he noted the ethical deficiencies of the American Bar soon after Watergate.[12] Partly as a result of his comments and exhortations the Ford Foundation funded courses on "professional responsibility" through the Council For Legal Education in Professional Responsibility, in every law school in the United States. Many of such courses operated through a "clinical" model in which students worked on real or simulated cases whilst they were at university under the supervision of teachers. It is submitted that only this model can really be helpful in discussing the detail of moral and ethical behaviour with students in the appropriate legal context. All other approaches hang around knowledge acquisition of conduct rules, rather than attitude and behaviour change among aspiring lawyers. Further discussion of this issue is therefore essential for the proper development of new codes of legal ethics, teaching of legal ethics and approaches to complaints and discipline.

3. FROM PROFESSIONALISM TO BUSINESS ENTERPRISE

According to Paterson the concept of professionalism is a neo-contractualist one including self regulation and autonomy, ethics and a quality of service which denotes expertise.[13] This concept relies on all three being present, the loss of any leading to a shift in the nature of a profession or, as now, a re-negotiation of the concept of professionalism. Gradually the legal profession in England and Wales has seen a number of changes which have affected its autonomous position. Firstly, reforms in relation to its conveyancing monopoly and its right to advertise, have led to an injection of competition within the profession; and between the profession and outside concerns such as the financial services market, which have led to a trend towards market forces and business enterprise. Secondly, as discontent from the public with the level of service that solicitors provide, and the high fees which they can command for

---

[11] See also Sheinman, L., "Looking for Legal Ethics", *Int.J. of the Legal Profession*, 1997, 139–154.

[12] Burger, W., "The 1973 Sonnet Memorial Lecture", 42 *Fordham L.Rev* 227 (1973–4).

[13] See Paterson, A., "Professionalism And The Legal Services Market", *International Journal of The Legal Profession*, 1996 Vol. 3 No. 1 and 2 137–168.

that service, has developed, the Government enacted the Courts and Legal Services Act l990 in order to take over part of the profession's own regulatory function.

Another shift towards business enterprise has been experienced as a result of the Legal Aid franchising specifications which operate as a legal equivalent of ISO 9002 to ensure that management and administrative systems are in place within law firms. These concentrate more on management structures than the quality of the legal work which is carried out within the firms, as do the practice Management Standards which the Law Society have endorsed for all law firms irrespective of whether legal aid work is undertaken. Consequently the organisation of the firm and the way in which the work is carried out and recorded is to a certain extent taken out of the hand of the solicitor and is dictated instead by the consumer in place of the consumer.[14] The consumer in question is of course the largest purchaser of legal services in England and Wales, the Legal Aid Board. In the case of legal aid work it will have, amongst other motives, the reduction of legal costs according to the principle of market forces.

The move towards quality assurance has led to the spotlight being turned on various aspects of legal practice which are then dissected to discover whether it is possible to measure quality within the legal profession. The charge that the profession is being deskilled as a result, and through this demystification is losing its identity and the appearance of exclusive expertise may be a fair one, although it may be a necessary step to convince the public that solicitors should be regarded as having particular expertise in the legal field. If the public have already lost faith in the ability of solicitors to provide a legal service which is better than one which could be offered by another provider, then quality assurance may be the only way to win the public and the Legal Aid Board around and therefore justify the high fees and continuing monopoly in certain types of work.

The introduction of block contracts for legal aid work could transform the present demand-led legal aid system into a system of competitive tendering between law firms and the Legal Aid Board more akin to the business environment than the traditional conception of a profession.[15] This is happening in "beauty contests" in the commercial context and in local authority funded areas of work with Compulsory Competitive Tendering. Legal Services have therefore become a saleable commodity, and the price fixing of the past is yet further eroded with solicitors openly price cutting in order to secure legal aid block contracts. This ethos will gradually filter through to non-legally aided firms as the culture changes in the legal services market.

Conditional fee arrangements will make a further incursion into the professional ethos of the English legal profession. As a result of proposed changes

---

[14] See Sommerlad, H., "Managerialism And The Legal Profession", *International Journal of The Legal Profession* vol.2 no. 2/3 l995 159–185.

[15] Ibid.

in the English Legal Aid system, conditional fee arrangements are likely to be much more important in the future. In order to undertake a case on this basis, a solicitor will have to make an assessment of the likelihood of success, since the risk of work undertaken by the firm will be carried by the solicitor. This will mean that a lawyer will be personally involved in the financial outlay of providing the funding for litigation.

The insurance industry will also be involved in insuring the risks of plaintiff litigants against the costs of the other side being awarded against them if they lose. The insurers will base their assessment of risk on that provided by the lawyer concerned. The lawyers' ability to continue to utilise insurance in this way is likely to depend, in the long run, on a correct assessment of such risks. In brief, the lawyer will be more careful, or more entrepreneurial, in relation to the conduct of cases depending upon the real possibility of risk assessment, the firm's ability to take on a large enough number of cases in order to spread the risk and other factors which are more related to the running of a business enterprise than the conduct of representation on behalf of litigants in judicial fora. Conditional fee arrangements set up a more major conflict of interests between clients and their own lawyers than has previously occurred. Although such approaches are not unknown, and contingency fees are the norm in the United States, the changes to the legal profession within England and Wales are bound to be considerable. The resultant effects on rules of conduct will be an interesting example of the profession accommodating the new entrepreneurial approach.

4. General Comparison of the Disciplinary Systems of the Bar in the US, the Netherlands, Scotland, England and Wales, and Germany

In Table 1 opposite, a rough comparison is provided of the numbers of legal practitioners per head of inhabitants in the United States, the Netherlands, Scotland, England and Wales, and Germany. The figures for England and Wales cover only solicitors. Another 10% could be added to the numbers of legal practitioners if barristers were taken into account. The Scottish figures also miss out the Bar. The Dutch Bar does not include notaries, public prosecutors or lawyers in public administration who all belong to different occupations. The figures for Germany also exclude public prosecutors and lawyers in public administration. Even so, it is interesting to note how different the ratios of practitioners to inhabitants are. The largest number of legal practitioners per head of population is in the United States. Both the Netherlands and Germany have a civil law system with special professions for prosecutors and public administration lawyers. Here the ratio of practitioners to inhabitants is quite different. Germany seems much closer to Scotland and England and Wales. The United States has two and half times as many lawyers per inhabitant than Scotland and England and Wales.

Table 1: General comparison of the disciplinary systems of the bar in the US, The Netherlands, Scotland, England and Wales and Germany[a]

	United States[b]	Netherlands[c]	Scotland	England and Wales	Germany
No. of practitioners	700,000	5,000	6,000	66,123	
Practitioners per 10,000 inhabitants	30	3	12	12.85	10
No. of complaints filed per year	50,000	1.400 (?)	1,321	18,017	
Complaints filed per year, per 100 practitioners	7	28 (?)	22	27	
Percentage of filed complaints heard	10(?)%	15 (?)%	32%	1.49%	
No. of complaints heard per year	5,000 (?)	200	420	268	
Complaints heard per year, per 100 practitioners	1 (?)	4	7	0.41	0.58
No. of reprimand etc. sanctions per year	1300	50	273		
Sanction per year, per 10 practitioners	0.2	1.0	4.6		
No. of serious sanctions per year	1000	14	13	92	
Serious sanctions per year, per 100 practitioners	0.15	0.30	0.3	0.14	

a. The figures are not all for the same year. The figures for US and Netherlands are "rough national coverages during the 1980s" (de Groot-Van Leeuwen, *L. International Journal of the Legal profession*, Vol 4 No. 1 / 2, 21,1997). The figures for Scotland and England and Wales are for 1995 as are the figures for Germany regarding complaints (the number of practitioners per 10,000 inhabitants was 1997 data).

b. There is a caveat to the reliability of the figures contained in Table 33. Abel points out that the number of states not reporting figures was substantial and varied on a yearly basis. Consequently the more reliable indicator from the figures in Table 33 is the ratio of complaints per practitioner at state level.

c. The comparison of the number of lawyers per 10,000 inhabitants in the US and The Netherlands is subject to the limitation that the Dutch figures represent only advocates rather than all practitioners

The number of complaints filed against the lawyers in each country, per 100 practitioners, also provides an interesting set of comparisons. This information is not available for Germany. England and Wales and the Netherlands show complaints in the region of 27 and 28 per 100 practitioners. Scotland is not far below this, but the United States has about a quarter of the complaints, per practitioner, as the Netherlands and England and Wales. Clearly, such comparisons are rough and do not take into account issues of culture, consumerism, complaints systems, or any other data which would affect these figures. Rough statistics of this nature therefore suggest new angles of enquiry rather than providing answers of themselves. Why should the number of complaints be so much less in the United States? Is the level of complaint really too high in the other three countries, or is it what one would expect?

The next heading 'Percentage of filed complaints heard' also provides a picture of major differences in approach in each of the complaints handling systems. In England and Wales, the largest proportion of complaints are dealt with by a system of conciliation (between 70 and 80%).[16] Of the complaints which are not dealt with by conciliation, another 20–25% are dealt with by a Committee made up of a mixture of lawyers and clients. Where it decides conduct issues alone, it has a preponderance of lawyers, where it decides issues of Inadequate Professional Services, it has a larger number of consumers than lawyers involved. Decisions are made on paper and therefore these cases cannot be taken into account as complaints "heard". If, however, these committees were taken into account, the position would be somewhere between that of Scotland at 32% and the Netherlands at 15%. The United States, at 10% of filed complaints heard, provides, once again, an interesting comparison. When looked at against the numbers of practitioners, Germany looks close to England and Wales and the United States whereas the Netherlands and Scotland are higher.

Finally, looking at serious sanctions per year per practitioner, further differences appear. England and Wales is closest to the United States, whereas the Netherlands and Scotland show similar results at double the rate of the other two.

5. Comparison between Legal and Medical Complaints

As a means of considering the level of complaints and systems of complaint handling in each country, within its own context, the idea of comparing complaints against doctors with complaints against lawyers is superficially attractive. It may reduce the effect of cultural or national differences which would otherwise play considerable importance in a comparison of different legal regimes.

[16] See Annual Reports of the Office for the Supervision of Solicitors and Solicitors Complaints Bureau, 1991 onwards.

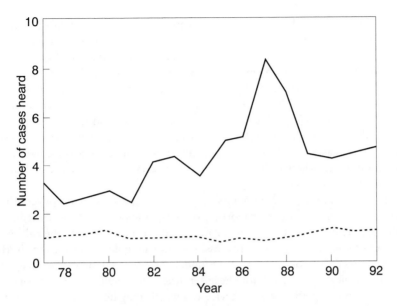

Fig. 1. Numbers of cases heard by the disciplinary committees of the bar and the medical profession in the Netherlands from 1977 to 1992.

Source: yearly reports of the respective disciplinary courts, adapted by ND/LdeG-vL.

Taking the work of Leny De Groot-van Leeuwen, I excerpt a graph of comparison of the numbers of complaints against lawyers and medics in the Netherlands over a time period, computed against the numbers of professionals in each profession. (See Fig. 1.)

According to de Groot-van Leeuwen, the disciplinary procedures of the medical profession in the Netherlands are largely copied from the example of the Bar although the type of sanctions differ. From the above chart it can be seen that the number of cases heard by the medical disciplinary committees rose from 296 in 1977 to 462 in 1987 and onwards to 720 in 1992. The chart shows the number of cases heard by the committees in both professions, per hundred professionals. The figures for the medical profession are much lower and more stable. The figures for the legal profession are much more volatile. Among the possible causes mentioned by de Groot-van Leeuwen are the growth of the Bar and the emancipation of the public, the increased accessibility of the committees and the decline of the quality of legal services. However, the growth of the Bar does not sufficiently explain the changes in proportion to number of cases. The clearest indication is in fact the rise in the number of members of the public who have sought legal assistance. There appears to be more of a constancy in the number per clients served. This would also seem to pre-empt the hypothesis about the decline in quality of the legal services.[17]

---

[17] de Groot-van Leeuwen, L.E., "The Legal Ethics Code and Disciplinary System in the Netherlands", *International Journal of the Legal Profession*, (1997) Vol 4 Nos. 1 /2, 16–17.

The figures in England and Wales comparing complaints against doctors and lawyers also provide some interest. It is noticeable that there are twice as many doctors per head of population as lawyers. The numbers of complaints per doctor were very much smaller, with one complaint per hundred as compared with twenty-seven complaints per hundred lawyers. Approximately 70% of complaints to the SCB are mediated by the Bureau and no further action is taken. For doctors approximately 50% of cases result in no further action.

Both doctors and lawyers have a forum which deals with serious complaints. .0785 cases per 100 medical practitioners went to the professional conduct committee, whereas 0.41 cases per 100 lawyers went to the Solicitors Disciplinary Tribunal.

All in all, many more complaints appear to be made against lawyers than doctors and a much larger proportion of complaints go to a serious tribunal with the possibility of striking the professional off the register or the roll. Any further comparison of the two professions must take into account that in the UK, most medical work is carried out under the National Health Service, and patients do not pay directly for these services. The result is that patients are less likely to complain about a service for which they do not make payment. Patients also need to be registered with a general practitioner and such registration relates not only to an individual but also to the rest of the family. Accordingly making a complaint against a practitioner on the medical side may mean that the entire family needs to find another doctor. Patients will often need to return to their doctors and so registration is important.

Although many lawyers will also be working for clients on Legal Aid, Legal Aid only covers a fairly small proportion of the population and even those who are eligible for Legal Aid may need to pay something towards their lawyer's work. One does not need to be registered with a particular lawyer either. So, if one lawyer is the subject of a complaint, the client may always go to another. It would therefore be wrong to make simplistic comparisons between the two professions, but some understanding of the complaints systems and numbers of complaints within each is helpful in understanding the cultural climate in which each exists. Together with information from other jurisdictions, some baseline data will enable further comparison and analysis in the future.

6. REGULATION, SELF-REGULATION AND DE-REGULATION

The snapshot across Europe shows a set of quite different positions. German codes of conduct are almost entirely based on full statute, recently revamped and taking into account the new situation of the old East Germany. Government involvement is strong and discipline is organised around the court's structure. In the Netherlands, codes of honour moved into codes of self-regulation, and the profession both makes its own rules and regulates its own discipline. Although there is a statutory basis which provides the structure for the profession, the passing of rules and maintenance of their enforcement is entirely based on the self-governance of the profession. The Scottish Bar and Law Society remain masters in their own houses in relation to the setting of rules, though a Legal Services Ombudsman can look at complaints against the way in which the professional bodies have dealt with complaints made to them.

The system in England and Wales shows a mixture of self-regulation, consumer and judicial involvement. As mentioned above, the Courts and Legal Services Act 1990 set out a structure in which changes to the rules of the Law Society and the Bar needed to go before the Lord Chancellor's Advisory Committee on Legal Education and Conduct (ACLEC). Until November 1997, it was thought that all the changes in rules needed to be seen by ACLEC, but in that month the Lord Chancellor passed down a decision made together with the four senior judges that this procedure was only applicable to a much more limited area of rule changes relating to the conduct of litigation and the rights of advocacy. The procedure involved ACLEC reviewing all changes and then making its recommendations to the four senior judges including the Lord Chancellor. Although there is still some uncertainty about the effect of the Lord Chancellor's decision, the power of that committee and the four senior judges seems to have been lessened. The importance of the committee is that it contains as many non-lawyer members on it, representing the consumer interest with regard to legal services, as lawyers. An important element in the recognition of the importance of consumer involvement in changes in conduct codes could be lost.

Under the English system, there is also a Legal Services Ombudsman who deals with complaints about complaint handling by the Bar and the Law Society. A further question which has been raised recently is whether there ought to be another "level of appeal" for solicitors who are found guilty of misconduct within the lower levels of committee decisions, without a hearing, but only on paper.[18] The English solicitors' profession therefore exhibits a large amount of formal legal regulation in its code of conduct, a code so large that its contents are unlikely to be known in its entirety by all members of the profession. The profession has recently moved from being entirely self regulating to a position where some changes in conduct rules have to go before an advisory committee, which also considers the entrance of competitors into the legal services market, and also advises on legal education and training.

These different systems present quite a range of approaches to the making of ethical rules, the governance of the professions and the policing of professional misconduct. Without further comparative study, it is impossible to say what effects such different approaches have on either the nature of the rules, or the obedience to them of practitioners. Clearly other issues of culture, pro-

---

[18] See Mears, *New Law Journal*, (1997) December.

fessional fragmentation, general obedience to law and authority will also be important in answering that question. But it is interesting to see the rather different approach currently being taken in the State of Victoria in Australia, and recognised elsewhere in this book, to this issue.

7. MULTI DISCIPLINARY PARTNERSHIPS, MULTI NATIONAL PARTNERSHIPS AND CONFLICTS OF INTERESTS

Multinational partnerships are now allowed in some of the countries of Europe and multidisciplinary partnerships are also allowed in some European countries. A multidisciplinary partnership allows lawyers to join with others who are not lawyers in the ownership and control of a law firm. A multinational partnership allows lawyers from different countries to join together in a similar way. Multidisciplinary partnerships may be important for the smaller firm as well as the larger firm; multinational partnerships are clearly more important for the large firms involved in transnational and international commercial work.

A multidisciplinary partnership on the "high street" could bring together lawyers, building societies, accountants, surveyors and estate agents, for example, in a "one stop shop". This could clearly produce an enhanced service to consumers who will not have to move between different types of professional as they seek a house, finance, and then conveyancing. But, tying in particular sets of services such as a particular firm of solicitors, a particular firm of surveyor or estate agents, and a particular building society or mortgage company could have the effect of setting up monopolistic or olligopolistic systems which could make it difficult for non-allied firms to compete. There might also be major conflicts of interest between the objectives of different professionals. Estate agents might want simply to sell houses, whereas solicitors want to be much more careful about what their clients were buying; and mortgage companies would want to know whether the buyers were likely to continue to pay the mortgage. Problems of confidentiality, as between the different parties would be much greater than they are now.

On the larger, more commerical scene, the largest firm of lawyers in France is owned by a firm of accountants. In England and Wales, and Scotland, there are already firms of solicitors which are closely allied to some of the major accountancy practices. Garrett & Co in association with Arthur Anderson started in 1993, Arnheim & Co with Price Waterhouse in 1996, and Tite and Lewis with Coopers and Lybrand in 1997. Although they have not merged so as to become a "multidisciplinary partnership" they already have the ethos, the connections and the approach of the accountancy practices with whom they are connected. In the Netherlands, Price Waterhouse is challenging the Dutch Bar's prohibition of partnership with accountants and Arthur Anderson is in litigation on the same issue.[19]

[19] Flood, J., "Megalawyering in the Global Order", (1996), Vol. 3, *Int.J.of the Legal Profession*, 119.

A more recent phenomenon is the direct merger between a large commercial firm in England and the largest of the German firms, Freshfields and Berends. This has been followed by rumours of other mergers. Previously a rather smaller firm, Harris, Cramer, Rosenblatt merged with a French firm and other alliances are being sought.

The Freshfields alliance produces interest because of the rules in Germany which allow multidisciplinary partnerships. This means that the German firm merged with Freshfields is allowed to have a partnership with non-lawyers, whereas Freshfields at present, as an English law firm working under the rules of the Law Society, is not allowed to do so.

At the international level, quite clearly the numbers of such alliances will cause more problems for conflicts of interests as large multinational commercial companies will find smaller numbers of available firms to go to in each country in order to avoid such conflicts. A conflict search for firms so joined would have to consider all clients and/or firms on the other side of all transactions or litigations with which any of the firms in the partnership have been concerned.

A common European approach to these issues would certainly be helpful.

8. CONCLUSION

Many of the current issues for legal ethics are similar across the countries in Europe. Conflicts of interests are a problem as are the continued survival of the sole practitioner. The compensation fund for clients of dishonest solicitors is the last bastion of pure altruism within the English legal profession. Perhaps, most important of all, the nature of legal ethics is under discussion among academics, legal professionals, regulatory bodies, and is receiving attention from the advisory body in relation to legal education and training.

Legal ethics are something of a barometer of de-professionalisation. Movements towards a commercial, or business approach, are reflected in greater regulation and more careful ethical codes. Regulatory bodies tend to be reactive rather than proactive, but the disputes over changes in ethical regulation often show up the background of power-mongering within the profession itself.

Index